WEALTH ANI

Wealth and Life completes an intellectual history of political economy begun in *Riches and Poverty* (1996). One of the main themes addressed in both books is the 'bitter argument between economists and human beings' provoked by Britain's industrial revolution. This book takes the argument from John Stuart Mill's contributions to the 'condition-of-England' debate in 1848 up to the decades prior to 1914 in the history of the economics profession as epitomised in the work of Alfred Marshall on economic well-being. The formal and informal writings of John Ruskin, Walter Bagehot, Stanley Jevons, Louis Mallet, Henry Sidgwick, and John Atkinson Hobson are also examined in a sequence of closely interlinked essays that ends with consideration of the twentieth-century fate of the debate between utilitarians and romantics in the hands of F. R. Leavis, Raymond Williams, and E. P. Thompson.

DONALD WINCH is one of Britain's most distinguished historians of ideas, and *Wealth and Life* brings to fruition a long-standing interest in the history of those intellectual pursuits that have shaped the understanding of Britain as an industrial society, and continue to influence cultural responses to the moral questions posed by economic life.

IDEAS IN CONTEXT 95

Wealth and Life

IDEAS IN CONTEXT

Edited by
Quentin Skinner and James Tully

The books in the series will discuss the emergence of intellectual traditions and of related new disciplines. The procedures, aims and vocabularies that were generated will be set in the context of the alternatives available within the contemporary frameworks of ideas and institutions. Through detailed studies of the evolution of such traditions, and their modification by different audiences, it is hoped that a new picture will form of the development of ideas in their concrete contexts. By this means, artificial distinctions between the history of philosophy, of the various sciences, of society and politics, and of literature may be seen to dissolve.

The series is published with the support of the Exxon Foundation.

A list of books in the series will be found at the end of the volume.

WEALTH AND LIFE

Essays on the Intellectual History of Political Economy in Britain, 1848–1914

DONALD WINCH

CAMBRIDGE
UNIVERSITY PRESS

CAMBRIDGE UNIVERSITY PRESS

Cambridge, New York, Melbourne, Madrid, Cape Town, Singapore, São Paulo, Delhi

Cambridge University Press
The Edinburgh Building, Cambridge CB2 8RU, UK

Published in the United States of America by Cambridge University Press, New York

www.cambridge.org
Information on this title: www.cambridge.org/9780521715393

First published 2009

Printed in the United Kingdom at the University Press, Cambridge

A catalogue record for this publication is available from the British Library

Library of Congress Cataloguing in Publication data
Winch, Donald.
Wealth and life : essays on the intellectual history of political
economy in Britain, 1848–1914 / Donald Winch.
p.   cm. – (Ideas in context ; 95)
Includes bibliographical references and index.
ISBN 978-0-521-88753-3 (hbk.)
1. Economics–Great Britain–History–19th century.   2. Great Britain–Economic
conditions–19th century.   3. Great Britain–Economic policy–19th century.
I. Title.   II. Series.
HB103.A2W57 2009
330.941′081–dc22   2008052013

ISBN 978-0-521-88753-3 hardback
ISBN 978-0-521-71539-3 paperback

To D. A. W.

Contents

Illustrations

Prologue: economists and human beings

THERE IS NO WEALTH BUT LIFE. Life, including all its powers of love, of joy, and of admiration. That country is the richest which nourishes the greatest number of noble and happy human beings; that man is richest who, having perfected the functions of his own life to the utmost, has also the widest helpful influence, both personal, and by means of his possessions, over the lives of others.

John Ruskin, *Unto this last*, 1862

I

With a crucial substitution of 'and' for 'but', the motto Ruskin chose for his own version of political economy suggested the title for this book, though since for him it was part of a damning indictment of the science and related arts which most of the cast who appear in these essays were cultivating, my purpose in using it is rather different. In echoing a sentiment expressed by Wordsworth in *The excursion* ('We live by Admiration, Hope, and Love'), Ruskin was adding his voice to what Arnold Toynbee later described in some famous lectures on the industrial revolution as a 'bitter argument between economists and human beings'. The argument was part of a broader assault on the allegedly self-interested, mechanical, and materialistic thinking of a despoiling industrial age – an assault that was to be hailed in the twentieth century as the 'romantic' or 'cultural' alternative to utilitarianism and political economy. Following a path indicated by a personal blend of the ideas of Carlyle and Wordsworth, Ruskin's campaign against political economy occupied his remaining decades of active life. Since these coincided with the last decades of the nineteenth century as well, one could say that he lived to falsify Toynbee's conclusion that by the 1880s the argument between economists and human beings had been resolved in favour of human beings. Indeed, many of those influenced by Ruskin's writings were still speaking as though resolution had not been achieved in the twentieth century. Wealth-producing and

wealth-distributing activities, and those who claimed to have developed
a science capable of explaining them, remained anathema to the life-
enhancing pursuits that Ruskin, and the cultural critics who were proud
to call themselves his descendants, sought to foster.

Although the conflict between wealth and life has preoccupied moralists of all persuasions over a far longer span of time, the period of modern
history that witnessed the rise to pre-eminence of Britain as a commercial,
financial, and industrial power furnished striking examples of that conflict played out against a dramatic backdrop. Since it also coincided with
the emergence of political economy as a more or less autonomous branch
of the moral sciences, it was inevitable that much of the debate on the
respective claims of wealth and life would take place around and in
opposition to the science that took material wealth as its province. That it
also took place *within* political economy is one of the themes addressed in
the following essays.

The argument between economists and human beings featured in the
final part of *Riches and poverty: an intellectual history of political economy in
Britain, 1750–1834*, to which this interconnected and overlapping set of
essays is a sequel. The essays do not form a unilinear sequence leading to
a triumphant set of conclusions. They can be read individually, but they
are meant to be read as they are numbered because the sequence has a
narrative logic that goes beyond mere chronology. This prologue provides
some contextual scenery and help with understanding that logic.

The first of the sections below (section II) says something about the
territory this book shares with its predecessor, and how that territory will
be explored in what follows. It also explains why 1848 has been chosen as a
starting date and why the 'condition-of-England' debate which preceded
and followed the startling events of that year provides the relevant context
for appreciating the focal significance of John Stuart Mill. Section III then
confronts the question of Mill's connection with those events, usually
treated as calamitous, that constitute the phenomenon traditionally known
as the Industrial Revolution at a time when the initial capitals were
obligatory. Section IV takes off from Mill's secular religion of humanity
to consider the role played by Christian providentialism in a popular
form of political economy that endorsed unqualified conclusions in
favour of free trade and *laissez-faire* and ran counter to the empiricism of
Mill's late nineteenth-century successors. Section V continues with the
apparently successful embodiment of the maxims of orthodox political
economy within British economic institutions and policies before other
challenges, in the form of depression, the rise of socialism, and tariff

nationalism, had to be faced by late nineteenth- and early twentieth-century economists. Section VI confronts the main theoretical dispute over the causes of exchange value, and gives reasons why one of the binary distinctions with which the dispute has become associated, the contrast between 'classical' and 'neo-classical' economics, does not feature as prominently in these essays as might be expected. Section VII shows how the essays in this book relate to other kinds of writing on these historical themes.

II

Riches and poverty attempted to sustain a narrative covering successive phases in the intellectual history of political economy. It tried to show how Adam Smith, in the *Wealth of nations*, fashioned a distinctive branch of the science of the legislator in the course of exploring the invisible connections linking the fortunes of rich and poor in commercial societies. Although the origins of the debate Smith transformed can be traced to the first half of the eighteenth century, the science he created was first put to serious use in providing guidance to legislators and those attempting to influence their actions during the last part of the century, roughly speaking between the American and French revolutions. The final third of the book followed the fortunes of a more controversial and tightly focused version of the science when it was taken up by Smith's English successors, Robert Malthus and David Ricardo, during the first three decades of the nineteenth century. Alongside the currency debates aroused by suspension of cash payments by the Bank of England in 1797, the Malthusian population principle, together with a posited law of diminishing returns in agriculture with which it was associated, gave the new science much of its purchase on urgent public events during the Napoleonic wars and the post-war period of depression and reconstruction. It also provoked the fierce opposition from the Lake poets and Carlyle that signalled the opening salvoes in the dispute Ruskin was to raise to new heights of bitterness during the second half of the century.

Apart from a brief epilogue on later developments, *Riches and poverty* ended in 1834, largely for symbolic reasons. This was the year in which Malthus and Coleridge, one of Malthus's most persistent romantic adversaries, died. It was also the year in which the Poor Law Amendment Act was passed, a landmark piece of legislation that its opponents regarded as one of the more malevolent clauses in Malthus's last will and testament. Perhaps even more ominously, the act authorised a bureaucratic manifestation of the utilitarian mind in the form of commissioners with a licence to collect evidence and argue for additional legislative and administrative powers. When first implemented during a period of depression in the manufacturing districts of Lancashire and the North of England generally, districts for which neither the old nor the new Poor Law was designed, it provoked demonstrations that merged with those associated with Chartism, the most challenging mass political movement of the 1830s and 40s.

At the risk of provoking questions about the missing intervening years, the opening and closing dates for the essays in this book chose themselves.[1] The beginning of the First World War and the violent dismantling of the Edwardian annexe to the Victorian era serve as an entirely conventional ending point. As a point of departure 1848 has equally conventional claims to attention: it was, of course, a year of Europe-wide, though short-lived, revolutions, sparked by the fall of the Orleanist monarchy in France in February, an event echoed in Britain by the last of a long sequence of mass meetings by supporters of the 'People's Charter' on Kennington Common on 10 April. In both countries economic depression during the late 1830s and 40s played a major part in underlining the discontents of the working classes, those excluded from the political nation on both sides of the Channel. The right of workers to associate 'in order to enjoy the advantages of their labour' was part of the French provisional government's original goals, and was followed in March by Louis Blanc's programme for co-operative workshops. The petition drawn up by the London Working Men's Association in 1838 to accompany demands for the six political points of the Charter refers throughout to economic grievances: regular employment at fair wages was one of the main goals they expected to achieve via the Charter.

It was to be sixty years before anyone thought of inventing the term 'hungry forties' to describe the decade, and when they did so it was with propagandist intent; they coined a phrase that allowed the discontents articulated by the Anti-Corn Law League in the period between its foundation in 1838 and the abolition of the Corn Laws in 1846 to be combined with the Irish famine of 1846–7 to form the basis of a campaign to prevent return to an era of taxes on food.[2] The period gave birth to an

---

[1] The intervening years are partially covered in the opening essay on Mill below. For a collection of primary sources covering the period that separates Ricardo from Mill, 1817 to 1848, together with an editorial assessment, see Terry Peach (ed.), *David Ricardo: critical responses*, 4 vols. (London: Routledge, 2003).

[2] The term was invented in 1904 by Jane Cobden Unwin as part of the free trade case against Joseph Chamberlain's campaign in favour of tariff reform and imperial preference; see *The hungry*

expression of its own under which these and other matters could be ranged: the 'condition-of-England question'. The expression first appeared in Carlyle's pamphlet on *Chartism* in 1839, the success of which led him to return four years later with more extensive commentary on the ominous spiritual and economic condition of the working classes in *Past and present*. Benjamin Disraeli's *Sybil or the two nations* (1845), Elizabeth Gaskell's *Mary Barton: a tale of Manchester life* (1848), Charles Kingsley's *Alton Locke: tailor and poet* (1850), and Charles Dickens's *Hard times: for these times* (1854) are the best-known novelistic tributes to the importance of Carlyle's theme. The last of these was actually 'inscribed' to Carlyle and was indebted to his writings for some of its attitudes to the 'dismal science' and antagonism to the 'cash nexus', two of Carlyle's more lasting coinages. *Hard times* has proved to be the most arresting expression of a state of affairs in which the moral defects of contemporary society, symbolised by its apparent commitment to a united brand of utilitarianism and political economy, are encapsulated in one of the novel's leading characters, Thomas Gradgrind.

The event that justifies 1848 as the starting point for this book, however, is the publication of John Stuart Mill's *Principles of political economy, with some of their applications to social philosophy*, a work that, in the English-speaking world at least, was to be a guiding light for all serious students of the science and its related art for the next two decades. Mill had begun work on this in 1846, and despite devoting six months to journalistic writings on the consequences of failure of the Irish potato crop, he still managed to complete a book that amounted to nearly half a million words in less than two years. It belongs alongside the other emblematic works cited in the previous paragraph, though it is understandable why a treatise of that size and complexity has received less attention from historians than the literary and more obviously polemical sources. In a conjectured adversarial arena containing only two camps labelled human beings or economists, Mill's *Principles* has to be placed in opposition to Carlyle's *Chartism*. Despite the lack of any supporting evidence, some cultural historians and literary critics in the twentieth century found it hard not to see in Mr Gradgrind a satirical portrait of the educational regimen imposed on the infant Mill by his father; they also maintained that the assault on political economy in *Hard times* had to

forties: life under the bread tax, descriptive letters and other testimonies from contemporary witnesses (London: T. Fisher Unwin, 1904).

have as its target Mill's book published a few years before.[3] As in the case of other artificially staged confrontations between political economy and 'romantic' dispositions, reality was more complex, offering scope for reversing the presumed moral polarities.

The first of the two essays devoted to Mill that comprise Part I of this book tackles that issue among others; and the opening essay (4) in Part II focuses on Ruskin's idiosyncratic decision, when planning his own serious foray into political economy, to make Mill the focus of his attack. Alfred Marshall, the author of the work that replaced Mill's *Principles* and rechristened political economy as the science of economics in 1890, was sufficiently conscious of the Carlyle–Ruskin critique to allow his scientific enterprise to be seen not merely as a response to it, but as an attempt to pre-empt any repetition of it. The pair of essays (9 and 10) on Marshall in Part IV of this book address that issue, and the second of them argues that Marshall's interest in well-being as well as wealth can be seen as an indirect response to the accusation that economics was incapable of coming to terms with the 'illth' associated with industrial forms of capitalism. The essays on Ruskin and Marshall are also necessary as background to an essay (11) in Part V on the economic heresies of J. A. Hobson, who thought of himself, and came to be regarded, as the chief twentieth-century standard-bearer for Ruskin's brand of 'economic humanism'. As a coda to these historical essays on the economist-versus-human being theme, an essay on the fate of Mr Gradgrind in the twentieth century has been included as an appendix to show how persistent some caricatures can be in cultural history. Fortunately, there are signs in the early years of the twenty-first century that the engagement of literary historians with the serious economic literature of the past is moving beyond the old stereotypes, making rapprochement with intellectual histories of economic debate possible.[4]

III

The success of the *Principles*, as part of Mill's larger achievement as philosopher-cum-moral scientist, justifies placing him in the position

---

[3] See pp. 373–4 below.

[4] See, for example, Philip Connell, *Romanticism, economics and the question of 'culture'* (Oxford: Oxford University Press, 2001). For commentary on how rapprochement has become possible and may yield insights into the Victorian novel, see Catherine Gallagher, *The body economic: life, death, and sensation in political economy and the Victorian novel* (Princeton: Princeton University Press, 2006).

here that Adam Smith occupied in the first two parts of *Riches and poverty*. The *Wealth of nations* was the model Mill chose for his *Principles*, a blending of an updated version of the science with applications to present – and, in Mill's case, conceivable future – social conditions. But Mill was far less deferential towards Smith than most of his successors as political economists have proved to be: he regarded the *Wealth of nations* as 'in many parts obsolete, and in all, imperfect'. The science had been substantially improved since Smith's death in 1790, chiefly as a result of the work of David Ricardo, whose opinions on value, distribution, and economic growth Mill accepted as the theoretical skeleton for his own work. Mill's equivalent to Smith's eighteenth-century science of the legislator differed so much in style and substance that detailed comparison would be pointless. In any event it was not a comparison that Mill had either the inclination or possibly even the information to mount.

It may suffice to say that Mill, whether as a youthful propagandist for the creed of Jeremy Bentham and his father, James Mill, or as a leader of radical liberal opinion during the mid-century decades, was a far more evangelising and combative figure than Smith. He brought these qualities to his self-imposed task of advancing the cause of intellectual and social progress in Victorian Britain, with the result that he became the last economist of note to combine intellectual leadership of the small community of devotees of the science with occupation of a role that went well beyond mere expertise in handling economic problems. This role is best described as that of 'public moralist', a term first coined by Stefan Collini in the 1980s that has become an indispensable part of the interpretative vocabulary. It is as an occupant of this role that Mill will largely be considered here, though the essays in Part I are not intended as surveys of what is now well-trodden ground so much as attempts to single out features of his work that were to prove fruitful or anathema in the eyes of those who figure in later essays.

No matter how successfully Mill occupied the role of public moralist, it is in the nature of things that publics tire of their moralists. Mill's *Principles* went through seven editions during the author's lifetime, including a cheap edition for working-class readers that sold over 100,000 copies before his death in 1873. By then the work had begun to lose its hold on devotees. More seriously, perhaps, his standing as a public moralist was both confirmed and compromised by the various causes with which he was associated as an MP between 1865 and 1868 and as a private citizen thereafter. He had taken the lead in advocating extension of the suffrage to women; and he had organised the campaign to prosecute Governor

Eyre for crimes committed when suppressing a revolt among ex-slaves in Jamaica. In what was perhaps his most impassioned political pamphlet, *England and Ireland*, written in the wake of the Fenian 'outrages' of 1867, Mill had advocated solutions to the Irish problem that earned him a reputation as a hothead who had capitulated to immoderate demands. In founding the Land Tenure Reform Association in 1869 Mill attached his name, and a good deal of the authority he brought to the subject as a political economist, to proposals for reform in England that were tantamount to property confiscation in the eyes of opponents who were too enraged to read them carefully.

Mill's preoccupation with land tenure reform in Ireland and England features in the second essay (3) in Part I, alongside another of his major concerns, public access to undisturbed natural environments. These interests can be cited as evidence of Mill's predisposition in favour of rural and agrarian issues as opposed to those connected with manufacturing in the new industrial cities. Raymond Williams and Noel Annan, an unlikely twentieth-century pairing in most matters, agreed in expressing impatience with Mill's apparent lack of concern with industrial problems. Williams, when writing his influential mid twentieth-century study of *Culture and society*, regretted that Mill spent so much time discoursing on 'civilisation' and its discontents instead of addressing the problems of 'industrialism'.[5] For Annan, if Mill had been capable of a true critique of his own times, 'surely one of [his essays] would have been concerned with urbanisation and industrialisation and their appalling problems'.[6] Mill's only mention of an 'industrial revolution' is a passing reference to the effect upon an underdeveloped region or nation of the opening up of foreign trade.[7] He devoted a good deal of attention to wage determination, strikes, and co-operative workshops, and he was concerned about the monotony and loss of opportunities for self-development associated with wage labour; but anyone interested in technological innovation, mechanisation, and factory production would be advised to turn, as Mill frequently did, to Charles Babbage's book *On the economy of manufactures*.[8]

---

[5] *Culture and society, 1780–1950*, 1958 (Penguin edn, 1961), p. 67.

[6] 'John Stuart Mill', originally published in 1964, as reprinted in J. B. Schneewind (ed.), *Mill: a collection of critical essays* (New York: Anchor Books, 1968), p. 33.

[7] 'The opening of a foreign trade . . . sometimes works a sort of industrial revolution in a country whose resources were previously undeveloped . . .'; *Principles*, CW, III, pp. 593–4.

[8] For Mill's appeal to Babbage's authority, see *Principles*, CW, II, pp. 106–7, 111–13, 124–6, 128–9, 131–2; III, pp. 770, 1008–10.

Mill does not fit the stereotypes that were later created to sustain a particular understanding of the industrial revolution. Awareness of the actual or potential benefits of technological innovation was accompanied by anxiety about the ways in which population increase could prevent wage-earners from enjoying them. Mill's evaluation of the cultural basis for Britain's industrial leadership was almost entirely negative: those factors that conferred superiority were at best a mixed blessing, at worst something that should not be envied or emulated by other nations. He also adopted Ricardo's stoicism in regarding Britain's wealth, the wealth that depended on unstable world markets, as genuine, though subject to vicissitudes that had to be endured if the larger benefits were to be secured. This meant that he was not prepared to adopt the incipient catastrophism he discerned in Carlyle and which was to become the defining feature of much subsequent commentary, from Friedrich Engels's diagnosis of the *Condition of the working class in England in 1844* onwards. Engels's account drew heavily on his own observations of Manchester life and British accounts of factory conditions; he also made incidental use of Carlyle's *Chartism* and *Past and present*. When later reworked in *Das Kapital*, of course, this diagnosis became an enduring element in all subsequent Marxian analyses of capitalism. English translations of these works by Marx and Engels did not appear until 1886 and 1892 respectively, with the French translation of *Capital* in 1873 acting as a halfway house for some early commentators. This delay, together with a natural preference for works addressed to a British audience, meant that the first native catastrophist interpretation of the industrial revolution was that of Toynbee, an unorthodox Anglican radical-liberal, whose *Lectures on the industrial revolution of the eighteenth century in England* were published posthumously in 1884. Toynbee did more than give the revolution its capital letters: he began the process whereby the phenomenon it described became central to late nineteenth- and twentieth-century British consciousness and historiography. For some of the economists, and more especially the economic historians, who figure in these pages the history of industrial Britain became, for the first time, a separate branch of inquiry, requiring them to follow in Toynbee's footsteps by looking for explanations of what was peculiar and instructive about British historical experience.

Toynbee admired the improved spirit of Mill's *Principles*, while regretting that the work was insufficiently emancipated from Ricardian methods. Mill's unenthusiastic view of the industrial revolution prevented him from joining what Ruskin later designated as the 'steam-whistle' party – those like Dickens or the historian, Macaulay, who treated technology as the key to an optimistic future for industrial societies. Mill famously declared in the *Principles* that no machine had so far lightened the day's work of anyone. It is therefore not surprising that evidence of his attending or commenting favourably on the Great Exhibition of 1851, the showcase for Britain's global industrial hegemony, has yet to be found. In correspondence and journalistic writings he was contemptuous of the whole self-seeking commercial creed of the Anglo-American world, and found almost anywhere on the Continent, but especially France, a more civilised place in which to live.

Mill, then, was not as insouciant about industrialisation and its consequences as some of his later critics contend. Nor should an interest in agrarian questions and land tenure reform be regarded as escapist or atavistic: it chimed well with some of the larger currents at work in British society and politics. Indeed, land tenure reform provides a case where an idea closely associated with Mill's political economy, the idea of an 'unearned increment' in the rental incomes of landowners, became embedded in popular political movements devoted to curbing the privileges of the landowning classes and improving access to land for a landless wage-earning class. An economic theorem, arising to a large extent from peculiarities in the English system of land tenure, penetrated deeply into English radicalism and socialism throughout the period covered by the essays in this book. Precisely for that reason it was important for a later generation of would-be professionals – those making a living, or hoping to do so, by teaching economics within a reformed university system – to clarify where the science stood on the emotive issues aroused by that theorem. The two essays (7 and 8) in Part III deal with that issue among others, and it also reappears in the second of the essays (10) on Marshall in Part IV.

IV

Mill's failure to be re-elected to parliament in 1868 could be attributed to the part he played in any of the causes mentioned so far, as well as to the well-publicised fact that he had contributed to the election expenses of Charles Bradlaugh, a notorious atheist. Controversy continued after Mill's death, when the nature and extent of Mill's own irreligion, or rather his support for a secular religion of humanity, was revealed to a wider public by the posthumous publication of his *Autobiography* and his *Three essays on religion*. In the twentieth and twenty-first centuries Mill's heterodox religious opinions have been used to cast doubt on his libertarian credentials; he has even been seen as the spokesman for a form of secularism that was as potentially autocratic as the official forms of atheistic Marxism were actually so.[9] Perhaps this illustrates a general rule: heterodoxy of the Mill variety draws more fire than straightforward infidelity. There is some irony in the fact that the arguments Mill used to warn against the authoritarian features of Auguste Comte's scheme for societies reconstructed along 'positive' lines and worshipping a religion of humanity have been applied to his own ideas. Strangely enough too, for a society that was more openly imbued with Christian values, the nineteenth-century reaction to Mill's irreligion, though it involved emotional recoil, was also more cerebral, certainly less ideological, than the modern attacks. But since all these statements need qualification, the religious dimension to political economy will feature as much in this book as it did in *Riches and poverty* – not as a central theme in its own right so much as an accompaniment to others. Not to recognise this dimension would be yet another example of what I characterised in the earlier book as premature secularisation.

The problems posed by Mill's irreligion are part of a larger difficulty. Although few would question the role played by religion in the intellectual history of the natural sciences during the nineteenth century, famously so in the case of Darwinian biology, the connections between economics and religion have largely been left to a few specialists, often writing against the grain of work on the same figures or subjects by their more secular-minded colleagues. These scholars – among whom Boyd Hilton and Anthony Waterman have taken leading roles, albeit in different directions – have succeeded in sensitising all but the most chronic secularists to the part played by religion in economics.[10] When considering the origins of university teaching in political economy, of course, it would be hard to deny that entry of any new branch of knowledge into the curricula of the ancient universities, from which until 1871 Dissenters and Jews were excluded, required a licence from the Established Church.

---

[9] See Maurice Cowling, *Mill and liberalism* (Cambridge: Cambridge University Press, 1963); and Linda Raeder, *John Stuart Mill and the religion of humanity* (Columbia: University of Missouri Press, 2002). A more moderate version of the thesis can be found in Joseph Hamburger, *John Stuart Mill on liberty and control* (Princeton: Princeton University Press, 1999).

[10] See Boyd Hilton, *The age of atonement: the influence of evangelicalism on social and economic thought, 1785–1865* (Oxford: Oxford University Press, 1988); A. M. C. Waterman, *Revolution, economics and religion: Christian political economy, 1798–1833* (Cambridge: Cambridge University Press, 1991); and *Political economy and Christian theology since the Enlightenment: essays in intellectual history* (London: Palgrave, 2004).

As Richard Whately, later Archbishop of Dublin, maintained in the lectures he gave as Drummond Professor of Political Economy at Oxford, a chair founded for this purpose:

> Convinced as I am, that the world, as it always in fact has been governed by political-economists of some kind, must ultimately be under the guidance of such as have systematically applied themselves to the science, I could not but regard it as a point of primary importance, to remove the impression existing in the minds of many, both of the friends and the adversaries of Christianity, as to the hostility between that and the conclusions of Political-Economy.[11]

Whately's object was to strengthen the alliance between science and Christian belief that Malthus had sustained throughout his writings, despite the criticism he faced from more fundamentalist Christians.

Whately's aim was first expressed when there was a fear that a secular and radical version of political economy, chiefly connected with Ricardo and James Mill, would monopolise the territory. William Whewell, with some assistance from Richard Jones, had also mounted a campaign against Ricardian methods and conclusions, doing so from an explicitly Christian standpoint. Open hostility was rare, though when it came it could be fierce. Mill's rejection of the idea that a Christian baptism (adult in this case) was essential to the moral legitimacy of the science shows that secularists could also become aggressive when put on the defensive.[12] Orthodox Christians who took up the science had no difficulty in accepting the rationale that Whately and others such as George Poulett Scrope and Thomas Chalmers, following in his train, supplied. A beneficent God provided providential guidance on the economic underpinnings of the moral order, just as He had done with every other aspect of that order. Based on that kind of reasoning, a broadly Christian dimension to the science of political economy that was popular in the eighteenth century endured up to and beyond the end of the nineteenth century.[13] Providence could provide a serious analogy for the workings of the economic order, but it was also prone to what can be called, in honour of Dickens's character in *Our mutual friend*, the Podsnap syndrome:

> As a so eminently respectable man, Mr Podsnap was sensible of its being required of him to take Providence under his protection. Consequently he always knew

---

[11] *Introductory lectures on political economy* (London: B. Fellowes, 1832), p. vi.
[12] See Mill's comments on John Lalor's *Money and morals* cited on pp. 59–60 below.
[13] On the eighteenth century, see Jacob Viner, *The role of providence in the social order* (Princeton: Princeton University Press, 1972); and for the first half of the nineteenth century, see Hilton, *Age of atonement*.

exactly what Providence meant. Inferior and less respectable men might fall short of that mark, but Mr Podsnap was always up to it. And it was very remarkable (and must have been very comfortable) that what Providence meant, was invariably what Mr Podsnap meant.

An inspiring notion of cosmic order, offering insight into its less obvious workings, could simply become a smug adaptation to whatever the wisdom of hindsight revealed and defence of the status quo required. It was bound to conflict with the views of those who, following Mill, thought of themselves as secular moral scientists whose speculations were disciplined by regard for inductive evidence rather than based on self-justifying moral intuitions. As will be shown in the essay (6) on William Stanley Jevons in Part II, however, the idea of design in the moral world did not collapse entirely in the face of scientific materialism and the rise of Darwinism.

While there has probably never been any abatement in the number of sermons delivered in condemnation of greed, material pride, charitable failure, and economic injustice, or in praise of brotherly love and equality in the sight of God, it is an interesting facet of the theme expressed in the title of this book that the weightiest condemnations of political economy came not from those with official church connections but from lay figures like Carlyle and Ruskin, whose own religious beliefs may have begun in orthodox fashion but certainly did not end there. It may also be worth noting that some of the bitterest criticism of the direction taken by political economy during the final quarter of the century came from economic fundamentalists who thought the English science had lost its way when it failed to maintain the intimate connection between economic law and morality. Creating a new relationship between economics and ethics outside any recognisable or acknowledged theological framework was often the path explored by late nineteenth-century economists, of whom Marshall is the most prominent among those who make an appearance here.

The best-known example of the connection between Christianity and political economy in the mid-century period can be found in the appeal of the Anti-Corn Law League and the movement founded by Richard Cobden that later emerged as the Manchester school. Cobdenism as an evangelising creed was not confined to the narrow economic case for abolishing the Corn Laws, curbing public expenditure on armaments, and making Britain the leader of a crusade in favour of cosmopolitan free trade. Indeed, as recent studies of the free trade movement have emphasised, it would not have been successful in achieving these aims

if it had been so confined.[14] Cobden characterised free trade as the
'International Law of the Almighty' and would not have devoted his life
to the cause if he had regarded that as an empty slogan. Alongside Adam
Smith, the only major intellectual influence on Cobden appears to have
been the teachings of his friend, the phrenologist George Combe, as
propounded in his highly successful popular treatment of the *Constitution
of man*, a work that confirmed the compatibility of material improvement with moral progress on every page. Providentialist conceptions of
a naturally harmonious world that needed to be purged of the artificial
evils of feudal privilege and protectionism supplied a sense of missionary
purpose that no secular theories of economic growth or market inter-
dependency could supply. They came in conflict with one another for this
very reason, especially when the science was taken up by a new kind of
student, keener to stress the professional neutrality of the science's methods
and conclusions, and less willing to engage in open political polemic.
When the new professionals laid claim to scientific disinterestedness, they
were met with charges from the amateurs of moral evasiveness, a conclusion that is easy to understand if economic laws are God's laws. Intellectual
error carries the taint of blasphemy as well.

No single essay is devoted to the Manchester school in this book, but
the first essay (7) in Part III deals with Louis Mallet, a leading exponent of
the Cobden creed as it developed after Cobden's death in 1865. Mallet
was a senior civil servant who, by adding a powerful infusion of doctrines
of economic harmony derived from the work of Frédéric Bastiat, became
one of the most rigid defenders of economic law as moral imperative.
Bastiat's teaching on the emancipatory logic of *libre échange*, as relayed by
Mallet and others, was taken up by followers of Herbert Spencer within
the Liberty and Property Defence League late in the century; they saw
themselves as defenders of the last bastions of Individualism in the face
of those pervasive tendencies towards Socialism (initial capitals essential
in those days) they discerned in British political and academic life during
the final two decades of the nineteenth century.

The partner to the essay on Mallet in Part III is one on Henry Sidgwick
(8) and what he called 'economic socialism'. Sidgwick, that most academic example of the moral philosopher as political economist, was an
unlikely champion of socialism in any of its more popular guises; but he
was determined 'to reduce to its proper limits the supposed opposition

---

[14] See Anthony Howe, *Free trade and liberal England* (Oxford: Oxford University Press, 1997); and
Frank Trentmann, *Paradoxes of civil society* (Oxford: Berghahn, 2000).

between orthodox political economy and what was vaguely called socialistic legislation'. This aim alone required an effort to distance the 'English' version of the science from its 'French', or Bastiat-influenced, opponent. In underlining the gap between the two approaches to political economy, Sidgwick was following Mill's closest disciple, John Elliot Cairnes. In turn, Sidgwick was followed by his Cambridge junior, Marshall, when advancing an economics that sought to remain aloof from the dogmatic *laissez-faire* fallacies of a largely Continental 'maximum satisfaction' school of thought (essay 10).

V

The triumph of Cobden's campaign to repeal the Corn Laws in 1846 had a double-edged effect on the public standing of political economy. On the one hand the prolonged burst of mid-century prosperity that followed repeal, as measured by the expansion of the import and export trades, gave a boost to the public image of the science. On the other, identification of the science with a single negative truth – that wealth is more likely to increase when domestic and international trade are not restricted by governments or private monopolies – rather than with open-ended inquiry into a wider range of unsolved social and economic problems, implied that the science had already completed its useful work. That was, indeed, the conclusion of the politician, Robert Lowe, when called upon to celebrate the centenary of the *Wealth of nations* in 1876, a celebration of the 'official' if not actual birthday of the science. Contesting this impression on behalf of the small tribe of academics teaching the science, Cairnes maintained that student recruitment had been inhibited by the popular association of political economy with *laissez-faire*. In 1870, when he took up his duties as professor at University College, London, he estimated, on the basis of student numbers attending courses in the capital, that the interest in economic studies was five or six times greater in the decaying town of Galway where he had also taught than it was in 'the metropolis of modern industrial civilization'. Severing association of the science with the dogma of *laissez-faire* required drastic measures: it had to be dismissed as a mere 'handy rule of practice' and the science had to be shown to have 'no more connection with our present industrial system than the science of mechanics has with our present system of railways'.[15]

---

[15] See pp. 195–6 below.

Unlike Cairnes, Walter Bagehot, the leading example of the Victorian economist as journalist, banker, and practical man of business, was not obliged to make his living by teaching; but he was equally concerned with the reasons why political economy lay 'dead in the public mind', and why modes of study of foreign provenance were proving more attractive to the young. The essay (5) centring on him in Part II has as its background the prolonged episode that normally goes under the title of *Methodenstreit* in honour of its association with the rise of the German historical school of economics. In Britain, largely due to the role played by two Irish political economists, Thomas Cliffe Leslie and J. K. Ingram, the dispute was Anglo-Irish in origin and flavour. It took the form of an attack on the hegemony of deductive reasoning in economics from perspectives that were variously historical, inductive, and 'sociological' in one of the many senses that clung to that relatively new word. Bagehot's response to this critique involved a bluff mixture of renewed emphasis on the hypothetical nature of the deductions made on the basis of 'economic man' assumptions, and an argument to the effect that the scope of the resulting explanations should be limited to 'a society of grown-up competitive commerce such as we have in England'.[16] While the former was a traditional rejoinder, and the latter came dressed in fashionable post-Darwinist language, it represented a retreat from earlier confidence about the universal applicability of economic theory, even when qualified, as Mill wished to see it qualified, by reference to the different role played by custom or competition in societies at different stages of development. Bagehot's limitation denied that the political economy of man as a 'money-making animal' had anything to offer to the understanding of new countries or what he conceived of as 'pre-economic' societies. This concession to historical and cultural relativism was eagerly grasped by some of the historicist critics of political economy, and for the same reason did not commend itself to a later generation of economic theorists who believed that more sensitive use of the new analytical tools offered insight into the economies of countries of new settlement as well as traditional societies such as India. It was almost a bread-and-butter issue for those whose academic appointments at Oxford and Cambridge were partially justified by the courses in political economy they mounted for students aiming to enter the Indian civil service.

Bagehot's concern with the methodological disputes that were damaging to the future of political economy did not prevent him from making

---

[16] See pp. 134–5 below.

some chauvinistic claims on behalf of the transformative effect of free trade on British living standards, and on the way in which the teachings of political economy, by contrast with the unenlightened habits of lesser breeds without the benefit of economic law, 'have settled down into the common sense of the nation, and have become irreversible'. The chauvinism made a good deal of sense to a British audience at the time. Victorians had come to believe they were peculiarly blessed in having embodied the findings of orthodox political economy within their institutions, making them part of their political habits and outlook. 'Sound' public finance, 'hard' money, and 'liberal' trade went along with 'good' (because limited) constitutional forms of governance. Free trade became the official policy of governments of all kinds after repeal of the Corn Laws and the Navigation Acts in 1846 and 1849 respectively. Even Ruskin, who on all other matters was determined to remain on a collision course with economic orthodoxy, declared himself to be 'an utterly fearless and unscrupulous free-trader', though the grounds he gave for this belief would have appeared strange to any economist. The public finances, both with respect to canons of taxation and the mechanisms and conventions surrounding control over expenditure, had been placed on that basis to which Gladstone, building on Pitt and Peel, was to lend his name. Much of this presupposed the existence of a banking system capable of protecting the internal and external value of the currency, and of acting in a manner that would minimise the effects of those financial crises that periodically afflicted a nation standing at the centre of the international monetary system. Bagehot himself, through his criticisms of the Bank of England in *Lombard Street,* had done much to consolidate the body of informed opinion that underpinned the slow and sometimes reluctant process by which the Bank came to accept its responsibilities for the British economy, and in lesser degree, by extension, for the international monetary system as a whole.[17]

The idea that Britain's peculiarities should be regarded as grounds for self-congratulation became more difficult to sustain during the final decades of the century. In addition to the depression that lasted from 1873 into the 1890s, there were clear signs of a loss of economic standing when compared with new world economic powers such as the United States and Germany. There was too a serious fear of socialism from the 1880s

---

[17] For detailed treatment of each of the broad themes mentioned here, see the individual essays in Donald Winch and Patrick K. O'Brien (eds.), *The political economy of British historical experience, 1688–1914* (Oxford: Oxford University Press for the British Academy, 2002).

onwards. Since two of the forms this took, Henry George's land reform
and 'single tax' campaigns and the revolutionary ideas of the German
Marxists, appeared to be based on Ricardian approaches to rent and the
labour theory of value, political economy seemed to be implicated on
both sides of the dispute, for and against socialism.

During the depression, defenders of free trade were called upon to keep
at bay protectionists advancing under cover of demands for 'fair trade'
and the abandonment of unilateralism in favour of reciprocity and
concern about empire. The line was held for the most part within the
economics community, despite Mill's concessions to the idea of temporary
'infant industry' tariffs. Sidgwick, acting in the spirit of Mill's open-
mindedness on the subject, had noted that 'Cobden's confident expectations that the example of England would be speedily followed by the
whole civilised world' had proved false. Sidgwick followed this up with an
expanded sympathetic treatment of the infant industry case – the case
that, implicitly at least, lay behind foreign unwillingness to follow Britain's
lead.[18] An important episode in the self-education of Marshall was the
extended trip to the United States he took in 1875 to make a study of the
effects of protection. Recognition that it could make economic sense for
other nations did not resolve the question of whether free trade was still
in the interests of Britain. These attempts to understand foreign alternatives to free trade policies could also be seen as flirtations with apostasy;
they were added to the charges levelled against academic economists by
diehard Cobdenites of the Mallet variety.

The first major break in the line did not occur until Joseph Chamberlain
mounted his campaign in favour of tariff reform and imperial preference
in the wake of the Boer war in 1903. Chamberlain's most significant
initiative as far as political economy was concerned lay in his success in
recruiting a small group of economic experts to his cause who were
capable of challenging the academic authority of the orthodox free traders.
The public nature of the dispute between rival economic perspectives
reopened those methodological divisions that had surfaced during the
celebrations of the centenary of the *Wealth of nations* in 1876, with the
liberal, cosmopolitan free traders mostly taking their stand on grounds of
economic theory, while their more conservative, neo-mercantilist opponents based themselves more on historical parallels and statistical evidence. Tariff reform was, of course, decisively rejected by the electorate
in 1906. Despite the use of slogans designed to reawaken memories of the

---

[18] See pp. 225–6 below.

'hungry forties', victory could not have been achieved via a straightforward replay of Cobden's campaign sixty years earlier, a campaign fought before a far less democratic electorate. In the closely associated battle for intellectual hegemony one could also say that victory went to the free traders, though since the votes in this contest need to be weighed rather than counted, proofs of a knock-down variety are harder to come by.[19] Success came with some bruising to professional egos. Marshall had shown some relish for public debate when taking on Henry George's populist land reform campaign in 1883, but regretted allowing himself to be drawn into the rough and tumble of the tariff reform debate twenty years later: it clashed with the professional ideal he hoped to disseminate, one of the themes of the second essay on him (10).

VI

The third essay (6) in Part II is concerned with the challenge of Jevons to Mill's legacy. The political economy dimension of this legacy centred on the theory of value, and in dealing with it one comes closest to what in any standard history of economic thought devoted to this period would be the main event: the beginning of the process known later as the 'marginal revolution' by which 'classical' political economy was replaced by 'neo-classical' economics. The scare quotes in that sentence signal the intellectual historian's need to distinguish retrospective labels from those which the historical agents themselves would have recognised, a distinction that carries less weight in other kinds of history devoted to economics. None of those now regarded by historians of economic thought as 'classical' economists, from Smith on to Mill and his two orthodox disciples, Henry Fawcett and Cairnes, described their own work as such. Nor did any of those now judged to be 'neo-classical' economists during the period in question use that term, though 'classical' was employed in the last decades of the century to characterise what was being replaced. The extraordinary lengths to which Marshall went in providing generous reinterpretations of his 'classical' predecessors played a large part in this. It lent point to Thorstein Veblen's coinage of the term 'neo-classical' in 1900 to describe the work of Marshall and others, though given later

---

[19] For a review of the evidence supporting the summary verdict registered here, see Howe, *Free trade and liberal England*, pp. 266–75. See too Frank Trentmann, 'National identity and consumer politics: free trade and tariff reform', in Winch and O'Brien (eds.), *The political economy of British historical experience*, pp. 212–40.

misunderstandings it might have been better if one of the other terms to which Veblen gave equal prominence – 'modernized classical economics', 'semi-' or 'quasi-classical economics' – had caught on.[20]

The more common contemporary division was simply between an 'old' and a 'new' generation of economists, and that is how the question will mainly be treated here. Several of the essays address this generational divide and one of them (9) is explicitly organised around the idea. It involved an uncertain combination of the main contested components, theoretical, methodological, and moral. But since the division was far less tidy than it can be made to appear in textbook histories of economic thought, the treatment given here does not centre on pre- and post-revolutionary dispositions. Minimum use of the term 'neo-classical economics', the retrospective label, is meant to be informative rather than perverse. Armed with the categories and criteria provided by modern economic theory, it would be possible to divide classical sheep from neo-classical goats, though there might still be some mixed forms. Jevons, for example, never completely emancipated himself from older classical notions, and Marshall was positively averse to being emancipated from them. There was never complete agreement on whether 'old' connoted ground-breaking rather than wrong-headed. Indeed, a significant part of the controversies of the period took the form of appeals to the 'true' lineage of the science, with the aim, to revert to Jevons's famous image, of shunting the car of economic science back on the right tracks. Finally, while there can be no doubt about Jevons's revolutionary intent when writing his *Theory of political economy*, whether the result was a revolution and precisely when it can be said to have happened, remain the subject of controversy.[21]

The main issues connected with disputes over the correct approach to the theory of value are covered here. No conception of economic life that dared to call itself a science would be complete without an answer to the fundamental questions raised by the underlying causes of exchange and use value. There are some important topics connected with the law of diminishing marginal utility, such as the case for progressive taxation, that could not be dealt with in any other way. But the main reason for minimising use of a binary division between pre- and post-marginal

[20] See Thorstein Veblen, 'The preconceptions of economic science', *Quarterly Journal of Economics*, 13 (1899), and 396–426 114 (1900), 240–69.

[21] See a collection of studies produced at the centenary of the so-called revolution in 1971: R. D. C. Black *et al.* (eds.), *The marginal revolution in economics: interpretation and evaluation* (Durham, NC: Duke University Press, 1973).

thinkers, classical and neo-classical economists, is a simple historical one: it adds little to an understanding of what happened and how it did so. And since I have no intention of condemning or recommending one or other of these binary choices, it seems best to retain the freedom that comes with agnosticism. For example, during one crucial phase in the process of transition, when the outcome was far from obvious, it was more appropriate to make a quadripartite distinction among approaches that can be roughly labelled as Franco-Swiss, German, Austrian, and English, where these connoted differences over the fundamental building-blocks on which any theory of economic life should be constructed. If the science was to be historical and inductive as opposed to a-historically deductive, the chief dispute was between its German and Anglo-French exponents, with the Austrians weighing in with the latter. If the foundation of the theory of value was to be utility or the subjective satisfactions associated with the consumption of material goods and services rather than an objective approach based on labour and the costs of production, the chief dispute was between adherents of the French and English deductive approaches, with the Austrians once more throwing their weight on to the French side.

As an added complication, the national labels did not correspond invariably with the nationality of the adherents and their respective heroes. Jevons's career exemplifies this. At the beginning of his investigations he believed he had discovered a new foundation in utility theory for explanations of exchange value. Some of his early attempts to describe the revolution involved replacement of the existing Anglocentric orthodoxy by a Francophile alternative – until, that is, Jevons was forced to acknowledge that he had British as well as German and other foreign anticipators and allies in his quest. While there can be no doubt about the nature of Jevons's disagreement with Mill's political economy on this issue, what the essay on him here tries to show is that Jevons's antipathy to Mill had deeper philosophical and religious roots. At the same time, as a guide to attitudes to questions of social and economic policy, the application of the classical and neo-classical labels to Mill and Jevons turns out not to have much power to discriminate – another reason for not allowing the labels to mislead.

On first inspection the essays (11 and 12) in Part V may not seem to be part of the Lord Mayor's procession and I hope they do not resemble the dustcart. They both have a connection with Hobson, one of whose claims on our attention has been mentioned already. As a self-advertising economic heretic (and, incidentally, one of the first to use Veblen's 'neo-classical' label pejoratively)[22], he represents a continuation of a line of dissent that can be traced back to Ruskin – though how far he can be regarded as a faithful disciple is one of the issues considered in the first of these essays. He also sustained a complex relationship with some of the leading academic economists of his day, notably with Jevons, Marshall, and some Austrian theorists. Hobson gives us an outsider's view of an emerging academic profession from which, notoriously, he was excluded. The concluding essay begins with Hobson's unflattering portrait of academic economics, and then proceeds to consider a number of the ways in which the insiders, some of the conformists who inhabited the earlier essays, earned their livings and attempted to organise themselves collectively as a profession through clubs, congresses, and professional journals.

This may be the place to suggest another sense in which *Wealth and life* may be an apposite title for this book. Without attempting in any case a full-blooded biographical approach, I have tried to convey how the studies of wealth carried out by my cast were linked to the stage and station in life they occupied at the time of writing. I have also kept the state of their personal as well as intellectual relations with one another in mind, doing so, where possible, by making extensive use of letters and informal writings as well as published works.

VII

As in the case of its predecessor, this book is conceived of as intellectual rather than as doctrinal history. Since the introductory chapter in the earlier book had something to say about current styles of writing intellectual history, I can be briefer here. One quick way of characterising the difference between these variants turns on something mentioned in connection with the marginal revolution, the emphasis placed on prospective as opposed to retrospective criteria of significance. We cannot write history without the benefit of hindsight, but we are free to decide whether to portray our historical actors according to the manner in which they led their intellectual lives – like us, looking forwards, sometimes short-sightedly so – or how they *might* have conducted themselves if they had possessed our intellectual tastes and knowledge of later outcomes. Doctrinal histories of political economy are committed more to the construction of genealogies that chart those routes that were or were not successful in anticipating our current interests and values. With this

[22] See J. A. Hobson, 'Neo-classical economics in Britain', *Political Science Quarterly*, 40 (1925), 337–83.

comes a tendency to create lines of descent that distinguish the acknowledged thoroughbreds from the also-rans, some of whom seemed more fleet of foot to their contemporaries than they do to us. Intellectual histories tend not only to be more tolerant of 'failure' in this respect, sometimes disgracefully so in the eyes of doctrinal historians: they are also less patronising towards their subjects. For those historians who take seriously their role as guardians of the relentless march of scientific truth, being patronising may seem at worst to be a venial sin.

Intellectual histories also tend to be more episodic than linear, where the episodes are measured in months and years, a human life span at best, but rarely a century or an epoch. They are 'humane' in one of its many senses in eschewing the God-like stance, or rather perhaps in this case, that of the modern textbook or the latest issue of a professional journal. One reason for favouring essays as opposed to chapters as the natural unit of measurement is that they match the episodic character of intellectual history, where an episode can be connected with an author or a debate and followed to a conclusion. As in my earlier work, I have attempted to connect economic speculation and advocacy with those other forms of thinking and feeling, moral and political, with which it was associated in the minds of the protagonists and contemporary readers of their work, without which, indeed, it would not have had significance.

While this book was planned as a sequel I do not expect readers to be as conscious as I am of the ways in which the two books have taken different paths. I take comfort from the apothegm attributed to Heraclitus that 'one cannot step twice into the same river'. Indeed, if it didn't sound like a post-modern sophism that concedes too much to the idea of *personal* flux, I might have accepted Cratylus's addendum to Heraclitus, namely that 'one cannot step *once* into the same river'.[23] But my interests have moved on, and there have been recent publications that give more effective treatment to some topics than I could have given them. In an even longer book, I would have liked to include essays on other figures or episodes such as the role of economists in parliamentary inquiries and royal commissions. The woman question appears fleetingly here, but there is clearly scope for essays on that and on women economists. And much else besides. Secondary literature is not mentioned in the texts of the main essays, but I hope the bibliographic notes at the end of the book will help those who wish to follow related threads.

[23] See Charles H. Kahn, *The art and thought of Heraclitus* (Cambridge: Cambridge University Press, 1979), pp. 168–9.

Another reason for favouring essays as the unit of account is that they acknowledge the obvious fact that many different argumentative narratives can be constructed around the same historical figures and debates. Discussions of the functions of money suggest that it is not for any author to say whether the unit of account he has chosen will also serve as a medium of exchange *and* a store of value. Although historians of economics have repeatedly studied the period considered here I am not convinced that the kinds of stories they tell fellow economists (or is it now merely other historians of economics?) are the only or most interesting ones that can be told. Intellectual history brings to light allusions and connections that tend to be overlooked in the existing literature. In attempting to bring such things to the fore I hope to make them more accessible to other kinds of historian and to readers who might not otherwise be drawn to the history of economic thought. Although I have long since given up any pretence to be an economist as well as a historian, I am still convinced that better service can be done to the nature of economists' modes of thought by revealing them to have been, like any genuine intellectual activity, genuinely problematic.

Unlike *Riches and poverty* this book has no epilogue forecasting how some of the themes that appear here were resolved at a later date. To a large extent I can legitimately claim that the long essay in the Appendix goes some way towards doing this, so far as the twentieth-century fate of the quarrel between economists and human beings is concerned at least. It picks up on the way the Ruskinian or romantic critique of utilitarianism and political economy was recycled for mid-twentieth century use by F. R. Leavis and two influential spokesmen for the cultural and political left, Raymond Williams and E. P. Thompson. For those who appreciate a bit more polemic with their history, the Appendix will supply that. But as is pointed out there, the romantic critique did not face up squarely to any of the post-Mill developments in economics that bulk large here – any bar one, that is, because after Ruskin the sole self-proclaimed heretic who appears in these essays, Hobson, provided the only acceptable way in which many on the non-Marxist left could absorb a dissident version of economics. This apart, there was merely an assumption in the background that the arguments of economists deserved the same moral condemnation as they had received earlier. That is certainly the case with R. H. Tawney, who provides an indispensable link in the chain that connects Ruskin via Hobson and an interpretation of the industrial revolution that combines Christianity and catastrophism with a very British type of early twentieth-century socialist morality. As a younger contemporary of

Marshall, faced with the economist's elevated claims on behalf of the discipline he had devoted his life to reconstructing, Tawney could only expostulate: 'There is no such thing as a science of economics, nor ever will be. It is just cant, and Marshall's talk as to the need for social problems to be studied by "the same order of mind which tests the stability of a battleship in bad weather" is twaddle.'[24] Tawney's Edwardian moralising now offends modern noses just as much as Marshall's late-Victorian version of the same: we scent cant in equal amounts. Twaddle is another matter, and there loyalty to my own upbringing as well as concern for the stability of tomorrow's battleships leads me to hope that there are more latter-day Marshalls than Tawneys designing and steering them.

[24] *R. H. Tawney's commonplace book*, ed. J. M. Winter and D. M. Joslin (Cambridge: Cambridge University Press 1972). See too Stefan Collini, 'Moral mind: R. H. Tawney' in his *English pasts* (Oxford: Oxford University Press, 1999), pp. 177–94.

PART I

Mill's Principles

2

Sentimental enemies, advanced intellects, and falling profits

Political Economy, in truth, has never pretended to give advice to mankind with no lights but its own; though people who knew nothing *but* political economy (and therefore knew that ill) have taken upon themselves to advise, and could only do so by such lights as they had. But the numerous sentimental enemies of political economy, and its still more numerous interested enemies in sentimental guise, have been very successful in gaining belief for this among other unmerited imputations against it.

John Stuart Mill, *Autobiography*[1]

I

One of Mill's retrospective claims for his *Principles of political economy* was to have succeeded in countering the unmerited imputations of sentimental enemies of the science. Before publication he said he would achieve this by avoiding 'the hard, abstract mode of treating such questions which has brought discredit upon political economists and has enabled those who are in the wrong to claim, and generally to receive, exclusive credit for high and benevolent feeling'.[2] Recapturing the high moral ground by exposing sentimentality and restoring political economy to its rightful place among the moral sciences, neither exaggerating nor minimising its value as a guide to present realities and future possibilities, was the task Mill set himself when he decided to write a work that would combine authoritative exposition with popular appeal. This essay deals with what led Mill to write his *Principles* when he did so and in the manner he chose.

The version of the science Mill had first learned as a thirteen-year-old from his father entailed bringing the 'superior lights' of Ricardo to bear

---

[1] CW, I, p. 242 [2] Letter to Napier, 9 November 1844, CW, XIII, p. 644

on Adam Smith's 'more superficial view of political economy'.[3] No
change of mind occurred on this front over the next three decades of
controversy within the science. That Mill continued to regard the *Wealth
of nations* as 'in many parts obsolete and in all, imperfect' is less surprising
perhaps than his fidelity to Ricardian formularies: 'What has been added
to the science since Ricardo, does not need to be substituted for his doctrines, but to be incorporated with them. They do not require alteration
or correction so much as fuller exposition and comment.'[4] Mill had
already supplied some of this in his *Essays on some unsettled questions in
political economy*, written in 1829–30 but only published in 1844 – essays
directed, as he said, at '*scientific* students of the science'.[5] When he wrote
his *Principles* the plan of incorporation expanded to include other significant post-Ricardian developments, one of which will be highlighted in
the penultimate section of this essay. It involved a variation on a central
Ricardian proposition connecting the downward tendencies of profit
levels with speculations about future growth prospects. Plotting such
tendencies was essential to Mill's diagnosis of the chief problems facing
the British economy, as it would have been to any serious economic
commentator. But using those tendencies to articulate a moral and political
ideal says something special about Mill's reasons for wanting to write his
Principles. For while it was necessary for him to show how the economic
remedies he favoured proceeded from sound economic analysis, his wider
goal included exhibiting 'the economical phenomena of society in the
relation in which they stand to the best social ideas of the present time'.[6]
Unlike his command over the Ricardian version of the abstract science,
Mill's confidence in being able to identify these social ideas was a more
recent acquisition, the result of a process of reappraisal that began with
the famous mental crisis he suffered during the winter of 1826–7, when
it seemed that none of the objects he had been educated to desire were
likely to give personal satisfaction.

As a young philosophic radical for whom political economy was a
badge of enlightenment, Mill took a hard-nosed line with the first sentimental enemies he encountered, the young Tories and Owenites against
whom he did battle in newspaper articles and in the London Debating
Society during the 1820s. Sentimentality was a sign of wishing to live in
an ideal rather than the actual world, an inability to think through difficult

---

[3] *Autobiography*, CW, I, p. 31.
[4] As stated in his review of De Quincey, with whom he agreed on Ricardo's pre-eminence; see CW,
IV, p. 394.
[5] Letter to W. Tait, 24 September 1833, CW, XII, p. 178.   [6] See *Principles*, CW, II, p. xcii.

things. As 'common terms of opprobrium' in the vocabulary of philo-sophic radicals, 'sentimentality' went alongside 'declamation' and 'vague generalities'.[7] Mill's early exposure to Ricardo's *Principles* equipped him with some robust arguments that could be used to good effect against anyone who failed to recognise that the Malthusian population principle operating in tandem with the law of diminishing returns in agriculture set the parameters within which the prospects for economic growth and future social improvement had to be considered. Birth control took the place of moral restraint (delayed marriage) as the chief remedy for low wages; and Mill's arrest for distributing literature on methods of con-traception at the age of seventeen shows that political economy was not a bookish form of philanthropy for him. Mill later summarised this neo-Malthusian position, a position shared by his generation of philosophic radicals, as follows:

[Malthus's] great doctrine, originally brought forward as an argument against the indefinite improvability of human affairs, we took up with ardent zeal in the contrary sense, indicating the sole means of realizing that improvability by secur-ing full employment at high wages to the whole labouring population through a voluntary restriction of the increase of their numbers.[8]

This doctrine marked the beginning of resistance to the idea that mass poverty was an irremediable evil, and in this respect alone did not deserve the common charge of being heartless or immoral.[9] Neo-Malthusianism was very much the hallmark of Mill's political economy, with implica-tions – as will be shown here and in the next essay – for many of the causes he espoused.

In opposition to the proto-socialist ideas of Owenites, according to which other classes were living on the produce of labour, Mill stressed the need for capital accumulation and hence for capitalists prepared to save and engage in 'productive' as opposed to 'unproductive' expenditure or consumption.[10] In answer to the Owenite panacea of co-operation he defended competition ('there may be competition for every thing – for good as well as ill: for fame and reputation, for the pleasures of beneficence, as well as for the pleasures of wealth').[11] Instead of calling for wholesale

---

[7] See *Autobiography*, CW, I, p. 113.   [8] *Ibid.*, p. 107
[9] *Newspaper writings* on 'Question of population', CW, XXII, p. 91
[10] 'On the words productive and unproductive' in *Essays on unsettled questions* was devoted to clarification of this distinction, and it became the basis for the equivalent chapter in the *Principles* (Book I, chapter 3) rehabilitating terminology that had come under fire since Adam Smith had made extensive use of it.
[11] Speech on co-operation in 1825, in *Journals and debating speeches*, CW, XXVI, p. 316.

replacement, what was needed was a 'fair comparison of the evils of the Competitive and the evils of the Cooperative system'.[12] Mill also defended the 'non-interference philosophy' on grounds of the superior knowledge economic agents had of their own affairs, while recognising that it had to give way in cases such as child factory employment, where 'it would be highly for the advantage of every body, if every body were to act in a certain manner, but in which it is not the interest of any *individual* to adopt the rule for the guidance of his own conduct, unless he has some security that all others will do so too'.[13]

In these early contests Mill was often little more than a skilful spokesman for his father's opinions. Although there was to be little change in his conclusions on the issues mentioned so far, Mill showed a degree of theoretical sophistication in his *Essays on unsettled questions* that went beyond anything to be found in his father's *Elements of political economy*. The rethinking that went into these essays was to stand him in good stead when he wrote the theoretical chapters in the first three books of the *Principles* on production, distribution, and exchange. During the 1830s, however, Mill was more preoccupied by a heady mixture of ideas that seemed incompatible with many of the doctrines he had first imbibed. So much so, indeed, that anyone who tried to follow his mental career after the crisis might well have concluded that political economy was low on any list of activities to which he would wish to devote his mature years. The crisis had exposed the ways in which education at his father's hands had exalted the capacity to reason over the 'cultivation of feeling'. Many of Mill's new personal and intellectual enthusiasms were located at the opposite end of any philosophical or political spectrum defined by the tripartite set of beliefs that comprised his earlier training: Benthamite principles of law and government; analytical psychology conducted along Hartleyan or associationist lines; and Ricardian political economy with its neo-Malthusian dimension being stressed. With the partial exception of the first of these three components, Mill's exposure to alternative views did not in fact result in abandonment of earlier positions, though it did entail an enhanced willingness to incorporate insights derived from other perspectives, and a degree of intellectual eclecticism that could be misleading to others if not to himself.[14]

---

[12] *Ibid.*, p. 319.   [13] *Newspaper writings*, CW, XXII, p. 400.
[14] For evidence of how Mill's behaviour during this period struck older friends within the Benthamite camp, Francis Place, Harriet Grote and John Roebuck, see the introduction to CW, VI, p. xxii.

This was obviously the case with Carlyle, with whom Mill struck up a close if uneven friendship in the 1830s. Initially, Carlyle's writings seemed to contain 'a haze of poetry and German metaphysics, in which almost the only clear thing was a strong animosity to most of the opinions which were the basis of my mode of thought; religious scepticism, utilitarianism, the doctrine of circumstances, and the attaching any importance to democracy, logic, or political economy'.[15] Later, Mill found himself falling into 'Carlylisms' and endorsing a view of Carlyle that was congenial to Carlyle's view of himself.[16] During the courtship stage of the relationship Mill readily conceded his friend's status as the soaring imaginative artist in contrast to his own more pedestrian role as political economist and logician. Mill also came to admire those 'philosophic' or 'speculative Tories', Wordsworth, Coleridge, and Southey, whose acquaintance he was pleased to make at much the same time. Wordsworth's nature poetry had personal therapeutic value to Mill during his crisis. As we shall see in the succeeding essay, the encounter with Wordsworth's Lake District left a permanent imprint on the opinions expressed in the *Principles*. As a result of friendships formed with two disciples of Coleridge, Frederick Denison Maurice and John Sterling, Mill became acquainted with those who, for a few years after 1848, called themselves 'Christian socialists' and whom he later described as 'Germano-Coleridgeans', those who exemplified the 'modes of thought of the European reaction against the philosophy of the eighteenth century' which he came to appreciate after his crisis. What these heterodox Anglicans – latent members of the 'clerisy' in Coleridge's ideal sense of that term – hoped to achieve through a revitalised established church was a challenging experience to someone who 'has not thrown off religious belief, but never had it'; and who had been taught to regard 'Church-of-Englandism' as an influence on education and politics that needed, at best, to be neutralised.[17]

II

Through Carlyle and the Coleridgeans Mill was exposed to Germanic styles of thinking later characterised as 'romantic'. But Mill's primary intellectual tastes were more Francophone. From his reading of the semi-socialist writings of the Saint-Simonians he absorbed terminology that

---

[15] *Autobiography* CW, I, p. 180.
[16] The best examples of Mill's recognition of this fault in himself can be found in letters to Carlyle, 18 May 1833, CW, XII, pp. 153–4, and 12 January 1834, XII, pp. 204–9.
[17] *Autobiography*, CW, I, p. 45

enabled him to situate his own work and the efforts of others on a larger
historical canvas designed to chart the main stages in the onward march
of the progressive mind. He became convinced that there was a 'law of
the successive transformations of human opinions'; and that he was living through an age of transition from a critical or revolutionary style of
thinking towards an organic or progressive one. Auguste Comte's version
of this idea depicted the sequence as one in which theological certainties
had been undermined by the negative metaphysics of the revolutionary
period. In turn, these metaphysical styles of thinking would be replaced
by a final phase in which all social institutions would be definitively
remodelled on the basis of positivistic interpretations of science, with a
comprehensive, holistic, and evolutionary form of sociology providing
the capstone to the entire edifice.

It was by this route that Mill learned, or rather relearned, an elementary lesson in historical or sociological relativism at a time when he was
being forced to concede that his father's deductive approach to the science
of politics based on the self-interest principle could not support claims
to universal validity. The defects in such an approach were too basic for
repair: amendments to the theoretical superstructure could not compensate 'for the want of sufficient breadth in its foundations'. Political
economy did not suffer from such serious faults because there was still
'one large class of social phenomena of which the immediately determining causes are principally those which act through the desire of wealth'.
All that was necessary was for political economists to be reminded that
societies differed in the scope allowed for this desire when compared with
the forces of custom; and that it was no longer possible to assume that
present economic institutions and practices would meet the needs of a
future, more improved state of society. Mill's updated version of the
science would recognise 'the very limited and temporary value of the old
political economy, which assumes private property and inheritance as
indefeasible facts, and freedom of production and exchange as the *dernier
mot* of social improvement'.[18]

The 1830s for Mill were a decade of intense involvement in party
politics. Denied more overt forms of participation by his position as a
civil servant at East India House, he used his journalistic skills to support
reform causes and the activities of the large group of radical MPs elected
after passage of the Reform Bill in 1832. This activist phase came to an
abrupt end in 1839 with the break-up of the parliamentary radicals and

---

[18] *Ibid.*, p. 174

the shattering of any hope of founding a party that could contest political space with Whigs, Tories, and the new extra-parliamentary forces in British politics represented by the Chartist movement and Cobden's Anti-Corn Law League. Mill formally withdrew from politics, shed his responsibilities for running the party's intellectual organ, the *London and Westminster Review*, and acted in accordance with his diagnosis that: 'We are entering upon times in which the progress of liberal opinions will again, as formerly, depend upon what is said and written, and no longer upon what is done, by their avowed friends.'[19] He began to devote most of his energies to finishing a work he had begun more than a decade before: *A system of logic, ratiocinative and inductive; being a connected view of the principles of evidence and the methods of scientific investigation* (*Logic* hereafter). This was to be his first mature contribution to the progress of liberal opinions, and it was based on the assumption that 'almost all differences of opinion when analysed were differences of method'. It followed that the person who could illuminate this subject would 'do most to forward that alliance among the most advanced intellects and characters of the age, which is the only definite object I ever have in literature or philosophy so far as I have any general object at all'.[20]

Mill had just begun work on the *Logic* when he confessed to those hopes. It was to take another dozen years of intermittent labour on the logic and history of science before ambition could be matched by performance; but the last thing that could be said of Mill during this period is that his interest in and admiration for alternative, more romantic modes of expression prevented him from sticking to his last, that of logician and philosopher of science. One of his modest boasts in 1840 was that 'if I have done any good a large share of it lies in the example of a professed logician and political economist who believes there are other things besides logic and political economy'.[21] When the *Logic* finally appeared in 1843 its success far exceeded Mill's expectations; he found a publisher willing to take on all the risks involved, and the healthy sales in university circles proved that he could capture a public beyond the sectarian audiences he had previously addressed. He was now free to look

[19] Letter to Macvey Napier, 30 July 1841, CW, XIII, p. 483.
[20] Letter to Sterling, 20–22 October 1831, CW, XII, pp. 78–9. This was also the conclusion of the essay on the definition and method of political economy (see IV, p. 324), the first of his non-journalistic writings which he thought of as 'classical' or canonical; see letter to Nichol, 17 January 1834, CW, XII, p. 211.
[21] Letter to R. B. Fox, 23 December 1840, CW, XIII, p. 453.

for other ways of forwarding the alliance between advanced intellects by capitalising on the reputation he had acquired.

A decade or more after the work appeared, when Mill was drafting his *Autobiography*, he could be more forthcoming about his motives. They were essentially to combat 'the German or *a priori* view of human knowledge and the knowing faculties' by means of a textbook defending the opposite position, one that 'derives all knowledge from experience, and all moral and intellectual qualities principally from the direction given to the associations'. Advanced intellects required such a defence because the idea that truth was innate and could be apprehended by intuition, regardless of experience, was

the great intellectual support of false doctrines and bad institutions. By the aid of this theory, every inveterate belief and every intense feeling, of which the origin is not remembered, is enabled to dispense with the obligation of justifying itself by reason, and is erected into its own all-sufficient voucher and justification. There never was such an instrument devised for consecrating all deep seated prejudices.[22]

Attacking the intuitionists in their stronghold, mathematics and the physical sciences, was a necessary preliminary to the argument in Book VI of the work, the culminating book on the logic of the moral sciences, which was designed to show that the naturalistic methods of the physical sciences were applicable to moral and social phenomena; and that progressive improvement in understanding was as much a feature of the moral sciences as it was in studies of the natural world.

In Book VI of the *Logic* Mill had outlined the various moral or social sciences available for cultivation by naturalistic methods. Comte's new science of sociology was given a blessing, largely at the expense of a separate 'science of government' conducted along the lines of his father's *Essay on government*. Mill proposed the addition of another new science to the array, ethology, a science of character formation that would act as a bridge between psychology on one side and the historical and social disciplines such as jurisprudence and sociology on the other. Mill was particularly attracted to this uncharted territory, partly as a result of an interest in the problem of free will and the formation of his own character; partly because his personal experience of English and French society and his knowledge, second-hand though it was, of India and Ireland, equipped him, or so he thought, with insight into political ethology, the study of

---

[22] *Autobiography*, CW, I, p. 232, emphasised again on p. 269.

the formation of national or group character on a comparative basis. He was later to apply ethology to the explanation of sex differences, carrying his campaign against 'intuitional metaphysics' further by showing how the differences between men and women could be explained by circumstances and earlier formative influences. One of his criticisms of Bentham's science of legislation was that it took 'next to no account of national character and the causes which form and maintain it' – a serious criticism because it precluded Bentham from giving proper consideration to 'the laws of a country as an instrument of national culture'.[23]

After a year or two of exploring the ethological possibilities, however, Mill was forced to concede that the time was not ripe for making progress with this new venture; that the aim of composing a tune that would allow advanced intellects to march in step could best be achieved by making use of his knowledge of one of the older branches of the moral sciences. Political economy had been cited in Book VI as one of those instances in which, despite the general consensus of social phenomena, it was legitimate to detach for separate treatment a class of causes relating to a particular psychological disposition: the desire to acquire or consume wealth with minimum effort when unimpeded by other motives. On such premises a hypothetical or deductive science could be constructed, using the indicative rather than imperative mood, a science capable of supporting a separate art yielding practical guidance when related branches of knowledge were called upon and allowances made for the failure of premises to match reality exactly.

Mill predicted correctly that he would make rapid progress with his *Principles* and was in ebullient mood by the time he had finished the first draft. As he reported rather breathlessly to a friend, the formula of combining the abstract science with practical illustrations had provided him with opportunities

to bring in, or rather to bring out, a great number of opinions on incidental matters, moral and social for which one has not often so good an opportunity, and I have used this privilege as freely as Adam Smith did, and I fully expect to offend and scandalize ten times as many people as I shall please, but that is 'all in day's work', and I always intended to make that use of any standing I might get among publicists.[24]

The book was published before the February revolution in France and was overtaken by the events that followed. Mill was pleased to discover

---

[23] 'Bentham', CW, X, p. 105.
[24] Letter to Henry S. Chapman, 9 March 1847, CW, XIII, pp. 708–9.

that 'the public mind became more open to the reception of novelties in opinion, and doctrines appeared moderate which would have been thought very startling a short time before'.[25] Scandalising his audience proved more difficult, but the shift in public opinion corroborated his decision to be forthright in expressing his views 'on incidental matters, moral and social'.

III

One of the reasons we know so much about Mill's aims in writing his *Principles* is that he found it necessary to justify his decision to some new allies, those who might have suspected that his choice of subject marked a retreat to a less emancipated self. To older English friends already versed in the science of political economy he mainly stressed the conventional nature of his aims, but in the case of people like Comte more elaborate justification was required. The trouble Mill took to convince Comte of the value of his new project reflects his unwillingness to jeopardise his relationship with someone he believed to be one of the most advanced intellects of the day. The ultimate goal of Comtean positivism was the reorganisation of society according to principles that would be established by a science combining study of the historical dynamics of social progress with the statics of social order, a distinction that Mill took over and employed for his own purposes in Book VI of the *Logic* on the moral sciences and in his *Principles*. As an adjunct to realisation of this, it was hoped that a religion of humanity would eventually replace existing otherworldly religions. Mill's broad acceptance of these features of Comte's way of thinking meant that the two men could for a time overlook those issues on which they were plainly at odds with one another. Mill was aware of Comte's suspicions of political economy on grounds of its 'critical' and 'revolutionary' associations; it belonged to a metaphysical stage in the unfolding of the laws of human progress that it was the obligation of a new generation, under Comte's leadership, to surmount. Anticipating such objections, Mill reassured Comte that his new work would stress 'the provisional character of all concrete conclusions', and make 'a special effort to distinguish the general laws of production, necessarily common to all industrial societies, from the principles of distribution and of the exchange of wealth, principles which by necessity assume a particular state

---

[25] *Autobiography*, CW, I, p. 241.

of society without prejudging whether this state must or even can last indefinitely'.[26]

Here then was the rationale for what became one of Mill's most characteristic innovations in the *Principles*, the distinction he introduced into a unified Ricardian framework between laws of production that resembled physical truths and laws of distribution that were matters of human will and hence subject to institutional adjustment. By making this distinction he hoped to achieve two objects: first, to break what had seemed to be an indissoluble link between political economy and a particular set of competitive and capitalistic institutions, what he had criticised in the work of an older generation of English economists as their attempt 'to construct a permanent fabric out of transitory materials'.[27] Secondly, and less obviously, he wanted to create the necessary space for inquiry into and publicity for those modes of distribution that would follow from different types of property relations, including industrial experiments along co-operative or socialistic lines of the kind being advocated by some French authors, and peasant proprietorships of the type that Mill had begun to advocate as a solution to Irish problems during and after the famine. Mill did not think he was limiting the role of political economy by making the distinction, because the science still had an important role to play in analysing the consequences of any chosen set of distributive rules.

In his early dealings with Comte one of the services Mill performed was to give advice on how the English public might best be tempted to broaden its intellectual tastes. For a practical-minded English audience, and a backward one that had not experienced any revolutionary break with the past, political economy presented in the manner Mill had in mind would serve the cause he shared with Comte far better than more frontal assaults on their moral and intellectual susceptibilities. Far from standing in the way of the development of sociology, then, political economy had the advantage

of preparing the positive education of many thinkers who are more or less seriously concerned with social questions . . . Moreover, I believe that today such a work has a good chance of taking possession of its particular field by displacing the treatises we have today, all essentially outdated even in terms of the present

---

[26] He opened the topic in April 1844; see CW, XIII, pp. 626, 630–1. For both sides of the correspondence, see the *Correspondence of John Stuart Mill and Auguste Comte*, trans. and ed. Oscar A. Haac (London: Transaction Publishers, 1997).

[27] Review of Martineau, CW, IV, p. 225.

state of public opinion; for even if the public does not soon find something a bit better, it will certainly turn away from this type of studies, and its disgust would then benefit only some systematic empiricism that denies all general theory in sociological matter.[28]

In other words, not only was Mill's plan suited to the English mentality, it would prevent something worse from happening, retrogression as a result of a collapse into what they both feared, mere empiricism unenlightened by theory.

Mill succeeded in obtaining a formal blessing from Comte for his treatise on 'l'économie industrielle des sociétés'. Mill's French, with its substitution of 'industrial' for 'political' as the relevant adjective, captures something of the reorientation that may have made his enterprise sound more acceptable to Comte. But as W. J. Ashley, the first editor of Mill's text to make use of the Mill–Comte correspondence, was to point out in 1909, Comte and Mill were seriously at odds over the meaning of *provisoire*/provisional. For Comte it meant temporary, even transitory, a period lasting until a positive science of sociology had been fully established. For Mill it meant as long as the existing state of human nature and the present system of private property appropriate to it were operative.[29] Mill was not conceding as much as he had earlier suggested, and when not required to adapt his language to Comte's susceptibilities, he could be more critical and assertive. French intellectuals might be streets ahead of their English counterparts in the boldness of their general opinions, but as Mill pointed out to Alexis de Tocqueville, another advanced intellect whom he first met and came to admire during the 1830s, they could not afford to ignore the English science:

It is my belief . . . that in political and social philosophy the French are not only original but the *only* people who are original on a large scale and that as soon as they shall have appropriated, and fitted into their theories, the stricter and closer deductions of the English School of political economy and some other matters of comparative detail they will give the law to the scientific world on these subjects. I do wish they would thoroughly master Ricardo and Bentham.[30]

Mill managed to combine apparent modesty with intellectual imperialism in the chapter he devoted to the subject in Book VI of the *Logic*.

---

[28] Letter to Comte, 6 June 1844, CW, XIII, p. 631 (p. 237 of Haac translation).
[29] See Ashley's introduction to his edition of the *Principles* (London: Longmans Green, 1909), p. xxiii.
[30] CW, XIII, p. 458. He had earlier advised two Saint-Simonians, Gustave d'Eichthal and Charles Duveyrier, that they had 'yet much to learn, in political economy from the English economists (inferior as they are to you in many points)'; see letter 30 May 1832, CW, XII, p. 109.

There was still 'one large class of social phenomena' that was susceptible of separate treatment; and while this class of events and type of behaviour was at present most marked in only two countries, Britain and America, the methods were applicable to other kinds of society:

Though many of its conclusions are only locally true, its method of investigation is applicable universally; and as whoever has solved a certain number of algebraic equations can without difficulty solve all others, so whoever knows the political economy of England, or even of Yorkshire, knows that of all nations, actual or possible, provided he have good sense enough not to expect the same conclusion to issue from varying premises.[31]

The major points of disagreement between Mill and Comte in the 1840s were given blunt expression in 1865 when Mill had fallen out with Comte over matters that cast serious doubt on the latter's credentials as an advanced intellect, notably in his attitude to equality between the sexes. In an extended critique, Mill noted that 'the weak side of [Comte's] philosophy comes out prominently in his strictures on the only systematic attempt yet made by any body of thinkers, to constitute a science, not indeed of social phenomena generally, but of one great class or division of them. We mean, of course, political economy.' Comte's criticisms of the science were based on ignorance of what had happened since Adam Smith left the scene; and his only point of substance, concerning the relativity of generalisations to a given state of social advancement, was one that 'no political economist would deny'. In the 1830s Mill was prepared to concede that there were *some* economists who needed the reminder: by 1865 they had all disappeared or been converted:

None of them pretend that the laws of wages, profits, and the like, set down in their treatises, would be strictly true, or many of them true at all in the savage state . . . or in a community composed of masters and slaves. But they do think, with good reason, that whoever understands the political economy of a country with the complicated and manifold civilisation of the nations of Europe, can deduce without difficulty the political economy of any other state of society, with the particular circumstances of which he is equally well acquainted.[32]

Simply by choosing to publish seven editions of his *Principles*, of course, Mill showed that his commitment to political economy, though still 'provisional' in his understanding of the word, had not suffered any depletion. In one of his last general pronouncements on the subject, his address as Rector to the students of the University of St Andrews in 1867,

[31] Review of Martineau, CW, IV, p. 226.   [32] *Auguste Comte and positivism*, CW, X, p. 305.

he commended political economy as the branch of the moral sciences that 'approaches nearer to the rank of a science, in the sense in which we apply that name to the physical sciences, than anything else connected with politics yet does'.[33] It met all the criteria he had laid down in Book VI of the *Logic* for a successful moral science conducted along naturalistic lines, and it still had important work to do.

IV

There are ample signs that by 1840, at the latest, Mill had fully taken the measure of the new sources of emancipation he had explored since his first mental crisis; and that he had reached a point at which he could present a personal amalgam of doctrines that would unite advanced intellects without further appeal to those sources. In another version of the Saint-Simonian differentiation between epochs, Mill contrasted the eighteenth-century ideas of his upbringing with the nineteenth-century influences he had explored after his crisis. The matching pair of essays he wrote on Bentham and Coleridge in 1838 and 1840 respectively as 'the two great seminal minds of England' provided another way of expressing this contrast. It was also a way of stating a problem that Mill had resolved by the time he wrote the second essay. For when read alongside letters and other writings belonging to the same period, the essay on Coleridge has many of the qualities of a farewell message, a final settling of accounts, a generous recognition of what had been learned prior to moving on. Reconciliation was now possible because the swings between opposite poles had settled on a sane middle solution that advanced intellects could share.

Anyone now capable of appreciating the mutually corrective symmetry of the tension between Bentham and Coleridge, between the styles of eighteenth- and nineteenth-century thinking they represented, had already found a stable position in order to do so. Mill's concluding praise for the Tory philosopher as someone who 'must often be a better Liberal than Liberals themselves' takes nothing back from what is said earlier, namely that on all the important philosophical issues dividing associ-ationists from romantic intuitionists the Germano-Coleridgeans had come to the wrong conclusions. Mill had been attracted to Coleridge's idea of a clerisy capable of providing cultural and intellectual authority. It continued to have some attractions, though by 1847 he was informing

---

[33] Inaugural address, CW, XXI, p. 245.

John Austin that he had 'ceased to think that a leisured class ... is an essential constituent of the best form of society'. It was more important that 'society at large should not be overworked, nor overanxious about the means of subsistence'.[34] Mill's essay on Coleridge was also the occasion for delivering the damning judgement that on political economy Coleridge wrote like an 'arrant driveller' who would have done well to avoid the subject altogether.

Another illustration of Mill's shift from supplicant to judge can be found in the contrast between the enthusiastic letter Mill sent to Sterling in 1831 reporting on his initial impressions after meeting Wordsworth in the Lake District, and the way in which he dealt with this in his *Autobiography* composed in the early 1850s. In the letter he said that 'all my differences with him ... would be differences of matter-of-fact or detail, while my differences with the radicals and utilitarians are differences of principle'; he summed up by saying that he and Wordsworth would 'be like two travellers pursuing the same course on the opposite banks of a river'. Writing about his relationship with Wordsworth and the other philosophic Tories twenty years later, however, Mill inserted a blunt hint to the effect that amid the grand imagery to be found in the *Ode: intimations of immortality* there was also 'bad philosophy'.[35] The early draft is more explicit. Speaking of the Coleridgeans, Mill says: 'But if I agreed with them much more than with Bentham on poetry and general culture, I was as much opposed to them as ever on religion, political philosophy, ethics and metaphysics'.[36] This is a fairly comprehensive list, suggesting that the river that divided him from such authors had come to seem a good deal wider during the intervening years.

But it is in Mill's shifting (and, ultimately, deteriorating) relationship with Carlyle that one sees most clearly what was happening to Mill's thinking as it was happening, and how Mill was emerging with renewed self-assurance. For the first few years, all diplomacy and modesty (almost to the point of self-abasement) was on Mill's side of the correspondence. He had to remind Carlyle tactfully from time to time that a personal commitment to many-sidedness was not synonymous with acceptance of Carlyle's idiosyncratic views. The correspondence surrounding the composition and publication of Carlyle's pamphlet on *Chartism* in 1839 has a special interest for two main reasons. First, the work was an early yet fairly complete statement of the authoritarian credo for which Carlyle

[34] Letter to Austin, 13 April 1847, CW, XIII, p. 713.
[35] See *Autobiography*, CW, I, pp. 152–3.   [36] *Ibid.*, p. 162.

later became famous or notorious. Secondly, as noted in the Prologue, *Chartism* and its sequel, *Past and present*, acquired emblematic status for many mid-century social commentators.[37] Mill endorsed that status by selecting Carlyle as an example of an influential form of social diagnosis whose attractions needed recognition. At the same time Carlyle became Mill's prime example of an approach that was inappropriate to any form of progressive modern society that advanced intellects could accept. Mill's decision to write his *Principles* in the way he did was intimately connected with his assessment of what needed to be put in place of the values for which Carlyle stood.

Some idea of the convoluted nature of the relationship between Mill and Carlyle is captured in the welcome Mill gave to the manuscript version of *Chartism*: 'It is a glorious piece of work, and will be a blessed gospel to many, if they read it and lay it to heart . . . I incline to think that the condition of the working classes has not deteriorated; but all that you say on the matter, ought to be said by those who think it, and the far greater part of it, I think too.' There is a hint of equivocation here, but it was pushed into the background by Mill's offer to publish the piece in the *London and Westminster* before he resigned as its editor: 'it would delight me much to let this be the last dying speech of a Radical Review. I do not think a radical review *ought* to die without saying all this – and no one else could say it half as well.'[38]

Carlyle was a little taken aback by Mill's enthusiasm. Although Mill had encouraged him to tackle this subject and advised him on various sources of information on working-class living standards, the story Carlyle was telling others was that 'Mill and his wooden set' would not publish anything that concluded living standards were falling.[39] While writing the piece Carlyle had decided that his views would be more acceptable to 'the better class of the Conservatives' than to Whigs or radicals.[40] Lockhart, editor of the *Quarterly Review*, gave him some encouragement, but after seeing the article was not prepared to risk publication, which is why Mill was given the chance to express an opinion. But rather than see

---

[37] See p. 5 above.

[38] Letter to Carlyle, early December 1839, CW, XIII, p. 414.

[39] If Mill's letter offering publication in the *London and Westminster Review* arrived before Carlyle wrote to Emerson in America on 8 December 1839, it is possible that he was informing Emerson that his article had been rejected *after* he had received Mill's plea for its inclusion; see letter to Emerson in the *Collected letters of Thomas and Jane Welsh Carlyle*, ed. Charles Richard Sanders (Durham, NC: Duke University Press, 1970–), XI, p. 226.

[40] Letter to Lockhart, *Ibid.*, p. 104.

his work appear in a periodical whose audience he disliked, a periodical he thought would founder when Mill gave up the editorship, Carlyle arranged for its publication as a pamphlet.

The title Carlyle gave his work was a late decision and not entirely apt: while it was being written he referred to it simply as a 'discourse' or a 'sermon' on the condition of the working classes. *Chartism* was inappropriate because Carlyle had little to say about the movement that bore that name; it was simply another of the age's cursed 'isms', a confused yet ominous reaction to a deeper malaise arising from a society in which the natural social bonds linking rich and poor, the wise and the ignorant, had been replaced by the cash nexus. He also thought its leaders were inadequate and ought to be replaced by men from a higher class – if only the aristocracy could be shaken out of dilettantism sufficiently to resume the duties that went with their historic role. Carlyle was unimpressed by the political aims of the movement: it would not do the working classes much good to gain entry into the place where the 'national palaver' took place, mainly because he set little store by representative institutions. He had finished his history of the French revolution a couple of years earlier, and there is more than a whiff of fear hanging over *Chartism*: the parallels between 1839 and 1789 were too close for comfort.[41]

Carlyle did not offer much by way of an economic diagnosis for depressed living conditions. Apart from drawing attention to the effect of Irish immigration on English wage levels he made a few remarks about steam engines creating work in the long run, but only for skilled workers. The closest he came to Mill's analysis of depression, as we shall see, was in a passing remark about the 'world-wide convulsive fluctuations' of English commerce. Carlyle had more knockabout fun at the expense of the 'Benthamee-Malthus' remedies and the reports of the Poor Law Commissioners he had been advised to read by Mill:

There is a phenomenon which one might call Paralytic Radicalism, in these days; which gauges with Statistic measuring-reed, sounds with Philosophic Politico-Economic plummet the deep dark sea of troubles; and having taught us rightly what an infinite sea of troubles it is, sums up with the practical inference, and use of consolation, That nothing whatever can be done in it by man, who has simply to sit still, and look wistfully to 'time and general laws', and thereupon, without so much as recommending suicide, coldly takes its leave of us.[42]

---

[41] 'These Chartisms, Radicalisms, Reform Bill, Tithe Bill . . . are *our* French Revolution'; see *Chartism and past and present* (London: Chapman Hall, 1888), p. 27; see also pp. 36, 41–2, 49.
[42] *Ibid.*, p. 58.

The new Poor Law was the acme of the prevailing *laissez-faire* mentality, which was in turn the fruit of the democracy launched by the 1832 Reform Act. Whether *laissez-faire* is an appropriate description of the thinking of a busy, meddling kind of commissioner such as Edwin Chadwick depends on where you are standing. The 'do-nothingism' Carlyle castigated was doing nothing that met his criteria of relevance. He was not lending support to the anti-Poor Law demonstrations; he judged the amendment Act, 'heretical and damnable as a whole truth', to be 'orthodox and laudable as a *half*-truth' – one that it was imperative to implement. The old Poor Law had become 'a bounty on unthrift, idleness, bastardy and beer-drinking'.[43] Malthusians and anti-Malthusians are ridiculed equally, though what Carlyle says about emigration, the only economic remedy endorsed in the pamphlet, presupposes acceptance of the idea of population pressure. But permanent relief from downward pressure on living standards could only emerge in a society in which the relations between classes were no longer purely commercial, in which the gospel of work commanded respect, and in which the moral duty of governors to govern was recognised. Those workers who were being drawn into movements like Chartism were calling for something more affirmative from their governors: 'An ever-toiling inferior, he would fain (though as yet he knows it not) find for himself a superior that should lovingly and wisely govern . . . It is for a manlike place and relation, in this world where he sees himself a man, that he struggles.'[44]

v

For Mill, as we have seen, failure to grasp the import of the Malthusian principle was a mark of sentimentality, of failure to face up to economic realities. Carlyle was too self-consciously a tough-minded devotee of power to be guilty of that kind of sentimentality. He did not share Mill's enthusiasm for Malthusianism and the new Poor Law, but he could not be described as an 'interested enemy in sentimental guise' because, unlike earlier romantic critics, he was not denying that pressure of numbers could ever be a cause of poverty. But it is with respect to Chartism that the differences between Mill and Carlyle are most obvious. For Mill it was a serious movement in its own right and to be welcomed as calling into question the established order: 'It was the revolt of nearly all the active talent, and a great part of the physical force, of the working classes,

[43] *Ibid.*, p. 13.   [44] *Ibid.*, p. 15.

against their whole relation to society.'[45] Far from thinking the movement badly led, Mill sought out William Lovett among the moderate leaders to offer his support, financial and otherwise.[46] He also thought that what the Chartists were demanding by way of political rights was worth seeking, though he made it clear that he would oppose working-class rule just as strongly as he opposed rule by any other class. Mill may have become less of a democrat than his father and Bentham had been, and temporarily given up politics for writing, but he could never have regarded parliamentary proceedings with the contempt shown by Carlyle.

In commending Carlyle to Comte, Mill said that Carlyle's point of view on the French revolution was 'imparfait mais progressif', diminishing this a few tones by adding, 'pour ce pays-ci'. Carlyle lacked any general doctrine apart from 'la critique de la critique'.[47] Decoded, this piece of Comte-speak describes someone who was progressive enough to be critical of critical thinking without having reached its proper antithesis, the positive scientific standpoint. Mill had not dissembled with Carlyle himself. Reviewing Carlyle's *French revolution* he praised the work's originality, and the epic, vivid, and pathetic qualities of the narrative prose. But he made no effort to conceal his opinion of the author's two cardinal weaknesses: an inability to understand the need for theory or 'general principles' when interpreting any complex chain of social or historical events; and his tendency 'to set too low a value on what constitutions and forms of government can do'.[48]

While Carlyle was working on another statement of his position on the condition of England for what became *Past and present*, Mill was preparing to write his first response to *Chartism* and other works of that kind, a counterblast to a 'prodigious current . . . of superficial philanthropy' generated by a variety of things, 'some good, some bad'. Writing to Chapman, he listed the following:

The anti-poor-law cry; the state of the houses of the poor, and their sanitary condition, as made known by Chadwick's official investigations; the conditions of large masses of people as shown by the enquiries of the Commissions about

[45] 'The claims of labour', CW, IV, p. 69.

[46] See letter to Lovett, 27 July 1842, CW, XIII, pp. 533–4. Mill was opposed to Oastler and Stephens, 'the worst portion of the Operative Radicals, almost confined . . . to a narrow district in the North'. But he praised the Working Men's Association which framed the Charter and began the agitation for it; they 'represented the best and most enlightened aspect of working-class Radicalism'; see 'Reorganisation of the reform party', CW, VI, pp. 485–6.

[47] Letter to Comte, 15 December 1842, CW, XIII, p. 562.

[48] Review of Carlyle's *French revolution*, CW, XX, p. 162.

the factories, mines, etc, then in another way the speculations of Carlyle, the Puseyites, and others, about the impossibility of any social stability or security if there is not a habitual bond of good offices and sympathy between the ruling classes and the ruled, especially the poor – which speculations would have had no effect whatever if there were no chartism and socialism to frighten the rich.

As the last remark indicates, Mill suspected that much of this could be attributed to fear of revolution plus a desire on the part of the landowning interest to take the wind out of the sails of the Anti-Corn Law League. Since he felt that the Corn Laws were already doomed, the main effect of this outpouring of literature was on the working classes, 'whom it greatly strengthens in the faith that it is other people's business to take care of them'. Much of the advance towards self-reliant positions that Mill associated with an unsentimental political economy was once more under threat: 'I never remember a time when any suggestion of anti-population doctrine or of forethought and self-command on the part of the poor was so contemptuously scouted as it is now.'[49] Mill had clearly worked himself up on the subject because the next day he wrote to the editor of the *Edinburgh Review* offering an article on the 'claims of labour' that promised to correct

speculations now afloat [that are] sadly deficient . . . in sobriety and wisdom – forgetful, in general, of the lessons of universal experience, and of some of those fundamental principles which one did think had been put for ever out of the reach of controversy by Adam Smith, Malthus, and others. The general tendency is to rivet firmly in the minds of the labouring people the persuasion that it is the business of others to take care of their condition, without any self control on their own part.

Mill also wanted 'to examine and controvert what appears to me an erroneous theory of the condition of the labouring classes'.[50] When it appeared in 1845, Mill's article cited Carlyle's *Chartism* and *Past and present* as works that were the most eloquent expression of this theory; they 'were openly, what much of his previous writings had been incidentally, an indignant remonstrance with the higher classes on their sins of omission against the lower; contrasted with what he deemed the superior efficiency, in that relation, of the rulers in older times'. What was being preached was not simply *ad hoc* forms of charity but 'a new moral order, or an old order revived, in which the possessors of property are to resume their place as the paternal guardians of those less fortunate'. But

---

[49] Quotations from a letter to Chapman, 8 November 1844, CW, XIII, p. 641.
[50] Quotations from a letter to Napier, 9 November 1844, CW, XIII, pp. 643–5.

with paternal care, he warned, comes paternal authority, the kind of society associated with feudal serfdom or slave-owning, where the best the patronised could hope for was the status of a grateful dependant.

Mill's response to Carlyle's denunciation of a normless world in which only the cash nexus ruled was to stress the positive resources and benefits of self-reliance, those qualities that could be enhanced by an education that went beyond knowledge of the Bible to include schools of industry that cultivated minds as well as hands. He drew attention to the contribution of the Scottish parochial schools in this respect and to the shameful contrast with England where no such provision existed. The working classes were as capable of foresight and rationality as their middle-class superiors:

A well-educated labouring class could, and we believe would, keep up its condition to a high standard of comfort, or at least at a great distance from physical destitution, by the exercise of the same degree of habitual prudence now commonly practised by the middle class. We believe, too, that if this were the case, the poor could do very well without those incessant attentions on the part of the rich, which constitute the new whole duty of man to his poorer neighbour.

Feudal relations suited to a static rural society were no longer appropriate to 'an age that produces railroads which, for a few shillings, will convey a labourer and his family fifty miles to find work; in which agricultural labourers read newspapers, and make speeches at public meetings called by themselves to discuss low wages'.[51]

VI

One influence at work on Mill eventually engulfed all others, though he could say little about it in public at the time. In 1830 he had fallen in love with Harriet Taylor, a woman with advanced opinions who had been given freedom by her husband to exchange them with her platonic admirer during their weekends and foreign expeditions together. The only freedom her husband refused to grant was Mill's wish to dedicate his *Principles* to Harriet and her desire to be the object of the dedication. It would have made Mill's dependence on her counsel more widely known at an earlier stage. After Harriet became his wife in 1851, Mill was able, with her encouragement and guidance, to plan to inform the world through the *Autobiography* he began to draft that the *Principles* was their

---

[51] All of the quotations are taken from 'The claims of labour', CW, IV, pp. 370, 372, 374, 378, 379, 380.

first 'joint production', and that a long chapter on 'the probable futurity
of the labouring classes' was entirely due to her: 'What was abstract and
purely scientific was generally mine; the properly human element came
from her: in all that concerned the application of philosophy to the
exigencies of human society and progress, I was her pupil, alike in
boldness of speculation and cautiousness of practical judgement.'[52]

Harriet altered how Mill saw and later came to write about the relationships that were part of his transition from crisis to maturity. She was
added to the Saint-Simonians as one of the sources through which Mill
came to appreciate progressive historicism, though her special gift was
to make it a 'living principle pervading and animating' the *Principles*.
She was also 'more courageous and farsighted than without her I should
have been, in anticipations of an order of things to come'. Harriet now
occupied the role of 'artist' or visionary in Mill's life, replacing Carlyle
along with earlier competitors for this role, and revealing Carlyle's limitations: she 'was more a poet than he, and more a thinker than I', her
'mind and nature included his, and infinitely more'. Whereas other artists
had required Mill's capacity to express their position in non-transcen-
dental terms, sifting error from truth along the way, Harriet 'struck out
truths far in advance of me, but in which I could not, as I had done
in those others, detect any mixture of error'.[53] She was understandably
annoyed when she learned how meek Mill had been in his correspondence with Comte and Carlyle. Mill credited her with preventing him
from 'modifying my early opinions too much'; and in this respect Harriet
helped to consolidate the gains. Mill's opinions now formed a stable
synthesis with hers that it was their joint task to transmit to the world
before the death they both anticipated from tuberculosis overtook them.

The parts of the *Principles* to which Harriet unmistakably contributed
are chiefly concentrated in the chapter in Book IV on the labouring
classes and the opening chapters of Book II on property and socialism.
Yet, as we have noted, the first of these, with one significant addition, was
fully prefigured in Mill's article on the claims of labour. To what Mill had
to say about the evils of dependency of the poor upon the rich, Harriet
added dependency of women on men: the attack on aristocratic paternalism in society at large became an attack on patriarchalism in the home
as well.[54] Mill needed no convincing on the abstract question of equality

---

[52] *Autobiography*, CW, I, p. 257.   [53] *Ibid.*, p. 253.
[54] 'The so-called protectors are now the only persons against whom, in any ordinary circumstances,
    protection is needed. The brutality and tyranny with which every police report is filled, are those

Fig. 1. John Stuart Mill: 'The ladies' advocate', *Punch*, 1 June 1867

between the sexes: Harriet gave the case the kind of passion that came from personal identification.

Mill acknowledged the 'seductive' qualities of the theory of dependency: the attractions of a society based on 'strong personal attachments and disinterested self-devotion', the chivalric aspect of feudalism. But as in the article on the claims of labour such visions were assigned to a bygone age, to the world of the clan, to 'a rude and imperfect state of the

of husbands to wives, of parents to children', *Principles*, CW, III, p. 761. Mill had collaborated with Harriet in writing eighteen newspaper articles on some prominent cases of male cruelty to women; see *Newspaper writings*, CW, XXV, pp. 1151–7, 1164–70, 1172–8, 1183–6.

social union', when protection of the weak by the strong had only positive qualities.[55] This is one of those places where Mill sounds less like a Saint-Simonian representing the nineteenth century than an eighteenth-century Scottish conjectural historian speaking the language of social stages. Outside rural parts of southern England, where deference still reigned, it was now totally inappropriate. The well-being of the working classes depended on their own 'mental self-cultivation'; and any advice offered had to be tendered to them as equals.[56] Spontaneous education was taking place, which meant that deference might be paid to superior intellect and knowledge, but the judgement of who was entitled to it could no longer be taken on trust.

From this point on, the 'joint' chapter becomes an exercise in hopeful extrapolation, with obvious backward connections to the other chapter that bears the strongest marks of Harriet's influence, the chapter in Book II on property and socialism. Education will lay the foundation for prudent population habits. Women will gain independence and new careers beyond those of wife and mother; the accidents of sex will no longer be the basis for unequal treatment under law. Even the 'animal instinct' underlying sexual relations will become less dominant. Wage-earners will increasingly manifest dissatisfaction with their wage-labour status and see it as a stepping-stone to something better. Capitalists too will acquire an interest in finding ways of overcoming the conflict of capital and labour. Inequalities of wealth will be reduced as property is increasingly diffused via peasant proprietor-ships and greater ease of access to land ownership. Since labour is more productive in large systems of manufacture and farming, it will be necessary to find ways of combining 'the civilizing and improving influences of association, and the efficiency and economy of production on a large scale' by co-operative enterprises that give workers a greater stake in them.

In later editions of the *Principles*, Mill chiefly added evidence relating to successful examples of co-operative associations, mainly French, though also including the Rochdale pioneers. What is also notable, however, is that Mill never retreated from the position he first articulated in youthful debates with the Owenites. It was a mistake on the part of socialists to condemn all forms of competition. It was capable of raising wages, and while it was not the best of stimuli perhaps, it was still a necessary stimulus at present – 'and no one can foresee the time when it will not be indispensable to progress'.[57] It should certainly not be looked upon as a 'baneful and anti-social' principle: to be 'protected against competition

---

[55] *Principles*, CW, III, p. 760.   [56] *Ibid.*, p. 763.   [57] *Ibid.*, p. 795.

is to be protected in idleness', in 'mental dullness'. With regard to the chapter on property in Book II on distribution, with its sections on some contemporary varieties of socialism, here too we know that Harriet had strong opinions that induced Mill to give socialist schemes a more favourable assessment in the second and later editions. This would be in line with her role in stressing progress in any assessment of what was possible, where the surviving correspondence allows us to overhear one of Mill's rare, yet still timid, demurrals: 'I cannot persuade myself that you do not greatly overrate the ease of making people unselfish.'[58] If the *Principles* was truly a joint work from the outset, she must either have approved of the more sober treatment given to socialism in the first edition, or was not paying enough attention to it when she read it for the first time. Perhaps it is best simply to say that the 1848 revolutions were an educative experience for both of them; that Harriet was keener to anticipate the socialist future to which the revolutions pointed; and he to proclaim their joint allegiance to it when she had died.[59]

We must respect Mill's recollection that the chapter on the future of the working classes was not part of his first draft, despite the connections between it and his article on the claims of labour written three years earlier. Ashley thought the chapter 'had little connection with what goes before'.[60] Further support for Ashley's view can be derived from the request by Christian socialists to publish the chapter separately as a pamphlet for distribution to the working classes, overlooking, perhaps, the defence of competition it contains. Mill and his wife discussed what changes would be made if separate publication were possible, and they agreed that they should do nothing to make the chapter seem like something written *for* the working classes rather than *about* them.[61] On the other hand, as against thinking of the chapter as an optional extra, it has to be said that Mill succeeded in finding a rounded way of embedding it in his work. It is the climax of Book IV entitled 'Influence of the progress of society on production and distribution' which was billed as adding

---

[58] Letter to Harriet, 21 March 1849, CW, XIV, p. 19.
[59] 'If the chapter in which I mention them [socialists] had been written after instead of before the late revolutions on the Continent I should have entered more fully into my opinions on Socialism and have done it much more justice'; letter to John Jay, CW, XIII, p. 741. J. M. Robson plausibly attributed the inconsistencies to be found in this chapter to Harriet's interventions, to her playing up of hopes for the future and being more critical of the present; see his *Improvement of mankind* (Toronto: Toronto University Press, 1968), p. 248.
[60] See the introduction to his edition of the *Principles*, p. xxi.
[61] In Mill's words, it should remain 'something written of but not *to* the working classes'; *Principles*, CW, III, pp. 1034–5.

'a theory of motion to our theory of equilibrium' in the earlier books.[62] And if the final chapter contains some novel opinions and projections on possible futures then so do the three chapters leading up to it, two of them dealing with the tendency of profits to a minimum, one with the stationary state. The first two have a bearing on Mill's diagnosis of the state of the British economy in 1848 and are best discussed in the present context; the third had a more speculative character that fits better with the subjects discussed in the succeeding essay.

VII

One of the ways in which Mill demonstrated that some recent contributions to the science were not in conflict with basic Ricardian principles was by incorporating a diagnosis of the state of the British economy expounded by Edward Gibbon Wakefield in support of his case for 'systematic' colonisation to Australia and New Zealand. Mill was an early supporter of these colonisation ventures and an active adherent to Wakefield's policies for restricting release of unoccupied land in such colonies and using the proceeds of land sales to subsidise immigration. This explains what might otherwise be a minor exotic feature of Book V of his *Principles*: prominent among the examples of exceptions to a general rule of *laissez-faire* is the Wakefield example of the public benefits of setting what was opaquely described as a 'sufficient' price on land to achieve an optimal combination of capital and labour in colonies of settlement.[63] Mill also accepted Wakefield's analysis of why the export of labour and capital to new colonies provided a remedy for a chronic problem facing the British economy: an excess of capital and population in relation to the current 'field of employment' that placed middle- and working-class incomes from profits and wages under persistent strain. Mill not only accepted this view of the problem, making it serve as his diagnosis for the deep depression affecting Britain in the late thirties and early forties, he placed it at the heart of his interpretation of the long-term prospects for an economy of the type Britain had become.[64]

---

[62] *Principles*, CW, III, p. 705. [63] Ibid., pp. 962–7.

[64] He hinted to Nichol (letter, 30 August 1834) that he needed to remodel his essay on gluts in the light of 'much new speculation' (CW, XII, p. 231), promising that Wakefield's ideas would be incorporated. Later, he maintained that he was persuaded to adopt this line of thinking by a pioneering article by William Ellis published in the *Westminster Review* in 1826, showing why, in a climate of capital abundance, working-class fears of machinery were misplaced; see *Principles*, CW, III, p. 736.

Before he wrote the *Principles*, Mill's clearest statement on these matters could be found in a review of a work by Robert Torrens published in 1843. Torrens, like Mill, was a convert to the Wakefield system, but his fears of long-term decline in Britain's manufacturing hegemony were more acute. Mill agreed that current difficulties needed to be placed against a larger historical canvas:

From the time when the mechanical inventions of the era of Watt and Arkwright made England the principal manufacturing nation of the globe, an ever larger and at length a preponderant part of her population have gained their subsistence by the production of manufactured articles for foreign markets. The condition of this great and growing mass of human beings has, during the whole period, been on the average considerably superior, as to the quantity of the produce of labour which they command, to the condition of the corresponding classes in other countries: but it has been subject to great vicissitudes, and chequered by occasional intervals of severe distress. We are now in one of the severest of these; one which has already surpassed the usual duration of such periods, and, long after most people expected it to terminate, shows no signs of termination.[65]

This contains the clue to Mill's unwillingness to accept Carlyle's gloomier thoughts on falling living standards in *Chartism*. It also served as an introduction to Mill's reasons for differing from Torrens in believing that the current depression was a sign that Britain was losing its manufacturing superiority. It could retain the productivity differential that justified its higher wage levels because it did not depend on cheap coal, inventions (many drawn to Britain by her abundant sources of finance), and manual dexterity alone. British economic superiority rested on a durable economic foundation: 'The Englishman is a more hard-working animal than a Frenchman or a German; he throws more of his energy, more (we may say) of his life, into his work.' But Mill's compliment to the native worker was decidedly backhanded: to match English patience and conscientiousness the foreign worker would have to become 'as careworn, as anxious, as joyless, as dull, as exclusively intent upon the main chance, as his British compeer. He will long be of inferior value as a mere machine, because, happily for him, he cares for pleasure as well as gain'.

What long-term remedies existed? Britain was vulnerable to foreign protectionism, and could reduce that risk by abolishing the Corn Laws. Improvements in domestic agriculture leading to a permanent reduction in food costs were less likely, and if attempted might increase rural unemployment. Introducing 'Scotch agriculture' into Ireland could have

---

[65] *Newspaper articles*, 28 January 1843, CW, XXIV, p. 837.

the effect of scattering 'the Irish labouring population as paupers and beggars over the Three Kingdoms'. The best solution was systematic colonisation along Wakefield's lines; it would revive 'the industrial state of a country in which both labour and capital are every year more and more redundant, by the transfer of large masses of both to her outlying possessions, there to raise raw produce for exchange against the manufactures of the parent nation'.[66] Mill held to this view tenaciously. It reappeared in his *Principles* and retained a prominent place there throughout all editions. Mill was convinced that state-supported emigration to 'new' British colonies was still necessary in the 1860s, long after the Irish famine had led to massive resort to this option in one part of the United Kingdom – the part, unfortunately, where, in Mill's opinion, the inhabitants were least well-adapted to the intrepid life of the pioneering colonist. Cheaper transport and better information about colonial opportunities had aided the process of voluntary emigration, but Mill held that state aid might still be needed 'to keep the communication open between hands needing work in England, and the work which needs hands elsewhere'. Since colonisation 'involves the future and permanent interests of civilization itself, and far outstretches the comparatively narrow limits of purely economical considerations', government intervention and expenditure were eminently justified.[67]

Wakefield's only mistake, according to Mill, lay in thinking that his doctrines were at odds with 'the principles of the best school of preceding political economists, instead of being, as they really are, corollaries from those principles'. What may be more telling, however, is Mill's admission that the corollaries 'would not always have been admitted by those political economists themselves'.[68] Incorporating Wakefield's position within orthodoxy required Mill to find a way of sharing Wakefield's diagnosis involving redundant labour and capital while holding together two cardinal doctrines associated with Ricardian macroeconomics. The first of these was an explanation for the secular decline in profit levels that treated it as dependent on what was happening to the cost of producing wage goods rather than anything connected with the market for final

---

[66] CW, XXIV, p. 840.   [67] See *Principles*, CW, III, pp. 963–7.
[68] *Principles* CW, III, p. 736; see too his letter to Chapman, 8 November 1844, CW, XII, p. 642, forecasting the line he was going to take. In his analysis of the class composition of British politics in 1839, delivered at the peak of his involvement with radical politics, he endorsed a view of the middle classes as the 'uneasy' classes that was probably derived from Wakefield's *England and America* (London: Richard Bentley, 1833). For Mill's endorsement of this work, see *Newspaper writings*, CW, XXIV, pp. 788–90.

goods. The second entailed rejection of the idea that general gluts were possible in an economy in which capital accumulation was taking place and aggregate output was growing. The latter was based on a set of propositions known as Say's law of markets, a law formulated by Jean-Baptiste Say and developed by James Mill and Ricardo in an attempt to ward off fallacies lurking around any belief in general, as opposed to partial, gluts. The law maintained that, outside conditions of acute monetary disorder, aggregate production always generated enough income to sustain an equivalent level of aggregate consumption. It was formulated as an answer to under-consumptionist diagnoses and remedies that became popular during the prolonged period of post-1815 depression and regularly resurfaced during later depressions, including the 1830s and 40s when Mill was writing his *Principles*. These were based on the idea that government expenditure, monetary reflation, or some other expedient to maintain 'unproductive' spending was necessary to offset a general tendency for capital to accumulate more rapidly than could be absorbed at current levels of aggregate demand. In Mill's day it was a position associated with the names of Malthus, Sismondi, and more recently Chalmers. Some of Mill's earliest economic writings were devoted to undermining underconsumptionism; a clarificatory essay on the influence of consumption on production was included in *Essays on unsettled questions*; and the arguments were recycled in the *Principles*. The importance of the underlying issue could hardly be exaggerated. Mill regarded the idea that 'the great end of legislation in matters of national wealth . . . was to create consumers' as one of those 'palpable absurdities' that had been unmasked by advances in the science of political economy: 'The point is fundamental; any difference of opinion on it involves radically different conceptions of political economy, especially in its practical aspect.'[69]

Glut had become one of those emotive words that stirred up unnecessary controversy among economists, 'giving a handle', as Mill put it, 'to the enemies of the science'. He advised one of his friends to avoid the word 'or anything which will bring you into seeming collision (though not real) with my father's and Say's doctrine respecting a general glut'.[70] Wakefield had been sparing in his use of the word, possibly as a result of Mill's

---

[69] For his earlier writings, see CW, IV, pp. 1–22, and XXII, p. 58. For the quoted phrases, see 'Of the influence of consumption on production', in *Essays on some unsettled questions*, CW, IV, pp. 262–3, and *Principles*, CW, III, p. 575. For his criticisms of Malthus, Chalmers, and Sismondi in the *Principles*, see CW, II, pp. 66–8, 75–7, and III, pp. 570–6.

[70] Letter to J. P. Nichol, 14 October 1834, CW, XII, p. 236. As he added: 'It may easily be shown that they were right; and yet that Chalmers and Wakefield are not wrong.'

advice, but he had certainly maintained that capital and labour could simultaneously be in excess supply. As Mill made clear in his essay on the influence of consumption upon production, the upholders of Say's law were not maintaining, in the face of abundant evidence to the contrary, that labour could never be unemployed or capital in the form of machinery or inventories left idle. What was merely a tautology in a barter economy where aggregate supply and demand were different sides of the same accounting convention was by no means such in a money economy subject to waves of nervousness about the future. Excess demand for money could exacerbate any mistaken business calculations that resulted in unsold stocks, short-time working, and unemployment. But in common with Ricardo, Mill took a grown-up view of such occurrences: 'This perpetual non-employment of a large proportion of capital is the price we pay for the division of labour. The purchase is worth what it costs; but the price is considerable.' He held no hope that such fluctuations would diminish in future.

Not only were periodic crises a normal feature of the system, they had useful purgative properties in societies that were, as Mill judged Britain to be, mature and secure economies where 'the rate of profit is habitually within, as it were, a hand's breadth of the minimum, and the country therefore on the very verge of the stationary state'. Periodic 'commercial revulsions' in which capital was wasted in speculative enterprises counteracted this tendency: even the railway gambling of the 1840s had its beneficial side. But Mill was more interested in regular agencies than these occasional purges: technological improvements, the importation of cheaper foreign goods, and 'the perpetual overflow of capital into colonies or foreign countries', especially when these led to a cheapening of goods consumed by wage-earners at home. The argument concerning the effect of cheaper wage goods had a Ricardian foundation, but the idea of an 'industrial state in which both labour and capital are every year more and more redundant' was not an orthodox Ricardian diagnosis. Nor was Mill's solution: 'the exportation of capital is an agent of great efficacy in extending the field of employment for that which remains: and it may be said truly that, up to a certain point, the more capital we send away, the more we shall possess and be able to retain at home'.[71] The chief moral drawn by Mill was a comforting one: 'It must greatly abate, or rather, altogether destroy, in countries where profits are low, the immense importance which used to be attached by political economists to the

[71] *Principles*, CW, III, p. 746.

effects which an event or a measure of government might have in adding to or subtracting from the capital of a country.'[72] Public support for schemes that would facilitate the export of capital and labour to colonies could be justified, and fears about the short-term effects of the introduction of machinery on wage-earners could be allayed.[73] As a young man, Mill, in common with his mentors, saw danger in any weakening of the opposition to public expenditure; it was still part of 'old corruption'. But the middle-aged Mill writing after parliament had been partially reformed, and while still highly critical of aristocratic influence, was less anxious to warn against public spending on some of his favourite schemes.

VIII

When faced with what he regarded as ignorant or interested attacks, Mill could be aggressive in his defence of political economy. One little-known critic who had the temerity to ask for Mill's assistance in completing his critique of the dogmatic fallacies of the science was told: 'I have read many such attempts: some of them more or less ingenious, others merely stupid, but all shewing equal incapacity of seeing through the most obvious paralogisms; and not only did none of them ... effect their object, but I have rarely found that anything was to be learnt from them, even incidentally.'[74] A more sympathetic victim of this aggression was an ex-assistant commissioner of the Irish poor law, John Lalor, the author in 1852 of a book with an intriguing title, *Money and morals: a book for the times*. A copy was sent to Mill as an act of homage, though Lalor knew that in taking his stand with the underconsumptionists he was contravening Mill's views on a major Ricardian theme. From Mill's perspective Lalor had made an unfortunate choice of where he wished to position himself, somewhere between Carlyle, Chalmers, and Mill. The book was dedicated to Carlyle ('though not free from error, a great teacher of great truths'); Chalmers was credited with beginning the 'baptism, so to speak, of political economy into Christianity, which was the main thing needful to bring about its regeneration'; and Mill's *Principles* was praised because 'it has indeed effected, scientifically and conclusively, that subordination of the doctrine of wealth to the doctrine of human welfare, which was the object so earnestly desired by Sismondi and Chalmers'.[75]

---

[72] *Ibid.*, p. 747.   [73] Quotations from *ibid.*, pp. 738, 746, 748.
[74] Letter to J. Britten, 1 July 1858, CW, XV, p. 555.
[75] *Money and morals* (London: John Chapman, 1852), pp. xxvii–xxviii.

Having gone to some lengths to distinguish his own position from the erroneous views of these two authors, Mill no doubt felt that he was being misunderstood as well as patronised by being yoked together with them. But his ire mostly fell on Lalor's suggestion, as Mill more emotively rephrased it, that 'pol[itical] ec[onomy], unless baptized into Christianity is a child of the devil'. It is hard to believe that Lalor could have been prepared for the ferocity of Mill's riposte: holding such views was 'quite inconsistent with any good opinion of me and my writings for in my opinion what is called Christianity is as thoroughly a child of the devil as any extant'. Mill cited Smith, Turgot, Say, Ricardo, and his father as examples of non-believers writing before Chalmers, none of whom could be charged with justifying 'universal selfishness', and 'none of whom regarded pol[itical] ec[onomy] as anything but a subordinate though necessary branch of utility or as you prefer to term it "the doctrine of human welfare" '.

Lalor's book has come to be regarded as one of the more interesting attempts to construct a theory of the trade cycle or commercial crisis on insights into the role of money and banking in a capitalist economy that owe something to Mill's essay on the influence of consumption on production. Mill could only see something less worthy of commendation:

I confess I do not see the good that is to be done by swelling the outcry against pol[itical] economists – or why they should be blamed because people do unjust or selfish things for the sake of money. I do not know what authority you have for saying that the clearing of Irish estates was 'perpetrated in the name of pol[itical] economy' any more than the clearing of English estates from the same motives in the time of the Tudors. But I do know that nearly all the pol[itical] economists supported a poor law in Ireland in order to give the landlords an interest in fighting against the causes of poverty.[76]

The last remark may have been a reminder to Lalor of his previous occupation, though why Mill bothered to do so in this way is obscure. As we shall see, he did not regard Irish landlords with any favour and extending the Poor Law to Ireland was not a policy he favoured. But it offers a good introduction to another of Mill's enduring preoccupations, land tenure reform in both parts of the United Kingdom, one of the main themes in the essay that follows.

---

[76] Letter to Lalor, 27 June 1852, CW, XIV, pp. 91–3.

3

Wild natural beauty, the religion of humanity, and unearned increments

We must needs think . . . that there is something out of joint, when so much is said of the value of refining and humanizing tastes to the labouring people – when it is proposed to plant parks and lay out gardens for them, that they may enjoy more freely nature's gift alike to rich and poor, of sun, sky, and vegetation; and along with this a counter-progress is constantly going on, of stopping up paths and enclosing commons. Is not this another case of giving with one hand, and taking back more largely with the other? We look with the utmost jealousy upon any further enclosure of commons. In the greater part of this island, exclusive of the mountain and moor districts, there certainly is not more land remaining in a state of natural wildness than is desirable.

John Stuart Mill, 'The claims of labour', *Edinburgh Review*, 1845.[1]

I

The above attack on 'legalized spoliation', Mill's description of enclosure of the commons in Britain, was written fully two decades before the foundation of the Commons Preservation Society in 1866. Alongside his disciple, Henry Fawcett, Mill took a leading part in the affairs of this society when they were both MPs. When Mill drew up the programme of the Land Tenure Reform Association in 1869, the aims of commons preservation were incorporated in a clause insisting that waste lands, and those lands requiring an Act of Parliament to enclose them, should be permanently reserved for national purposes, leaving the less fertile land around cities to be 'retained in a state of wild natural beauty, for the general enjoyment of the community, and encouragement in all classes of healthful rural tastes, and of the higher order of pleasures'.[2] Protecting the rights of all people to enjoy nature from the threats posed by pressure of

---

[1] CW, IV, p. 384.   [2] See 'Land tenure reform', CW, V, pp. 689–95.

population and the social and economic predations of urban landowners brought together Mill's environmentalist concerns and the long-standing anti-landlord antagonisms of a Ricardian who was also a philosophic radical.

Mill had been a keen amateur botanist since youth; he had acquired this hobby, along with a taste for mountain scenery, during his first visit to the Pyrenees as a fourteen-year-old. Later these tastes were moulded as much by necessity as pleasure. One of the palliatives he took for the tubercular condition he believed would kill him in the 1850s was extensive walking tours, during which botanising was his chief activity, enabling him to become an amateur expert on the flora of Britain and several European countries.[3] The hobby was chiefly pursued nearer to home in the Surrey hills, but one of the most important walking tours he undertook in Britain, undoubtedly, was the one that resulted in a visit to Wordsworth in the Lake District. The part played by Wordsworth's poetry in lifting Mill from depression by impressing on him the enduring rewards attached to the active pursuit of the 'culture of the feelings' is eloquently documented in the *Autobiography*. The pilgrimage he made to the Lake District in 1831 was undertaken with vivid recollections of Wordsworth's earlier and shorter poems in mind, and the poet's didactic tourist guide, a *Description of the scenery of the lakes in the north of England*, in hand.[4]

Memories of the visit left a small but significant mark on Mill's *Principles*. The visit occurred before Mill immersed himself in the literature on land tenure throughout Europe, partly prompted by a search for a solution to the problems revealed by the Irish famine in which he found himself at one with William Thornton, a previously unknown colleague at the East India Office.[5] Wordsworth's brief paean to the 'perfect Republic of Shepherds and Agriculturists' in the *Description* came to mind when Mill was advocating replacement of the cottier system by peasant proprietorship as a partial solution to Irish problems, and when

---

[3] For the records of Mill's botanical interests, see CW, XXXI. As Alexander Bain pointed out: 'Plant hunting was to him what sports are to other persons'; see *John Stuart Mill: a criticism* (London: Longmans, 1882), p. 152.

[4] For the journal Mill kept while in the Lake District, see CW, XXVII. The best accounts of the episode can be found in the editorial introduction to this volume and Anna J. Mill, 'John Stuart Mill's visit to Wordsworth, 1831', *Modern Language Review*, 44 (1949), 341–50. The same author was also the first to examine the aesthetic that accompanied Mill's interest in Wordsworth; see 'John Stuart Mill and the picturesque', *Victorian Studies*, 14 (1970), 151–63.

[5] See William T. Thornton, *Over-population and its remedy: an inquiry into the distress prevailing among the labouring classes of the British island and into the means of remedying it* (London: Longmans, 1846); and *A plea for peasant proprietors*, 1848 (London: Macmillan, 1874).

he was incorporating the results of his inquiry into systems of land tenure into the *Principles*. The Lakeland 'statesmen' are cited there as showing what could have been achieved elsewhere if the yeoman ideal had not given way to English prejudices in favour of large-scale agriculture as the best means of feeding a rising population. The political economy on which Mill had been raised operated with a model that took for granted the 'natural' tripartite system of ownership and reward embodied in English agriculture, according to which landowners received contractual rents paid by tenant farmers in search of profit on their capital and employing wage labour in order to do so. If anything, Mill outdid Wordsworth in his praise for the alternative to this, for whereas the poet was elegiacally recalling the situation as it existed sixty years before, Mill took it to be a fair representation of the existing state of affairs: 'No other agricultural population in England could have furnished the originals of Wordsworth's peasantry.' The memory of his visit in 1831, when he had recorded that 'no penury' was visible among that peasantry, remained with him in the 1840s when marshalling evidence in favour of peasant proprietorship on a pan-European scale and against the background of his official, if second-hand, knowledge of peasant agriculture in India.[6]

Clearly, this was not Wordsworth's most important influence on Mill. He gave poetic form to what Mill described as 'one of the strongest of my pleasurable susceptibilities – the love of rural objects and natural scenery'.[7] Mill's environmental interests not only predate Wordsworth's influence, they have a deeper and decidedly unromantic provenance as well: they derive directly from the neo-Malthusian anxieties mentioned in the previous essay. Reconciling Wordsworth with Malthus – reconciling a romantic ecology with one based squarely on political economy – was not, at first sight, an easy task. But it is not a bad short description of what Mill achieved as an environmentalist.

II

Mill maintained that the law of diminishing returns in agriculture and other activities involving the use of natural resources was 'the most important proposition in political economy'.[8] As an essential part of the Ricardian theory of economic growth and income distribution, it remained an article of faith with Mill from his earliest jousts with critics of political

---

[6] *Principles*, CW, II, pp. 252 3.   [7] *Autobiography*, CW, I, p. 150.   [8] *Principles*, CW, II, p. 174.

economy in the 1820s to his later engagements with socialists in his posthumous chapters on the subject. Half a century after he had been arrested for distributing birth control literature, Mill continued to believe that restraining the Malthusian devil was essential to any prospect for a permanent rise in working-class living standards. We have seen how neo-Malthusianism underlay his long-standing interest in state-assisted emigration and systematic colonisation. It also surfaces in less expected places. For example, in that sustained attack on the 'tyranny of mass opinion', his essay *On liberty*, Mill argued that the full weight of public disapproval should be brought to bear on irresponsible parents, those who placed the future of fellow wage-earners in jeopardy by having more children than they could support or educate properly. He was even prepared to countenance legislation 'to forbid marriage unless the parties can show that they have the means of supporting a family'.[9] Mill's interest in peasant proprietorship and in some experiments in co-operative socialism derived strength from his belief that parental irresponsibility would be more clearly perceived and hence controlled under those arrangements. What had happened to French birth rates provided proof. Removing the burden of large families was an integral part of his feminism too. Since he regarded sexual intercourse chiefly as an 'animal' demand made on women by their husbands, it followed that working-class wives could not be held responsible for having large families. Feminism was linked with environmentalism because Mill, departing from his usual denial that we know what attributes are essential to woman's 'nature', was convinced that 'as in so many other things ... women will be much more unwilling than men to submit to the expulsion of all beauty from common life'.[10]

Neo-Malthusianism accounts too for Mill's disqualification from membership of what Ruskin was later to describe and dismiss as the 'steam-whistle party', those who celebrated industrial and scientific progress and entertained optimistic visions of the prospects held out by further technological innovation.[11] Mill could be equally dismissive of those, like Samuel Laing, who recognised that 'the Norwegian, and German, and French state of society are [*sic*] much better for the happiness of all concerned than the struggling, go-ahead English and American state', but who at the same time were 'always measuring the merit of all things by their tendency to increase the number of steam engines, and to make

---

[9] *Ibid.*, p. 371.   [10] Letter to Charles W. Wilkinson, 24 October 1869, CW, XVII, p. 1659.
[11] Ruskin's phrase was originally applied to Dickens; see the Appendix, p. 368 below.

human beings as good machines and therefore as mere machines'.[12] Any optimism Mill felt about social improvement based on technological change was hedged around with qualifications, chief among them being those connected with population:

Hitherto it is questionable if all the mechanical inventions yet made have lightened the day's toil of any human being. They have enabled a greater population to live the same life of drudgery and imprisonment, and an increased number of manufacturers and others to make fortunes. They have increased the comforts of the middle classes. But they have not yet begun to effect those great changes in human destiny, which it is in their nature and in their futurity to accomplish. Only when, in addition to just institutions, the increase of mankind shall be under the deliberate guidance of judicious foresight, can the conquests made from the powers of nature by the intellect and energy of scientific discoverers, become the common property of the species, and the means of improving and elevating the universal lot.

On this subject one could say that the public moralist was at war with the political economist, though it would be more accurate to cite it as a case where the abstract 'science' had no authority over the 'art' of public policy and the choice of the ultimate ends of social existence. As he said of the latter in the *Principles:*

I confess that I am not charmed with the ideal of life held out by those who think that the normal state of human beings is that of struggling to get on; that the trampling, crushing, elbowing and treading on each other's heels, which form the existing type of social life, are the more desirable lot of human kind, or anything but the disagreeable symptoms of one of the phases of industrial progress.[13]

Worship of the 'idol' of production, that 'disposition to sacrifice every thing to accumulation' and the 'exclusive and engrossing selfishness which accompanies it', was one of Mill's earliest strictures on the mentality and culture of his fellow countrymen.[14] He added the 'dollar-hunting' habits of Americans later, and classified America alongside Britain as the two chief examples of the 'industrial' mentality, where this refers to the pursuit of economic gain. Mill asserted a gospel of leisure over Carlyle's gospel of work, a doctrine that he later would describe as pure cant: what could be laudable about work for work's sake?[15] In a more sane society the effort involved in satisfying the demand for luxury would be questioned.

---

[12] Letter to Sarah Austin, 26 February 1844, CW, XIII, p. 622.
[13] Quotations from *Principles*, CW, III, pp. 754–6.
[14] Letters to d'Eichthal, 15 May and 8 October 1829, CW, XII, pp. 31, 37.
[15] See 'The Negro question', CW, XXI, pp. 90–1.

A more just society would ensure that the burden of physical labour was distributed fairly. As we saw in the previous essay, Mill thought the price paid for superior English productivity was too high when measured by the loss of pleasure from relaxation.[16] A further statement by Mill in his *Principles* illustrates the depth of his commitment to this goal:

> Most fitting . . . is it, that while riches are power, and to grow as rich as possible the universal object of ambition, the path to its attainment should be open to all, without favour or partiality. But the best state for human nature is that in which, while no one is poor, no one desires to be richer, nor has any reason to fear being thrust back, by the efforts of others to push themselves forward.[17]

The importance Mill attached to the law of diminishing returns, despite recognising ways in which its operation could be temporarily suspended, places him among those who thought the trajectory of economic growth in 'old' countries would eventually be asymptotic, confined within limits, rather than exponential or open-ended. Under these conditions, control over birth rates was required to ensure the maintenance of rising living standards. Consciously or unconsciously, steam-whistlers took the view that all bottlenecks could be overcome by technologies that enabled inorganic materials and processes to act as substitutes for those based on natural resources.[18] There is a well-known statement by Macaulay that helps to bring the contemporary difference of opinion into closer focus. In responding to Southey's gloomy diagnosis of the state of British society in 1830, Macaulay asserted that he was 'unable to find any satisfactory record of any great nation, past or present, in which the working classes have been in a more comfortable situation than in England during the last thirty years'. He prophesied that a century hence the English would have a population of 50 million, 'better fed, clad, and lodged than the English of our time', with cultivation 'rich as that of a flower-garden' being 'carried up to the very tops of Ben Nevis and Helvellyn'.[19] These were the very places – especially Helvellyn, a Lakeland fell standing over Thirlmere, the first of the lakes to be taken over by Manchester to supply its water needs – that acquired emblematic significance to Victorian environmentalists.

---

[16] See p. 55 above.   [17] *Principles*, CW, III, p. 754.

[18] The contrast between asymptotic and exponential growth paths invoked here is derived from the work of E. A. Wrigley; see *Continuity, chance and change* (Cambridge: Cambridge University Press, 1988) and *People, cities, and wealth* (Oxford: Blackwell, 1987).

[19] See his review of Southey's *Colloquies* in *Lord Macaulay's essays* (London: Longmans Green, 1886), p. 120.

Mill was one of the earliest political economists to stress environmental limits and costs when discussing economic growth. It took more than a century for the argument to be stated in anywhere near such a fundamentalist fashion again. Mill's way of conducting the case took its cue from the concept of a stationary state as the *ne plus ultra* of economic growth, an integral part of earlier debates provoked by Adam Smith and continued by Malthus and Ricardo. As we have seen, Mill believed that the British economy was now fated to be 'within a hand's breadth' of this state, and was only prevented from entering it by periodic 'revulsions' in which capital was wasted in speculative enterprises.[20] He was arguing for the replacement of such accidental palliatives by regular agencies that included the export of capital to colonies and countries capable of meeting Britain's need to import food and raw materials.

These were solutions for the short and middle term. In the long run, instead of wishing to see the onset of this stationary state postponed irregularly or even indefinitely, Mill invited his progressive-minded readers to embrace a positive vision of stationarity in which, although there would be no net additions to population size or the capital stock, all future improvements in technology would be directed towards the reduction of effort and improvements in the quality of life. In other words, Mill's stationary state was to be a virtuous version of an idea that had been used by his mentors as a bogeyman to support those measures, such as free trade and the reduction of public expenditure that would sustain capital accumulation and widen, if not remove, the organic bottleneck to further capital accumulation and growth. One lengthy quotation from Mill's defence of a zero-growth society conveys the substance of those environmentalist values he believed to be under threat from further economic growth.

There is room in the world, no doubt, and even in old countries for a great increase of population, supposing the arts of life to go on improving, and capital to increase. But even if innocuous, I confess I see little reason for desiring it. The density of population necessary to enable mankind to obtain, in the greatest degree, all the advantages both of cooperation and of social intercourse, has, in all the most populous countries, been attained. A population may be too crowded, though all be amply supplied with food and raiment. It is not good for man to be kept perforce at all times in the presence of his species. A world from which solitude is extirpated, is a very poor ideal. Solitude, in the sense of being often alone, is essential to any depth of meditation or of character; and solitude in the presence of natural beauty and grandeur, is the cradle of thoughts and aspirations

---

[20] See pp. 56–9 above.

which are not only good for the individual, but which society could ill do without. Nor is there much satisfaction in contemplating the world with nothing left to the spontaneous activity of nature; with every rood of land brought into cultivation, which is capable of growing food for human beings; every flowery waste or natural pasture ploughed up, all quadrupeds or birds which are not domesticated for man's use exterminated as his rivals for food, every hedgerow or superfluous tree rooted out, and scarcely a place left where a wild shrub or flower could grow without being eradicated as a weed in the name of improved agriculture. If the earth must lose that great portion of its pleasantness which it owes to things that the unlimited increase of wealth and population would extirpate from it, for the mere purpose of enabling it to support a larger, but not a better or a happier population, I sincerely hope, for the sake of posterity that they will be content to be stationary, long before necessity compels it.[21]

The final remark about 'necessity' may suggest a grim Malthusian version of the asymptote, but the rest of the passage has little or no connection with what one would normally associate with an economic analysis of optimal population size – judged, as Mill was also prepared to judge it, by reference to trends in real wages. It is also worth bearing in mind that when Mill first wrote this passage, the population of England, Scotland, and Wales – though it had increased faster than ever before (or since) during the first decades of the nineteenth century – was still no more than 18 million. The language is clearly 'romantic' and the emphasis on the 'spontaneous activity of nature' and of 'solitude in the presence of natural beauty and grandeur' marks it as a Wordsworthian evaluation of the benefits of communing with nature. Macaulay, once more, provides the steam-whistler view: he could find little to praise in Wordsworth's posthumously published *Prelude*; it was merely a repetition of the 'old raptures about mountain scenery and cataracts; the old flimsy philosophy about the effect of scenery on the mind; the old crazy, mystical metaphysics'.[22] Mill, by contrast, was prepared to share the raptures while giving the mystical metaphysics a more solid basis of his own construction – one that consorted better with ethics, his interest in the natural and moral sciences, and his hopes for a religion of humanity.

III

Although the romantic influence contributed an important emotional and aesthetic dimension to Mill's thinking, it came as a supplementary

---

[21] *Principles*, CW, III, p. 756.
[22] See the *Life and letters of Lord Macaulay*, ed. George Otto Trevelyan (London: Longmans Green, 1901), p. 614.

revelation to the central tenets of his upbringing. When listing the subjects on which he remained at odds with philosophic Tories, Mill mentioned ethics and religion, beliefs that account for the gulf separating his environmentalist ethic from that associated with Wordsworth and his more orthodox followers. It would be impossible to envisage a Wordsworthian ethic that did not include a profound belief in a Christian deity.[23] We have no direct evidence of Wordsworth's reaction to his meetings with his youthful admirer, though Mill reported that he was impressed by what his host had to say about 'states of society and forms of government'.[24] Even if Mill concealed or diluted some of his opinions, these topics were bound to be divisive. Opposition to Malthusianism, for example, was an enduring feature of the Lake poets' views on politics and morals. Malthus's depiction of the laws of nature as requiring constant exertion to avoid misery and vice proved especially challenging to Wordsworth's more benevolent view of Nature's healing qualities.[25] By coincidence, a few weeks before Mill arrived in the Lake District, Wordsworth had been condemning the influence of Malthus on current Poor Law debates, a position he was to expound more fully in a postscript to the 1835 edition of his poems, where the malign connection between political economy and the Poor Law Amendment Act was noted, and the virtues of 'a christian government standing *in loco parentis* towards all its subjects' extolled.[26] This was, of course, a version of the paternalist position that Mill was to attack when Carlyle published a more heroic version of it a few years later.

Like Coleridge and Southey, Wordsworth loosely associated much that he disliked about the modern world with utilitarianism and political economy. When opposing the extension of the railway into the heart of the Lake District in 1844, for example, he employed the conventional charge that utilitarianism served 'as a mask for cupidity and gambling speculations'. He also expressed the hope that since man did not live by

[23] Indeed, charges that his poetry was guilty of pantheism led Wordsworth to modify his earlier poems to ensure that a more orthodox Anglican message could not be missed; see S. Gill, *William Wordsworth: a life* (Oxford: Oxford University Press, 1989), pp. 344, 398–9, 416–19.

[24] Letter to Sterling, 20–22 October 1831, CW, XII, p. 81.

[25] For detailed examination of the ambiguities of Wordsworth's relationship with Malthus, see the study by Philip Connell, *Romanticism, economics and the question of 'culture'* (Oxford: Oxford University Press, 2001), ch. 1.

[26] See letter to Lady Beaumont, 8 July 1831, in the *Letters of William and Dorothy Wordsworth*, ed. A. G. Hill, 8 vols. (Oxford: Oxford University Press, 1978–88), V, pp. 405–6; and the *Prose works of William Wordsworth*, ed. W. J. B. Owen and J. W. Smythe, 3 vols. (Oxford: Oxford University Press, 1974), III, pp. 240 8.

bread alone, political economy would not be allowed to decide whether
the Lake District would be violated by working-class day-trippers from
Manchester in search of cheap amusements.[27] Mill's support for the
Commons Preservation Society on grounds of the benefits it would bring
to the working classes may suggest a different set of priorities, though
Wordsworth too hoped that Manchester's operatives could learn to
appreciate natural beauty closer to home, in their 'neighbouring fields'.
Epping Forest, Hampstead Heath, Wimbledon Common, and Banstead
Downs may not have the 'sublime' connotations of the Lake District,
but their preservation as open spaces was as much a public achievement
as any later associated with the National Trust, the body that grew out
of the Commons Preservation Society and was founded by some of
Wordsworth's followers in 1895 with conservation of the Lake District
very much a first priority.

Speaking purely as an economist, Mill was always in favour of strict
parliamentary regulation of the monopoly powers of the railway companies. This included choice of routes, with their environmental impact
on sites of natural beauty and botanical interest forming one of the criteria.
For example, Mill opposed one of the London-to-Brighton routes that
would have passed through the vale of Norbury at the foot of Box Hill,
a district known to him through residence and botanising trips to the
North Downs. In good radical fashion he contrasted lack of concern
with damage to the environments open to the poor with parliamentary
willingness to spend £11,000 on two Correggios for the new National
Gallery. Mill was aware that such comments could arouse a chorus of
denunciation of political economists and utilitarians for lacking imagination and taste, to which his response was that a 'sense of beauty' scarcely
existed in Britain, and that purchase of the Correggios was a case of judging
quality by price, a common aristocratic failing. He pilloried Sir Thomas
Maryon Wilson, an urban developer, for enclosing part of Hampstead
Heath, and the Archbishop of Canterbury, William Howley, for enclosing part of the Addington hills near Croydon. Incitement of the people
of Croydon to 'sally out with axe in hand' to level the fences erected by
the Archbishop 'to exclude them from what was morally as much their
birthright as any man's estate' could well have compounded Mill's
teenage offence of distributing birth control literature.[28]

Mill followed his father's advice in concealing his lack of orthodox
religious belief from public view. This did not apply to his dealings with

---

[27] See *Prose works*, III, p. 352.   [28] See Mill's *Notes on the newspapers*, CW, VI, pp. 249–50, 328.

friends or acquaintances. Southey had no hesitation in branding Mill an atheist after their meeting in the Lake District, claiming that Mill had confessed to this. Southey's reported reaction to this revelation is very much what might be expected: 'I can live in charity with all men, but I should seem to act as absurdly in taking the opinion of any person who is dogmatically a disbeliever in God and in a future state of reward and punishment, upon any of the vital interests of society, as if I were to take that of a man born blind upon optics. The foundation of my system of opinion is Christian faith.'[29]

Being thoroughly acquainted with the conventional objections to utilitarianism as a narrow selfish ethic, Mill was keen to demonstrate that his version of the doctrine provided equivalent, usually superior answers to questions that involved our concern for others, including past and future generations. One way in which he accomplished this can be found in his defence of his interpretation of the doctrine in *Utilitarianism*, the first part of which is an extended exercise in comparing moral criteria with those furnished by more conventional Christian accounts of morality. Mill took the high ground here by portraying Christ's teachings as containing the essence of ethics: 'To do as one would be done by, and to love one's neighbour as oneself, constitute the ideal perfection of morality', freed from the 'selfish' and immoral doctrines of personal reward and punishment that were part of the teachings of the corrupted Pauline church.[30] This functional interpretation came without the central message that Christians would draw from Christ's sacrifice. Mill seems to have arrived at this conclusion in 1833 when he read the New Testament seriously for the first time. To Carlyle he wrote that he had 'unbounded reverence' for the Christ of the gospels when contrasted with the 'namby-pamby Christ of the poor modern Christians'.[31] Compared with this, Mill's altruistic religion of humanity entailed more strenuous demands on personal character to make the right kind of disinterested choices involving private and public good. He denied that he wrote in any 'hostile spirit' towards Christianity, 'though undoubtedly both good ethics and good metaphysics will sap Christianity if it persists in allying itself with bad'.[32]

The full extent of Mill's religious unorthodoxy was not disclosed until he published *Auguste Comte on positivism* in 1865 and his stepdaughter,

---

[29] Letter cited in Anna J. Mill, 'John Stuart Mill's visit to Wordsworth', p. 344n.
[30] *Utilitarianism*, CW, X, p. 218. [31] Letter to Carlyle, 5 October 1833, CW, XII, p. 182.
[32] Letter to Bain, 14 November 1859, XV, pp. 645–6.

Helen Taylor, released the *Three essays on religion* after his death. Readers
of the former would have noticed Mill's commendation of the idea that
'a religion may exist without belief in a God, and that a religion without
a God may be, even to Christians, an instructive and profitable object
of contemplation'. Comte's concept of a *Grand Etre* entailed veneration
for the collective existence embodied in the past, present, and future of
humanity; and it included a duty of care for those 'animal races which
enter into real society with man' as well. Mill's Benthamite training would
have extended this category to include all animals capable of suffering
pain, whether or not they had a connection with man.[33] The botanist in
Mill gave him reason for condemning Comte's 'overweening presumption' in proposing that all animals and plants that could not be justified
for existing human use should be eliminated.

As if any one could presume to assert that the smallest weed may not, as
knowledge advances, be found to have some property serviceable to man. When
we consider that the united power of the whole human race cannot reproduce a
species once eradicated – that is what is once done, in the extirpation of races,
can never be repaired; one can only be thankful that amidst all which the past
rulers of mankind have to answer for, they have never come to the measure of
the great regenerator of Humanity; mankind have not yet been under the rule
of one who assumes that he knows all there is to be known, and that when he has
put himself at the head of humanity, the book of human knowledge may be
closed.[34]

As the person who had some responsibility for introducing Comte to
the English-speaking public, Mill was anxious to warn against these
megalomaniac tendencies. *Utilitarianism* does this in a veiled fashion:
having said that he entertained 'the strongest objections to the system of
politics and morals' contained in Comte's *Système de politique positive*,
Mill concluded darkly that the version of the religion of humanity
advanced there could prove to be so binding 'as to interfere unduly with
human freedom and individuality'.[35] The purpose of *Auguste Comte and
positivism* was to remove any remaining doubt on this subject by showing
that Comte's later effusions as grand pontiff of humanity constituted 'the
completest system of spiritual and temporal despotism, which ever yet
emanated from a human brain'.[36]

---

[33] For Bentham's defence of animal rights, see his *Introduction to the principles of morals and legislation* (London: W. Pickering, 1823), ch. 17.

[34] *Auguste Comte and positivism*, CW, X, pp. 357–8.   [35] *Utilitarianism*, CW, X, p. 232.

[36] *Autobiography*, CW, I, p. 221.

Three essays on religion was as much a part of the joint legacy with Harriet as the *Autobiography, On liberty*, and the *Subjection of women*. Having exercised caution on the subject of religion in his published writings, Mill would have thought it cowardly not to leave a record of his/ their views on this subject. He admired the courage of infidels such as Richard Carlile or G. J. Holyoake in taking punishment for their beliefs, even though he could not respect all the arguments they employed to defend infidelity.[37] The reception given to Mill's posthumous essays by Christians and secular admirers alike proves how wise he was not to court publicity for his views during his lifetime. Agnostic admirers, led by John Morley, regretted the unnecessary concessions to Christianity, especially those in the last-written of the essays, that on 'Theism', with its con-clusion that the rational sceptic was permitted an imaginative form of hope that God exists even if he was denied adequate grounds for belief.[38] Although this essay was regarded by some of Mill's friends as 'hard to reconcile with his former self', there was little that was truly novel in the other two.[39] The most polished of them, 'Nature', confirmed what he had maintained in his *Examination of the philosophy of Sir William Hamilton*, as well as in less formal writings, namely that Mill diverged sharply from more conventional approaches to Nature's wonders and the lessons they were capable of teaching humanity. Nature could be malign as well as benign: 'nearly all the things which men are hanged or imprisoned for doing to one another, are nature's every day performances'.[40] If the results of natural laws were taken as evidence of the existence of God, the only conclusion any respecter of inductive evidence could draw would be that omnipotence and benevolence could not both be attributes of the deity. The idea that following Nature had any moral as opposed to prudential force receives some severe handling. At best the evidence supported the idea of a deity with limited powers who needed the active support of human creatures in the Manichaean struggle between good and evil, where evil was moral rather than natural and therefore fell within the scope of 'enlightened infidelity' to overcome. A religion of this kind, with

[37] On Carlile, see Mill's letter to Comte, December 1842, CW, XIII, p. 562; and 'Debate on Church', 15 February 1828, CW, XVI, pp. 419–27; and on Holyoake, see 'Enlightened infidelity', unpublished letter to *Reasoner*, some time after 2 June 1847 in *Newspaper writings*, CW, XXIV, pp. 1082–4.

[38] See Morley's 'Mr Mill's *Three essays on religion*', *Fortnightly Review*, November 1874, January 1875; and Lipkes's chapter on Morley, in J. Lipkes, *Politics, religion and classical political economy in Britain* (London: Macmillan, 1989).

[39] Bain regarded 'Theism' as 'a more extraordinary departure from opinions that he had been known to maintain, than had been his Bentham and Coleridge articles'; see *John Stuart Mill*, p. 158.

[40] *Three essays on religion*, CW, X, p. 385.

the life of Christ acting as moral inspiration, was 'excellently fitted to aid and fortify that real, though purely human religion, which sometimes calls itself the Religion of Humanity and sometimes that of Duty'.[41]

The original importance of Christianity to environmentalism derives from its role in pointing to the providential aspect to Nature, the one embodied in pre-Darwinian notions of purpose, harmony, and design. If Nature contained God's message of peace and order there were powerful reasons for protecting it from man's overweening pride in his own scientific knowledge. Christian environmentalists could fortify secular notions of despoliation with charges of sacrilege. When Mill reproved Comte for his attitude towards plants that had no current human use, his case was confined to pointing out the uncertainty attached to existing scientific knowledge. Similarly, while Mill recognised the elevated pleasures of communing in solitude with nature, they did not require him to believe in God. When Christian aesthetes such as Ruskin deployed the ideas of infinity, unity, repose, symmetry, purity, moderation, and adaptation to ends in a theory of beauty, Mill simply appropriated them, with due acknowledgement, as proof of the normal processes of psychological association and recollection. In any version of utilitarianism that recognised qualitative differences in pleasure they deserved special status (beyond mere agreeableness) for their superior character and capacity to grant 'deeper delight to the imagination'.[42] But there was no need to invoke a deity to explain such emotions. Mill was looking for a secular and scientifically based environmental ethic that was adapted to a post-Christian era. The pleasures and terrors of the sublime in nature were the effect of sheer scale and power when compared with what fell within the range of human achievement. But aesthetic uplift from such feelings could be purchased at the expense of ethical discrimination. As he said in a deadly aside that may have had Ruskin's position in view: 'Those in whom awe produces admiration may be aesthetically developed, but they are morally uncultivated.'[43] Finally, while Mill may have made some concessions to Christianity that his followers could not accept, he was not willing to admit that Epicurean short-sightedness was a defect in non-Christian versions of religion when it came to judging the results of human action on the environment:

---

[41] *Ibid.*, p. 488.
[42] See Mill's references to Ruskin's *Modern painters* in the notes on his reissue of James Mill's *Analysis of the phenomena of the human mind*, in *Miscellaneous writings*, CW, XXXI, pp. 224–6.
[43] *Three essays on religion*, CW, X, p. 384.

the supposition, that human beings in general are not capable of feeling deep and even the deepest interest in things which they will never live to see, is a view of human nature as false as it is abject. Let it be remembered that if individual life is short, the life of the human species is not short; its indefinite duration is practically equivalent to endlessness; and being combined with indefinite capability of improvement, it offers to the imagination and sympathies a large enough object to satisfy any reasonable demand for grandeur of aspiration. If such an object appears small to a mind accustomed to dream of infinite and eternal beatitudes, it will expand into far other dimensions when those baseless fancies shall have receded into the past.[44]

IV

While the Established Church and its endowed educational appendages were always fair game for Mill (until the ancient universities showed signs of reformation), religion was not one of those subjects on which he openly set out to 'offend and scandalize' readers during his lifetime. He reserved this stance for the conventional targets of philosophic radicalism very much as originally delineated by Bentham and his father. Hence the stream of ridicule regularly directed at aristocratic institutions and habits in his newspaper writings; and the attacks on the privileges and bulwarks of landownership, as represented by the Corn Laws, game laws, and laws of inheritance, especially primogeniture and entail. In his *Principles* Mill articulated proposals for curbing inheritance rights that would, if implemented, 'pull down all large fortunes in two generations'.[45] Bain is our informant on this claim, and he also tells us that Mill was surprised and disappointed when the anticipated 'outcry about his doctrines on Property' failed to materialise. Bain astutely attributed failure to utopianism ('the dream of a future too distant to affect the living') and 'views that were too wild and revolutionary to be entertained'.[46]

There was much in the *Principles* to alarm established interests and to disturb readers who were deeply attached to the status quo; but it was often in the form of standard Ricardian propositions to which a radical twist had been imparted. This is plainly the case with Mill's ideas on land as a factor of production with marked peculiarities that differentiated it from capital and labour. Whereas these could be increased indefinitely, land was limited in extent and quality. The theory of rent, therefore, was reserved for what was 'differential and peculiar' about production when

[44] *Ibid.*, p. 420. [45] *Principles*, Book II, chapter 2, sections 3–4, CW, II, pp. 218–26.
[46] Bain, *John Stuart Mill*, p. 89.

compared with the 'natural and necessary' elements represented in wages and profits.[47] It followed that social expediency played a larger role in relation to the former than in the case of the latter. Mill denied that landed property could be the subject of an absolute right. An economic justification could only be given where the proprietor was an improving landowner rather than 'a sinecurist quartered on it'.[48] English landowners were, he grudgingly conceded, 'not unfrequently' improvers, though the law of primogeniture often prevented those who inherited land from acquiring the funds necessary to invest in improvements. In Ireland the economic conditions that might justify estate ownership were completely absent, a sweeping judgement that Mill kept in all editions of the *Principles*, merely adding a note in later editions that vaguely mentioned 'moral and economical' improvements that had taken place since 1848. Land was the least 'sacred' form of property: 'No man made the land. It is the original inheritance of the whole species.'[49]

Mill held that the only landownership right that ought to be respected was the right to fair market compensation in cases where the community decided to appropriate or control the use of land for whatever reason. Even if an exclusive right were granted for purposes of cultivation, it did not carry with it the privilege of curbing public access: 'The pretension of two Dukes to shut up a part of the Highlands, and exclude the rest of mankind from many square miles of mountain scenery to prevent disturbance to wild animals, is an abuse.' While rent was a justifiable form of return on any improvements made by the landowner himself, 'he is morally bound, and should, whenever the case admits, be legally compelled to make his interest and pleasure consistent with the public good'.[50] This was a subject on which Mill credited Coleridge with reviving a conservative insight into the public trust that attached to landed property. It meant that the state had a special interest and duty in superintending land tenure and the system by which agricultural cultivation was carried on.[51]

Here Mill's prolonged though intermittent engagement with Irish problems, from the famine in 1846–7 up to Gladstone's first Irish Land Act in 1870, was a major predisposing factor. It was powerfully reinforced by the knowledge he acquired as a civil servant at India House, where the administrative problems of dealing with a peasant-based form of agriculture bulked large. Since he regarded his father as 'the originator of

---

[47] *Principles*, CW, III, p. 495. [48] *Ibid*, p. 228. [49] *Ibid*., p. 230.
[50] *Ibid*., p. 232. [51] 'Coleridge', CW, X, pp. 157–8.

all sound statesmanship' on these subjects, he was prepared to borrow freely from his father's ideas when required.[52] In 1819, in his *History of British India*, James Mill had proposed a Ricardian solution to the Indian land revenue problem that amounted to a form of land nationalisation. He advised the East India Company to make the most of the fortunate historical circumstance in which it found itself in India, where there was no obvious equivalent of the English landowner. By acting as the ultimate owner of land, and by levying taxes directly on *ryots*, or peasant cultivators, based on assessments of the pure or Ricardian rent for the 'original and indestructible properties of the soil', the needs of state could be met without placing excessive burden on cultivators.[53] A land revenue system based on the assessment of its 'pure' rent-earning properties was one that entailed minimum burden on the cultivator (it took only what would otherwise be paid to a private landowner) and minimum distortion of the ordinary market calculations of wage-earners and profit-recipients. During their overlapping periods of service as employees of the Company in the period between 1819 and 1857, both Mills were committed to preventing encroachment on the *ryotwari* system in operation, chiefly in Madras and Bombay, by advocates of the *zemindari* alternative in Bengal based on English notions of private property. As Mill expressed this in his *Principles*, those who attempted to create what was termed a 'permanent settlement' in India had 'flattered themselves that they had created, throughout the Bengal provinces, English landlords, and it proved that they had only created Irish ones'.[54]

In the book that provided his son's first exposure to political economy, the *Elements of political economy*, James Mill had floated a tax proposal with the same underlying Ricardian justification for implementation in Britain. It involved a distinction between the expected rental income on which the original purchase of land had been settled, and any increment in rent attributable to actions by the 'legislature' which resulted in an 'increase in the amount of population and the demand for food'. While the former was rightly interpreted as belonging to the landowner, the latter, 'arising from the circumstances of the community, and from nothing in which the landholders themselves have any peculiar share',

[52] *Autobiography*, CW, I, p. 213.
[53] For Mill's application of the rent doctrine to India, see D. Winch (ed.), *James Mill: selected economic writings* (Edinburgh: Oliver and Boyd, 1966), pp. 391–5. The classic study of this episode remains that by Eric Stokes, *The English Utilitarians and India* (Oxford: Clarendon Press, 1959), especially ch. 2.
[54] *Principles*, CW, II, p. 321.

could legitimately be regarded as 'peculiarly fitted for appropriation to the purposes of the state'.

Although Ricardo had maintained that under a system of agricultural protection the interests of landowners conflicted with those of the rest of the community, he remained a gradualist on the implementation of reform of the Corn Laws and was unconvinced by James Mill's proposals of the feasibility of taxing the unearned element in rental income under British conditions.[55] As part of radical teaching on the way in which, under aristocratic forms of government, the ruling 'few' regularly plundered the interests of the subject 'many', Mill senior laid particular stress on this conflict of interests, and his son followed suit. Thus whereas Ricardo had advocated a fixed duty on corn, together with a scheme for a gradual reduction in its level, the youthful John Stuart Mill was not prepared to countenance this 'measure of indulgence' towards landowners.[56] At best he conceded the tactical value of not stressing conflict of interests 'in order to soothe the landlords, and persuade them that it is not their interest to resist the march of improvement'.[57] This did not affect assessment of the facts of the case: the Corn Laws involved a direct clash of pecuniary interests; they imposed a simple tax on consumers, at least half of which ended up in the pockets of the landlords. Mill also followed his father rather than Ricardo in believing that a tax on the unearned increment could be applied to British circumstances. In the *Principles* a few pages were devoted to establishing the proposition that such a tax represented 'no violation of the principles on which private property is granted'.[58]

The four lengthy chapters Mill devoted to systems of land tenure in his *Principles* were, as he half-recognised, 'disproportioned to the dimensions of this work'.[59] Taken in conjunction with the two chapters that preceded them on custom versus competition and slavery as a mode of production, the scope of Ricardian economics had considerably expanded in what might be described, in honour of Mill's Comtean phase, as a comparative and 'sociological' direction, though 'Smithian' would have done quite as well if Mill had been more prepared to acknowledge that source. Given the special significance he attached to land, it is clear that the solutions he favoured, whether in Ireland or England, could never be determined by

---

[55] For James Mill's proposals and Ricardo's criticisms of them, see *Elements of political economy* as reprinted with Ricardo's notes in Winch (ed.), *James Mill*, pp. 338–42.
[56] 'The corn laws', *Westminster Review*, 1825, as reprinted in CW, IV, p. 69.
[57] 'The new corn law', *Westminster Review*, 1827, as reprinted in CW, IV, p. 148.
[58] *Principles*, CW, III, pp. 819–22.   [59] *Principles*, CW, II, p. 336.

economic logic alone. There is a parallel here between Mill's qualified acceptance of the case for further industrial growth and his unwilling-ness to discuss agrarian arrangements simply in terms of their economic rationale. The economic benefits England derived from 'high farming' could be purchased at too large a social cost in the form of exclusion of the working classes from roles that allowed scope for the social benefits of ownership, non-dependency, and self-development.

v

Even the most casual reader of Mill's *Principles* would have gathered that peasant proprietorship was one of his 'crotchets'. But it was not until the last six years of his life that Mill began to enjoy public notoriety for the radical nature of his opinions on land tenure. Two significant events occurring in 1867 help to explain this: the deterioration in Anglo-Irish relations that led up to the Fenian 'outrages' in that year and passage of the second Reform Act. In the case of Ireland there was a genuine devel-opment in Mill's opinions as well as a shift in the tactics he employed to advance them in public. In the case of English land tenure reform, it was more a matter of thinking that extension of the suffrage to urban working-class males now offered an opportunity to give legislative substance to radical opinions Mill had imbibed from his father at an early age. Boldness on this subject had always gone hand in hand with filial piety. Public circumstances now required and favoured radical initiatives: what had always been true in principle could now be offered as a practical blueprint.

Mill's interest in Ireland effectively dates from the sequence of leading articles he wrote for the *Morning Chronicle* during the famine of 1846–7. Before that he appears to have shared the conventional English economic diagnosis of Irish poverty, namely that Ireland lacked a system of *grande culture* that enabled plots to be consolidated and capital to be applied to improve productivity. Ireland seemed to exemplify Malthus's analysis of the consequences of a population 'forced' by the deceptive ease with which a subsistence based on potato cultivation could be obtained, and where a degraded version of the 'cow system' left the poor with few resources to withstand crop failure. Mill's articles marked a decisive shift away from such diagnoses: he advocated government purchase of waste land from the worst kind of unimproving Irish landowner for redistri-bution as fixed-tenure peasant proprietorships, along European lines, to the better kind of Irish subsistence farmer. The 'English' solution had now become the 'Tory' solution, and it had to be answered by drawing

attention to the falsity of the claim that sub-dividing property was synonymous with population growth and poverty.[60] Imposing the English
solution on Irish agrarian conditions would have involved a major exercise
in social engineering. Mill's aims were equally ambitious, but they were
not confined to seeking the most efficient economic solution. Trans-
mutation of the Irish cottar into a day-labourer on the English pattern, he
maintained, was 'rather a scheme for the improvement of Irish agriculture, than of the condition of the Irish people'. Such proposals had 'no
charm for infusing forethought, frugality, or self-restraint, into a people
devoid of them'.[61] Ownership of the land being cultivated would have
the desired effect. English ideas and prejudices were not applicable to
a society where competition merely had destructive effects on the peasantry, and where different customs dictated different solutions. Peasant
proprietorships were preferable to state-supported emigration and the
extension of the Poor Law to Ireland: bad Irish habits would be encouraged
by the latter, and Mill's estimate of the Irish character led him to think
that it was not suited to colonisation ventures. While these habits and
the Irish character could be accounted for in good associationist manner
as part of the legacy of English exploitation and neglect, Mill could hardly
be accused of sentimentalising the victims.

There was little further development in Mill's position on Irish land
until the 1860s. After the famine, in common with many other commentators, he was content to place his hopes on a mixed system combining commercial farming with peasant proprietorship. It required a
recurrence of agrarian difficulties, more evidence of the failure of attempts
to promote contractual solutions, and the assistance of John Elliot
Cairnes's incisive notes on the Irish land question to bring Mill (and the
1865 edition of his *Principles*) up to speed once more. Had it not been for
the violence associated with Fenianism, things might have rested there.
The events connected with this galvanised Mill into political action in the
same way that the Governor Eyre scandal in Jamaica had done. Frustrated
by what he saw as the insouciance of the British public towards Irish
grievances, he became convinced that the Anglo-Irish union could only
be preserved by acceptance of the most radical measures of land reform.
English insularity and indifference on the one side, and Fenian outrage on
the other, suggested the need to frighten the English public into accepting

[60] See Mill's attack on John Wilson Croker's use of biased evidence relating to France since
primogeniture was abolished, in an appendix to Book II of the *Principles*, CW, II, pp. 433–51.
[61] *Principles*, CW, II, p. 326.

Gladstone's more moderate measures. The pamphlet Mill wrote on the subject, *England and Ireland*, went well beyond any of the solutions he had previously supported in parliament and in his *Principles*. He now endorsed fixity of tenure for all Irish tenants, with 'fair' rents being adjudicated by a government commission with powers to offer Consols in compensation to landowners who would rather sell up than submit to adjudication. The pamphlet earned him a reputation as a rabble-rouser and as the supporter of a sequence of dangerous 'isms' that were a mirror image of the truth: Irish nationalism, anarchism, and communism.

There was method in Mill's madness and some good family ancestry as well. Frightening the ruling classes into accepting a moderate measure by threatening something more revolutionary was a tactic self-consciously employed by Mill's father when managing extra-parliamentary pressure groups during the Reform Bill crisis of 1831–2.[62] By taking an extreme position Mill was able to boast that he had assisted acceptance of the more moderate solution embodied in Gladstone's first Irish Land Act in 1870.[63] Had he lived to see it, he might have made similar claims for the second Land Act of 1881 which granted fixity of tenure. That his position was tactical can be seen from the way in which, in private, he recognised that other proposals were more likely to be adopted. The intemperate language and radical proposals contained in *England and Ireland* were not reflected in his parliamentary speeches on the Irish Land Bill.

It was widely feared that any recognition of tenants' customary rights in Ireland would have dangerous implications for landed property in England and Scotland. For Gladstone and others it was safer to construct a ring fence around the issue by recognising Irish peculiarities rather than by continuing to press for English 'contractual' solutions. While anything that disturbed English complacency would have pleased the incendiarist in Mill, the parallels that weighed more with him were between Ireland and India rather than Ireland and England. The *ryotwari* solution showed that it was possible for English rulers to shake off 'insular prejudices' by

governing another country according to its wants, and not according to common English habits and notions. It is what they have had to do in India; and those Englishmen who know something of India, are even now those who understand Ireland best. Persons who know both countries, have remarked many points of resemblance between the Irish and the Hindoo character; there certainly are many between the agricultural economy of Ireland and that of India.[64]

---

[62] See J. Hamburger, *James Mill and the art of revolution* (New Haven: Yale University Press, 1963).
[63] See Mill's claim in *Autobiography*, CW, I, p. 280. [64] *England and Ireland*, CW, VI, p. 519.

Mill was not alone in seeking to advance on the Irish problem of tenant right across Indian territory. George Campbell, Chief Commissioner of the Central Provinces of India, did so in less extreme fashion in a pamphlet on *Irish land* that was to prove more helpful to Gladstone when preparing his Irish land bills than Mill's less measured utterances on the subject.

VI

The second Reform Act helped to concentrate Mill's mind on the kinds of reforms that might now gain momentum as a result of extension of the suffrage to male members of the urban working classes. Chief among these were the reforms called for by the Land Tenure Reform Association. The statement of aims he drew up began by proclaiming that: 'Of all our leading institutions, none are more unsuited than the Land Laws to the state of society of which the Reform Act of 1867 is the harbinger.'[65] The programme went well beyond the familiar Cobdenite or Liberal case, largely aimed at a middle-class audience, for 'free trade' in land. It included state purchase of land for the purposes of sub-division, the construction of smallholdings on crown land, reclamation of wasteland for the same purpose, and the formation of agrarian co-operatives to reap the advantages of scale. Capping all these was a clause pledging support for taxation of the unearned increment, which was pushed through by Mill in an attempt to counter the demands of the rival working-class organisation, the Land and Labour League, for outright land nationalisation with the object of distributing wasteland for agricultural use. Mill opposed this on two grounds. First, he thought that state management was unfit for the task: for the time being administration of commons and wasteland was as much responsibility as bureaucracy could bear.[66] Secondly, he placed a higher priority on commons preservation than cultivation; and in his dealings with the leaders of the League, he came to the conclusion that 'there will be more difficulty than ever in preserving the commons. The working-class speakers are filled with exaggerated ideas of the value

---

[65] 'Land tenure reform', CW, V, p. 689.
[66] '. . . I do not know that it may not be reserved for us in the future; but at present I decidedly do not think it expedient. I have so poor an opinion of State management, or municipal management either, that I am afraid many years would elapse before the revenue realized for the State would be sufficient to pay the indemnity which would justly be claimed by the dispossessed proprietors.' See speech on land tenure reform, 15 May 1871, as reprinted in *Public and parliamentary speeches*, CW, XXIX, p. 419.

of the waste lands for cultivation, and apparently do not care at all for the preservation of natural beauty.' It was against this background that he hoped that women's suffrage would counter this male tendency to 'submit to the expulsion of all beauty from common life'.[67]

The programme of the Land Tenure Reform Association represents the high-water mark of Mill's radicalism on such matters. Alongside the cause of female emancipation, the activities of the Association absorbed most of his energies during the final years of his life, with his step-daughter, Helen Taylor, taking an active part in causes alongside him. They also became members of a new Radical Club founded by Fawcett in 1870, with Charles Wentworth Dilke as its secretary, a club that had as the first clause in its constitution the right of women to be members. Half its membership was drawn from 'the most radical of the Liberal Party in the House of Commons; the remainder composed of representatives of the Radical press, and the leaders of advanced liberal thought from the Universities and elsewhere'.[68] The Club and the Association contained several of Mill's friends and disciples, but it is not clear how many of them were entirely at one with him. Unearned increments could divide as well as unite.

As the representatives of Ricardian orthodoxy within Mill's personal circle, Fawcett and Cairnes regarded the rental return on landed property as subject to laws that differed from those governing other types of property. For Cairnes, it involved 'a factitious value incident to the progress of society' that justified state intervention 'to supply that which the principle of unrestricted competition has failed to supply'.[69] But there was less than complete agreement with Mill on what precise form that intervention should take. Fawcett stopped short of taxation of the unearned increment, and opposed land nationalisation schemes on grounds that were probably more rigid than Mill's own reservations about increasing the state's role in such matters.[70] Cairnes and Mill were broadly in accord when it came to finding solutions to the Irish land problem, but while Cairnes favoured official regulation of rents in Ireland, he was only prepared to defend the *principle* on which taxation of the unearned increment

---

[67] Letter to Fawcett, October 24 1869, CW, XVII, p. 1659.
[68] Letter from Mrs Fawcett to Helen Taylor, cited in CW, XVII, pp. 1698–9. Other members included Cairnes, Morley, Frank Harrison Hill (editor of the *Daily News*), Leslie Stephen, Leonard Courtney, Henry Sidgwick, W. C. Sidgwick, and McCullagh Torrens.
[69] See 'Political economy and land', as reprinted in his *Essays in political economy: theoretical and applied* (London: Macmillan, 1873), pp. 192, 198.
[70] On the unearned increment, see H. Fawcett, *Manual of political economy* (London: Macmillan, 1883), pp. 286–7. See also 'The nationalisation of land', *Fortnightly Review*, 72 (1872), 627–43.

was based.[71] If we are to believe the testimony of Dilke, Mill found more unqualified support from younger members of the Land Tenure Reform Association like himself. Dilke criticised Mrs Fawcett for downplaying Mill's activities in the fields of land reform, education, and trade unions during the last years of his life, those fields in which the Fawcetts failed to follow Mill's lead. Dilke claimed that 'in his last years [Mill] was very far from being an individualist, was abreast of the most modern tendencies in a socialist direction, and, so far from being stationary in his opinions was moving in the van. Indeed he was perhaps the first English politician to inaugurate a movement dealing with the land question, which was socialistic in its aims.'[72] This overlooks Mill's pursuit of his father's lead, but it consorts with other ways in which, as we shall see in Essay 8, Mill left a lingering belief that he might have been more socialist in his sympathies than followers such as Cairnes and Henry Sidgwick were prepared to accept.

On the wider issues raised by peasant proprietorship Mill formed close alliances and friendships with William Thornton and Cliffe Leslie, neither of whom had orthodox commitments as economists. Indeed, both men were critics of Ricardian orthodoxy and the methods of reasoning that underpinned it. Both attacked the wage-fund theory before Mill himself renounced it; and as we shall see in Essay 5 Leslie was to become one of the leading Anglo-Irish advocates of an alternative historical and inductive mode of inquiry. Though grateful for the support Mill gave to his inductive research, especially that conducted during his travels to European countries, the formative intellectual influences on Leslie were Henry Maine's historical jurisprudence and the work of comparative agrarian historians such as Leonce de Lavergne and Emil de Laveleye.[73] Especially when confronting the problems raised by land tenure, agrarian economic history and the new versions of evolutionary historical jurisprudence furnished evidence that could be used either to reinforce or

---

[71] See his appendix to 'Political economy and land', pp. 230–1 and his obituary assessment of Mill's political economy in *The Examiner*, as reprinted in Bain, *John Stuart Mill*, pp. 200–1.

[72] See 'John Stuart Mill, 1869–73', *Cosmopolis*, 5 (1897), p. 631. It was to Dilke that Mill expressed his concern at the height of the campaign for land tenure reform in England that the Bombay *ryotwari* system was once more under threat from those who favoured the *zemindari* alternative. He attributed this to 'a strong reaction in favour of setting up landlords everywhere' and dreaded to think what would happen when an Irish landlord, the sixth Earl of Mayo, took over as Viceroy; see *Later letters*, CW, XVII, p. 15.

[73] See the preface he wrote to his *Essays in political and moral philosophy* (Dublin: Hodges, Foster, and Figges, 1879), p. vi. On this, see R. D. C. Black, 'The political economy of Thomas Edward Cliffe Leslie (1826–82): a reassessment', *European Journal of the History of Economic Thought*, 9 (2002), p. 334.

undermine conclusions derived from Ricardian rent theory. Mill provides an example of how Maine could be used opportunistically and counter to Maine's own wishes. Leslie's use of Maine could have been equally opportunist, but his version of Maine valued the essential insights he supplied into an economic past and present that could not be uncovered by the timeless and placeless abstractions of economic theory. After Mill's death Leslie was frank in giving his opinion on the failure of Mill's entire intellectual enterprise: 'It was not possible to weld the abstractions of Ricardo and the actual forces governing economic phenomena into a consistent and scientific system; or to furnish an adequate theory of the origin and growth of human ideas without investigation of the entire history of human society.'[74]

Despite a generous bequest in Mill's will, the Land Tenure Reform Association died with him. This was certainly not true of the cause itself. Or rather, perhaps, in view of the long history of land tenure reform initiatives in Britain, it would be better to say that Mill set on foot a relay race with some of the characteristics of a game of leapfrog, a combination that may account for some of the resulting confusion. Mill passed the baton to a new generation when he recruited Alfred Russel Wallace, the co-discoverer of the theory of natural selection in biology, as a supporter of the Association. Wallace was responsible for inclusion of a clause that incorporated preservation of 'all natural objects or artificial constructions attached to the soil, which are of historical, scientific or artistic interest'. Conservation and preservation of the kind embodied in the founding of the National Trust in 1895 might have had more radical connotations if the programme of the Association had been implemented *en bloc* in the 1870s. Wallace carried the fight into the last quarter of the century by means of his own Land Nationalisation Society formed in 1881, a society to which Helen Taylor subscribed. Wallace in turn passed the baton to a more famous land reformer, Henry George, while attempting later to distinguish his own reforms from the 'no compensation' programme endorsed by the Georgist Land Restoration League.[75] George's lectures

---

[74] For Leslie's reflections on Mill, see the preface to *Essays in political and moral philosophy* and 'John Stuart Mill', *The Academy*, 5 June 1875, as reprinted in his *Essays on political economy* (Dublin: Hodges, Foster, and Figges, 1888), p. 57. In a letter written to Leon Walras he stated that much as he honoured Mill's character, a close study of Mill's *Principles* had convinced him that Mill was a writer who was often incapable of dealing with the problems he raised, citing the doctrine that 'demand for goods is not demand for labour' as a prime example of this; see letter to Walras, 7 September 1874, in *Correspondence of Leon Walras*, ed. W. Jaffé, 3 vols. (Amsterdam: North Holland Publishing Company, 1965), I, pp. 424–6.

[75] See A. R. Wallace, *Land nationalization: its necessity and its aims* (London: Swan Sonnenschein, 1882).

drew large audiences in the 1880s, and he made one notable convert among the early Fabians, Bernard Shaw. Sidney Webb, on the other hand, chose to credit Mill with the ideas that became central to Fabian economics, particularly after the Fabians decided to do without the benefit of Karl Marx's analysis of capitalism's inherent contradictions. The 'law of economic rent' and the taxation of unearned incomes became 'the very corner-stone of collectivist economy', a position by which Webb was still prepared to stand as late as 1920.[76] A few years earlier in an essay on the 'historic groundwork of Socialism' included in *Fabian essays*, one of the early founding documents for the Fabian Society, Sidney Webb nominated the 1848 edition of Mill's *Principles* as 'the boundary of the old individualist Economics'. Every subsequent edition of the book had become more socialistic, and the *Autobiography* confirmed Mill's 'development from a mere political democrat to a convinced Socialist'.[77] Having decided to accept a Jevonsian rather than a Marxian theory of value, Webb and his closest confederate, George Bernard Shaw, granted a large space in the Fabian programme for a version of the Ricardo–Mill 'law of economic rent' as the basis of proposals for taxing unearned increments in all forms of income.

Whether this was Mill's legacy, and whether Webb's claim to it was legitimate, matters less than the way in which it embarrassed others, especially those academics who were anxious to lay claim to the neutrality or disinterestedness of the science of political economy. Mill had aimed to bring science and art into closer and more fruitful relationship with one another. By the end of his career, however, largely as a result of his campaigns and 'crotchets', all the careful methodological discriminations between economics and ethics, between the indicative and imperative moods, seem to have become blurred, making it more difficult to arrive at a just estimate of what belonged to the science as opposed to what was personal to Mill.

* * *

Each of the essays in Part II deals with an aspect of this problem. On the surface, the subject of the first of them, John Ruskin, could hardly have been less ambivalent: Mill was an enemy to be annihilated. Yet even here,

---

[76] See the Webbs' *History of trade unionism*, rev. edn, 1920 (Kelley reprint, 1973), p. 162; and the preface to the 1920 edition of *Fabian essays*: 'Tested by a whole generation of further experience and criticism, I conclude that, in 1889, we knew our Political Economy, and that our Political Economy was sound' (London: George Allen and Unwin, 1948), p. xviii.

[77] See Webb's contribution to G. B. Shaw (ed.), *Fabian essays* (London: Walter Scott, 1889), pp. 54–5.

when outright rejection was the avowed aim, Ruskin betrayed signs of having learned more from Mill than he found it convenient to admit.

Ruskin's onslaught on the 'soi-disant' or 'commercial' science was less accurately directed at Mill than it would have been if Walter Bagehot, the subject of the second essay, had been the target. Bagehot showed even fewer signs of doubt about how to judge Mill as an economist or politician. He did so by means of an appeal over Mill's head to Ricardo, the economist Bagehot most admired, and whose realistic grasp on the inner dynamics of the financial world matched his own understanding of business psychology. Admirable though Mill might be in his own way, he could offer nothing of this quality. Bagehot combined this rather atavistic attachment to Ricardo with a sense of superiority to Mill that came from being conscious of what it meant to inhabit an intellectual world that was post-Darwinian, fully aware of the legal and biological insights associated with the writings of Henry Maine and Darwin himself.

William Stanley Jevons, the third subject in Part II, was conscious of the same source of superiority over Mill, and in his case it was confirmed by an extensive knowledge of other mid- to late-Victorian developments in mathematics, logic, and the physical sciences. Jevons had also built up a tank of resentment against Mill that was large enough to fuel his dislike for a large part of his foreshortened career.

Finally, looking even further forward to the essays in Part IV, we find Marshall maintaining that his own 'tendency to socialism' as well as much of his understanding of political economy derived from Mill's writings. He also hinted that after further exposure to the writings of socialists he found the message of *On liberty* more relevant to his thinking than the posthumous chapters on socialism.

PART II

Three responses to Mill

Fig. 2. John Ruskin. Photograph by
Elliott and Fry taken in 1867 when
Ruskin was 48.

Fig. 3. Walter Bagehot. Mezzotint by
Norman Hirst from a photograph *c.* 1865
when Bagehot was 39.

Fig. 4. William Stanley Jevons. Photographed
by himself in Australia *c.* 1858 when he was 23.

4

'Poor cretinous wretch': Ruskin's aversion to Mill

I

My title is selected solely for its brevity from a fusillade of abusive remarks that Ruskin directed at Mill in private communications and published writings over two or three decades. With the publication of articles in the *Cornhill Magazine* in 1860, collected together two years later as *Unto this last: four essays on the first principles of political economy*, Ruskin became the latest scourge of the science with which Mill's name was closely connected. Ruskin – not much given to understatement – came to regard the science as 'the most cretinous, speechless, paralysing plague that has yet touched the brains of mankind'.[1] No wonder then that its founding father came in for similar abuse: Adam Smith was that 'half-bred and half-witted Scotchman' who had taught the 'deliberate blasphemy' that 'thou shalt hate the Lord thy God, damn His laws, and covet thy neighbour's goods'.[2] Such denigration of the dismal science had been standard fare since Southey, Coleridge, Wordsworth, and Carlyle had declared political economy to be anathema during the first half of the century; it was part of the 'bitter argument' between economists and human beings about which Toynbee spoke in retrospective mood in the 1880s. In the long aftermath of his initial attack Ruskin did his best to position himself before the Victorian public as the humane alternative to everything for which he took Mill to stand: liberalism, utilitarianism, scientific materialism, and a non- or anti-Christian stand on morals. He was adding his voice to that of Carlyle, his mentor in such matters, and using the kind of personal invective against Mill that the Lake poets had earlier reserved for Malthus.[3]

---

[1] Letter to Dr J. Brown, August 1862, cited in JRW, XVII, p. lxxxii.
[2] *Fors clavigera*, JRW, XXVIII, p. 764. For a sample of similar statements about Smith, see also JRW, XXIX, pp. 134, 212, 282.
[3] For the earlier romantic assault on Malthus, see D. Winch, *Riches and poverty* (Cambridge: Cambridge University Press, 1996), pp. 225–8, 288–348, 395–401.

Unlike most of his predecessors, with the possible exception of Coleridge, Ruskin entertained a serious ambition to construct an alternative version of the science. He came to regard *Unto this last* as the work that would stand 'surest and longest of all work of mine'. When republishing the follow-up sequence of articles he wrote for *Fraser's Magazine* as *Munera pulveris* in 1872, he announced his resolution 'to make it the central work of my life to write an exhaustive treatise on Political Economy'.[4] Although he failed to make good this promise, *Unto this last*, a becalmed publishing venture for the first decade or so of its life, caught some strong breezes towards the end of the century when Ruskin acquired a following among those who wished to add a more overtly ethical dimension to economic inquiry. In this fashion *Unto this last* did, indeed, come to stand 'surest and longest', ensuring Ruskin a prominent place in what became known as the 'culture-and-society' critique of Victorian capitalism.[5]

Mill himself is usually granted a walk-on part in the reconstructed version of this critical tradition, mainly by virtue of his appreciative essay on Coleridge and his championing of Wordsworth as 'the poet of unpoetical natures, possessed of quiet and contemplative tastes'.[6] For these services Mill has been awarded the status of a flawed or failed romantic, capable of appreciating the private consolations of literature, but lacking those liberating qualities that would have allowed him to uphold (or anticipate) an alternative vision of society.[7] As with all such attempts to reconstruct cultural traditions, these retrospective judgements are often profoundly tendentious – as, of course, was Ruskin's contemporary verdict. But if the cue had been taken from Ruskin himself, Mill would have had an entirely different part to play. Mill was not merely the latest manifestation of the 'paralysing plague'; he was, quite literally, 'the root of nearly all immediate evil among us in England'.[8] When expressing this opinion in correspondence, knowing that the recipient took a different view, Ruskin gave an assurance that he was in deadly earnest. In dealing with someone for whom the personal was always public, and the public

---

[4] See JRW, XVII, p. 143.   [5] On this critique, see the Appendix, pp. 368–86 below.

[6] *Autobiography*, CW, I, p. 153.

[7] For this judgement on Mill, see Raymond Williams, *Culture and society* (Penguin edn, 1961), ch. 3.

[8] See letter to Charles Eliot Norton, 12 September 1869, *Correspondence of John Ruskin and Charles Eliot Norton*, ed. J. L Bradley and I. Ousby (Cambridge: Cambridge University Press, 1987), p. 172. The letter went on to say that Ruskin objected to Mill 'being looked up to as "the greatest thinker" when he is in truth an utterly shallow and wretched segment of a human creature incapable of understanding *Any*thing in the ultimate conditions of it – and countenancing with an unhappy fortune – whatever is fatallest [*sic*] in the popular error of English mind'.

always personal, there is no alternative – short of declaring him mentally unhinged – to an approach that takes such remarks as an accurate depiction of his state of mind.

Ruskin's opinions on Mill provide an initial focus for this essay because they were an integral part of his relationship with political economy: his readers were being invited to make a choice of allegiance between himself and Mill. Yet whatever Ruskin may have come to believe about the deficiencies of the science, Mill was still an odd choice of opponent – a choice for which some explanation seems required. In attempting to supply that explanation here it may be possible to appreciate the genuine peculiarities of Ruskin's position, the wilful or rhetorical artifices involved as well as the genuine insights it contained. And since Ruskin became an emblematic public figure during his lifetime, it is also possible to employ his opinions on Mill as a point of entry into another theme: the fate of the Ruskinian critique once it had passed into the hands of some immediate followers who became economists.

II

Although the public sources of Ruskin's antipathy to Mill were multiple, as with so much that was significant about Ruskin, the story has a domestic beginning. Ruskin's father had suppressed two of his son's letters on economic subjects to *The Times* in 1852, and viewed the articles that appeared in the *Cornhill* and *Fraser's Magazine* with apprehension, or what his son described at the time as 'terrified complacency'.[9] Frustration aroused by knowledge or fear of disapproval at home was compounded by the hostility with which the Victorian public greeted Ruskin's attacks on political economy. At times it must have seemed as though only Carlyle was cheering from the sidelines, an act of generosity from master to acknowledged pupil that Ruskin rewarded by dedicating *Munera pulveris* to him. Mill first appears as the target at a very precise moment in this story: the moment when Thackeray, editor of the *Cornhill*, informed Ruskin that the fourth essay would have to be the last, and when he offered more space as compensation.[10] To answer critics who said that the

---

[9] See the letters sent by Ruskin and his father to Sir Walter and Lady Trevelyan in V. Surtees (ed.), *Reflections of a friendship: John Ruskin's letters to Pauline Trevelyan, 1848–1866* (London: Allen and Unwin, 1979), pp. 150, 157, 159.

[10] John Tyree Fain was the first to suggest this dating in his *Ruskin and the economists* (Nashville: Vanderbilt Press, 1956), p. 104.

earlier articles showed complete ignorance of political economy, Ruskin returned to Smith, Ricardo, and Mill to prove them wrong.[11]

At this juncture, after a second failure, when the articles for *Fraser's* had also been discontinued on grounds of their unpopularity, domestic events played another part. The death of Ruskin's father in 1864 removed a restraining hand while at the same time furnishing the son with ample means to choose the way in which he presented his ideas to the public, free from the interference of editors and the readerships they served. Inheritance of John James Ruskin's fortune allowed Ruskin to become his own publisher, making available to the world his every passing thought in the series of letters that comprise *Time and tide* and *Fors clavigera*, works initially addressed to a member of the working classes seeking the advice of his social superior on the affairs of the day. *Fors clavigera* is the source of the statement about Adam Smith quoted at the outset, and there is more there, and in *Time and tide*, that reveals Ruskin's irritated preoccupation with Mill over a period of more than two decades.[12]

No one still believes, as his father did, that these post-1860 writings were an unfortunate digression from Ruskin's career as an art critic. Ruskin became an avid reader of Carlyle's *Heroes and hero worship* and *Past and present* in the 1840s, the period when he began the search for an occupation that he thought would be more useful to society than his current concerns. That it took him some time to settle on his new vocation could account for his anxiety to put his ideas on Victorian society into permanent shape once he had found it. Ruskin's inability to share the enthusiasm of those who saw the Great Exhibition of 1851 as a triumph of British industrial ingenuity and manufacturing supremacy, his scorn for what he described as the 'steam-whistle party', were significant signs of what was to come. In 1857 he gave lectures in Manchester which were first published as the *Political economy of art* (later as *A joy for ever*), having expressed similar views on this subject in one of the works that had earned him the attention of the Victorian public, the treatment of

---

[11] A collection of contemporary reviews can be found in J. L. Bradley (ed.), *Ruskin: the critical heritage* (London: Routledge, 1984). The *Saturday Review* had dwelt on Ruskin's ignorance of these authors: 'The world may have been mistaken in looking upon Adam Smith, Mr Ricardo, and Mr Mill as some of the clearest and most useful thinkers that England ever produced, but they are . . . entitled to better treatment than, like Sydney Smith's dean, to be preached to death by a mad governess' (p. 274).

[12] See, for example, the description of 'the modern Liberal politico-economist of the Stuart Mill school' as 'essentially of the type of a flat-fish – one eyeless side of him always in the mud and one eye, on the side that *has* eyes, down in the corner of his mouth, – not a desirable guide for man or beast'; see *Fors clavigera*, JRW, XXVII, p. 180.

'Nature of the Gothic' in the *Stones of Venice*. But it was only with the fourth essay in *Unto this last* that Ruskin's invective began to be concentrated on political economy. The writings that precede this abound with condemnations of the vulgarity, impermanence, adulteration, exploitation, and speculative excess that Ruskin invariably associated with urban, competitive, and technology-driven employments, but there was none of the antagonism towards the science of political economy shown later.

There must have been a copy of the *Wealth of nations* on Ruskin's father's bookshelves: John James was certainly advised to make a careful study of it when he was a young man. His adviser told him that it would counteract the narrow mentality associated with his chosen profession, the wine trade, making him 'an honourable and distinguished merchant' as opposed to 'a mere trader'.[13] It was to this honourable station that his son later proposed that all merchants and manufacturers should aspire. John Ruskin himself needed no antidote to professional deformation. As he freely acknowledged, his father's wealth, based on exploitation of the Spanish peasants who grew the grapes he sold as sherry, made it unnecessary for him to follow any profession, unless it was as lecturer and man of letters. As late as 1856, in a typical mixture of generosity and arrogance, John could write to a friend that 'I have reasoned out a good many principles of a general philosophy and political economy by myself, and I have *always* found myself in concurrence with Bacon and Adam Smith as soon as I have settled social principles to my own satisfaction; and as I believe those two people to have been no fools, I see no reason for concluding that I am one myself.'[14]

This self-confirmatory style of reading served Ruskin well in the *Political economy of art* when criticising a revived version of Bernard Mandeville's argument on the beneficial employment effects of luxury expenditure: the response Ruskin gave is impeccably Smithian, though couched in the moralistic language he had made his own.[15] Ruskin told his readers that he had read the *Wealth of nations* 'some twenty years ago', and that he did not think it worth mentioning modern works. Most of his economic principles were 'accepted by existing authorities on the science', and the works he had seen since reading Smith were 'encumbered with inquiries into accidental or minor commercial results'. The science had its uses,

---

[13] Letter from T. Brown to John James Ruskin 18 February 1807, in *Praeterita*, JRW, XXXV, p. 125.
[14] Letter to Acland, 27 April 1856, JRW, XXXVI, p. 238.
[15] See note 5 on the invention of new wants in JRW, XVI, pp. 123–4.

and could easily be taught to the young, but it was not worth diverting too much effort from higher intellectual and aesthetic pursuits to do so: 'no profound study seems compatible with the work in which I am usually employed'. Ruskin preserved this stance of effortless superiority in his only reference to Mill's *Principles* in these lectures. He referred to its treatment of the distinction between productive and unproductive labour as something he had noted when he 'chanced . . . on opening' the book the other day.[16] This was disingenuous: his reading of political economy was sporadic and often jaundiced, but chance had little to do with it.

The late 1850s was probably the period when Ruskin first did any extended reading in post-Smithian political economy, and when he did so he found much with which he could agree in Mill's *Principles*. The sparse marginal notes he made on a copy of the first edition confirm this view. 'Good', 'very good', 'excellent', and even 'admirable' are more frequent than the comments on those sentences with which Ruskin wished take issue, and most of the latter are confined to what are often verbal quibbles with the preliminary remarks and the early definitional chapters of Book I.[17] As may be clear from the earlier essays on Mill, it would not be difficult to cull a number of quotations from the *Principles* expressing ideas that are indistinguishable in substance if not style from positions later to be thought of as Ruskinian. The most obvious examples are Mill's dislike of the prospect of a world permanently devoted to competitive striving; his opinion that improvements in machinery had so far increased the gap between rich and poor without relieving the burden of physical labour; and his examination of the possibilities of a zero-growth society in which the quality of life would take precedence over the cruder, though still as yet essential, quantitative measures of improvement. There are no marginal comments on these topics in Ruskin's copy, but his frequent return to them later shows how much they disturbed him once Mill had become his chief target.

When mentioning Mill's *Principles* in the concluding essay of *Unto this last*, Ruskin said that its virtues chiefly proceeded from its inconsistencies: '[Mill] deserves honour among economists by inadvertently disclaiming the principle which he states, and tacitly introducing the moral consid-erations with which he declares his science has no connection.' Ruskin also grudgingly acknowledged that Mill had 'partially glanced at' the probable

---

[16] See *A joy for ever*, JRW, XVI, pp. 9, 17, 131.
[17] Copy held by British Library, c. 60.l.10; see too the summary of the marginalia in JRW, XXXIV, pp. 708–9.

future of the labouring classes in his forty-page chapter on the subject; and that the related treatment of a conceivable stationary state in which the natural environment would be protected from the damage inflicted by continued population growth differed 'from the common writing of political economists in admitting some value in the aspect of nature, and expressing regret at the probability of the destruction of natural scenery'.[18]

The letters Ruskin wrote to Charles Eliot Norton at this time shed some light on this phase of his relationship with Mill's writings. Norton was the recipient of the letter in which Ruskin described Mill as the 'root of nearly all immediate evil'; he was on friendly terms with Mill, a fact known to Ruskin and one that he used to josh Norton about his familiarity with and support for Mill's political economy.[19] He accused Norton of confusing economy with morality when defending Mill: 'you do not clearly see that I do not (in my books) dispute Mill's morality; but I flatly deny his *Economical science*'. This was Ruskin's priority while the ambition to write a treatise was uppermost in his mind, and it led him to challenge Norton, then editor of the *North American Monthly*, to use his pages to demonstrate which version of the science, his or Mill's, was capable of revealing laws 'as inevitable as gravitation'.[20]

Ruskin had good reason to be grudging about Mill's chapter on the labouring classes. As we have seen, it contains Mill's rejection of paternalistic interpretations of the responsibilities of the rich as upheld by the earlier romantics.[21] The growth of intelligence within the working classes, Mill said, ensured that they were no longer in 'leading strings', a reference to Carlyle's image of them as a horse that needed to be bridled by a firm yet kind master. In other words, Mill had in essence replied to Ruskin's position a decade before Ruskin himself had expressed it.[22] Reading Mill before and after he had resolved to write an exhaustive treatise must have been a strange experience for Ruskin, making it easier for him to be more

---

[18] *Unto this last*, JRW, XVII, p. 110.

[19] For some indication of Norton's position on related matters see his *Considerations on some recent social theories* (Boston: Little, Brown, 1853). Mill's *Principles* is cited on co-operation and the future of the working classes, and a simple version of his position on competition endorsed: 'In dwelling upon the evils of competition many have become blind to the fact of its necessary existence and to the good which results from it'; see pp. 83, 85–6, 114.

[20] See letter to Charles Eliot Norton, 18 August 1869, *Correspondence of John Ruskin and Charles Eliot Norton*, p. 155; see further letters on same subject pp. 62, 142, 152, 168, 172, 174.

[21] See pp. 48–9 above.

[22] Ruskin's awareness of this can be seen in his return to Mill's chapter on later occasions; see *Fors clavigera*, JRW, XXVIII, pp. 405–6, 699: '. . . let Mr John Stuart Mill have the disordering of [the modern British workman], so that "no one shall be guided or governed, or directed in the way they should go" – and they sink to lower and lower depth   till the dance becomes Death's'.

sympathetic in the privacy of his study than he chose to be in print after
he had announced his intentions.[23] Ruskin's summary judgement on
Mill's cretinous qualities, therefore, conceals an enduring pattern of fas-
cinated dislike that needs to be examined as part of the wider background
to his decision to write his own version of Mill's *Principles*.

III

Why did so much of Ruskin's pent-up anger come to be directed at Mill?
That he started at the top of the range – he descended to lesser lights such
as Fawcett subsequently – could simply be a mark of his ambitions. After
all, the aim to which he dedicated the rest of his life was hardly a minor
one, and dislodging Mill from his pedestal would be no mean feat for
a variety of reasons. Mill was the crusading figure from whom the radical
and liberal Victorian intelligentsia and a large number of working-class
radicals and trade unionists learned not only their political economy but
many of their opinions on politics and morals as well. As Ruskin said,
echoing Carlyle, Mill was 'The Greatest Thinker in England', with the
capital letters adding weight to the irony intended.[24] Cheap 'people's
editions' of the *Principles* and the essay *On liberty* were issued in 1865 to
meet working-class demand.[25] When Ruskin began his series of letters to
the working classes in *Time and tide*, later extended in *Fors clavigera*, he
was competing for the attention of the same audience – though he claimed
to be addressing the workmen of the future rather than those 'who have
been produced by the instructions of Mr John Stuart Mill'.[26] Although
Mill died in the year that *Fors clavigera* first appeared, his presence as a
public figure, still capable of arousing controversy, was sustained by use
of his work in universities and by the posthumous publication of his
autobiography and his final reflections on religion and socialism.[27]

Ruskin refers to some of these late writings, but the revived memory
of some crucial sentences in two chapters in the *Principles* seems to have

---

[23] See *Munera pulveris*, JRW, XVII, p. 143.   [24] *Fors clavigera*, JRW, XXVII, pp. 64–5.

[25] In 1865, when Ruskin was becoming heavily involved in political and economic questions, Mill's
publications were much in evidence. New editions of *Representative government* and of the *Logic*,
as well as *On liberty* and the *Principles* appeared, with new works on *Auguste Comte and positivism*
and the *Examination of Sir William Hamilton's philosophy* also making their first appearance.

[26] *Fors clavigera*, JRW, XXVII, p. 669.

[27] On the general issue of Mill's reputation, before and after death, see Stefan Collini, *Public
moralists: political thought and intellectual life in Britain, 1850–1930* (Oxford: Oxford University
Press, 1991), ch. 4, 8. For his influence on trade unionists, see E. Biagini, 'British trade unions and
popular political economy, 1860–1880', *Historical Journal*, 30 (1987), 811–40.

been enough to keep his indignation going: the first on rent and landed property and the second, already mentioned, on the future of the working classes. The latter contains not only the rejection of the aristocratic 'theory of dependence', but hints of other opinions on women and co-operative forms of socialism that Mill was to reinforce in later editions and other writings. It contains, for example, some remarks on the effect of improved intelligence in promoting the 'social independence of women', thereby opening up careers beyond the domestic ones – remarks that were to be developed in the *Subjection of women*. Ruskin reverts to these remarks on several occasions; as well he might, given the marked contrast between them and the account of women's duties given in *Sesame and lilies*. In *Fors clavigera* Mill is taken to be representative of all those 'restless' spirits who by complaining about the limitations placed on women's paid employment encourage mothers to neglect their children and other wifely duties.[28] Ruskin also hints that the chastity of young men and women may have been placed at risk by Mill's advocacy of birth control, the subject of renewed adverse comment in the obituary disputes.[29]

Before turning to some policy questions on which there was a greater measure of agreement than one would gather from the tone of Ruskin's remarks, it is worth recalling the issue on which they clashed in public. What brought them into direct conflict in 1865–6 was the campaign by the Jamaica Committee, led by Mill, to prosecute Governor Eyre for imposing the death penalty on those responsible for a revolt by ex-slaves in Jamaica. Ruskin had allowed himself to be recruited to Eyre's side by Carlyle, using one of the lines of attack on Mill that Carlyle had initiated: what was all this liberal palaver about the treatment of ex-slaves in Jamaica when Mill was an exponent of a science that justified wage slavery at home? Nor is it difficult to find other significant political differences that were not conducted in public. Chief among these would be Mill's dismay over Louis Napoleon's *coup d'état* and Ruskin's initial welcome to a potentially heroic Carlylean regime that would restore some discipline in France. It is also mirrored in their divergent attitudes to America and

---

[28] The 1871 preface to *Sesame and lilies* contains what could be a veiled reference to Mill's parliamentary activities and his pamphlet on the *Subjection of women* when Ruskin speaks of 'those questions [which] have arisen respecting the education and claims of women which have greatly troubled simple minds and excited restless ones'; see JRW, XVIII, p. 35.

[29] See *Fors clavigera*, JRW, XXVII, pp. 431, 536. For the birth control element in the obituary disputes, see Collini, *Public moralists*, pp. 312–14.

to the cause of the North in the American civil war, where, as in the case of Jamaica, slavery was the central issue.[30]

On the basis of this evidence one might conclude that it was Mill's prominence as the leader of radical liberal opinion, far more than his dominant role as the exponent of the science of political economy, that made him the prime target for a self-confessed 'violent Tory of the old school', a 'violent Illiberal' who was too anxious to destroy many things to qualify as a Conservative.[31] There is a good deal of truth in this as long as one remembers that just as Ruskin was a distinctly peculiar kind of Tory, Mill was a distinctly peculiar kind of Liberal, with both having claims to the 'radical' prefix: neither can be considered as representative Victorian thinkers. Politics in the everyday sense seems to have played the following part in shaping Ruskin's attitude to Mill: once new sources of political disagreement had entered the picture in the 1860s, Ruskin found it more difficult to acknowledge borrowings and points of agreement.

An illustration of this can be found in Ruskin's treatment of the essay *On liberty*. Liberty was one of those slogans Ruskin associated with the horrors of the French revolution, and its widespread use as a catchphrase frequently acted as a red rag to him. Although he later characterised 'liberty' as Mill's 'Cockney English' for something quite different, namely *libertas*, he had, in the fifth volume of *Modern painters* in 1860, commended Mill's essay by saying that he found no need to enlarge on the meaning of 'individual, that is to say, distinct and separate in character, though joined in purpose' because 'all that I should care to say has been already said admirably by Mr J. S. Mill'.[32] He also approved of the treatment given to freedom of thought, conceding that 'some important truths are there beautifully expressed, but many, quite vital, are omitted; and the balance, therefore, is wrongly struck'.[33] What was lacking was an equivalent treatment of the virtues of discipline or 'restraint'. It went alongside Ruskin's observations on the increased unwillingness of mere authority to command deference, something that was welcomed by Mill, but had a more threatening aspect to Ruskin.[34]

---

[30] They agreed in disliking some aspects of American go-getting, though it is significant that Mill withdrew his most outspoken statement on 'dollar-hunters' from the *Principles;* see CW, III, p. 754n.

[31] See opening sentence of *Praeterita* in JRW, XXXV, p. 13 and *Fors clavigera*, JRW, XXVII, pp. 14–15.

[32] JRW, VII, p. 229.

[33] *Cestrus of Aglaia*, JRW, XIX, p. 127; for the marginal comments, see JRW, XXXIV, pp. 707–8.

[34] See *Fors clavigera*, JRW, XXVII, p. 211; XXVIII, pp. 405, 699.

Finally, there are the questions that centre on institutional reform of social and economic life, those fundamental issues of property, equality, and income and wealth redistribution that were central, in different ways, to both men's visions. Fortifying his distinction between laws of production and laws of distribution, Mill added to the chapters in the *Principles* dealing with the latter topics, becoming steadily warmer, as we have seen, towards socialist experiments and his own schemes for taxing inheritances. More generally, as he made plain in the *Autobiography*, he believed that: 'The social problem of the future' would be 'how to unite the greatest individual liberty of action, with a common ownership in the raw material of the globe, and an equal participation of all in the benefits of combined labour'.[35] Although Ruskin always differentiated his proposals for social reform from contemporary forms of socialism, and thought equality was an impossible goal, he endorsed a number of specific solutions which are close to those advocated by Mill: the virtues of *petite* as opposed to *grande culture*, peasant proprietorship, and compensation for tenants' improvements being obvious examples.

On the question of rent and private property in land, however, Ruskin, while agreeing with Mill's solution to the Irish land problem ('Mill right at last, and attacked for being so') found him guilty of equivocation on grounds that are almost as contorted as those that emerged from the Eyre controversy. Mill had written that while rent was a justifiable form of return on any improvements made by the landowner himself, 'he is morally bound, and should, whenever the case admits, be legally compelled to make his interest and pleasure consistent with the public good'.[36] Quoting this in 1867, Ruskin accused Mill of an 'immense involuntary error', of 'cunningly', later dishonestly, masking the consequences of his own conclusions 'for fear of fostering political agitation'.[37] Yet as we have seen in an earlier essay, Mill was simply following his father in employing the conclusions of the Ricardian theory to support a case for land tenure reform that would break the power of the absentee landowners in Ireland and reduce the concentration of landownership in Britain generally.[38] He would have welcomed and was actively engaged in political agitation himself on such matters.

Ruskin's solution to the same problem was to allow landowners to occupy their estates, but to receive a government salary for their custodial

---

[35] CW, I, p. 239.   [36] *Principles*, CW, II, p. 232.   [37] *Time and tide*, JRW, XVII, pp. 442–5.
[38] Fain astutely asks how Mill could be right in the pamphlet on *England and Ireland*, but guilty of equivocation in his *Principles* when the same doctrine is being applied; see *Ruskin and the economists*, pp. 118–19.

services, thereby divorcing their income from rents that varied with market conditions. Mill's equivocation, in Ruskin's view, centred on his acceptance of rent under existing contractual arrangements. From Mill's perspective it was simply a matter of acknowledging the legal claim and what followed from it, namely proper compensation for land taken over for public purposes. The idea of landownership as a public trust had been espoused by Coleridge in the first two decades of the century, and Mill described Coleridge's proposals in the House of Commons as based on a theory of property 'compared with which anything which I ever hinted at is the merest milk and water'.[39] In later speeches on the Irish land question, and in the *Principles*, however, he rejected attempts to attach duties to landownership by 'erecting it into a sort of magistracy, either moral or legal' by reminding his readers that if landowners were to be treated as 'public functionaries', the public could decide to do without their services.[40] Ruskin rightly denied that his proposals involved nationalisation or even the replacement of existing landowners: merely separating their incomes from market-determined rents would satisfy his aims. By endorsing primogeniture as a sacred right he was able to bypass any question of public appropriation, with or without compensation. The defence of private property in land in *Fors clavigera* is an uncompromising one, modified, in Coleridge's manner, by an appeal to the consciences of landowners.

IV

Such divergences and convergences in matters of everyday politics and economic policy did not have to coincide with disagreement on the nature and scope of the science of political economy. But in his most fundamental challenge to what he now called a 'bastard' or 'soi-disant' science, Ruskin contrasted 'commercial' or 'mercantile' political economy with his own loftier version – a science that had Greek roots in Plato's *Republic* and Xenophon's *Oekonomicus*. The fusion of *oekonomia*, the household science, with *politeia* allowed Ruskin to unite these separate spheres in a manner that captures an important feature of his position.[41]

---

[39] See *Speeches*, CW, XXVIII, p. 82.   [40] *Principles*, CW, II, p. 230.
[41] For a broader treatment of the rhetorical resources opened up to Ruskin and others by their reading of Xenophon, see Jane Garnett, 'Political and domestic economy in Victorian social thought: Ruskin and Xenophon', in Stefan Collini, Richard Whatmore, and Brian Young (eds.), *Economy, polity, and society: British intellectual history 1750–1950* (Cambridge: Cambridge University Press, 2000), pp. 205–23.

He conceded that the mercantile science was true within its own restricted limits, but declared that he was 'uninterested' in the results.[42] The 'economic man' assumption on which its theories were built ignored the social affections, making the science inapplicable 'to the present phase of the world' – a neat reversal of Mill's belief, or hope at least, that the 'coarse stimuli' needed to drive present 'coarse minds' would give way to more co-operative institutions and behaviour in future.[43] Ruskin was still wavering, then, between finding political economy trivially correct within its narrow sphere and the far more serious charge that it was a blasphemous symbol of all that was wrong with the modern world. The economists may not have invented Mammon, but they had done nothing to discourage the extension of his realm. The latter charge became more common as Ruskin warmed to his theme, ending in his condemnation of the 'pig philosophy'.

As he had shown first in the *Political economy of art*, Ruskin's political economy was to be a 'paternal' science concerned with the wise or just management of the nation's labour and other natural resources along the lines of a well-conducted household or estate in which servants were assigned tasks that made best use of their time, talents, and capacity to trust loving superiors. In return they were to be rewarded according to a fixed scale of wages akin to the fees paid to professionals, thereby ensuring that good workers could not be undercut by bad ones. Wages would not vary with demand: those who were unskilled or deficient in other ways would simply not be offered employment. They would be retrained in government schools or given assistance at the public expense, with the recalcitrant being 'set, under compulsion of the strictest nature, the more painful and degrading forms of necessary toil, especially to that in mines and other places of danger' until they had learned their lesson.[44] Recognising that arduous physical labour could not be abolished, though some of it ought to be shared on a token basis with other classes, and assuming that slavery was no longer an option in Britain, all 'mechanical and foul employment' should be performed by criminals, thereby relieving the 'innocent population'.[45] Liberty and equality, as already noted, were rejected as undesirable or impossible aims, and fraternity, the only one of the three French revolutionary slogans Ruskin could accept, meant little unless it respected the paternity principle. 'Discipline and Interference

---

[42] *A joy for ever*, JRW, XVI, p. 26.   [43] *Principles*, CW, III, p. 754.
[44] *Unto this last*, JRW, XVII, p. 22.   [45] *Munera pulveris*, JRW, XVII, p. 234.

lie at the very root of all human progress or power.'[46] They represented
the principle of life in contrast with the 'let-alone' principle of death
based on competition and indifference to others. As reward for disciplined
obedience the masses had unconditional rights to education, employment,
and relief during old age and sickness. These are the topics on which
Ruskin was later welcomed as a socialist and credited with anticipating the
welfare state, though with historical overtones more redolent of Bismarck
than Beveridge.[47]

The Platonic, Tory, or illiberal element in all this was based on a belief
in the persistence of a class with the natural qualities of rulers, the 'lordly'
element in society when contrasted with its 'servile' components.[48]
A household ruled by a *pater* or *mater familias*, a king or a queen acting *in
loco parentis*, or an army led by a general who was loved by his soldiers,
could be emulated by manufacturers in dealings with their operatives,
provided they set a good example by ceasing to pursue short-term speculative gains and avoided plutocratic modes of consumption. During the
transitional period they might have to suffer losses by continuing to
provide employment, despite falling demand for their products. By acting
in this manner, merchants and manufacturers could attain the status
and trust granted to the liberal professions; they would become known
for their public service in meeting the needs of the nation rather than, as
at present, for their covetousness and dishonesty. The assumption that
commerce and manufacturing were permeated with fraud and the naked
use of unequal bargaining power to deprive the weaker party of the legitimate reward for his labour was developed into the broader claim that all
exchanges within the existing economic framework were a form of robbery.
To this Ruskin later added that interest on capital should be condemned
in the same terms employed by Aristotle and the Bible when denouncing
usury.[49] The human costs associated with the division of labour had been
a feature of Ruskin's thinking for a longer period, and since he could
not have borrowed the idea of 'alienation' from Plato, Xenophon, Hor-
ace, or Cicero, his usual sources, and certainly not from Marx, it is not

---

[46] *A joy for ever*, JRW, XVI, p. 26.
[47] See, however, Jose Harris's evidence on the Ruskinian dimension to Beveridge's own thinking,
with the further implication that some of the more authoritarian features of Ruskin's position
were, perhaps with some regret, regarded as inapplicable to countries with strong representative
institutions; 'Ruskin and social reform', in Dinah Birch (ed.), *Ruskin and the dawn of the modern*
(Oxford: Oxford University Press, 1999), pp. 23, 29–31.
[48] *Munera pulveris*, JRW, XVII, p. 236.
[49] R. G. Sillar was the acknowledged source of this development in Ruskin's views; see *Munera
pulveris*, JRW, XVII, p. 220n.

impossible that what Ruskin says about the moral disadvantages of the division of labour was based on another buried memory of his reading of the *Wealth of nations*.[50]

V

It is hardly necessary to say that Ruskin did little to make his ideas palatable to economists. As we shall see, some reactions, like that of Bagehot to *Unto this last*, were only to be expected.[51] But others who were not devotees of the science, amateur or semi-professional, shared Bagehot's dismissive judgement. George Eliot, for example, though a great admirer of Ruskin's work on modern painting and much impressed by the literary panache of the *Political economy of art*, could still feel that it contained some 'stupendous specimens of arrogant absurdity on some economical points'.[52] The one person whose reaction to Ruskin would be most interesting – Mill himself – never bothered to respond or even notice any of Ruskin's attacks on political economy. But Mill was aware of Ruskin's work as a critic of art and architecture and had cited *Modern painters* to make a point about female painters in his work on the *Subjection of women*. In his lone summary judgement on Ruskin he considered that 'now that Carlyle has written himself out, and become a mere commentator on himself', only Ruskin and Comte could be considered as original authors, adding, however, that 'to the practical doctrines and tendencies of both these, there are the gravest objections'.[53] This diary observation was made in 1854, several years before Ruskin had got into his stride. Mill may have felt that his demonstration of the irrelevance of the paternalistic theory in the *Principles* was an adequate answer to Ruskin as well as Carlyle.

It might appear, then, as though the 'bitter argument' had reached deadlock. Ruskin had provoked what he may have intended to provoke: blank rejection by those from whom he welcomed rejection. Nevertheless, during the period in which Ruskin entertained serious ambitions of setting the science to rights, he offered solutions to one of the fundamental questions that was exciting controversy between the new and old generations of economists: the theory of value. Ruskin showed only sporadic interest in what economists were writing after Mill had left the

[50] The classic statement of the problem can be found in the *Wealth of nations*, Book V, ch. 1.
[51] See p. 136 below.
[52] Letter to Sara Hennell, 17 January 1858, in G. Haight (ed.), *The Yale Edition of the George Eliot Letters*, 9 vols. (New Haven: Yale University Press, 1954–78), II, p. 422.
[53] CW, XXVII, p. 645.

stage. There are some disparaging remarks about Fawcett, and one or two references to Jevons as the author of some new-fangled attempt to capture human enjoyment in diagrams. Significantly, in the latter case, Ruskin's knowledge of Jevons was derived not from Jevons himself but from a hostile review of Jevons.[54] In so far as economists feature in his comments on value it is the older sources, Smith and Ricardo, which are mentioned rather than any of the new utility theorists. They too became less visible amid the wide range of classical and biblical sources that Ruskin increasingly called upon to expound his views. Nevertheless, comparison of what he has to say on value with what economists of both old and new persuasions were maintaining on the same subject may help to bring out other distinctive features of Ruskin's economic vision.

From an economist's point of view, much the most interesting aspect of Ruskin's critique of modern industrial capitalism centres not on his paternalistic proposals or even his opinions on exploitation through unequal exchange and the illegitimacy of taking interest on invested capital. As we shall see, the most conspicuous example of a Ruskinian economist in the succeeding generation, Hobson, discarded both these positions as excess baggage.[55] More interest attaches to Ruskin's treatment of value, wealth, and 'illth', the last of these being Ruskin's term to describe the moral and other costs associated with the pursuit of commercially defined wealth and the consumption of worthless goods. Controversy within the economics community centred on utility (demand-side factors) as an alternative to labour or cost of production (supply-side factors) when advancing answers to the question: what *causes* goods to have value and how are their relative prices determined? This was often confused with other questions: what would constitute the best or invariable *measure* of value? and what is the 'just' price or reward? Ricardo and Malthus had engaged in the search for an invariable measure, but Mill had judged this to be an impossible quest that was no longer of great interest.[56] Ruskin tends to confuse questions of cause, measure, and the justness of market valuations, and was in good company when confusing the first two.

Since a good deal of Ruskin's economics turned on moral-cum-aesthetic states of mind when explaining the uses and misuses of wealth; and since his writings often take the form of advice to consumers on how they should distinguish between goods and services that were life-enhancing and those that bred illth, this might suggest placing him close to the

[54] The review was by Cairnes; see pp. 159–60 below.   [55] See pp. 315–17 below.
[56] See the chapter 'Of a measure of value' in *Principles*, CW, III, pp. 577–81.

new utility theorists with their interest in subjective tastes. That under-represents Ruskin's position because his advice to consumers was also designed to concentrate spending exclusively on goods produced under circumstances that were life-enhancing to producers as well. A proleptic reading of this suggests parallels with ethical investment policies, consumer boycotts of goods produced under sweated conditions, and campaigns in favour of environmentally friendly goods, with the moral or psychic benefits being enjoyed by the investor/consumer as well as the producers.

There is, however, a more historical reading of Ruskin's concerns that sees them as one of the lessons he derived from his reading of Xenophon. Here the fortunes of master, mistress, and servant are linked together within a self-sufficient household or estate that exists outside any market framework, and where the economic problems of deciding what to produce and how it should be consumed are fused by being determined by a single authority, the *pater* or *mater familias*. The economists' problem stood at the opposite end of this spectrum: what were the collective consequences of myriads of households making decisions on the basis of the opportunities offered in the markets for goods and labour – a world subject to continual changes in tastes and technology, but with no master intelligence to guide its fortunes. Jevons's theory, for example, was designed as a guide to achieving an optimal allocation of expenditure or effort between competing calls on consumers' incomes or labourers' time. As with the basic theory of utility on which it was based, it was a theory that purported to explain how consumers or wage-earners actually behaved; but it could also be used hedonistically to advise them on how they ought to behave if they wished to maximise the pleasure and minimise the pain entailed in their economic activities.

Another factor distancing Ruskin from the new economics associated with utility theory can be seen in his deliberations on the essentially normative or metaphysical question of what is the best measure or guide to 'just' prices and wages. On this subject Ruskin was understandably attracted to Smith's labour measure of value via time (an hour's labour 'may be said' to represent an equal sacrifice to all concerned), though with the important proviso that instead of speaking of wages as compensation for the disagreeableness of labour, Ruskin wanted to include the possibility of making labour joyful.[57] Anyone who enters these troubled waters

---

[57] *Unto this last*, JRW, XVII, p. 50. Fain argues that Ruskin followed implicitly Smith's treatment of real and nominal price; see his comparison of JRW, XVII, pp. 95–6 with chapter 5 of Book I of the *Wealth of nations*; see *Ruskin and the economists*, pp. 145–6.

finds it necessary to adopt positions on subjects that had perplexed many people since Aristotle first talked about value in use and natural lawyers enunciated the famous water/diamond paradox in the seventeenth century. One by-product of what was later called the marginal revolution was that it enabled every first-year student to resolve the paradox by distinguishing between marginal utility, the anticipated satisfaction attached to an additional unit of consumption (low in the case of water when abundant, high in the case of diamonds when in short supply), and total utility, the satisfaction attached to all units of consumption (high in the case of water, and low in the case of diamonds). This became the alternative to the Ricardian solution, which maintained that while utility was a prerequisite for all economic goods, it was not the cause of exchange value. The clue to that lay in the real costs involved in producing goods, whether measured in money or labour effort. Market values might fluctuate on a day-to-day basis, but under long-run competitive conditions the exchange value of goods whose supply could be augmented would conform to their costs of production. If supply rather than demand was the ultimate determinant of the majority of exchange values (leaving aside uniquely scarce goods and those produced under monopoly conditions), this provided good reason for not attending to the minutiae of the shifting preferences of consumers between an almost infinite variety of goods and services. It was sufficient to say that markets performed an allocative function, with Ricardo, for example, believing that once the inertia associated with custom or ignorance had been overcome, the market usually worked with a high degree of responsiveness to rising or falling profits and prices. Value in use, therefore, was a separate question from value in exchange. It was a separation that offered opportunities to Ruskin to satirise modern society by giving his own version of the water/diamond paradox: what kind of society was it when pornographic prints were able to command a higher exchange value than the priceless fragments of Tintoretto's work peeling off Venetian walls?[58]

What engaged the economists on both sides of the emerging divide was a search for the relationship between supply and demand that would best explain how prices or the rewards to land, labour, and capital were established and how they changed. There was also a concern, more prominent in the work of the classical authors, with how the relative values of important commodities, especially those, like food, that dominated wage-earners' budgets, might change over time. They thought, quite

---

[58] *Munera pulveris*, JRW, XVII, pp. 132–5.

rightly, that it provided the clue to prospects for raising mass living standards in a world where the law of diminishing returns in agriculture set limits to improvements which could only be shifted outwards by improvements in technology, acceptance of free trade in foodstuffs, and individual efforts to control the rate of population increase. Ruskin seems to have accepted diminishing returns and descried the Malthusian problem of establishing an optimal relationship between population and natural resources, without proposing any stable solutions of his own, apart from the idea of allowing a new kind of 'bishop' to preside over the marriage ceremony and report on the conduct of the families under their pastoral jurisdiction.[59]

Ruskin had the businessman's practical knowledge needed to grasp the simple logic of everyday market behaviour, not only from what he learned about the wine trade at his father's table, but from the market he knew best, the art market. One could add too that this market provided the classic location to observe that polar case for any labour theory of value, the market for old masters, the price of which depended entirely on demand factors like fashion and the willingness of rich people to pay high prices to own them rather than let them hang on (or peel off) someone else's walls. It was for that reason that Ricardo and his followers explicitly denied the applicability of the labour theory to such uniquely 'rare' or non-reproducible goods.[60] Ruskin's position was an identical one, though worked out without benefit of the longer debate by economists. Ruskin did not shun discussions of actual exchange values when relevant. He had a precise knowledge of what prices he or his father should pay for drawings or paintings, and how they might appreciate over time. He also recognised the intellectual problem of relating value to price to be an 'intensely complex, curious, and interesting' one. But having pronounced it to be 'too complex to be examined yet', he never got round to doing so.[61] If he had completed his ambitious plan to write an exhaustive treatise he would have had to face up to that task more squarely.

---

[59] In *Unto this last* he distanced himself from such remedial measures as colonisation, cultivation of waste land, and discouragement to marriage: 'Melancholy' was his word for the 'speculations of political economists on the population question' (JRW, XVII, p. 106); but unlike his predecessors in this line of thinking, Southey for example, Ruskin, while not mentioning Malthus, restated the Malthusian problem of optimal population increase as follows: 'But the radical question is, not how much habitable land is in the world, but how many human beings ought to be maintained on a given space of habitable land.'

[60] See *Principles of political economy* in *The works and correspondence of David Ricardo*, ed. P. Sraffa, 11 vols. (Cambridge: Cambridge University Press, 1951–73), I, p. 12.

[61] *Unto this last*, JRW, XVII, p. 69.

But perhaps Ruskin was wise not to get side-tracked. It would have diverted him from his special concerns, which lay not in exchange value but 'intrinsic' or 'vital' value, something that was a matter of absolute rightness or wrongness in a Platonic sense.[62] On this subject Ruskin could call on the knowledge, and the authority it had conferred on him with the public, when delivering reasoned, but essentially *ex cathedra* judgements on the intrinsic worth of paintings, painters, and styles of architecture. Indeed, he took this one step further by speaking of those invariant values we *ought* to attach to goods if we were guided by our higher selves, those selves he sought to educate.[63] Ruskin was quite right in saying that the pure versions of the science of political economy had nothing to offer on such matters, which is why classical economists operated with a clear line drawn between use value and exchange value. Much to the annoyance of Jevons, Mill had gone one step further by denying that 'the laws of human enjoyment', the 'laws of the consumption of wealth', were a legitimate part of the economists' province.[64] The reasons why Mill *qua* economist could find no place for such laws in his scheme of things, and was not impressed by what he saw on the subject in the work of Jevons, go to the heart of his position as an exponent of a 'positive' or experiential methodology for the social sciences.[65] In essence the answer can be found in Ricardo's blunt rejection of earlier attempts to make utility the measure of value: 'Value in use cannot be measured by any known standard; it is differently estimated by different persons.'[66] The newer theories of value seemed to offer no scope for objective comparisons over time, and yet entailed what seemed an impossible examination of the subjective tastes of individuals, compounded by the need to make assumptions about the inter-personal comparability of the satisfactions to be derived from consumption.

VI

There is one remaining area in which one might seek signs of convergence between Ruskin's economics and that of orthodox economists. Ruskin's

---

[62] *Munera pulveris*, JRW, XVII, pp. 135, 153.

[63] '. . . wealth is never to be attached to the *accidental object of a morbid* desire, but only the *constant object of a legitimate one'*; see *ibid.*, p. 165.

[64] CW, IV, p. 318.

[65] For a fuller examination of the reasons why Mill refused to accept the new approach, see N. De Marchi, 'Mill and Cairnes and the emergence of marginalism in England', in R. D. C. Black *et al.* (eds.), *The marginal revolution in economics* (Durham, NC: Duke University Press, 1973), pp. 78–97.

[66] For Ricardo's fullest defence of this position, see *Works*, VIII, pp. 276–7.

slogan – 'There is no wealth but life' – is based on a non-theological version of the ethic of the Sermon on the Mount concerning our duties of love. Mill, as we have seen, had already appropriated this as a perfect statement of the utilitarian ethic.[67] Ruskin, however, thought that it contrasted with orthodox political economy in being purged of any basis in a covetous version of the self-interest principle. There are some well-known difficulties arising from the problem of distinguishing selfishness from self-interestedness, and the connections, positive or negative, between self-love and love for others. They were dissected by eighteenth-century moral philosophers, not least among them being Adam Smith, and were to remain at the heart of philosophical debate on how far hedonistic morals could serve altruistic ends. Some impeccable eighteenth- and nineteenth-century theological sources, including those belonging to the Evangelical tradition in which Ruskin had been raised, provided examples of providentialist accounts of the social order that treated self-interest in the normal enlarged sense as essential to the Divine plan. By taking self-interestedness to mean only a narrow and inherently dishonest form of selfishness that often involved the naked use of superior bargaining power, Ruskin was exploiting a rhetorical opportunity rather than engaging with these earlier discriminations.

What lends operational (i.e. non-rhetorical) significance to Ruskin's covetous interpretation – in principle at least – are his observations on the ways in which wealth could be purchased at the expense of illth, goods being counterbalanced by bads, those forms of production and consumption that were at the expense of life. Although his normal practice is absolutist, on such matters Ruskin resorts to an implicit language of quantity and degree when speaking of additions and subtractions, the pluses and minuses in the calculation. Followed further, this track leads from his usual Manichaen either/or treatment of moral absolutes into one that economists find more congenial, the world of more or less, a world in which optimal solutions that minimise sacrifice or maximise welfare subject to constraints are sought. Ruskin's attitude to such balancing acts was hostile: in jurisprudential terms, he treated them as part of the inferior realm of equity rather than justice. Nevertheless, any counterpositioning of wealth against illth in this world, as opposed to a planned utopia in which no conflict between priorities is permitted to occur, implies the ability on somebody's part to perform such balancing acts. The marginal revolution is relevant here because it provided a means of

---

[67] See p. 71 above.

making the concept of maxima and minima behind the idea of an optimal solution more explicit and precise than it had been earlier.

Mill too, as we have seen, was particularly keen to draw attention to the human and environmental costs of economic growth – costs that were not registered or regulated by market mechanisms. Sidgwick and Marshall went further in codifying this to form a branch of economics later known as welfare economics. It was an integral part of their conception of how economics could articulate the public interest and protect the unorganised consumer against the better-organised battalions serving labour and capital. In this sense it was meant to show how economics could clarify the public debate on wealth and illth. It implied the existence of a realm of public accountability, a condition that could be met in modern democracies by parliamentary bodies and methods of inquiry. It is doubtful if these methods would have commanded Ruskin's confidence. Not only was he proud never to have exercised his right to the suffrage, he followed Carlyle in his disdain for parliament as a mere talking shop. Here again, some later Ruskinians regretted the authoritarian element in Ruskin's thinking, while hankering after greater powers, and certainly retaining a belief in the enlightenment of professional experts.[68]

'Liberty', when used in political or economic settings, could be a catchword. Ruskin suspected that it was being used as a cover for licence. There also seems to have been some change in Ruskin's position between the time when he could praise the freedom enjoyed by craftsmen working on Gothic masterpieces to learn from the process of personal experimentation, and a later period when the control of the master-designer-architect was stressed. The absence of any consideration of the secondary or developmental benefits of liberty to those exercising it might well have led, as Ruskin no doubt hoped it would, to a barrier being created between his own vision and that of economists. As we might expect, economists of all varieties made a great deal of the virtues of learning by doing. Within the limits set by his scheme of paternal hierarchy Ruskin encouraged workmen to be authors of their own fate, but he frequently expressed horror when faced with conceptions of an order emerging from the impersonal forces released by individual action, where this was always seen as competitive rather than co-operative, destructive rather than constructive. Or rather, Ruskin conceived of it only fleetingly when

---

[68] For further consideration of this authoritarian dimension in Ruskinian thinking, see pp. 316–18 below.

observing the flying spindles of an Italian textile factory in 1858.[69] He thought that the activities of the factory marked 'the beginning of liberty in Italy'.

In the whirr of those wheels there is a power which no policy can resist; and in the giddiness of the shuttle more might [be achieved] than in the glance of the bayonet. People will let themselves be kept in ignorance as long as knowledge must be paid for, or can only be had by exertion; but not when knowledge will make clothes cheaper, or build villas faster.

In a more mature society such as Britain, Ruskin seems to have believed that the benefits of liberty had been carried beyond the point of exhaustion and were now part of the menace threatening the modern world.

VII

With the exception of Carlyle, the initial reaction to Ruskin's economic writings had been largely one of indifference, bemusement, or hostility, either based on an appreciation of the necessary limitations of political economy in its purer theoretical forms, or on more conventional wisdom concerning the benefits of *laissez-faire* and the virtues of self-help. By the 1890s, however, newer kinds of conventional wisdom were being formulated that were less individualistic in orientation, with the result that Ruskin began to develop a personal following. Through his lectures at Oxford while Slade Professor of Art in the 1870s, and again briefly in 1883–4, he exerted a moral influence on a number of young men who were to occupy important positions in the university extension movement, various reformist campaigns, and the civil service. Some of the practical experiments Ruskin had initiated, such as the Hinksey Road project and the Guild of St George, were at best symbolic gestures or partial successes; but they left more permanent residues in the work of others, notably through the journal *Saint George* and the Ruskin reading societies. The end of the mid-century economic boom and the long period of depression that began in 1873, particularly in agriculture, also created a climate in which critical voices of all kinds were once more being given a sympathetic hearing. An analysis that owed a debt to Carlyle's commentary on the 'condition-of-England' in the 1840s proved capable of being recycled in new forms to suit end-of-century social and economic unease.

---

[69] See the remarkable letter to his father on 11 July 1858, in J. Hayman (ed.), *John Ruskin, letters from the Continent, 1858* (Toronto: Toronto University Press, 1982), p. 79.

Of the many figures who attempted to spread Ruskin's gospel, two in particular, Edward Cook and Alec Wedderburn, were to perform the greatest long-term service. During Ruskin's lifetime they began to assemble material that would appear later in their library edition of his collected writings. When this began to be published in its luxuriant thirty-nine-volume form in 1903 they were able to bring together a number of gratifying references to Ruskin by dissident economists and other social commentators to support their claim that Ruskin's heresies were now 'accepted doctrine'. Or as another of their sources, Edward Freeman, late Regius Professor of History at Oxford, was quoted as saying: 'The Political Economy of today is the political economy of John Ruskin, and not the political economy of John Bright or even of John Stuart Mill.'[70] Cook played the leading role in this, with the result that the portrait of Ruskin that emerged bore a family resemblance to Cook's own 'New Liberal' sympathies, combining support for a 'sane Imperialism' with social reforms that reflected the interventionist trend of legislation away from the priorities of the Manchester school.[71] Ruskin was once thought to be a socialist: was it not accepted that we were all socialists now? Chamberlain's radical 'unauthorized programme' of 1885 was mentioned as a sign of the times, as was his most recent heresy on tariff reform. Although protectionism derived no support from Ruskin, the implication was that *Manchesterthum* was in retreat on this front as well, and that tariff reform might be legitimised by a shift of public opinion similar to that which had brought renewed relevance and respectability to Ruskin's ideas. Other changes in a Ruskinian direction noted by Cook were the acceptance of the state as a model employer; its role in organising municipal schemes of public relief work; endorsement of the concept of 'fair' or trade union wages; the proposals for old-age pensions; and acceptance of the need for greater state involvement in land tenure issues to establish fair rents, fixity of tenure, and compensation for tenants' improvements. He also pointed out that *Unto this last* was now selling around 2,000 copies every year.

Cook noted something that Ruskin had ignored but which Cook felt he had helped to stimulate: the established creed among economists was under attack from 'historical' and 'realistic' schools of thought in Germany

---

[70] JRW, XVII, p. cxi.
[71] On Cook, see J. Saxon Mills, *Sir Edward Cook, KBE* (London: Constable, 1921); and the commentary on his role as Ruskin's editor in T. Hilton, *John Ruskin: the later years* (New Haven: Yale University Press, 2000), pp. 415, 466, 484, 494–7, 515, 555–8, 594.

and by Comtists at home. J. K. Ingram's one-sentence reference to Ruskin in his *History of political economy* was duly pressed into service, along with a longer citation of his programme for the absorption of political economy within a sociological framework.[72] It went well with those biological aspects of Ruskin's 'vitalism' that had been recognised by Patrick Geddes in another work cited by Cook. In 1885, during one of Ruskin's bouts of insanity, someone had the idea of organising a round-robin letter of support from some economists who wished to express their indebtedness to his writings.[73] Together with a couple of appreciative articles on Ruskin that had appeared in the new professional economic journals, it was to furnish Cook with more evidence to suggest that Ruskin had propounded the political economy of the future. Cook also made selective use of recent studies of Ruskin and a book by Hobson that will have to be examined more carefully later than Cook chose to do.

In this process of launching Ruskin on his posthumous career as the prophet of various late-Victorian and Edwardian intellectual and political trends, the original Ruskin message took on qualities and colouration that would have been unrecognisable or unacceptable to the master himself. Almost the first, and certainly the most incongruous example of this kind of opportunistic absorption of Ruskin can be found in the pamphlet by Geddes mentioned by Cook. It came with the promising title, *John Ruskin, economist*, and was suitably critical of the economics Ruskin had attacked. But Geddes, a biologist-cum-sociologist-cum-town planner, was keen to assimilate Ruskin into his own post-Darwinian view of man's place in nature: 'our disciple of Plato and scholar of Turner has also become the highest practical exponent of Darwin'. His 'sentimental' works 'at once analyse the conditions and attack the problems of the evolution of society by heredity and sexual selection'. Geddes either did not know or did not care to know about Ruskin's rejection of Darwin along with most modern science. Ruskin would not have been flattered by Geddes's description of his work as a contribution to 'physical economics', an economics that when speaking of 'vital' or 'intrinsic' value was seeking to measure the physiological and psychological properties of sensory stimuli by means of a calorimeter 'varying according to Fechner's law'. Nor would Ruskin

---

[72] 'Ruskin had not merely protested against the egoistic spirit of the prevalent doctrine, but had pointed to some of its real weaknesses as a scientific theory'; *History of political economy* (Edinburgh: A. and C. Black, 1888), p. ???

[73] The signatories were W. J. Ashley, C. Bastable, H. S. Foxwell, E. Laveleye, ? MacCunn, A. L. Perry, J. E. Symes and F. A. Walker; see JRW, XVII, p. cvi note.

have felt comfortable in being lumped together with such other critics of economic orthodoxy as Ingram, de Laveleye, Cliffe Leslie, and Jevons.[74]

William Smart, a Ruskinian economist who wrote a work entitled *A disciple of Plato* published in 1883, only rates a passing mention in Cook's account. When Smart wrote his tribute to Ruskin his discipular credentials were impeccable. He was the manager of the Mile-End Thread works in Glasgow, president of the city's Ruskin Society, and a founder-member of the Guild of St George. Smart's pamphlet is chiefly remarkable for the final pages and for Ruskin's churlish comment on them. Smart had concluded by saying that economists of the post-Mill variety no longer appealed to 'eternal laws to settle any question'; and that they were as right in their way as Ruskin was in his. With co-operation as an industrial principle having become the accepted hope of the future, it was no longer necessary to continue Ruskin's quarrel: 'things being as they are, we may go by economical rules; but things being not as they should be, we shall occasionally break them'.[75] Edward Caird, Professor of Moral Philosophy at Glasgow and Smart's mentor, took the same position.[76] As practical examples of the way in which the two perspectives had converged, Smart made the mistake of citing the agreement between Ruskin and Mill on peasant proprietorship and compensation for tenants' improvements. The olive branch was firmly rejected by Ruskin: 'There is no word I want to add or change up to page 41 [where these examples appeared]; but, as regards what follows, I would like to add that, while I admit there is such a thing as mercantile theory, distinguished from social, I have always said that neither Mill, Fawcett, nor Bastiat knew the contemptible science they professed to teach.' No truce with such a science could be honourable.

Smart later wrote an autobiography entitled *Second thoughts of an economist* which summed up the way in which he had managed to pursue Ruskinian ideals while remaining committed to his work as a teacher of the 'contemptible science'. When he informed Ruskin of his choice of occupation, he received a single-word rebuke: 'You'.[77] It is not difficult to imagine Ruskin's sense of betrayal if he ever learned that Smart had become not merely an economist but the first holder of the Adam Smith chair of the subject in Glasgow. *Second thoughts* is the testimony of

---

[74] *John Ruskin, economist*, Round Table Series, no. 3. 1884, quotations on pp. 32, 35, 38, and 42.
[75] *A disciple of Plato: a critical study of John Ruskin* (Glasgow: Wilson and McCormick, 1883), p. 42.
[76] See E. Caird, 'Political economy, old and new', *Quarterly Journal of Economics*, 3 (1888), 213–15.
[77] *Second thoughts of an economist*, with a biographical sketch by Thomas Jones (London: Macmillan, 1916), p. 4.

a Christian who was convinced that the Bible-inspired ethic he shared with Ruskin could be made part of the economics he taught, wrote, and practised in a life that exemplifies many of the practical philanthropic enthusiasms of men of his formation and generation. Ruskin could not have faulted Smart's practical efforts on behalf of Ruskinian ideals. He founded a Toynbee Hall in Glasgow; encouraged access to higher education for women and working-class men; and worked for the protection of women whose wages in sweated trades were not covered by trade union activity. He also campaigned for the regulation of intemperance through model public houses; and organised the purchase and administration of municipal housing for working-class tenants on the basis of the kind of arrangements Ruskin made with Octavia Hill in London. Smart's work on municipal housing drew him to the attention of the prime minister, Balfour, and later led to his becoming one of the hardest working members of the 1905 Poor Law Commission, a task which later led to his compilation of the two-volume *Economic annals of the nineteenth century*. He established his credentials as an economist by translating the work of the Austrian marginalists, learning German in order to do so, but later pledged allegiance to Marshall's version of this theory, writing a textbook on the burning issue of the day, the distribution of wealth and income, and took the orthodox position in resisting Chamberlain's tariff reform proposals.

On the question of free trade there was no open conflict between Smart's two loyalties: after all, Ruskin claimed to be 'an utterly fearless and unscrupulous free-trader' on the grounds that it would result, via some mysterious process, in an 'end to competition' between nations, with any acquired or natural comparative advantages becoming permanent.[78] This is one of the many pieces of evidence that support the view that the ideal Ruskinian economy was a static one in which full employment and abundance for all could be achieved according to the existing state of technology and via a once-for-all redistribution of tasks, tastes, and incomes. Mill's ideal stationary state shows that Ruskin was not alone in this. But Mill's state would have been one in which there was a revolving equilibrium allowing improvements in technology to be redirected towards increased leisure and improvements in the quality of life. It would also have had more egalitarian or socialistic features than Ruskin would have found congenial. Smart became convinced that whatever the attractions of the Ruskinian work ethic, the new theories of value and distribution

---

[78] *Unto this last*, JRW, XVII, p. 72n.

had replaced Ruskin's attractive personal insights into 'value as life-giving power'. After citing this slogan Smart added that 'I quote this passage, partly on account of its suggestiveness, partly to show how impossible it would be to reconcile any such definition of value with ordinary language or with economic science.'[79]

Ruskin might have had an earlier economic disciple than Smart: Arnold Toynbee, who went through a period of interest in Ruskin while working on the Hinksey Road project as an undergraduate at Oxford, actually becoming a foreman. This alone meant little: Oscar Wilde worked on the same project and enjoyed similar access to the master. Understandably, Cook, in his biography of Ruskin, mentions Toynbee but not the recently disgraced Wilde.[80] Toynbee proved to be exactly the kind of person Ruskin had in mind when as Slade professor he set out to show what noble aims Oxford undergraduates should pursue. As any reading of Toynbee's lectures on the industrial revolution will confirm, however, his choice of route diverged from Ruskin's. The closest he comes to Ruskin in the lectures is via Carlyle's 'cash-nexus'. In rejecting Carlyle's 'feudal' solution Toynbee adopted a position that shows the influence Mill and, more remotely, Adam Smith, still had upon him: 'the old economic conditions had to be destroyed before new moral relations could come into existence'. The old order was based on what Smith had described as 'servile dependency', his version of Mill's 'leading strings'. Those whirring wheels that Ruskin himself had noticed briefly in Italy could be part of the process of liberation. In Toynbee's rendition, dependency had to be eliminated by the cash nexus before a 'new and higher form of social union' could emerge, one based on 'the voluntary association of free men'.[81] The advent of trade unions was creating conditions of greater equality between employers and employees that would lay the groundwork for settling disputes by means of boards of conciliation. The people, rather than Carlyle, had been right when agitating for the vote. Competition was neither good nor evil in itself; it needed to be studied and controlled.

Toynbee's democratic sympathies, pragmatic turn of mind, and his fairly commonplace belief in a progressive version of history separated him from Ruskin. To Ruskin history was more a cyclical story of the rise

---

[79] *An introduction to the theory of value* (London: Macmillan, 1891), p. 4n.
[80] See *Life of John Ruskin*, 2 vols. (London: Allen and Co, 1911), II, p. 191.
[81] *Lectures on the industrial revolution*, 7th impression (London: Longmans Green, 1923), pp. 163, 209–10, 215.

and fall of civilisations, with perfection in art forms providing an infallible sign of the cruelty and corruption that presaged decline. As in some apocalyptic versions of this position, there was little point in waiting for the historical process to deliver favourable conditions for social change. If simultaneous mass conversion of the ruling classes was not possible, the only remedy was for the faith to be kept alive by small bands of followers such as could be found in the Guilds of St George. Toynbee's strategy was a more conventional one of building on small advances to create larger ones. His lectures, personal example, and early death created for him a following among a generation of Oxford economic historians which, for a time, rivalled that of Ruskin; and his example was to prove capable of sustaining careers that combined academic work with active participation in reformist movements.[82]

VIII

Ruskin receives a passing mention but is not the subject of an article in Palgrave's *Dictionary of political economy* published in the 1890s, an encyclopedia of the subjects and figures then thought significant. There are two early and relatively sympathetic articles on Ruskin's economics in the two first professional journals published in English, the Harvard-based *Quarterly Journal of Economics* and the official organ of the Royal Economic Society, the *Economic Journal*. The first of these considers Ruskin's views on interest as fallacious: like rent, interest was the logical consequence of private property. If Ruskin wanted to attack this he should have done so instead of making private property the foundation of all forms of justice. The affinities between Ruskin and the socialism of the German historical school were mentioned, and his services in discrediting 'economic man' assumptions recognised, leading to the conclusion which Cook chose to quote: 'the future political economy may not build from him directly, yet it will be rather with Ruskin's earth than with Ricardo's straw that its bricks for building shall be made'.[83] The second article accepted the challenge by considering whether Ruskinian clay was up to the job, and concluded that, confusions of usury with interest apart, Ruskin had established the case for making economics an explicitly ethical science when it came to judging the outcome of consumer choices.[84]

---

[82] For Toynbee's influence, see D. C. Coleman, *History and the economic past: an account of the rise and decline of economic history in Britain* (Oxford: Oxford University Press, 1987), pp. 59–62.
[83] See F. J. Stimson, 'Ruskin as a political economist', *Quarterly Journal of Economics*, 2 (1888), 426–9.
[84] See C. E. Devas, 'Lessons from Ruskin', *EJ*, 8 (1898), 28–36.

The obituary of Ruskin by James Bonar that appeared in the *Economic Journal* was suitably gentle with Ruskin's 'very fallible judgements on matters beyond his knowledge', and appreciative of the way in which he had shown up the limitations of an older version of abstract economics. But the conclusion reveals why Bonar was not one of the sources quoted by Cook: 'Most economists will agree that the economics of Ruskin are to be read with the same reservations as the Apocrypha; they may be used for examples of life and instructions of manners, but we must not apply them to establish any doctrine.' Ruskinian ideas were hardly more visible in the pages of the Oxford-based Christian Social Union journal, the *Economic Review*, a periodical dedicated to publishing articles on 'Economic Morals from the point of view of Christian teaching'.[85] The only article entirely devoted to Ruskin was prompted by the publication of Cook's biography. Inspirational or prophetic qualities were claimed, but it was acknowledged that 'the scientific economist of today, it would seem, finds little to demand his attention in such books as *Unto this last* and *Munera pulveris*'.[86]

On the basis of this evidence, drawn from a period in which Ruskin enjoyed his first major burst of acquiring disciples, one has to say that Ruskin was the dog that did not bark for most economists. Hobson, as we shall see, did not fare much better, though he had the advantage of a superior grasp of orthodox economic thinking than Ruskin. None of the attempts at reconciliation met with Ruskin's personal approval: the ethical absolutes with which he was concerned were far too important to be compromised by the lesser explanatory concerns of a science which he believed to have a dubious role, not so much in explaining, but in explaining away what he thought it essential to contest. It is still possible to ask what might have happened if economics had shown itself capable of encompassing what Ruskin said any genuine political economy should encompass. It would literally have become the master human science, regulating all aspects of our relationships with one another as in the harmonious stasis of the Xenophonic household. Economists, especially those, like Marshall, who harboured imperial longings for a revised version of their science, could not be accused of excessive modesty; but they were incapable of entertaining dreams of conquering worlds quite as ambitious as Ruskin's.

---

[85] See the editorial programme in *Economic Review*, 1 (1890), 1.

[86] G. Hislop, 'The social teaching of Ruskin', *Economic Review*, 24 (1914), 30–8. An earlier 'Footnote to Ruskin' by H. W. Blunt (*Economic Review*, 10 (1900), 355–62) is more critical still; it accuses Ruskin of adopting a Malthusian version of a determinate wage-fund derived from the fixity of food supply, thereby ignoring the problem of determining 'efficiency wages'.

5

'Last man of the ante-Mill period':
Walter Bagehot

I

In the obituary of Mill that Bagehot wrote for *The Economist*, the journal he had edited for the previous dozen years or so, having inherited this role from James Wilson, his father-in-law, he said that he had 'long been in the habit of calling himself the last man of the ante-Mill period'.[1] Unlike most of his contemporaries and the younger generation, his knowledge of political economy predated the first publication of Mill's *Principles*. That he had obtained highest honours in the intellectual and moral sciences at University College, London (UCL) in 1848, an advanced centre as far as these modern subjects were concerned, lends some support to this boast. It certainly gave him confidence to write a supremely self-assured review of Mill's *Principles* at the age of twenty-two, the year he obtained his MA.

Being ante-Mill reflects Bagehot's self-understanding, though, as his review shows, it did not imply being anti-Mill. He was alert to all, and appreciative of many, of Mill's innovations within the Ricardian framework, and devoted a good deal of his space to Mill's 'peculiar opinions'. These were accurately summarised as follows:

[Mill] is the first among great English economists who has ventured to maintain that the present division of the industrial community into labourers and capitalists is neither destined nor adapted for a long continued existence; that a large production of wealth is much less important than a good distribution of it; that a state of industry in which both capital and population are stationary is as favourable to national well-being as one in which they are advancing; that fixed customs are perpetually modifying the effects which unrestrained competition would of itself inevitably produce; that a large body of peasant proprietors is usually a source of great national advantage; and that a system of emigration on a great scale would be productive of much benefit to the English peasantry by

---

[1] 'The late Mr Mill', CWWB, III, p. 558.

raising their habitual standard of comfort, and therefore putting a check on the reckless increase of a miserable population.[2]

On most of these issues Bagehot was later to take a tougher, more business-like line than Mill. The economist as man of business – commercial and financial rather than manufacturing – would be one description of Bagehot, and it was the source of his high regard for Ricardo. As he said, Adam Smith may have discovered the country, but Ricardo was the first to supply a proper map of its contours.[3] Reporting Bagehot's conversation, Robert Giffen, his successor to the editorship of *The Economist*, recounted that Bagehot regarded Ricardo as 'by far the best writer on the subject, in spite of defects in expression and other difficulties'.[4] Attempting to restore Ricardo 'to his proper position as an authority' was not a fashionable revisionist move in the 1870s, but it lends substance to the ante-Mill claim and scotches any doubts based on the fact that Ricardo died three years before Bagehot was born in 1826. What Bagehot most admired was Ricardo's 'Jewish genius for the mathematics of money-dealing': he had the rare quality, conferred by race and his stock-jobbing background, of combining a business mentality with the ability to handle the necessary abstractions of economic theory.[5] As we shall see, showing why Ricardo's deductive approach was both necessary as well as necessarily limited in its sphere of application lay at the heart of Bagehot's own contribution to the debate on the future of political economy that began, or rather was resumed, in the 1870s. Mill's capacity for close reasoning in the *Logic* could hardly be denied. When writing his obituary Bagehot did not deny the substance of George Grote's encomium on the subject, citation of which supplied some of the padding he used to fill the allotted space. But Mill did not possess Ricardo's qualifications, and if race and knowledge of the business world played the formative role assigned to it by Bagehot, could not have acquired them. What he had instead was 'philosophical acumen', inherited from Scotland via his father, and 'the French gift of precise and graceful explanation' acquired from his extensive contacts with France.[6]

The 1848 review, via a patronising route, arrived at the judgement that Mill deserved to stand alongside Smith and Ricardo as an equal. Bagehot's final verdict on Mill's *Principles* was less flattering. Mill added little to

---

[2] See review of Mill's *Principles*, CWWB, XI, pp. 157–8; and letters to W. C. Roscoe and R. H. Hutton on the subject, CWWB, XII, pp. 279–82, 292–7.
[3] See *Economic studies*, CWWB, XI, p. 236.   [4] 'Bagehot as an economist', CWWB, XI, p. 213.
[5] *Economic studies*, CWWB, XI, p. 344.   [6] 'The late Mr Mill', CWWB, III, pp. 556–7.

Ricardo by way of theory, and much that was new was due more to his powers of synthesis and expository skills than to genuine originality. Mill's 'remoteness from mercantile life' and his eagerness to inquire into 'things far less sublunary than money' disqualified him from 'giving the finishing touches to a theory of "the great commerce"'. Finishing touches were all that was necessary, and Bagehot considered himself to be in a position to supply them, an ambition concealed behind one of those epigrams to which he was so attached: Mill was 'open to the charge of having widened the old political economy either too much or not enough'.[7]

II

Before considering what lay behind this judgement, it is worth noting one important subject on which Bagehot did learn something from Mill that he could not have learned from Ricardo: he accepted one of Mill's assumptions about the world they shared that had not been part of Ricardo's way of thinking. The topic in question has already figured in an earlier essay (2) and it concerned the state of the market for capital in Britain by the third quarter of the century when compared with what Ricardo had assumed to be the case during the immediate post-Napoleonic war period. It is only possible to make sense of Ricardo's policy priorities by reference to the existence of acute capital scarcity in Britain. Whether on the effect of the Corn Laws in lowering the rate of profit, the main source of capital accumulation, or on the high taxes made necessary by the levels of public debt accumulated during the war, Ricardo persistently emphasised the dangers of capital flight, taking comfort only from 'feelings, which I should be sorry to see weakened, [which] induce most men of property to be satisfied with a low rate of profit in their own country, rather than seek a more advantageous employment for their wealth in foreign nations'. Coming from a person who had professional experience in foreign capital transactions, and whose normal assumption was that well-informed economic agents were quick to exploit opportunities for gain, this statement based on 'feelings' was a significant one. Bagehot cited it later when pointing out that: 'A class of cosmopolitan capitalists has grown up which scarcely feels them at all.'[8]

---

[7] *Economic studies*, CWWB, XI, p. 237.
[8] *Ibid.*, pp. 275–6; and D. Ricardo, *Principles of political economy*, as reprinted in *The works and correspondence of David Ricardo*, ed. P. Sraffa, 11 vols. (Cambridge: Cambridge University Press, 1951–73), I, pp. 136–7.

The origins of this can be traced back to Bagehot's review of Mill's 'peculiar opinions', where he commended Mill's counter to those who stressed the perpetual need for economy in public expenditure. In Bagehot's rendition this read: 'it is of no consequence that taxation entrench on the capital of a country, if the capital appropriated by government [was] about to expatriate itself on account of a prevailing low rate of profit'.[9] This was a reference to Mill's observation that in a mature and secure economy 'the rate of profit is habitually within, as it were, a hand's breadth of the minimum'; and the distinctly non-Ricardian corollary he drew from it: 'the exportation of capital is an agent of great efficacy in extending the field of employment for that which remains: and it may be said truly that, up to a certain point, the more capital we send away, the more we shall possess and be able to retain at home'.[10] The youthful, even bumptious, Bagehot had welcomed Mill's shift of emphasis and some of the policy conclusions Mill associated with it.

After more than two decades of experience as a banker and City analyst, and having completed his description of the workings of the London money market in *Lombard Street* in 1873, he had developed the argument in a direction that was entirely his own. He accepted Mill's practical conclusions while rejecting the more idealistic ones associated with the idea of a virtuous stationary state. Although Bagehot advised successive Chancellors of the Exchequer via their permanent civil servants at the Treasury, he was better known for his advice on short-term funding via the new Treasury Bill than as the stern voice of orthodox economy. As Richard Holt Hutton (his close friend from UCL days) said, Bagehot preached that 'in the case of a rich country like England, efficiency was vastly more important than the mere reduction of expenditure, and held that Mr Gladstone and other great Chancellors of the Exchequer made a great deal too much of saving for saving's sake'.[11] When he came to write about the postulates of English political economy, the speed with which capital could be transferred within the British economy and abroad became the main feature of a 'society of grown-up competitive commerce' for which the abstractions of the English science were perfectly suited. Bagehot recognised that freedom of capital movement presupposed the 'transferability of labour' (the first of his postulates), but his main emphasis fell on capital and those intermediaries who controlled its direction.

---

[9] Review of Mill's *Principles*, CWWB, XI, p. 190.
[10] Mill's *Principles*, CW, III, p. 746 and pp. 58–9 above.
[11] 'Memoir of Walter Bagehot', CWWB, XV, p. 120.

England had led the way in all this, and now commanded a 'great speculative fund', the latest results of which were to be seen in the railways
being constructed throughout the world. On this the normally sceptical
and frequently cynical Bagehot could wax both patriotic and lyrical: 'the
emigration of young men with English capital, and to manage English
capital, is one of the great instruments of world-wide trade and one of
the binding forces of the future'.[12]

Unknown to Bagehot, this was a vision of global capitalism seen from
its financial hub that matched that of Marx, and it came with a similar
accent on exuberance and instability rather than precise market equili-
bration.[13] The capitalist was 'the general of the army; he fixes on the plan
of operations, organises its means, and superintends its execution'. Those
who were 'taken with the conspicuousness of the working classes' often
overlooked this when they boasted that labour had made Birmingham or
Manchester. With clear reference to Mill's *Principles* and other writings
that it had inspired, Bagehot said that

some even of our gravest economic literature is dangerously tainted with superficial
sentiment. It speaks much of the sufferings of the working men which are seen,
and little of those of the capitalist which are not seen. But the capitalist, being a
higher and more thinking kind of man, is probably of more sensitive organisation than the labourer, and pecuniary anxiety is a more racking thing than any
physical kind of pain short of extreme hunger.[14]

Mill was still in his sights when he claimed that co-operative schemes
designed to eliminate the capitalist had often found it necessary 'to invent
a capitalist in disguise': 'A body of separate labourers has many of the
characteristics of a mob; but one acting under the control of a capitalist
has many of those of an army.'[15] The future lay in the hands of 'a thinking
man in a dark office' who controls what happens through his knowledge
of how money is managed. Mill's 'pleasant' stationary state was bluntly
dismissed: 'with this political economy has nothing to do. It deals with
men here and now.'[16] This was one case where Mill's widening of the
science had over-extended it. As another of Bagehot's friends, the banker-
economist, Robert Palgrave, pointed out: 'Towards the working classes

---

[12] *Economic studies*, CWWB, XI, p. 279.
[13] For example, the capital that had flowed into coal and iron during the railway boom had done so
more than adequately, and 'instead of reducing these profits only to an average level, it reduced
them below that level; and this happens commonly, for the speculative enterprise which brings
in the new capital is a strong, eager, and rushing force, and rarely stops exactly where it should.'
Ibid., p. 239.
[14] *Ibid.*, p. 387   [15] *Ibid.*, p. 312.   [16] *Ibid.*, p. 334.

and their trade unions, he was never hostile; but he was not demonstratively sympathetic. His sympathies lay with the capitalist-employers: the people who "spend their minds on little else than on thinking whether other people will pay their debts".[17] It followed *a fortiori* that Mill's speculations on a possible co-operative socialist future formed no part of Bagehot's agenda, whether as hope or fear. The potential political dangers of an enfranchised working class, on the other hand, were of great concern to him, especially after the passage of the Second Reform Bill in 1867.

Bagehot never became part of Mill's intimate circle, though they met at the Political Economy Club after Bagehot's election to it in 1864. During the sixties Bagehot made several unsuccessful attempts to be elected as a Liberal member of parliament, one of them for the new University of London constituency created by the 1867 reform, for which graduates of the university were eligible. Bagehot followed Mill's parliamentary career in anonymous articles for *The Economist*, making it clear that although he differed strongly from many of Mill's 'advanced' opinions, he would have voted for him as a candidate, 'partly because we know no man whose voice is better entitled to be heard in the senate of a great country, and partly because *our* senate is conspicuously distinguished by the absence of that original, philosophic, and thorough-going honesty of thought which Mr Mill would bring to it'.[18] Perhaps there was a tinge of personal regret in all this, and as Hutton said, with more than a hint of disapproval, '[Bagehot] always seemed to me to think far more of the intellectual and moral tone of governments than he did of the intellectual and moral interests of the people governed.'[19]

It was not Mill's crusades that Bagehot admired (though he shared Mill's reaction to Carlyle's worship of naked force during the Governor Eyre controversy) so much as those ways in which he stood out against the 'official creed of the advanced Liberal party'.[20] Unlike some other radicals, Mill did not favour wholesale substitution of direct for indirect taxation. Nor did he support the blanket non-interventionist and anti-militarist side of Cobdenism; there was nothing wrong with England's use of its power to support the cause of liberty abroad; and it was more important to achieve efficiency than economy in the use of funds spent on the army and navy. In the early sixties Bagehot had advocated various

---

[17] Article on Bagehot by R. H. I. Palgrave in his *Dictionary of political economy*, 3 vols. (London: Macmillan, 1894), I, pp. 80–1.
[18] 'Mr Mill's address to the electors of Westminster', CWWB, III, p. 541.
[19] 'Hutton on Bagehot', CWWB, XV, p. 118.
[20] Bagehot on 'Mr Carlyle on Mr Eyre', CWWB, III, pp. 563–5.

'fancy' franchises himself, and he supported Mill's campaign for the representation of minorities as protection against 'class ascendancy' through numbers. But he was not in favour of the scheme of proportional representation endorsed by Mill; it was a device that could aid party managers. He also felt that Mill was playing with fire in wanting to guarantee the working classes control over half the national representation. This would thrust power into the wrong hands 'whenever they chose to pull together and whenever, as a matter of bad political economy, of vicious temper, of jobbing, of ultra-montanism, of anti-Saxonism, – or from any motive of intrigue whatever – they could induce any considerable section of the Irish members to coalesce with them'.[21] Bagehot did not believe that Mill's proposals for the reform of Irish land tenure would have the desired political or economic effect: 'land, like so many other things, is a blessing only to those who can use it, and a poison to those who cannot'.[22] And if Mill had been able to guess the identity of the author behind the cloak of anonymity, he would not have been pleased by the following dismissal of his case for female suffrage.

We need scarcely say a word as to his claim for the extension of the suffrage to all adult women: – no party, and scarcely any individual politician save himself, holds this theory, and it will be long before it becomes a practical question. When it does, we entertain little doubt that Mr Mill will have altered his views on the matter, as he has done on the ballot; for he will probably have discovered that out of the two or three million of women whom he would thus endow – including half-a-million of maid-servants – not above ten thousand would have any political opinions at all, or any *political* preferences for one candidate over another; and that in consequence to give them votes would merely be giving extra votes vicariously to their fathers, their husbands, their masters, their lovers, or their priests.[23]

Conventional in sentiment, if not expression, though this argument was, Bagehot did not join the chorus of critics who held that in forsaking his study for the hustings the philosopher MP had allowed himself to be corrupted by demagoguery. After all, he had been keen to add a seat in parliament to his editorial and banking chairs himself. It was more a matter of Mill being 'easily excitable and susceptible; the evil that is in his mind at the moment seems to him the greatest evil'.[24]

---

[21] 'Mr Mill's address to the electors of Westminster', CWWB, III, pp. 545–6.
[22] 'Mr Mill on Ireland', CWWB, III, p. 550.
[23] 'Mr Mill's address to the electors of Westminster', CWWB, III, pp. 542–3.
[24] 'Mr Mill on Ireland', CWWB, III, p. 547.

Across a broader front, in his Burkean interpretation of the peculiar suitability of the English constitution to English 'stupidity' and deferential habits, Bagehot's *English constitution* was partially written to correct Mill's failure to appreciate the significance of the Cabinet in his *Considerations on representative government*. Yet Mill and Bagehot shared a concern for the quality of parliamentary life and public debate in an era before mass party organisation had tipped the balance towards opinion outside parliament. They also shared an admiration for Gladstone. But Bagehot's thorough-going reliance on the merits of the double truth, the contrast between outer show and inner management, in his description of the workings of the constitution was far too Burkean, even Machiavellian, for someone more puritanically committed to the cause of future improvement. Mill would probably have agreed with Hutton's comments on his friend's concern with the tone of governors rather than with the intellectual and moral interests of the governed.

III

Although Bagehot clearly had enough material to write a rounded portrait of Mill, particularly when the latter's *Autobiography* became available, this was one of the projected studies he failed to complete before his premature death in 1877 at the age of fifty-one. Alongside the essays on basic postulates it would have completed a quartet of biographical assessments that began with a fairly thorough if not always accurate study of Smith, and went on to include more ephemeral studies of Malthus and Ricardo. He had begun work on the essays two years earlier and probably had the forthcoming centenary of the *Wealth of nations* in mind as the occasion for their publication.[25] Bagehot wanted to contribute to the debate on the past and future of the discipline independently of the centenary, but in common with other parties to the debate, he found the event too good an opportunity to be missed for public rehearsal of fundamental methodological issues alongside discussion of Smith's legacy and achievements. By comparison with other contributors, however, what makes Bagehot's position of interest is the way in which he managed to be both ante- and post-Mill in his intellectual sympathies, without believing that the core assumptions and methods of the science needed to be

---

[25] See letters to John Morley, November 1875 and June 1876, proposing a series of articles for the *Fortnightly Review*, including one on Smith, designed to be collected together later as a book; CWWB, XIII, pp. 672–3, 676–7.

fundamentally reconstructed. He was ante-Mill in his attachment to Ricardian abstractions, where Mill had become over-keen on broadening the inquiry into matters of 'social philosophy'; and he was most plainly post-Mill, as Jevons was later to pride himself in being, in the importance he attached to work inspired by Darwin in biology and by Henry Maine on historical jurisprudence. This would have been obvious to readers of *Physics and politics; or thoughts on the application of the principles of 'natural selection' and 'inheritance' to political society*, which had appeared in 1872. Four years earlier in a minor work on *Universal money* he had drawn attention to the bearing such ideas had on political economy:

The greatest want of our present political economy in England is that someone should do for it what Sir Henry Maine has done so well for 'ancient law'. We want someone to connect our theoretical account of the origins of things with the real origin. Our theory is right enough; our notion of what is best to be done is correct, but our notions of the way practices began and customs grew up are often erroneous enough.[26]

In *Physics and politics* he wanted to show 'how, upon one or two great points, the new ideas are modifying two old sciences – politics and political economy'.[27] 'Things' and 'points' have an air of knowing vagueness about them, and they refer to those places where Bagehot was to charge Mill with being behind the scientific times in not widening the boundaries of political economy enough.

Work on *Physics and politics* had been interrupted by illness and one of the purposes of what was published posthumously by Hutton as *Economic studies* was to add an economic dimension to the legal and political arguments in the earlier work.[28] There Bagehot had contrasted a patriarchal 'pre-economic age' with modern society, dwelling more on chance variations in individual and national character formation than would be expected of an exercise in what would later be called some version of pre-economic history or economic anthropology. *Physics and politics* culminates in the 'age of discussion' rather than in the complexities of life in Manchester or the City of London. Combining Huxley's *Elementary physiology* and Maudsley's *Physiology and pathology of mind* with Maine and some Lamarckian notions on how acquired faculties were passed on to progeny had seen Bagehot through to his conclusion. To fill the remaining lacunae in his *Economic studies*, he called upon a different range of scientific work: the ethnology of Lubbock, Catlin, Drew, and

[26] *A universal money*, CWWB, XI, p. 58. [27] See *Physics and politics*, CWWB, VII, p. 17.
[28] On this, see Giffen's comments, CWWB, XI, pp. 210–11.

Peschel, supplemented by Francis Galton on the families of judges and the domestication of animals. The object was to underline the stark contrast between primitive immobility/insecurity and modern fluidity/ stability, those properties essential to civilised economic existence.

If the essays on postulates show Bagehot to have been *au courant* in naturalistic vein, the essay he wrote on 'Adam Smith as a person' revealed a more familiar aspect of his authorial personality: the journalist as self-conscious man of letters. Bagehot's cultivated air of distance becomes obvious from his announcement that the *Wealth of nations* was 'a very amusing book about old times'.[29] That says as much about his conversational tone when addressing a *Fortnightly Review* readership as it does about Smith's reputation at the time. Nor is it difficult to fathom Bagehot's reasons for announcing that the *Wealth of nations* was now more an object of historical curiosity than a contribution to modern understanding. As a guide to enlightened economic policies the science to which this work had given rise had proved more influential than a sceptical Smith had been prepared to hope. Paradoxes in Smith's time, ideas that continued to perplex benighted foreigners, were now commonplace on his native heath. The main struggle being over, it was time to pay homage to the person responsible for starting the process that had brought free trade, as well as the principles of sound government finance and monetary practice, to such a triumphant conclusion in Britain. Bagehot had been excited by the activities of the Anti-Corn Law League as an undergraduate, and the journal he inherited from James Wilson had been founded as the independent London voice of Cobden's free trade movement. Free trade then was part of the stock-in-trade of the family business, with Smith being recognised as a clear-sighted if rather faint-hearted senior partner who had been unable to envisage just how successful the campaign against protectionism could be when taken up as a middle-class crusade. In the hundred years since the *Wealth of nations* had been published it had had a 'wonderful effect'.

The life of almost everyone in England – perhaps of everyone – is different in consequence of it. The whole commercial policy of the country is not so much founded on it as instinct with it. Ideas which are paradoxes everywhere else in the world are accepted axioms here as results of it. No other form of political philosophy has ever had one thousandth part of the influence on us; its teachings have settled down into the common sense of the nation, and have become irreversible.[30]

---

[29] CWWB, III, p. 106.
[30] *Economic studies*, CWWB, XI, p. 222, and repeated with different wording on p. 280.

Complacent, chauvinistic, and condescending though some of Bagehot's judgements may sound, they signal a minor landmark in the long history of Smith's changing role in the national imagination: the beginning of attempts to confront Smith's authorial personality without undue piety, and to treat the *Wealth of nations* in conjunction with Smith's other writings from a historical rather than a doctrinal or policy perspective. The journalistic fluency, even flippancy, Bagehot brought to this task was the other side of the historical distance he assumed was now possible. Taking a cue from Bagehot's epigrams, it was a distance not available to those less contented with the status quo, or to those even more contented with it than he proved to be.

Bagehot certainly recognised the scope of Smith's original enterprise: 'Scarcely any philosopher has imagined a vaster dream.' This had been lost sight of since Dugald Stewart's early appraisal of Smith's intellectual ambitions. Employing the new mid-Victorian language, Bagehot drew attention to the 'great scheme of evolution' which underpinned the entire plan, a scheme that comprehended 'the origins and progress of all the sciences, the laws, the politics, and all the other aids and forces' which showed 'how, from being a savage, man rose to be a Scotchman'.[31] As this last intended witticism indicates, Bagehot was addressing an English audience and deploying the amused irony that was his trademark as an author. To men of the world such as the author presumed himself and his readers to be, Smith was 'an awkward Scotch professor, apparently choked with books and absorbed in abstractions', whose only charms were a 'lumbering *bonhomie*'. He was the kind of absent-minded and silent man who excelled as a lecturer but was the most unlikely candidate to become the author of anything as down to earth as the *Wealth of nations*, or to take a practical part in public life, as he subsequently did as a commissioner of customs. Yet somehow Smith had conjured 'an enduring particular result' from his 'comprehensive and diffused ambition', investigating 'the progress of opulence as part of the growth and progress of all things'.[32]

Bagehot's speculations about Smith's personality were based on the factual evidence provided by Stewart, suitably enlivened and foreshortened

---

[31] 'Adam Smith as a person', CWWB, III, p. 91. Bagehot could claim to have written extensively on the Scottish mind; he compared Smith with Macaulay and Chalmers as Scots, and wrote on the Scottish education of the group who might be called Smith's grandchildren in 'The first Edinburgh reviewers'; see CWWB, I, pp. 309–41.

[32] 'Adam Smith as a person', CWWB, III, p. 86.

in the interests of entertaining his readers.[33] He doubted whether Smith's lectures on *belles-lettres* and the moral faculties were of 'much intrinsic merit', and his opinion of the *Theory of moral sentiments* was that the Victorian reader would find 'little to interest him in this celebrated [but 'rather pompous'] book'. He characterised it as belonging to the intuitive or Scottish moral sense school in opposition to utilitarianism, and thought its arguments were based on 'an obvious confusion of two familiar sentiments' that could be disposed of epigrammatically: 'We often sympathise where we cannot approve, and approve where we cannot sympathise.' Smith's attempt to save this theory required 'a little epicycle' in the form of the 'impartial spectator', an unconvincing fiction because 'if he sympathises he is not impartial, and if he is impartial he does not sympathise'.[34] Speaking perhaps as someone for whom Darwin's theory of natural selection had actually confirmed his theism, Bagehot regarded Smith as exactly the kind of indifferent Christian that Calvinism produces, with the 'complacent optimism' of the eighteenth century supplying an alternative creed that fell short of Hume's outright irreligion.[35]

The chief merit of Smith's first book, according to Bagehot, was that it earned him a tutorship that delivered him from the *longueurs* of teaching at Glasgow. It also enabled him to travel in France where he met the *Économistes* and added the problems of that powerful yet troubled monarchy to the knowledge of the practical world he had gleaned from the merchant community in Glasgow. Compared with the work on moral philosophy, Smith's second book had the merit of being 'entirely plain and manly', superior in this respect to anything written by Hume, who lacked Smith's anglicising advantages acquired at Oxford. It embodied a mixture of theory and common sense, strikingly illustrated with curious observations, and exactly calculated 'to put certain broad conclusions into the minds of hard-headed men, which are all which they need know, and all which they for the most part will ever care for'.[36] Smith was economics for businessmen; Ricardo, 'the true founder of abstract political economy', was for the connoisseur.[37]

---

[33] For example, Bagehot recounted that Smith's commissionership was a sinecure, and that it prevented him from writing anything during the last fourteen years of his life. Neither of these statements is true, as the extensive revisions to the *Theory of moral sentiments* show. Even a friend and admirer such as Giffen doubted if Bagehot's sketch of Smith was 'adequate'; see CWWB, XI, p. 212.

[34] 'Adam Smith as a person', CWWB, III, p. 96.

[35] For Bagehot's religious beliefs, see the account given by Hutton, CWWB, XV, pp. 83–133.

[36] 'Adam Smith as a person', CWWB, III, p. 110.   [37] *Economic studies*, CWWB, XI, p. 342.

Another sign of the distance Bagehot achieved can be found in his reference to Henry Buckle, who had anticipated Bagehot in placing both of Smith's main works within a broader philosophical context, doing so with more *gravitas* than Bagehot. Buckle had dealt with the 'Scotch intellect' at length in his mammoth *History of civilization in England* (1857–61); and since the *Wealth of nations* was described there as 'probably the most important book which has ever been written', he can hardly be accused of taking a parochial view of Smith's claims on posterity.[38] But Buckle commanded none of Bagehot's first-hand authority when dealing with political economy. Moreover, in regarding both of Smith's works as examples of the virtues of adopting a deductive approach to human affairs, with selfishness as the central axiom of the economic work and sympathy providing the basis for the deductions in moral philosophy, Smith became a prime illustration of Buckle's rationalist-materialist version of the history of progress. It made Buckle an easy target for Bagehot, who by comparing Smith's speculations on the theme of progress with 'the dream of the late Mr Buckle' consigned them both to an eighteenth-century world in retreat.[39] Readers of *Physics and politics* would have known that it began with an inversion of 'Mr Buckle's idea that material forces have been the main-springs of progress, and moral causes secondary', and continued with a stress on those small variations introduced by force of will that could accumulate over time.[40]

IV

Bagehot was fully aware of the unsatisfactory state of affairs in political economy when he wrote his appreciation of Smith. Indeed, the related essay on the postulates of English political economy is best known for its statement that the science lay 'dead in the public mind'; that it was failing to excite the interest or inspire the confidence of earlier days. New methods of investigation originating from abroad were proving more attractive to a younger generation no longer in thrall to Smith and Ricardo in political economy, or to Austin and Bentham in jurisprudence (an interesting linkage in view of Bagehot's approval of Maine, and one that inducts Smith firmly into the later camp despite what Bagehot had said about the *Theory of moral sentiments*). For 'no theory, economic or

---

[38] H. T. Buckle, *History of civilization in England*, 2 vols. (London: Parker, Son and Bourn, 1861), II, p. 443.
[39] 'Adam Smith as a person', CWWB, III, p. 86. [40] See *Physics and politics*, CWWB, VII, pp. 22–3.

political, can now be both insular and secure; foreign thoughts come soon
and trouble us; there will always be doubt here as to what is only believed
here'.[41]

Bagehot proposed two solutions to overcome this hostility or indifference, one with a venerable (forty years at least) ancestry, the other new
and more fashionable, representing his understanding of recent developments associated with Maine and a variety of post-Darwinian sciences.
First, he reiterated arguments about the hypothetical status of the abstract
deductive science based on 'economic man' assumptions that can be
traced back to the earliest attempts to legislate for the post-Ricardo shape
of the science in the 1820s and 30s. Bagehot considered John Elliot
Cairnes's restatement of Mill's position in his *Character and logical method
of political economy* to be the best treatment of the subject.[42] During the
final period of his life Cairnes held the chair of political economy at
Bagehot's *alma mater*. The inaugural lecture he gave in 1870 could well
have been the inspiration for Bagehot's emphasis on the Englishness of
political economy and the neglect into which it had fallen as a result of
the successes of the free trade movement.[43]

What Bagehot added to the familiar defence of deductions based on
abstract assumptions was a radical form of relativism derived from his
contrast between the conditions that ruled in primitive economies and
those that suited, as we have seen, 'a society of grown-up competitive
commerce such as we have in England'.[44] He was forsaking claims to
universal applicability, thereby reducing vulnerability to attacks from
those who maintained that the science could not be used to understand
very different kinds of society. Bagehot readily conceded this, not merely
in the case of 'pre-economic' societies but in 'new countries' as well,
where the Ricardian assumption of diminishing returns was not met and
the Malthusian thesis was inapplicable. This confined political economy
to a 'money-making' mentality that was amenable to Bagehot's appreciation

---

[41] CWWB, XI, p. 224.
[42] Cairnes had sent Bagehot a copy of his last book, *Some leading principles*; see CWWB, XIII,
pp. 653–4. Bagehot's obituary of Cairnes stated that 'he defines better, as we think, than any
previous writer, the exact sort of science which political economy is, the kind of reasoning which it
uses, and the nature of the relation which it, as an abstract science, bears to the concrete world'; see
CWWB, XI, pp. 401–3.
[43] 'Every great step in the progress of economic science . . . has been won by English thinkers; and
while we have led the van in economic speculation, we have also been the first to apply with
boldness our theories to practice.' See *Essays in political economy* (London: Macmillan, 1873), p. 232
and the statement about neglect of the science on p. 236.
[44] *Economic studies*, CWWB, XI, p. 235.

of business psychology. By making the science more specific in its applicability, even nationally or racially specific, Bagehot could arrive at his chief conclusion – expressed, once more, in an epigram. Once the postulates of the science were properly understood 'we shall then find that our political economy is not a questionable thing of unlimited extent, but a most certain and useful thing of limited extent'.[45]

From this more secure position it was possible to attack some of the proposed alternative methods of inquiry. The simplifications or abstractions from motives other than those operating in grown-up economies were necessary because neither the 'all-case' nor 'single-case' inductive methods were capable of yielding scientific results, as he believed the examples of Newton in astronomy, Lyell in geology, and Darwin in biology showed. He refused to call these alternative methods 'historical', a term he found ambiguous. When rightly conceived, the historical method, the one employed by Maine, was not in conflict with the use of abstraction, an indication of why Bagehot did not feel it necessary to choose between Bentham and Maine in legal matters.[46] Just as the natural scientist was aware that outside the pages of a manual on theoretical mechanics perfectly rigid bodies and elastic planes did not exist, so the economist was justified in dealing with 'an immaterial subject, which in the existing world cannot be found either'. It was a sound scientific maxim based on common sense to take simple cases first. Being more complex than the physical sciences, and with its practitioners being subject to 'practical impulses', it was open to misuse. Confirmatory evidence was more difficult to find and more readily open to divergent interpretation. Bagehot conceded, however, that English exponents of the science had 'not been as fertile as they should have been' in verifying their abstractions.[47]

The economist did not inquire into the origin of human wants or ask whether only the best of those wants ought to be encouraged: 'He regards a pot of beer and a picture, a book of religion and a pack of cards, as all equally "wealth", and therefore, for his purpose, equally worthy of regard.'[48] This conformed to Cairnes's stress on scientific neutrality with respect to the subjective wants of individuals and the moral goals pursued by society as a whole. It was not possible to use political economy to prove, as some unnamed foreign anti-socialist authors (presumably he meant Bastiat, another subject on which Cairnes had written) had attempted to do, that the economic world was a good one, still less that

---

[45] *Ibid.*, p. 238.   [46] *Ibid.*, pp. 230–3.   [47] *Ibid.*, pp. 226, 236, 280–1.   [48] *Ibid.*, p. 287.

it was the best of all possible worlds.[49] Bagehot also wished to defend political economy against those he described as 'uncultured moralists', those who failed to understand that economists 'dealt not with man, the moral being, but with man, the money-making animal'.[50] Bagehot had taken up Ruskin's challenge when *Unto this last* had first appeared in serial form in 1860, and had done so under a headline that left the reader in no doubt about the text: 'Aesthetic Twaddle versus Economic Science'. The article began with one of Bagehot's favourite words, stupidity: 'In the faculty of writing nonsense, stupidity is no match for genius.'[51]

V

These methodological issues were to surface during the discussions that followed the centenary dinner organised by the Political Economy Club in 1876. Although Bagehot did not speak on that occasion, in one way or another all those who did so confirmed his diagnosis of the divided and inauspicious state of English political economy.[52] As a celebration of Smith's achievements the occasion could not be faulted by anyone who was content with the nineteenth-century legends that had become attached to Smith's name. And judged simply by the social and political standing of those present, the event could hardly have been more successful. Gladstone took the chair alongside several who had served in his first ministry, a number of other MPs, the Duke of Argyll, some bankers, civil servants, lawyers, and journalists, and a large contingent of visitors which included the French Minister of Finance. All that was lacking was a member of the royal family. As befitted their status, those present by virtue of their academic credentials, the six holders of chairs of political economy at London, Oxford, Cambridge, Belfast, Manchester, and Edinburgh, plus a Belgian visitor, were beneath the salt. Only two of them spoke, the ebullient and highly politicised holder of the Oxford chair, J. E. Thorold Rogers and, out of politeness to foreigners perhaps, the Belgian guest, de Laveleye.

Discussion proceeded along two separable lines that can be labelled respectively as practical-normative and methodological. Most of the speakers, led by Gladstone and Robert Lowe, an ex-Chancellor of the Exchequer, were concerned with what practical results had flowed from

[49] *Ibid.*, p. 238. On Bastiat and Cairnes's attack on him, see pp. 195–7 below.
[50] *Ibid.*, p. 283.   [51] CWWB, IX, p. 315.
[52] The articles on basic postulates had appeared before the dinner took place in May 1876, and he made arrangements to ensure that further articles appeared in print soon afterwards.

the *Wealth of nations* and what further objectives remained to be secured. They were chiefly interested in discerning where the founder of the science would have stood on some prominent issues of current concern: the impending legislation on educational endowments at Oxford, limited liability for joint-stock companies, landlord–tenant relations, the threat or opportunity posed by trade unions, and the merits of securing multilateral free trade via the second-best route of bilateral treaties. The link between these policy concerns was the question of how far recent legislative trends constituted a legitimate departure from the *laissez-faire* maxims Smith's work was thought to embody. Smith was being canonised officially – for the first if not the last time – as the patron saint of Victorian economic orthodoxy, with most of the speakers taking the view that *laissez-faire* was the most important inference to be drawn from the laws of political economy. Gladstone was exceptional among those on the top table in arguing that the country could not and should not be governed by such laws alone, while Lowe merely paused amid eulogy to regret that Smith had 'found exceptions to his own rules that did not really exist'.[53] If Smith's reservations could be dismissed in this way, there was little hope that any of the qualifications expressed on the subject by economists such as Mill and Cairnes would have gained a hearing. Lowe actually devoted some attention to Mill's uncomplimentary statement about the work being celebrated, namely that it was 'in many parts obsolete, and in all, imperfect'.[54]

As Lowe made clear, the implications for the future of the science were not promising: 'I am not sanguine as to any very large or any very startling development of Political Economy ... The controversies that we now have ... although they offer a capital exercise for the logical faculties, are not of the same thrilling importance as those of earlier days; the great work has been done.'[55] The Cairnes–Bagehot diagnosis of why the subject lay dead in the public mind was being confirmed, and those academics present who might have hoped that their devotion to teaching and writing would at least earn them a respectable living were not being given much encouragement, logical gymnastics training apart.

Lowe's provocative after-dinner speech also succeeded in triggering and prefiguring the disputes that were to divide devotees of the science for the

[53] *Political Economy Club: revised report of the proceedings of the dinner of 31 May, 1876, held in celebration of the hundredth year of the publication of the 'Wealth of Nations', Right Hon W. E. Gladstone in the chair* (London: Longmans, 1876), p. 11.
[54] See p. 30 above.   [55] *Political Economy Club: revised report*, pp. 20–1.

next two decades or more. He had made his position clear in parliament when speaking about the Irish land bill in 1870: 'Political economy belongs to no nation . . . It will assert itself whether you wish it or not. It is founded on the attributes of the human mind, and no power can change it.'[56] At the dinner he maintained that Smith possessed 'the unique merit . . . of having founded a deductive and demonstrative science of human actions and conduct' that was capable of predicting economic outcomes accurately. The truths he had propounded would last 'as long as mankind shall seek after truth'. Political economy was the only one of the moral sciences to be raised to the dignity of a deductive science, despite the noble efforts of Bentham and James Mill 'to raise politics to a like eminence'.[57] He also managed a glancing blow at what 'it is the barbarous jargon of the day to call Sociology', a tilt at the English Comtists represented at the dinner by Frederic Harrison and T. E. Cliffe Leslie, a partial sympathiser, who had criticised Lowe's dogmatic utterance when it was made in parliament. Lowe may have planned his opening speech as a pre-emptive strike against those present whom he knew would take the opposite position.

Emile de Laveleye was one of these. He agreed with Lowe in holding that the part of the science cultivated by the 'école orthodoxe', that dealing with the production of riches, was now complete. This was amply confirmed by the spectacular statistics relating to English prosperity in recent decades. But the second task of the science, 'la repartition de la richesse', remained to be tackled, and was being tackled by another school that could be variously labelled as the 'socialists of the chair' (*Kathedersozialisten*) or as the 'historical' or 'realist' school in Germany, with its disciples in Italy, France, and England. He proceeded to give a long list of those troublesome foreign authors about whom Bagehot had written without mentioning names. He described them as anxious to extend the scope of the science by dealing with 'les rapports de l' économie politique avec la morale, avec l'idée du juste, avec le droit, avec la religion, avec l'histoire, et la attachant a l'ensemble de la science sociale'. The proprieties of the occasion were maintained, however, by de Laveleye's emollient conclusion that 'les deux écoles invoquent également l'autorité d'Adam Smith et, avec raison, d'après moi, car son ouvrage immortel est un exemple si parfait et si fécond en conséquences utiles de l'alliance des deux méthodes scientifiques – la méthode déductive et la méthode inductive'.[58]

---

[56] *Hansard*, 3rd series, 1196–7 (4 April 1870).
[57] *Political Economy Club: revised report*, p. 7.   [58] *Ibid.*, p. 31.

James Thorold Rogers's reply to Lowe was less conciliatory: 'There is . . . nothing more significant than the difference of the process by which Adam Smith collected his inferences, and that by which his followers or commentators have arrived at theirs.' Smith avoided hypotheses and concentrated on the historical record, as Rogers, the latest editor of the *Wealth of nations*, thought he could show on the basis of his verification of Smith's sources. This confirmed his judgement that Smith was an inductive philosopher 'to be looked on . . . as the practical Bacon of Economical science'.[59] Most of the errors into which Smith's followers had fallen could be attributed to 'purely abstract speculation', with Ricardo's theory of rent being the main culprit. This meant that 'Smith is far more frequently in the right than his critics are'. Any remaining blemishes were due either to the rudimentary evidence at his disposal, or (on the subject of value) to 'his exaggerated sympathy with the economical theories of his French friends and teachers'.[60] As the friend, indeed brother-in-law of Cobden, Rogers was able to offer a token olive branch to the opposition by saying that they could still unite in praising Smith's contribution to the cause of free trade.

If Lowe had fused Bagehot's two heroes, Smith and Ricardo, into a composite figure, de Laveleye and Rogers were intent on prising them apart. Smith had not merely discovered the country but had used the proper methods to explore it. Ricardo's map had already led his followers astray. Although Bagehot had taken the opposite view, the report he wrote on the dinner for *The Economist* did not mention any of the disagreements that had emerged.[61] Perhaps he had written it ahead of the dinner. It differed little from the longer piece he wrote on Smith that appeared a month later, with some additional detail on the 'uncultured moralists'. On this occasion they were identified as Carlyle, Matthew Arnold, and all those 'sentimentalists who are never so sure that they are right as when they differ from what political economy teaches'. Those who had forecast impending ruin during the debate on the 'condition of England' in the 1840s had been proved wrong. For reasons that Smith had foreseen, 'we were [then] on the eve of the greatest prosperity which we have ever seen'.[62]

[59] *Ibid.*, p. 33.   [60] *Ibid.*, p. 32.
[61] 'Centenary of the *Wealth of Nations*', CWWB, III, pp. 113–19. The dispute was mentioned in the only other newspaper account of the event; see *Pall Mall Gazette*, 30 May 1876 in which it was noted that the dinner had occurred at an 'inauspicious moment in the history of the science'.
[62] 'Centenary of the *Wealth of Nations*', CWWB, III, p. 117.

Bagehot's solution to the methodological problem had solved little. After the dinner the dispute thundered on in the periodical press. Lowe expanded on his insults to the sociologists and other advocates of complementary social sciences:

Political economy is separated from all the moral sciences, not by the arbitrary act of its founders, but the nature of things themselves . . . In love, or war, or politics, or religion, or morals it is impossible to foretell how mankind will act; and therefore on these subjects it is impossible to reason deductively. But once place a man's ear within the ring of pounds, shillings, and pence, and his conduct can be counted on to the greatest nicety.[63]

As we shall see in the succeeding essay, Jevons made these and other divergences uncovered during the centenary dinner the theme of his inaugural lecture when he succeeded to Cairnes's chair at UCL in 1876; his object was to show that 'the future of political economy is not likely to be such a blank as some of the speakers at the centennial dinner would lead us to suppose'.[64] Cliffe Leslie had already made his position clear in articles written in the 1860s and during the Irish land bill debates, and was to renew his attack on Lowe, Buckle, and Bagehot after the dinner. The Anglo-Irish *Methodenstreit* had begun in earnest.

VI

The extent to which any scientific proposition in political economy, and the policy conclusions to which it might point, was history- or culture-bound – Bagehot's chief and only concession to the critics of orthodoxy – was seized upon by some of them as a damaging concession. But they were to find that relativism was a double-edged weapon with which they could also both arm and wound themselves. Absolutists such as Lowe could adopt impregnable positions based on 'the nature of things themselves', and Bagehot could rest content with his own Whig history of the discipline by treating Smith as an historical curiosity on the assumption that what was still serviceable in the *Wealth of nations* had been preserved in the more advanced work of his orthodox successors. Believing that post-Smithian economics was a snare and a delusion, Leslie could not accept such complacency. But in seeking to rescue Smith from his followers he was obliged to give reasons why some parts of Smith's legacy

---

[63] See 'Recent attacks on political economy', *The Nineteenth Century* 4 (1878), 864.
[64] See 'The future of political economy', *Fortnightly Review*, November 1876, as reprinted in *The principles of economics* (London: Macmillan, 1905), p. 206, and pp. 161–2 below.

were still of contemporary relevance, while others had to be excused or condemned on grounds of changing circumstances or erroneous philosophical underpinnings. The task was not an impossible one, but it required an effort to assemble the relevant evidence. When the evidence fell short of the mark, neither the historical reconstruction nor the contemporary support derived from it carried conviction. Where such efforts were merely polemical, Smith's authority became that of mere icon or stalking-horse.

Leslie is the key early figure in the Anglo-Irish dispute, partly because he was responsible for linking it with his interest in Irish economic conditions, partly because he shared with Bagehot one important source or influence: a legal education and enthusiasm for the work of Henry Maine, the undisputed British pioneer of the application of evolutionary perspectives to law. An almost exact contemporary of Bagehot, he had been a law student at the Inns of Court when Maine was giving those comparative-historical lectures on jurisprudence which were later to appear as *Ancient law*. When Bagehot was returning from his law studies at Lincoln's Inn to run the family bank, Leslie was taking up a chair of jurisprudence and political economy at Queen's College, Belfast, while continuing to reside in London most of the year. Leslie matched Bagehot's identification with Ricardo by taking on those items of Smith's clothing that were still capable of being put to good use. They were relevant to his academic calling (the combination of jurisprudence and political economy in his academic title corresponds with two of the duties attached to Smith's chair in Glasgow), and his use of them went well beyond strategic display of the founder's brand name. Considering the textual resources available to Leslie, few could fault his pertinacity in reconstructing Smith's original enterprise. Like Smith, he emphasised the subordinate role of political economy within 'a science of the legislator', bringing Smith into closer relation with *Kameralwissenschaft* as depicted in the work of Roscher and the German historical school.[65] Dugald Stewart's account of the role of 'conjectural history' in Smith's work allowed Leslie to conceive of a way in which he could effect his own reconciliation of Maine's historical programme with an inductive form of political economy.[66] What had been for Bagehot some quaint eighteenth-century

---

[65] See 'The history of German political economy', in *Essays in political and moral philosophy*, (1879), reissued as *Essays in political economy*, ed. J. K. Ingram and C. F. Bastable (Dublin: Dublin University Press, 1888), p. 87.

[66] For example, having reviewed the components of Smith's teaching, he concluded 'that his conception of the true scope and method of jurisprudence agreed with his conception of the true

speculations of a rationalistic kind on the theme of social progress became for Leslie a neglected insight into the chief problem now facing political economy. Buckle's misunderstanding had been compounded, not resolved, by Bagehot. An appreciation of the historical themes of Book III of the *Wealth of nations* on the progress of opulence would place the chapters in Book I that centred on prices, rents, wages, and profits as determined by market equilibrating processes in proper perspective.[67] Bagehot may have undermined Lowe's boast that political economy belonged to no country by showing that it belonged to one country that was in the van of progress, but he had failed to deal with the intermediate stages of economic progress, and ignored the consequences for the superstructure of the science.[68]

In answer to Buckle, Lowe, and Bagehot, Leslie offered a 'true history of human ideas' by showing that 'selfishness was not the fundamental principle of Adam Smith's theory'. Smith's conclusions were not deduced from an assumption of universal economic man; his method, as Rogers had claimed, was 'in a large measure inductive'. Nevertheless, Leslie still had to locate that 'vein of unsound a priori speculation' in Smith that allowed the opposition to claim legitimate descent.[69] The origins of Smith's mistake could be traced – and in being traced neutralised – to the influence of the 'code of nature' idea of the Greeks, embellished by the Roman lawyers, and bolstered in the eighteenth century by a combination of natural theology and the arguments of those political philosophers who reasoned on the basis of 'an assumed state of nature'. Thus although Smith's 'economic system was part of a complete system of social, or, as he called it, moral philosophy', the system combined two opposed methods of reasoning: an a priori method based on the pre-existence of social harmony, and the inductive or sociological method which Leslie, following Maine, traced to Montesquieu; hence the divided legacy that allowed Ricardo to claim allegiance to Smith by disregarding what had been shown by Maine's writings on natural law to be erroneous. Smith's references to the 'invisible hand' and the emphasis on the harmony

---

scope and method of economic inquiry'; see 'The wealth of nations and the slave power', in *ibid.*, p. 15.

[67] 'The political economy of Adam Smith', in *ibid.*, pp. 35–9.

[68] See 'Mr Bagehot', in *ibid.*, pp. 63–4; 'On the philosophical method of political economy', in *ibid.*, pp. 179–82; and 'Political economy and sociology', in *ibid.*, p. 207.

[69] See 'The political economy of Adam Smith', p. 23. See also the uses made of Smith in articles written before and after the centennial dinner: 'On the philosophical method of political economy', 'Political economy and sociology', and 'The known and the unknown in the economic world'.

produced by unintended consequences in both his major works had produced the dogmatic nineteenth-century *laissez-faire* position of which Lowe was now the best representative or worst example.

Fortunately, there was that other inductive strand derived from Smith's 'philosophical love of truth, and of interrogating nature itself in its real phenomena', an approach that had been adopted by the followers of Montesquieu in Scotland who formed 'a new school of political and jural philosophy'.[70] Though lacking the sophisticated examples of induction associated with nineteenth-century natural science and the historical investigations of Maine, Smith had curbed the tendency to ignore or minimise the frictions and forces disturbing market equilibrium by acknowledging that competition had not eliminated the inequalities produced by differential bargaining power and disabling policies and institutions. Equilibrating forces were confined to primitive economies and to 'an almost stationary condition of industry and neighbourhood trade, in which few changes in the mode of production or the channels of trade took place', where this too could be explained by reference to the rudimentary state of modern industry when Smith wrote.

Two followers of Maine, then, Bagehot and Leslie, reached diametrically opposed conclusions on the basis of similar evidence about modern economies. Relativism supported absolutism with respect to English conditions in one case, and in the other it served to undermine any confident use of deductive forms of theory. Whereas for Leslie the indeterminacy of wages and profits that accompanied the increasingly heterogeneous development of modern industry was leading away from the abstract method, for Bagehot it was making it the only method appropriate to the modern science. Of the two, there is no doubt that Bagehot remained closer to Maine's own, more conservative political leanings. Maine was increasingly annoyed by those who cited his work on India, a status-oriented society, as part of an attack on the legitimacy of political economy as a guide to civilised societies, like Britain, governed by contract and characterised by private property.[71] Maine said that he thought of *Physics and politics* as 'practically an old friend' when he was sent a copy of the second edition, and he did not think he was over-influenced by Bagehot's warm allusions to himself.[72]

---

[70] *ibid.*, pp. 31–2, instanced by Lord Kames, John Miller, and James Dalrymple.
[71] See *Village-communities in the east and west*, 4th edn (London: John Murray, 1881), pp. 191–7; and more especially 'The effects of observation of India on modern European thought', a lecture given in 1875 which is included in the above edition, pp. 223–33.
[72] Letter to Bagehot, January 1873, CWWB, XIII, pp. 640–1.

Irish land tenure problems provided another test case. Leslie, with Mill's support, had challenged Lowe's universalism in arguing that the laws of political economy applied to Ireland, regardless of local peculiarities.[73] For this and other reasons connected with friendship, Leslie counted himself indebted to Mill as well as Maine, while recognising, after Mill's death at least, that the influence of Mill's Benthamite upbringing continued to separate them.[74] For Bagehot it was more a question of asking whether or not the Irish as a race evinced those adult qualities that were necessary for any novel economic remedy to be successful. Faced with Mill's most radical proposals on the subject, he had registered the following verdict:

A race disciplined to labour, trained in the elements of forethought, if it should obtain the possession of land, would improve both in industry and prudence. But a race, from whatever cause, and by whatever history, improvident, reckless, and thoughtless, if given land without supervision, will only use it to become more idle, more reckless, more improvident . . . To which of the two classes the Irish population belong no one doubts. They have been trained and disciplined in the bad use of land – they have acquired worse habits of labour, probably than any other race of equal mind.[75]

As Palgrave rather tactfully pointed out, although Bagehot was one of the first economists in England to recognise the importance of Darwinism to economics, 'in most cases he is more careful to dwell on the contrast between the old and the new than to show how the one passed into the other or how the phenomena of the one shed light on the phenomena of the other'.[76] Leslie, following Smith, had attempted the larger task, and in this he was to set an example to the rising generation of economic historians.

VII

Bagehot's Whig history, or rather perhaps, Whig biography of political economy was conservative in its implications for future development. Although he believed there had been intellectual advances since the *Wealth of nations*, he was not prepared to endorse the newer mathematical theories of value associated with the names of Jevons and Walras. Jevons had raised his revolutionary standard against the Ricardo–Mill stranglehold five

---

[73] Mill had done so in parliament in 1870 and had followed this up when commending Leslie's comparative-historical treatment of *Land systems and industrial economy;* see CW, V, pp. 671–85.
[74] See obituary article in *Essays in political economy*, pp. 54–9.
[75] 'Mr Mill on Ireland', CWWB, XI, 550.   [76] *Dictionary of political economy*, I, p. 80.

years before the centenary dinner, but the new theory went unnoticed during the post-prandial engagements. Bagehot alluded to it in passing in his essays on the postulates, but merely to say that anyone who thought 'what is ordinarily taught in England objectionable, because it is too little concrete in its method, and looks too unlike life and business, had better try the new doctrine, which he will find to be much worse on these points than the old'.[77] It is not clear what work by Walras, if any, Bagehot had read, but he had been acquainted with Jevons for over a decade and had a high regard for his work as an applied economist, especially on monetary subjects. They shared a common background as UCL alumni, and Jevons was related to Henry Roscoe and Hutton, who were to remain Bagehot's best friends within the Unitarian community in which they had both been brought up. Bagehot had invited Jevons to contribute to *The Economist*, and he supported Jevons in his successful application for the Cobden chair at Owens College, Manchester, in 1863, drawing attention to Jevons's ability to combine 'an equal knowledge of the abstract theory of Political Economy and an equally accurate acquaintance with the statistics of present facts', chiefly as revealed by his study of the effect of gold discoveries on the price level.[78] In return Jevons complimented the author of *Lombard Street*, and they acted harmoniously as co-examiners for the Ricardo scholarship at UCL in 1875. Bagehot's praise for Jevons's knowledge of 'abstract theory' predates publication of his main mathematical work, his *Theory of political economy*, but he had that work in mind when he cited Jevons and Walras as examples of doctrines that were even less concrete than the old ones. Countering the 'mathematical' critics was mentioned as one of the original aims of his economic studies, but he had nothing to say on the subject when he came to write them. The final fragment on exchange value does not move outside the ambit of Mill–Cairnes arguments around the meaning of the cost of production. Utility theory is not mentioned, and while the determination of wages features there, no reader would gather that it had recently been the subject of considerable dissension. Bagehot was not *au courant* with the latest economic literature.

Bagehot must have felt he was occupying a satisfying middle position, unmoved by the historical and mathematical extremists on either side of him. Maine provided a way of retaining the orthodox substance of the science while avoiding the abrasive stance of Lowe – a quality Bagehot

---

[77] *Economic studies*, CWWB, XI, p. 234
[78] See letters to Jevons, 10 March 1866, CWWB, XIII, pp. 606–8.

rather admired in the man himself.[79] Bagehot's defence of the postulates of the science in their established form places him where he often sought to place himself in his political writings, namely on the conservative wing of a liberal (indeed, Liberal) position. Given his ante-Mill opinions on Ricardo, it was impossible for him to endorse the attempts of Rogers, Leslie, and Jevons, for their different reasons, to treat Ricardo as the villain of the historical piece, as an aberrant post-Smithian development. But he had no constructive ideas on the future outside applications of known principles. Standing in the solid middle of these disputes probably accounts too for the historical tolerance towards Smith he managed to achieve, limited though it was by his desire to be entertaining. It permitted him a little more generosity to Smith than Mill had shown when the science was being developed, but did not allow him to follow Leslie and others, for whom resurrecting Smith's methods and conclusions had contemporary significance.

Bagehot's ante-Mill stance may have something to do with this as well. For those who had learned their political economy from Mill and were still actively engaged in the business of deciding what kind of science political economy should become, Mill was the ghost of Banquo at the centenary dinner. How this ghost should be exorcised, how the gap left by Mill's death should be filled, was a matter of more moment to them than it was to Bagehot. Mill cast an ambivalent shadow over the 1876 proceedings because he had become the source of much confusion on matters of theory, policy, and method – a subject already encountered that will be further explored in later essays. Leslie was more significant as an indication of one future line of development than Bagehot proved to be – the line that resulted in more attention being paid to historical and institutional factors by economists and economic historians alike. When Sidgwick reviewed the outcome of earlier methodological disputes in the 1890s, Bagehot was credited with suggesting 'an attractive modus vivendi' between the extremes of deductivism and the historical school. Unfortunately, his proposals were no longer capable of supporting life. Any genuinely pre-economic society could just as well be called 'pre-historic', and any society that could boast a history of some kind had evidently reached a stage when the concepts of deductive economics had become relevant. Against the 'aggressive' historicists, Sidgwick made the shrewd observation that the harder they pressed the distinction between their

---

[79] 'The quality of his mind is to put everything in the most lively, most exciting, and most startling form'; see 'Mr Lowe', CWWB, III, p. 572.

own work on earlier ages and that of economists on present-day societies, the more they were conceding the independence of modern economics and the irrelevance of their own historical work to advanced communities.[80] Here was a prime case of the sword proving double-edged, and here too was the uneasy basis for the accommodation between the two camps that eventually prevailed, though it meant accepting less than Leslie and later historical economists and economic historians continued to press for – a fully historicised and inductive version of the science of economics.

Following in Sidgwick's footsteps, John Neville Keynes, whose judicious survey of the entire debate in his *Scope and method of political economy* set the tone on these subjects in the period running up to the First World War (increasingly one of boredom, it has to be said), considered it unwise on Bagehot's part to have restricted the scope of the science by use of the 'economic man' assumption. The concept of a pre-economic society was opaque and unduly restrictive: 'We are compelled to recognize eras of varying economic types, and the existence of primitive societies in which industrial organization is but rudimentary; but until we find an age or a society in which exchanges – even in a disguised form – are unknown, and appropriated wealth does not exist, we have not in a strict sense reached the pre-economic.' He was also able to cite Maine against Bagehot when noting that Maine had argued that 'familiar economical conceptions', such as property, rent, profits, exchange, and competition were to be found in India, despite their appearance in guises that were unfamiliar to the occidental eye.[81] No better defence of the continuing relevance of political economy to recruits into the Indian civil service could be given, unless it was that of Alfred Marshall based partly on his experience of teaching recruits into the Indian civil service at Oxford.[82]

Whether or not the *Wealth of nations* was merely an amusing book about old times, or still managed to provide valuable insight, its centenary had been a fortuitous occasion for rehearsing issues that would undoubtedly

---

[80] See his article on 'Political economy', in Palgrave, *Dictionary of political economy*, III, pp. 135–6.

[81] See J. N. Keynes, *Scope and method of political economy*, 4th edn (London: Macmillan, 1917), pp. 306–10; see also pp. 15–17, 117–18, 209, 231, 242–3 for further comment on Bagehot.

[82] It was Marshall's opinion that what was needed in India was an annual export of half-a-dozen young men with 'a good grounding in economics', men capable of understanding the 'main bearings of those modern economic forces which are revolutionising the West, and are making great changes in the East'; see his evidence to the committee of inquiry into the Indian currency in *Official Papers by Alfred Marshall* (London: Macmillan for the Royal Economic Society, 1926), p. 325.

have been raised without this excuse. Looking back to the centenary from the 1890s, it was easier to notice, as Keynes did, that Smith said nothing in the *Wealth of nations* about the right method to use in political economy. Surely it was obvious that like everybody else he employed both induction and deduction, and that in this respect Lowe and Leslie had been wrong to stress one at the expense of the other. This was Marshall's conclusion too, and it consorted well with his penchant for believing that moderation and good sense had characterised the English tradition of political economy from the outset. However much Marshall may have begun his own theoretical work by transforming the arithmetical and verbal formulations of Ricardo and Mill on value into mathematics, he claimed that his appreciation of Smith's achievement had grown with further acquaintance. Devotees of Smith could hardly quarrel with Marshall's considered verdict, namely that Smith was singly responsible for taking 'the greatest step that economics has ever taken' towards becoming a science.[83] As Marshall confided to L. L. Price, one of the period's new historians of economics, another sub-discipline that had benefited from the *Methodenstreit*, the more he compared Smith with predecessors and successors 'the more I worshipped him. It was his balance, his sense of proportion, his power of seeing the many in the one and the one in the many, his skill in using analysis to interpret history and history to correct analysis ... that seemed to mark him out as unique; very much as similar qualities have more recently given a similar position to Darwin.'[84] No praise from Marshall could be higher: Smith was everything Marshall hoped to be himself.

While Bagehot's work on the money market in *Lombard Street* retained its reputation, therefore, *Economic studies* fared less well. Marshall was embarrassed by having to make good his promise to Bagehot's widow to write an introduction to a new edition of a work he thought was thoroughly outdated.[85] The man of the world had proved too worldly, and what was post-Mill in his thinking was too fragmentary, too simplistically committed to a binary distinction between the children and the adults, to settle any issue. Last man of the ante-Mill era he may have been, but his bid to supply a guide to the post-Mill era had been overtaken by others on either side of him. Those who live by epigrams often die by them.

---

[83] *PE*, I, pp. 756–7   [84] See letter to Price, 19 August 1892, *Correspondence*, II, pp. 80–1.
[85] See letters to Keynes, 10 August and 27 August 1889, *Correspondence*, I, pp. 294, 298.

6

'As much a matter of heart as head': Jevons's antipathy

I

It is well known that Jevons, especially during the final decade of his tragically foreshortened life, was preoccupied with countering Mill's malign influence as a philosopher. John Maynard Keynes judged the preoccupation to be based on a violent aversion pursued 'almost to the point of morbidity'; and he traced its origins to Jevons's failure to win the first prize in political economy when he took his BA at University College, London (UCL) as a mature student, twenty-five years old. Relying on the testimony of his father, who had co-examined with Jevons, Keynes suggested that continued repression of Jevons's own ideas as a result of having to base his teaching and examining on syllabi dominated by Mill's writings 'brought his feeling against Mill to boiling point'.[1] Jevons certainly made a vow in 1860 to be avenged for the exam result by publishing his own *Theory of political economy*, a work he was confident would 're-establish the science on a sensible basis'.[2] A few weeks before the examination he was convinced he had discovered '*the true theory of Economy* so thorough-going that I cannot now read other books on the subject without indignation' – an indignation that could only be stoked by Mill's complacent announcement in the main textbook for the course that the theory of value was complete, leaving nothing 'for the present or any future writer to clear up'.[3] It was to be eleven years before the *Theory* appeared, and it concluded with a denunciation of 'the noxious influence of authority' in which Mill was held responsible, alongside Ricardo, James Mill, and Henry Fawcett, for inhibiting free inquiry and the development of the science.[4] The second edition published in 1879 reinforced this by

[1] 'William Stanley Jevons', in *Essays in biography*, as reprinted in JMK, X, p. 136.
[2] Letter to Herbert Jevons, 25 July 1860, PC, II, pp. 415–16.
[3] Letter to Herbert Jevons, 1 June 1860, PC, II, p. 410; and Mill's *Principles*, CW, III, p. 456.
[4] *Theory of political economy*, 2nd edn (London: Macmillan, 1879), pp. 299–300.

means of a new preface in which Jevons recorded the results of his research into the pre-history of value theorising, culminating in his celebrated pronouncement that Ricardo and his 'equally able and wrong-headed admirer', Mill, were responsible for shunting the car of economics onto the wrong track. Jevons's revolutionary manifesto was expressed, then, as a proposition derived from his own recently established genealogy of economic theorising. If the science was to regain its rightful lineage it would have to abandon the dominant native mode in favour of an alternative he associated chiefly with a line of French economists:

the only hope of attaining a true system of Economics is to fling aside, once and for ever, the mazy and preposterous assumptions of the Ricardian School. Our English Economists have been living in a fool's paradise. The truth is with the French School, and the sooner we recognise the fact, the better it will be for all the world, except perhaps the few writers who are too far committed to the old erroneous doctrines to allow of renunciation.[5]

Standing the Ricardo–Mill tradition on its head, Jevons maintained that 'value depends entirely on utility'. The laws of human enjoyment explored by Bentham as part of a concern with the intensity, duration, certainty, and propinquity of pleasures and pains could provide a psychological foundation for a theory of economic maximisation that had universal application. The pure or abstract version of the science of political economy under static conditions turned on 'the mechanics of utility and self-interest'. Pleasure maximisation and pain minimisation was *the* problem for any basic theory of economic life. With his newly acquired understanding of the pre-history of the utility tradition he could express his aim as one of making explicit the mathematics that underlay Bastiat's simple harmonious circle of 'wants, efforts, satisfaction'.[6] Reduced to its essence, economic behaviour entailed an inquiry into the way in which we achieve an optimal relationship between our efforts and our wants.

Amid the bold programmatics of Jevons's aim to transform economics into a quantitative and hence a mathematical science it is easy to overlook the modesty with which he presented his initial findings. Unlike Mill (and Marshall later) Jevons did not claim to be advancing 'a systematic view of Economics' and was never able to complete a later attempt to do so. The posthumously published work entitled the *Principles of economics* is better described by the sub-title assigned to it by his editor, *a fragment of a treatise on the industrial mechanism of society and other papers.* Jevons

---

[5] *Ibid.,* p. xlix.   [6] *Ibid.,* p. 44; the other quoted phrases can be found on pp. 2 and 23.

was also frank in conceding that it was not possible to 'weigh, nor gauge, nor test the feelings of the mind: there is no unit of labour, or suffering, or enjoyment'. Nevertheless, even if we had no direct unit of measurement, the feelings that underlay our buying and selling behaviour were quantitative; and they could be estimated by our willingness to pay various prices to meet our needs: 'The will is our pendulum, and its oscillations are minutely registered in the price lists of the markets.' He conceded, however, that economics dealt only with 'the lowest rank of feelings': it had nothing to say about the 'higher calculus of moral right and wrong' that 'would be needed to show how [man] may best employ that wealth for the good of others as well as himself'.[7]

Keynes's memoir focused almost exclusively on the economic side of Jevons's combative stance, his championing of the principle of 'final' or marginal utility over labour or cost-of-production approaches to the theory of value. Jevons himself laid greater stress on his divergence from Mill's *Logic*.[8] Keynes recognised that logic and scientific method occupied at least as much of Jevons's attention as his work on economics and statistics, but judged Jevons's book on the *Principles of science* not to have stood the test of time as well as his work in these fields. This book, by far Jevons's longest, has acquired admirers since Keynes wrote.[9] But regardless of reputation, it is simply not possible to understand Jevons's attitude to Mill without taking account of the role played by logic and scientific method in forming it. In this respect Jevons was at one with Mill in thinking that systematic differences of opinion in the mental and moral sciences were as likely to turn on different conceptions of the appropriate philosophic method as on questions of fact: 'They differ not solely in what they believe themselves to see, but in the quarter whence they obtained the light by which they think they see it.'[10]

If attention is concentrated on Jevons's economics, the new light he brought to abstract political economy appears to be essentially mathematical,

---

[7] The quotations come from the *Theory*, pp. 8, 13–15, and 29.

[8] See letter to Foxwell, 7 February 1875: 'In regard to what I have said of Mill, I must allow that I should not have expressed so strong an opinion had I been thinking only of his political economy. There is much that is erroneous in his "Principles" . . . but the book is not the maze of self contradictions which his Logic undoubtedly is'; see PC, IV, p. 101. Keynes explicitly denied this when it was put to him by Clara Collet, who knew Jevons during his period as professor at UCL; see JMK, X, p. 138n.

[9] Computing revived interest in Jevons's logical machine, and Jevons's view of scientific inquiry has been seen as an anticipation of Karl Popper's hypothetico-deductive interpretation of its procedures. See W. Mays and D. P. Henry, 'Jevons and logic', *Mind*, 62 (1953), 484–505; and W. Mays, 'Jevons's conception of scientific method', *Manchester School*, 30 (1962), 223–49.

[10] 'On the definition of political economy', as reprinted in CW, IV, p. 324.

and in the case of his applied economics, statistical, with differential calculus facilitating the former and time series, index numbers, and the law of error the latter. Jevons's *Principles of science*, on the other hand, raises broader philosophical questions and encompasses issues of intellectual taste and personal belief as well. Critical remarks on Mill's views on scientific method are scattered throughout this work, but Jevons's most concentrated attempt to undermine Mill's reputation was made in four articles he published in the *Contemporary Review* (1877–9) under the general title of 'John Stuart Mill's philosophy tested'.[11] Here Jevons made one of his frequent complaints that he had 'been compelled by the traditional requirements of the University of London' to employ Mill's works as textbooks for the previous two decades. During the last of these he had come to the conclusion that 'Mill's authority is doing immense injury to the cause of philosophy and good intellectual training in England'. He pledged himself to the task of destroying the 'citadel of [Mill's] logical reputation' as the only means of exposing 'the disconnected and worthless character of his philosophy'.[12]

II

Jevons began by considering three of Mill's most characteristic doctrines in the *Logic*: the demonstration that the rules of geometry conformed with the normal principles of induction; that perceptions of resemblance are essential to the comparisons which underlie our scientific beliefs; and his classification of the various experimental methods available to natural and moral scientists. The fourth essay was devoted to destroying Mill's claims in *Utilitarianism* to have put this philosophy of public affairs on a new footing. On this subject Jevons saw himself, with considerable justification, as a more faithful adherent to the letter and spirit of Bentham's felicific calculus. He took some satisfaction from imagining what damage Bentham would have inflicted on his soi-disant disciple if he had been faced with Mill's 'genial' but unrigorous version of the greatest happiness

---

[11] The articles appeared over a period that stretched from December 1877 to November 1879, and during that period Jevons also inserted 'A fragment on Mill's logic' in the *Owens College Magazine*, January 1879, 81–7. They were republished posthumously in a work entitled *Pure logic; and other minor works*, edited by Robert Adamson, Jevons's colleague at Owens College, and Harriet A. Jevons, his widow (London: Macmillan, 1890). Adamson had consulted the Jevons MSS notes, but considered only one fragment criticising Mill's treatment of the 'method of difference' as worthy of inclusion. The remaining notes passed into the care of Wolfe Mays before he donated them to the Jevons Papers at the John Rylands Library in Manchester.

[12] See *Pure logic*, p. 202.

principle. Mill's qualitative distinction between forms of pleasure was singled out for special condemnation and ridicule.[13]

That this did not exhaust Jevons's interest in the subject can be gauged from the notes he gathered as preparation for a book he hoped to publish after the *Principles of science*. These notes give a more precise chronology for his disenchantment with Mill. They tell us that he first read and dissented from the *Principles of political economy* in 1857, and that by 1868 he had discovered Mill's fallibility as a logician. The contemporaneous record contained in his journal and correspondence broadly confirms these recollections. By 1866, he claimed to be in a position to reveal 'the true logic of the future'; and two years later he composed an early version of the four articles that were to appear in the *Contemporary Review* (the finished articles, as we shall see, were supplemented by evidence derived from Mill's posthumous publications), only to have them rejected by the periodical to which they were originally submitted.[14] In drawing attention to this fact, Jevons was partly concerned to show that there was nothing 'hasty or ill-considered' about his assault, and partly to reveal that he was prepared to publish it during Mill's lifetime – though he also admitted that 'it is probably fortunate for me that I was not allowed prematurely into a controversy of so serious a nature'.[15]

Ten years later he returned to the task, spurred on by 'an accidental discussion' that took place in the columns of the *Spectator*. What provoked this discussion was a letter from someone who signed himself 'G.S.B.' attacking Mill's opinions in the posthumously published *Three essays on religion* on the illusory but captivating qualities of the belief in immortality. This had provoked a defence from W. T. Malleson, one of Mill's admirers, to which in turn Jevons had responded. He accepted Malleson's characterisation of Mill as being scrupulously honest, while pressing home the charge that Mill was guilty of confusion or logical inaccuracy. He illustrated this by drawing attention to the two conflicting definitions of religion given in the essay entitled 'Utility of religion'. In the first of these Mill had said that 'the essence of religion is the strong and earnest direction of the emotions and desires towards an ideal object'. In the second he had spoken of religion as 'the product of the craving to know whether . . . imaginative conceptions have realities answering to them in some other world than ours'.[16] On Jevons's reading, this entailed

---

[13] *Ibid.*, pp. 268–94   [14] See letters to Herbert Jevons, 1 June 1860, PC, II, p. 410; and PC, I, p. 204.
[15] Jevons Papers, John Rylands Library, JA6/5/42–97.
[16] See *The Spectator*, 17 and 20 October 1877. Jevons's letter was published on 27 October, to which Malleson wrote a further reply on 3 November.

a contradiction: ideal and reality were being separated, without any sign that Mill believed it was possible to construct a bridge between them.

Jevons's unpublished notes add to the information we have on how he would have constructed a bridge that would be fit for modern scientists to cross from one world to the other. But Jevons's distaste for any discussion of the utility of religion is prefigured in the preface he wrote to the *Principles of science* and in the peroration to the book.

> We have heard much of what has been aptly called the Reign of Law, and the necessity and uniformity of natural forces has been not uncommonly interpreted as involving the non-existence of an intelligent and benevolent Power, capable of interfering with the course of natural events. Fears have been expressed that the progress of Scientific Method must therefore result in dissipating the fondest beliefs of the human heart. Even the 'Utility of Religion' is seriously proposed as a subject for discussion.[17]

'Reign of Law' was a term given currency by the Duke of Argyll in a book with that title containing a theistic interpretation of natural or scientific laws. Jevons closed his own work with a ringing declaration that 'atheism and materialism are no necessary results of Scientific Method'. Despite being convinced of the progress marked by Darwin's theory of natural selection, and his admiration for Herbert Spencer's evolutionary theory of morals, Jevons clung to one distinctive, though negative, conclusion: 'we cannot disprove the possibility of Divine interference in the course of nature'. The advances of science in recent years had done nothing 'to reduce the number of strange things that we may believe'. Indeed, if we remained faithful to the scientific method it would guide us in the investigation of 'those instincts of the human mind, by which man is led to work as if the approval of a Higher Being were the aim of life'.[18] The innocent 'as if' in this sentence could be a significant statement of faith: it bears the stamp of Jevons's continued adherence to an aspect of his ancestral religion, Unitarianism.[19] We also know that one of the works he did not live to complete was a tenth Bridgewater treatise along the lines of the ninth of these, written by Charles Babbage. Like its predecessors in the series, it would have shown the compatibility of modern science with religion – though not, in Jevons's case, of the biblical variety.[20]

[17] *Principles of science*, 2nd edn (London: Macmillan, 1877), p. ix.
[18] *Ibid.*, p. 769. The quotations appear on pp. 465, 467, and 470 of *Pure logic*.
[19] The case for believing that Unitarianism had special affinity to marginalism is rehearsed in J. Lipkes, 'Religion and the reception of marginalism in Britain', *Forum for Social Economics*, 26 (1997), 21–42.
[20] See H. A. Jevons (ed.), *Letters and journal of W. Stanley Jevons* (London: Macmillan, 1886), pp. 451–5.

This was no late-life conversion: Jevons gave enthusiastic support to Sir John Herschel's protest against the assumptions of a fundamentalist 'Theological declaration of scientific men' being circulated in 1864. Herschel objected to his failure to sign the declaration being construed as a profession of infidelity. Jevons expressed this in a rhetorical question: 'Is it worthy of Religion to assume that it must be discarded by all who freely seek after the Truth?'[21]

What also seems clear is that publication of Mill's *Autobiography* in 1873, in which Mill's irreligion was frankly avowed and later confirmed by the *Three essays on religion*, acted as the final spur, or last straw, to Jevons. Both of these works feature in the *Contemporary Review* articles.[22] In the unused notes he condemns the essays in the following terms:

> I cannot avoid coming to the conclusion that Mill in his own showing should never have published these essays. If Mill believed that there was probably no God, believed that a belief in a good God as far as belief can be ascertained is beneficial, then truth is not good, and Mill should have endeavoured to hide his own belief and persuade people to the contrary.
>
> . . .
>
> There is this obvious difficulty; either Mr Mill must have considered his own argument not fitted to shake the belief of other people, or else he ought not to have published them. If it is desirable for us to cultivate a warm confident belief Mr Mill cannot have helped us in doing so by proving that there really is no God.[23]

This helped to convince Jevons that he should

> no longer consent to live silently under the incubus of bad logic and bad philosophy which Mill's Works have laid upon us. On almost every subject of social importance – religion, morals, political philosophy, political economy, metaphysics, logic – he has expressed unhesitating opinions, and his sayings are quoted by his admirers as if they were the oracles of a perfectly wise and logical mind.[24]

An erroneous political economy was only a small part of this charge, and since Jevons had exposed the theoretical shortcomings of the Ricardo school in the *Theory of political economy*, he did not propose to expend much energy on it in the work he planned. If anything, he was inclined to be generous: 'Mill's Political Economy is the work which will be most esteemed in the future.'[25] The nub of Jevons's objections to what he was

---

[21] Letter to Herschel, 27 September, 1864, PC, III, p. 60. Ironically, perhaps, Herschel later refused to join Jevons and some other natural scientists in Manchester in forming an organisation dedicated to increasing 'the influence possessed by men of science in national affairs'; see PC, III, pp. 236–7.
[22] See *Pure logic*, pp. 200–1, 248–9, 278, 286.   [23] Jevons Papers, JA6/5/76.
[24] *Pure logic*, p. 201.   [25] See Jevons Papers, notes JA6/6/14.

frank in describing in his notes as 'the *evil* of [Mill's] philosophical character' lay elsewhere.

An intricate story needs to be told before we can return to the proximate source of Jevons's antipathy to Mill. But before embarking on that narrative, it may be helpful to recall our starting point. Keynes was right in diagnosing that there was a personal or psychological dimension to Jevons's aversion. But 'morbidity' seems exaggerated when seen against a background that concentrates on Jevons's economics, especially when we bear in mind those features of the Ricardian inheritance he was content to leave untouched.[26] Keynes belonged to the first generation of British intellectuals to be drawn to Freud's concept of the unconscious, and the marks of this are clear in other parts of his memoir on Jevons. He suggested, for example, that Jevons's fears about the exhaustion of natural resources in the *Coal question* could be traced to a form of anal retentiveness – though he was too polite to use that term in a memoir first delivered before Jevons's son and other friends.[27] Yet even the uncensored parts of Jevons's private journal and his letters to family members show that we do not need Freud to explain Jevons's convoluted state of mind: the patient could do so quite effectively himself, even if he did not use 'introvert' to describe it. The title of this essay comes from a statement in one of his letters admitting that his preoccupation with Mill's errors could not entirely be accounted for on intellectual grounds.[28] The letters also reveal another psychological dimension to his relationship with Mill for which the over-used term *Schadenfreude*, or better still, some fluctuating mixture of envy, admiration, and resentment, seems an appropriate label.

III

Jevons's first and only meeting with Mill took place in the lobby of the House of Commons in 1866, where they discussed Jevons's forecast of the rate of depletion of Britain's coal stocks, the leading, even sensational, theme of his book on the question. Mill spoke on the subject in parliament, citing Jevons's book and endorsing his recommendation that retirement of the national debt should be given higher priority in the light

---

[26] A point made by R. D. C. Black when demurring from Keynes in his introduction to the *Theory of political economy* (Harmondsworth: Penguin Books, 1971), p. 29.
[27] See JMK, X, p. 117. He further illustrated this retentiveness by reference to Jevons's propensity to hoard paper.
[28] See letter to Broadfield, 7 April 1878, PC, IV, p. 250.

of his forecasts, a position accepted by Gladstone in his budget of the same year. At the age of thirty, this was Jevons's first taste of public recognition, and it led him to confide the following prayerful mixture of pride and humility to his journal:

What is this poor mind of mine with all its wavering hopes and fears, that its thoughts should be quoted and approved by a great philosopher in the parliament of so great a nation? Do not grant me intellectual power O God unless it be joined to awe of Thee and thy Truth, and to an ever present love of others.[29]

In a letter acknowledging and minimising the significance of the plaudits that came with this public exposure, he wrote that he would gladly exchange them 'for a few kind words from a loving girl'. A proposal of marriage had been turned down a few months before.

The episode gave a major boost to Jevons's career. Having emigrated to Australia for five years at the tender age of eighteen on the basis of a training in the chemistry of assaying, partly as an act of filial piety, partly to rescue the family fortunes; having distinguished himself in a wide range of disciplines at UCL on his return; having obtained recognition from the established authorities for his statistical work on the effect of the Californian gold discoveries on the value of gold, while seeing his first effort to expound his new mathematical theory of economics in 1862 completely overlooked; having sunk to the level of being forced to offer his services as a freelance researcher in London at 3 shillings an hour; and having semi-reluctantly taken a jack-of-all-trades tutorship, reliant on students' fees, at Owens College, Manchester in 1863, Jevons was now able to apply for the Cobden chair of political economy, and hold it in conjunction with the chair of logic, mental and moral philosophy at the same institution. He was armed with testimonials from former teachers, from leading scientists such as Herschel, and from senior members of the small fraternity of economists, including a fellow-alumnus of UCL, Walter Bagehot, as well as William Newmarch, James Thorold Rogers, John Elliot Cairnes, Henry Fawcett, and, above all perhaps, John Stuart Mill. He even obtained a testimonial from another of his heroes, Herbert Spencer, though that said more about the writer than its subject.

Appointment to the Manchester chair provided Jevons with a measure of financial security that had been missing since his father's iron business had been declared bankrupt. The capital he had acquired as a result of the savings from his well-paid occupation in Australia was used to support his unmarried sister and to invest in his own education. He could also now solve the problem of persistent loneliness from which he suffered as a young man living abroad or in lodgings in London: he found a loving girl who was prepared to marry him. In choosing as his partner Harriet Taylor, the daughter of the founder of the *Manchester Guardian*, he succeeded in adding a further link between his own family and that of another powerful branch of the Liverpool–Manchester Unitarian aristocracy. Jevons had at last arrived, and he had done so by hoeing not one hard row but several, in fields as apparently disparate as economics (pure and applied), meteorology, geology, statistics, and logic.[30]

By 1876 the years spent in Manchester had enabled Jevons to build a considerable scientific reputation and earn enough from his popular writings to entertain forgoing salary in return for the advantages that came with taking a lower-paid chair at UCL, a move within the same dissenting milieu he enjoyed in Manchester. At the cost of losing two-thirds of his Manchester income, he could do less teaching and be closer to the metropolitan intellectual circles that now mattered most to him. Taken in conjunction with poor health and a desire to concentrate on what he increasingly called his 'literary' writings, the income from his textbooks, the periodical press, and investments helped him to take the next logical step: he resigned his UCL post in 1880 to concentrate on full-time writing.[31] Unfortunately, he died in a drowning accident two years later, just short of the age of forty-seven. Had he lived longer his life would have been a good example of a successful career sealed by early retirement.

It does not seem entirely fortuitous that Jevons connected the move to London with the theme of this essay in a letter to a friend announcing his intention. By moving to London, he would be able to attend the meetings of the Political Economy Club more regularly. Not only did the club include every leading economist, but as he reminded his friend: 'Mill's opinions were all disseminated and discussed there many years ago, indeed he was a very prominent member.'[32] It would be placing far too much

---

[30] 'Apparently', because the links between these separate pursuits are in some cases close, notably in connection with metereology, where statistical expertise could be carried over into the study of monetary and commercial statistics. The underlying unity of Jevons's enterprise is, of course, a major theme of all significant studies of Jevons's career. On the connections between Jevons's philosophy of natural science and his practice as an economist, see, for example, Mays, 'Jevons's conception of scientific method'.

[31] Keynes (JMK, X, p. 145) cites the cumulative circulation figures up to 1936 for his various works: the *Theory of political economy* (7,000), *Principles of science* (9,000), and *The state in relation to labour* (9,000).

[32] Letter to Broadfield, 6 October 1875, PC, IV, p. 134.

emphasis on a passing remark, however characteristic, to say that Jevons was engaged in a ritual slaying of the father, literally hoping to take the place vacated by Mill's death a few years earlier. But he was certainly keen to reap the benefits he thought Mill and his circle had enjoyed during their period of dominance. In this sense it was another move in his general campaign to further his own ideas at the expense of those associated with Mill.

Morbid or not, there is something over-insistent, even unbalanced, about Jevons's references to Mill and to the conspiratorial successes of the 'Mill faction'. After all, had 'they' not awarded him the Ricardo scholarship in 1860? That his cousin, Richard Holt Hutton, was one of the examiners on this occasion could not have harmed his case. Overlooking the role played by Mill, Fawcett, and Cairnes in supporting his candidacy for the Manchester chair, Jevons exaggerated the deliberateness and effectiveness of the faction in placing their supporters in other professorial and examining posts.[33] Although Jevons could not know this, Mill did not use the Political Economy Club as a vehicle for disseminating his own opinions. Those who observed his behaviour there spoke of his unwillingness to claim authority for his views, and of his interest in the opinions of the younger dissidents, especially Cliffe Leslie and William Thornton. Charles Dilke could also have told Jevons that during his period as a member there were often rows between Mill and Fawcett of a 'semi-socialist' versus individualist nature.[34] But perhaps the most puzzling aspect of Jevons's charges is that he could speak of the faction as having created an atmosphere of 'despotic calm' at a time when the divisions within the political economy community were coming to a head as a result of the wage-fund controversy and the first significant shots in the battle over the relative merits of inductive and deductive methods that were discussed in the preceding essay.

Cairnes noted this discrepancy in his review of the *Theory of political economy* in 1872. Had there ever been a period like the previous twenty years in which there was such widespread questioning of fundamental principles? Anarchy rather than stagnation seemed a better description of the current state of affairs. The only exceptions Cairnes could think of were the popular works of Fawcett and his wife; he did not cite his own writings in support of orthodoxy, and the reference to the Fawcetts

---

[33] See Neil de Marchi's 'The noxious influence of authority: a correction of Jevons' charge', *Journal of Law and Economics*, 16 (1973), 179–89.

[34] See *Political Economy Club: minutes of proceedings* (London, 1921), VI, reminiscences of Lord Courtney, pp. 326, 328; and extracts from the life of Sir Charles Dilke, pp. 309–10.

shows that he was not willing to be lumped together with them. Jevons responded by reiterating his experience as an examiner at the University of London, and by citing an anonymous critic who shared his views on 'the Intellectual Tyranny associated with the name of Mill'.[35] Among the critics of orthodoxy instanced by Cairnes were William Thornton and Francis Longe, two of the authors responsible for persuading Mill to make his famous recantation of the wage-fund theory in 1869. Jevons could have supported his case by pointing out that, despite this recantation, Mill had not revised the last edition of his *Principles* in the light of it. Instead, and very much later, when mounting his final attack on Mill, Jevons used the episode as evidence that Mill was always willing to favour candour over consistency. Mill did leave a confused legacy towards the end of his life, but Jevons damned him for what he did, and could equally have damned him for what he had failed to do.

Jevons made only passing reference to the wage-fund controversy in the preface to the first edition of his *Theory*, but a good deal happened in the seven years that elapsed before Jevons produced the second edition. First, as has been noted, he undertook extensive research on the antecedents, at home and abroad, of his own theory of exchange value, especially mathematical treatments of it. Articles by and correspondence with Fleeming Jenkin in 1868 had been enough to convince him that he needed to put his own work into publishable shape if he was to claim any credit for its originality. But his subsequent inquiries revealed that several other authors in what he had once thought to be a lonely quest had preceded him. Many of them were French or German authors, and he used this fact to underline the dormant situation in Britain, though since he now had to add to the list of British authors who were proceeding along similar lines, the contrast was weakened. Secondly, he paid more attention to the critics of the wage-fund theory, without choosing to go beyond the hints of a new wage theory included in the first edition. Thirdly, he recognised the existence, in the shape of the writings of Cliffe Leslie and J. K. Ingram, of a quite different kind of challenge to orthodoxy from his own.

IV

At this point then we make contact with the *Methodenstreit* once more, a congenial subject for someone who had recently published a book on the

---

[35] See letter to Cairnes, 14 January 1872, PC, III, pp. 245–7. Cairnes's review appeared in the *Fortnightly Review* and is reprinted in PC, VII, pp. 146–52.

principles of science, one of the main conclusions of which was that 'induction is simply an inverse employment of deduction'.[36] In that work, however, there was no equivalent to Book VI of Mill's *Logic* dealing with the methods appropriate to the moral or social sciences. No obvious equivalent that is, though it was clearly Jevons's intention to follow this up with work on the methods appropriate to economics and other social sciences. The methodological divisions revealed during the dinner organised by the Political Economy Club in 1876 to celebrate the hundredth birthday of the *Wealth of nations* provided an opportunity to move in this direction. Like Bagehot, Jevons had been a silent witness at the dinner itself, but he used his inaugural lecture on 'The future of political economy' delivered at UCL in the same year to register his own verdict, some of the conclusions of which were to reappear in the preface to the second edition of the *Theory*. Chaos rather than despotic calm now became the main diagnosis of the state of the discipline, and Jevons was quick to offer a solution that would prevent the dispute from continuing along sterile binary lines. There was no need to be exclusive when it came to choosing between methods; there was room for all positions on an enlarged, but sub-divided map of an expanding realm. Physical science had shown the way: 'It is no more one science than statics, dynamics, the theory of heat, optics, magneto-electricity, telegraphy, navigation, and photographic chemistry are one science.' Economics could similarly be divided into various branches such as 'commercial statistics, the mathematical theory of economics, systematic and descriptive economics, economic sociology, and fiscal science', following Spencer's laws of increasing differentiation of function.[37]

With the exception of sociology, by 1876 Jevons had contributed to each of these sub-divisions. Robert Lowe had sneered at the Comtean neologism during the centenary dinner, but Jevons was prepared to make significant concessions to its advocates, Cliffe Leslie and Ingram at home, Laveleye and Lavergne abroad: 'The present economical state of society cannot possibly be explained by theory alone. We must take account of the long past out of which we are constantly emerging. Whether we call it sociology or not, we must have some scientific treatment of the principles of evolution as manifested in every branch of social existence.'[38] While 'sociology' could raise hackles, 'evolution' was a banner under which many

---

[36] *Principles of science*, p. xxviii.   [37] *Theory*, p. xvii
[38] 'The future of political economy', as reprinted in *Principles of economics* (London: Macmillan, 1905), p. 195.

could march, whether they were followers of Spencer or Darwin, or those, such as Cliffe Leslie, who were impressed by what Maine had done for historical jurisprudence. Jevons used the analogy with jurisprudence to point up a moral for economics: Benthamite systems of analytical jurisprudence could happily co-exist with Maine's investigations into the origin and development of law.[39] But it was the Spencer–Darwin route that Jevons was to pursue himself when he made his own excursions into what he regarded as the sociological dimension.

When seen from either side of the *Methodenstreit*, Jevons occupied a middle position that was unsatisfactory to most other participants. Neither the orthodox defenders of deductive methods, nor their historicist critics could accept his mathematical innovations. Even Bagehot, as we have noted, though well disposed towards Jevons's monetary and statistical studies, could not follow him on the use of mathematics: that appeared to mark a further move away from everyday reality and the categories of common sense.[40] Jevons's claim for his own brand of the abstract theory that the laws dealing with the relationship between human wants and available resources applied 'more or less completely, to all human beings of whom we have any knowledge', regardless of historical and institutional circumstances, ran directly counter to Bagehot's view that political economy applied only to 'a society of grown-up competitive commerce such as we have in England'. It was even more provocative to the new proponents of historicism, for whom the relativism of all economic thinking was a core assumption.[41] To them a history of the human beings that inhabited Jevons's universe would always be in danger of reading like a recurring decimal, a charge they had made against the universalistic pretensions of Ricardianism.

Jevons took no further part in what he probably regarded as sterile and divisive disputes. He had settled his own position, taken comfort from its conformity with practice in the physical sciences, given a blessing to pluralism, and knew where he stood on the more important questions raised by evolution. When he returned to the subject for purposes of

---

[39] 'Future of political economy' in *Principles*, p. 197.   [40] See p. 145 above.

[41] For Jevons's view, see *Principles of economics*, pp. 196–7. Cliffe Leslie was confident, on the basis of the mathematical authority of Ingram, that mathematics could not be applied to economic problems. Ingram maintained that Jevons 'scarcely apprehended the full meaning of the historical method, which he erroneously contrasted with the "theoretical" and apparently supposed to be concerned only with verifying and illustrating certain abstract doctrines resting on independent bases'. See letter from Leslie to Jevons, 27 July 1879, PC, V, p. 68l, and his review of Jevons's *Theory* in PC, VII, pp. 157–61. For Ingram's assessment of Jevons, see *History of political economy* (Edinburgh: A. and C. Black, 1907), pp. 231–3.

attacking Mill it was largely to expose the barrenness of Mill's vestigial Comtism and his lack of genuine understanding of the import of the Spencer–Darwin discoveries.

V

For the reasons noted earlier, Jevons did not feel quite as strongly about Mill's *Principles*: he continued to recommend that his students read this work.[42] He also recommended it for the Bankers' Institute examinations, and cited this as evidence of a fair-mindedness he thought had been lacking in the opposition:

Thus however violent may be my attacks on the logic of Mill I cannot be accused of one sidedness. Nor am I inconsistent, for it is one thing to put forward views for the rational judgement of competent readers; it is another thing to force those views upon young men by means of examinations. The Mill faction never scrupled at putting their lecturers and examiners wherever they could, but I believe it only requires a little clear logic and a little time to overthrow them.[43]

It may be worth recalling that this statement was made some twenty years after he had vowed to avenge himself for his own injuries at the hands of the UCL examiners. Jevons could hold a grudge, and Keynes took the evidence of this, plus his father's testimony, too literally. The publication of lecture notes on the course Jevons gave at Manchester show that while he followed the order of Mill's presentation of the subject, this did not prevent him from incorporating his own theories in his teaching.[44]

In the unused notes, Jevons praised Mill's *Principles* in the following terms:

Where the author is simply expounding a doctrine, adducing evidence, criticising opponents, or otherwise dealing with plain matters, nothing can exceed the lucidity of his statements, and the alluring easy character of his style. The more abstract arguments are agreeably relieved by a moderate amount of illustrations and the practical tendency of doctrines is always kept in view. Perhaps the best of all the divisions of the work is the fifth book treating of the influence of government, and of taxation. The errors contained in this book are comparatively few, and his treatment of the functions of government has but one fault – brevity.[45]

---

[42] 'it will be well to adopt as a textbook Mr J. S. Mill's work on Political Economy. That is the generally recognised treatise on the subject'; inaugural lecture at Manchester, PC, VII, p. 59. See too Jevons's preface to Luigi Cossa's *Guide to the study of political economy*, translated from the 2nd Italian edition (London: Macmillan, 1880): 'the judicious student of Economics must necessarily select the works of Adam Smith, of Ricardo, of J. S. Mill, of Cairnes, or someone of a very few leading English economists, and must study them, so to say, completely'.

[43] Letter to Foxwell, 14 November 1879, PC, V, pp. 80–1.

[44] See the editorial comment of R. D. C. Black in PC, VI, pp. ix–x.   [45] Jevons Papers, JA6/6/14.

Jevons was also prepared to acknowledge the appeal of other writings by Mill, including the essays on Bentham and Coleridge, which he described from a literary standpoint 'as near perfection' as it was possible to be: 'There are no writings on philosophical subjects which it is more easy and agreeable to read. Indeed, I must candidly allow that intensely as I feel the evil of his philosophical character, there is no writer to whose works I more readily recur, or am more surely led to read on when I have once begun.' In obituary style, he acknowledged that we shall not look upon his like again, which could explain why the final item in the collection of unused papers is a newspaper cutting describing Mill's funeral in Avignon.

It is significant that Book V, Mill's treatment of the exceptions to the general presumption in favour of *laissez-faire*, was Jevons's favourite. He was to repair its defect of brevity by exploring the same territory in his *State in relation to labour* and in some of the essays that were collected together as *Methods of social reform* after his death. On matters involving the art of legislation corresponding to the science, Mill and Jevons agreed on the non-existence of what the former had described as *axiomata media* and the latter said was the lack of any 'royal road to legislation': 'in social philosophy, or rather in practical legislation, the first step is to throw aside all supposed absolute rights or inflexible principles. The fact is that legislation is not a science at all; it is no more a science than the making of a ship or a steam-engine, or an electrical machine is a science.'[46]

This dictated that policy questions had to be tackled purely on a pragmatic basis. Jevons's proposal for 'experimental legislation' also conformed to Mill's preference for local, small-scale trials in matters of social reform. Whatever differences there may have been in the two men's conceptions of utilitarianism as a philosophical doctrine, there were substantial similarities in the way in which they applied it to analyse the costs and benefits, or as Jevons usually expressed it, the good and evil, of specific public measures and institutions. Moreover, despite Jevons's objections to Mill's willingness to allow qualitative questions to intrude on the quantitative sphere delineated by Bentham, Jevons was often more forthright in his comments on moral habits and practices that he considered

---

[46] See *State in relation to labour*, 3rd edn (London: Macmillan, 1894), quotations on pp. 171 and 9. Mill's equivalent to this ran as follows: 'I suspect there are none [*axiomata media*] which do not vary with time, place, and circumstances. I doubt if much more can be done in a scientific treatment of the question than to point out a certain number of *pro*'s and a certain number of *con*'s of a more or less general application, leaving the balance to be struck in each particular case as it arises.' Letter to John Austin, 13 April 1847, CW, XIII, p. 712.

evil. This is notably the case with those essays that deal with the coarse-ness of drink-sodden working-class amusements in England, where the remedies required public initiatives to create musical events and free public libraries and museums as well as to regulate the drink trade, where competition had had the effect of increasing levels of intemperance. On such subjects Jevons brought the mature skills of a statistically minded social investigator to bear, on problems that came close to his heart as a music-lover with personal experience of civic enterprises and contem-porary modes of self-improvement. In dealing with the reasons why public enterprise suited the postal and telegraph services, but would not suit the railways, it would be hard to show that Jevons differed much in argumentative style from Mill's excursions into the problems of regu-lating public utilities. There is some point in noting why Jevons became more willing to countenance state action as he grew older, but any attempt at a minute contrast between Mill and Jevons on such matters does not seem likely to be fruitful.

On one subject, however, the employment of women in factories, there was a difference. Whereas Mill, in common with the Fawcetts, man and wife, was opposed to legislative restrictions on grounds of sexual equality, Jevons was in favour of 'complete exclusion of mothers of children under the age of three years from factories and workshops' in the interests of reducing infant mortality.[47] The statistics he collected, which he inter-preted as showing a causal relationship between infant mortality and the number of child-bearing women employed in factories, provided new ammunition here; but as Jevons's wife pointed out, it was his personal experience of the beneficial moral influence of the domestic sphere that supplied the fervour.[48] Provided that the marriage partners enjoyed equality, Mill would have endorsed this sentiment; and he also accepted that within a companionate marriage it was part of the bargain that women should take on the main responsibility for household manage-ment and childcare, renouncing 'not all other objects and occupations,

---

[47] See 'Married women in factories' in *Methods of social reform* (London: Macmillan, 1904), pp. 151–72 and his letter to the *Manchester Guardian* in answer to his critics, 10 January 1882, PC, V, pp. 163–7. Here Jevons did support Mrs Bright's proposals that women who voted in municipal elections should vote in parliamentary ones as well, but he did not see the connection with the issues he had raised, and he added that 'whether women are to have votes or not, there can be no doubt that the proper place of a good housewife is in her house' (p. 165). For a more detailed and critical treatment of this issue as part of a general study of 'Women in Jevons's political economy', see the chapter by Michael V. White in P. Groenewegen (ed.), *Feminism and political economy in Victorian England* (Aldershot: Edward Elgar, 1994), pp. 46–78.
[48] *Letters and journal*, pp. 448–9.

but all which are not consistent with the requirements of this'.[49] As a teacher in a co-educational institution, UCL, Jevons was in favour of higher education for women, but he was hardly unusual in not sharing Mill's passion for female emancipation in all other spheres. It may give some indication of the size of the gap separating him from Mill that he cited the *Subjection of women* in his unused notes to illustrate how the author was prone to 'extreme and sometimes grotesque views'.[50]

VI

On some practical issues Jevons acknowledged that he was simply following where Mill had led. This is well illustrated by the trouble he got into with Manchester radicals in 1866 for some remarks made during an inaugural lecture, sponsored by the Cobden memorial committee, which was designed to disseminate knowledge of the principles of political economy to members of the working classes. One of the main themes was the threat to liberty posed by the growing power of trade unions, with liberty being defined not 'vulgarly' as the privilege of voting in parliamentary elections, but in the fashion portrayed in Mill's *On liberty*, 'that noble essay which is perhaps the best of his great works'.[51] It connoted liberty of conscience and opinion and the liberty of combination as long as the results did not harm others. Jevons's chief object was to point out those ways in which 'our working classes, with their growing numbers and powers of combination, may be led by ignorance to arrest the true growth of our liberty, political and commercial'. The theme was a sensitive one in the wake of the 'Sheffield outrages' of 1865–6, mentioned by Jevons in the lecture (explosions aimed at blacklegs and others out of tune with militant interpretations of trade union rulings), especially when the campaign for an extension of the suffrage that eventually led to the Second Reform Act was just getting under way. When challenged in the press by 'A British Workman', a 'Cobdenite', and a pioneer of the trade union movement, on the grounds that he had taken the employers' position and defiled the memory of Cobden, Jevons denied the charges. Like Cobden he was in favour of free trade in land and improvements in mass education. He was not opposed to the formation of trade unions on a voluntary basis. He was merely adding his 'small voice' to that of men like Mill, Fawcett, and others who were saying that 'a new era will open to the

---

[49] *Subjection of women*, CW, XXI, p. 298.   [50] Jevons Papers, JA6/5/42–97.
[51] See PC, VII, p. 42.

workmen of England when they take measures for sharing in the possession, management, and profits of capital'.[52] Co-operative enterprises were, of course, one of Mill's 'crotchets' and in the more cautious form of industrial partnerships they became part of Jevons's solution to industrial unrest.[53]

What lends interest to this case is that it is one in which the wage-fund theory recanted by Mill, defended by Fawcett, and dismissed by Jevons might have been expected to make some difference. If it did, the result can only be described as a hardening of Jevons's attitude towards the activities of trade unions in fixing wages. As Philip Wicksteed, one of Jevons's chief followers, later maintained, 'Jevons had a strong dislike and suspicion of trade unions, based on economic theory'.[54] That probably understates the case. Jevons was certainly more forthright than Mill in registering a negative verdict on the capacity of trade unions to raise wages: 'On the whole, then, we conclude that it is quite impossible for trade unions in general to effect any permanent increase of wages, and that success in maintaining exclusive monopolies leads to great loss and injury to the community in general.'[55] It also follows that he showed none of Mill's interest in the possibilities of a socialist future. The subject hardly arises in his correspondence or published writings, and the only reference to it in a lecture to a Mechanics Institute dismisses 'socialistic ideas' on 'individualistic' grounds:

Schemes had been proposed with the view of arranging people in the places they should hold; and that promotion should be conducted on some arbitrary system, but competition, after all, seemed to offer something better. He thought all would admit that the motive for pushing their way and exerting their talents was what really conduced to the wealth of the country.[56]

On the subject of another of Mill's major preoccupations, land reform, Jevons supported Gladstone's Irish land legislation.[57] The theory of rent was part of the Ricardian legacy that Jevons was content to express in the new mathematical, or diagrammatic, language. In one of the articles he

[52] Jevons's critics and the answers he gave to them are in PC, III, pp. 123–38, and 143, 153 where Mill is cited once more.

[53] See *State in relation to labour*, ch. 6; see also the essays on 'Industrial partnerships', in *Methods of social reform* (London: Macmillan, 1883).

[54] See P. Wicksteed, *Common sense of political economy*, 2 vols. (London: George Routledge, 1938), II, p. 807.

[55] *State in relation to labour*, p. 109.   [56] See PC, VII, p. 64.

[57] 'My impression is increasing to the effect that landlordism is a terrible burden on the country, and that the just laws of England are rather a myth.' See PC, V. p. 54. For further comment on Gladstone and the Irish land problem, see PC, V, pp. 150, 178, 196

wrote as a young man in Australia, he had commended a land-leasing system as a means of taxing increases in rent, citing Mill, 'the great modern authority in political economy'.[58] That he showed no interest in this form of taxation when he returned to Britain proves little: it does not differentiate him from Fawcett and many economists writing towards the end of the century. It may be more significant that he could not even be bothered to read Henry George's *Progress and poverty*.[59] Nor on the other hand was he prepared to adopt the apologetic opinions of Bastiat on landownership, despite warmness towards this author on grounds of his emphasis on exchange as the key to value.[60] What may be more telling are some brief unpublished jottings he penned on land. One of these rejects Mill's views on the virtues of smallholdings, chiefly because machinery was necessary to advanced agriculture: 'Are we to maintain an old system in order to make labour for poor men – in all other cases economists are aware of the fallacy.'[61] Another expresses exasperation with the amount of attention given to land reform. Compared with regulation of the drink trade and education for the poor, it was not a major element in any personal scheme of reform: 'We must surely give up the notion that we in this country live upon the land – we live upon the world – and upon our coal mines.'[62]

This represents a shift of focus when compared with Mill's emphasis on the agricultural bottleneck, but it does not mean that Jevons was rejecting the Malthusian principle upon which Mill had laid so much stress. In carefully delineating the proper sphere of the abstract science of economics, Jevons had formally announced that the population principle, despite 'its truth and vast importance', no longer played any part in an inquiry that took the following as its central problem: 'Given, a certain population, with various needs and powers of production, in possession of certain lands and other sources of material; required, the mode of employing their labour which will maximise the utility of the produce.'[63] As many later critics of neo-classical economics were later to maintain, this could be read as a sign of the formalism that accompanied adoption of mathematical modes of thinking, allowing what was tractable according

---

[58] PC, VII, p. 7.
[59] 'I have not read George's pamphlet nor his book; but from glancing over the latter I am not inclined to take it up while so many better books are available.' See letter to Rylett, 2 July 1882, PC, V, p. 197.
[60] 'I do not think you need trouble yourself much about Bastiat's opinions in regard to land. They are not, in my opinion, well founded.' PC, V, pp. 196–7.
[61] See Jevons Papers, JA6/14/51.   [62] Jevons Papers, JA6/14/11.   [63] *Theory*, pp. 288–9.

to a particular technique to determine the scientific agenda.[64] In Jevons's case it was simply an example of his penchant for sub-division of the discipline into different branches. His work on the British coal industry was an extended exercise in Malthusian projection, in which he argued that the beneficial feedback mechanisms associated with population growth under a manufacturing system, those currently being enjoyed by Britain, would eventually give way to more sombre conclusions as the price of coal rose. This was Jevons's equivalent to Mill's concerns about population pressure and diminishing returns in agriculture, and it represented a move towards the energy source that was essential to Britain's manufacturing pre-eminence – a reflection, perhaps, of Jevons's family background, Manchester residence, and scientific interests in industrial technology. Compared with Mill's lack of confidence in the capacity of technology to give permanent relief to living standards, Jevons had plenty: he visited the Great Exhibition of 1851 on several occasions and was a keen visitor to other international exhibitions as well, the last of which was the Electrical Exhibition in Paris in 1881. What is strange, then, is why Jevons proved so unwilling to explore the implications of increasing returns in manufacturing, and was not prepared to entertain the idea that alternative technologies would be found to relieve the energy bottleneck posed by declining coal stocks.

Together with his work on trade cycles, the interest Jevons had in long-term growth trends shows that he was not seeking to confine economics to static allocation problems. Similarly, his inquiry into infant mortality rates was clearly at heart a Malthusian inquiry. Improvidence, misdirected charity, and the failure to stand by the 1834 principles of poor relief remained almost as much of a theme in Jevons's writings on poverty as it had been in the writings of Malthus, Ricardo, and Mill.[65]

Although Jevons could pronounce confidently on legislative matters when he had made a special study of them, he was neither as self-assured nor as radical as Mill and Fawcett when it came to expressing opinions on wider constitutional and other political issues, such as those raised by Ireland or foreign affairs.[66] Jevons's Manchester critics were right to suspect that he was lukewarm on the suffrage question. By contrast with advanced liberals of the Mill–Fawcett variety, he appears to have been a

---

[64] The first economist to make this observation when faced with Jevons's limitation was Cliffe Leslie; see his review of the *Theory* as reprinted in PC, VII, p. 158.

[65] PC, III, p. 255.

[66] 'Being an economist and not a politician, I hardly like to venture upon the wide and stormy field of the Irish Question.' See letter to Rylett, 2 July 1882, PC, V, p. 197.

middle-of-the-road Gladstonian liberal, a conventional and patriotic member of the Victorian middle classes who had taken pride in his membership of the volunteers in 1859 when there were fears of an outbreak of war between Britain and France. He retained a strong respect for the traditional elements in the British constitution. When Mill and Fawcett were about to add women to the proposals for an extension of the suffrage in 1867, Jevons was confiding the following hesitant statement of his political inclinations to his journal:

> What side am I to take . . . or can I take both? I cannot consent with the radical party to obliterate a glorious past – nor can I consent with the conservatives to prolong abuses into the present. I wish with all my heart to aid in securing all that is good for the masses, yet to give them all they wish and are striving for is to endanger much that is good beyond their comprehension. I cannot pretend to underestimate the good that the English monarchy and aristocracy with all the liberal policy actuating it, does for the human race, and yet I cannot but fear the pretensions of democracy against are strong and in some respects even properly strong.[67]

This was to some extent a reflection of a more professional ethic that accompanied the academic status Jevons had acquired but which Mill neither sought nor desired. Not only should economics and politics be distinguished, in Jevons's opinion, but also politics did not have the characteristics necessary to make it a science: 'About politics, I confess myself in a fog. . . . I prefer to leave *la haute politique* alone, as a subject which admits of no scientific treatment. I have enough to think and write about which I can somewhat understand, without troubling myself about things which I cannot understand.'[68]

VII

Jevons's mixture of admiration and resentment towards Mill may have turned antipathy into something more complex, but we know that the aversion was sufficiently strong for him to plan yet one more settling of the score. It is apparent from the frequency with which Jevons felt it necessary to justify his attack on Mill that he was aware of the danger of

---

[67] PC, I, pp. 207–8. See also his comment in a letter dated 28 December 1866 (PC, III, p. 150): 'It is very difficult to know what view to take of this Reform agitation. I am not a democrat as perhaps you know and don't much care to adopt popular views to please the mob. However I don't think any reform bill that is likely to pass will really upset our system here, while it may lead to many real improvements.'

[68] PC, IV, p. 293.

appearing to be gratuitous if not obsessive. Had he not been, his friends and opponents would have supplied the correction. Robert Adamson, his colleague at Manchester, warned him to be more careful when speaking of Mill ('your language regarding him is a little bitter'), though the effect on this occasion was merely to make Jevons substitute 'difficult and tedious' for 'unutterably tedious' when referring to Mill's chapters on international values.[69] After reading the *Contemporary Review* articles, Sidgwick, who had met and got on well with Jevons during one of his examining trips to Cambridge, and whose *Methods of ethics* was praised in the *Contemporary Review* articles, had written to say that Mill was not unique among philosophers in infringing the law of non-contradiction, mentioning Spencer as another example. Jevons replied as follows:

I am pleased to have your ideas about my attack on Mill, but while quite agreeing that most philosophical writers break the law of non-contradiction, I should hold in Herbert Spencer's case, the breaches are in matters of detail and that after striking off all errors there remains a new and true philosophy. In Mill, con-tradiction is of the essence of his method, I am sorry to hold.[70]

Other readers of the same articles took to the pages of *Mind* to correct Jevons, including the editor himself, George Croom Robertson, who delivered a sarcastic reproof and a challenge. If Jevons had been aware of the deficiencies of Mill's logic for twenty years, and if these defects were so widely understood, even among those who think highly of Mill on other grounds, 'for whose benefit, then, one wonders is this series of papers to be written?' Yes, Mill had engaged in some heavy criticism himself in his *Examination of Sir William Hamilton's philosophy*, but it had been in a positive cause. Why did Jevons not indicate what his own alternative was: 'will he for once in a way, tell us quite plainly what he considers are all the elements of a *true* empirical philosophy?' This would fill a gap in Jevons's *Principles of science*, and it could be accomplished 'without the accompaniment of a war-dance over the prostrate form of Mill'. The 'prejudiced and unthinking' might appreciate such perform-ances, but 'at the end Mill will be found to hold just the place that he holds now in the estimation of serious thinkers who know what is and what is not. Will Prof. Jevons retain *his* place?'[71] Coming from a pupil of Alexander Bain, Mill's friend, this might have been expected. Jevons responded shrewdly with a question of his own: if Robertson was aware of

---

[69] Adamson also drew Jevons's attention to passages where Mill was alive to some of the criticisms that Jevons was levelling against his theories; see letters from Adamson in PC, V, pp. 60–2.
[70] See letter to Sidgwick, 28 February 1879, PC, V, p. 24.   [71] *Mind*, 3 (1878), 141–4.

Mill's inconsistencies, how could he object to an attack on them? He felt under no obligation as a critic to construct an alternative system, though he could hardly be accused of not going some way towards this in his *Principles*.

Some of these comments and criticisms were in Jevons's mind when he was summoning up his dwindling energies to mount the final assault. In the unused notes he mentions being criticised for 'needless warmth and strength of language' in the *Contemporary Review* articles: 'If so I much regret the fact and will endeavour, in the present work to keep within due limits.' On the other hand, he drew attention to Mill's advocacy of frank expression of views in *On liberty*, and his 'free and unsparing criticism' of Hamilton. The conspiracy idea reappears at this juncture. Mill and Morley might 'descant upon the mischievous influence of sectarian feeling', but 'it would be difficult to point to any modern philosopher who was more distinctly the head of a definite and compact school of followers'. In defending 'the propriety of my work both in purpose and in manner', Jevons did so in the full knowledge that it was

> an invidious and unwelcome task to attack a man of great and pure reputation; it gives an opportunity for all kinds of misconstruction, and such has not been altogether wanting. But after years of consideration I decided to incur whatever risk there might be in attacking not only one who was supposed to be a great logician and philosopher but one who was undoubtedly the acknowledged master of a powerful and well united sect.[72]

There is something to be said for Robertson's challenge, ill-intentioned though it may have been at the time. By the end of the 1870s Jevons was a well-established figure with ample achievements to his credit, while Mill's reputation was well past its peak. Jevons could simply have done what others, notably Sidgwick, were to do when reminiscing about their own intellectual histories and the intellectual history of the disciplines with which they were associated. He could have delivered a funeral oration showing why Mill, despite his accomplishments, was now an outdated figure. By Jevons's standards there is no doubt that he was a pre-scientific one. Mill's knowledge of the natural sciences was largely second-hand; and he had not appreciated the analogies between the physical and social

---

[72] Jevons Papers, JA6/5/42–97. Jevons was right about the risks. The following statement in Justin McCarthy's book on *England under Gladstone* was to give offence to his widow: '[Jevons] owed his success in life largely to Mr Mill's generous recognition of his ability as a young man and it was regrettable that he should have devoted much of the latter part of his life to a futile and ungrateful attempt to lower Mr Mill's reputation as a thinker and philosopher.' See R. Könekamp, 'The work of Harriet Ann Jevons (1838–1910) after her husband's death', *Manchester School*, 50 (1982), 393.

sciences that licensed a parallel use of mathematics in economics. Nor was he capable of grasping the mathematical features of Jevons's logic.[73] As an interpreter of scientific procedures he suffered from the defect of not being able to appreciate the significance of the theory of probability, a major deficiency when economic and social inquiry was increasingly adopting ever more sophisticated statistical methods.[74] He was not impervious to the attractions of Darwin's theory of natural selection, and his step-daughter maintained, in her preface to the *Three essays on religion*, that if they had been written after the works of Darwin and Maine had appeared, Mill would have noted the 'coincidence of thought' with these authors.

Jevons may not have known about Mill's acceptance of Darwin's 'hypothesis'; he makes no reference to it in his attack. He cited Darwin's criticism of Mill in the *Descent of man*, a criticism delivered more in sorrow than in anger as a result of Darwin's admiration for Mill's liberalism: 'The ignoring of all transmitted mental qualities will, as it seems to me, be hereafter judged as a most serious blemish in the works of Mr Mill.'[75] To this could have been added Mill's unwillingness to countenance a sexual division of labour based on 'transmitted mental qualities'. Jevons dismissed the claims of the step-daughter as 'amiable and pardonable bias': 'The fact is that the whole tone of Mill's moral and political writings is totally opposed to the teaching of Darwin and Spencer, Tylor and Maine.'[76] Mill was 'the last great philosophic writer conspicuous for his ignorance of the principles of evolution'. Placing him between two of his own heroes, Jevons found Mill lacking in the virtues of either; he had discarded much that was admirable in Bentham, while failing to appreciate that Spencer's evolutionist principle embodied

---

[73] Mill's testimonial for Jevons in 1866 states that if he had a fault to find 'it would be that the expenditure of power was greater than any result to be obtained' by the use of symbols in his formal logic; see PC, III, p. 120. He was more forthcoming about Jevons's 'useless complications' and use of a notation 'implying the existence of a greater precision in the data than the questions admit of' in a letter to Cairnes, 5 December 1871, CW, XVII, pp. 1862–3.

[74] See *Principles of science*, pp. 200–1, 222–3 for Jevons's criticisms of Mill's incomprehension.

[75] *Descent of man* (1871), as reprinted by Prometheus Books (New York, 1998), p. 101n. Frances Power Cobbe, a Christian and a conservative feminist who took issue with the moral implications of Darwinism, reported that Darwin had told her 'Mill could learn some things from physical science; and that it is in the struggle for existence and (especially) for the possession of women that men acquire their vigour and courage'; see *Life of Frances Power Cobbe by herself*, 2 vols. (Boston: Houghton Mifflin, 1894), II, p. 445. On the divergence between Mill and Darwin on these subjects see my 'Darwin fallen among political economists', *Proceedings of the American Philosophical Society*, 145 (2001), 415–37.

[76] *Pure logic*, p. 290.

'a more truthful philosophy of morals than was possible before his time'.[77] These two great bodies of thought could now be reconciled. Spencer's *Data of ethics* published in 1879 was welcomed by Jevons precisely because it revealed that 'a definite step has been made in a matter debated since the dawn of intellect. The moral sense doctrine, so rudely treated by Bentham, is no longer incapable of reconciliation with the greatest happiness principle, only it now becomes a moving and developable moral sense.' In the unused notes Jevons spoke of Spencer's philosophy as being 'infinitely to be preferred to that of Mill', and it was with the 'grotesque' essays on religion to hand that he thought the comparison showed Mill at his weakest.

The murderous cruelty of Nature; the self dependence of poor little mortals, destined to struggle with Nature in the hope of reforming her; the evanescent mocking hope that perhaps after all the state of things may not be quite so bad; there may possibly exist a God or even a Jesus Christ; and we must make the best of this faint possibility. This is cheerful indeed and this is what we reach by following philosophy devoid of logic. Mill represents human beings as so many little gods who though they have free will, must set to work vigorously to reform themselves and each other, unless they wish everything to go to the bad. He actually seems to have realised in a certain way this view of things, and to have fallen into despair whenever the controversies of the day went against himself and the small band of philosophic radicals with whom he acted. It never seemed to have occurred to him that things are not necessarily just as they seem to be at the moment. He ignored the existence of any Forces which might be working behind and within, and of which we ourselves might be the slight instruments and creatures.

   The Spencerian philosophy leads, however, (at least it leads me) to a totally different view of things. Murderous though nature may still seem, she carefully kills off those in preference who are detriment. Mankind degenerates when forced to inhabit the Arctic regions like the Esquimaux. But I see nothing in this to exclude the existence of a Benevolent Power. In retrograding the being becomes more suited to his circumstances: more capable therefore of happiness. The machine-producing machine of evolution would be working badly if it turned out machines unfitted to the environment. But however this be we must accept a philosophy which is true, and we may well be thankful that things are not worse. We are not little self dependent gods fighting with malignant nature, and sure, one would think, to be crushed. On the contrary we are ourselves the products, the manifestations of an all prevailing tendency towards the Good and the Beautiful. We are the latest springs of creations, and as in the workings of maternal nature we look for an explanation of every material phenomenon, so are we to look for explanations of those feelings of good which are in the human heart.[78]

[77] *Ibid.*, pp. 289–91.   [78] Jevons Papers, JA6/5/42–97.

The published version of this ends by equating the good and the beautiful with happiness, the Benthamite measure: 'Creation is not yet concluded, and there is no one of us who may not become conscious in his heart that he is no Automaton, no mere lump of Protoplasm, but the Creature of a Creator.'[79] Jevons was well on the way to his Bridgewater treatise.[80]

What mattered to Jevons were the deficiencies of Mill's Comtean religion of humanity when compared with what Jevons took to be the message of Spencer's evolutionary theory of morals. Jevons had undergone some changes in his moral philosophy, some wavering even in his faith. As a young man he described himself as a 'dependent moralist', one who denied the existence of a 'moral sense' that could be separated from 'our animal feelings', an orthodox Benthamite conclusion.[81] His journal contains evidence of early disenchantment with the gospels and revealed religion, and in letters to his sister, Henrietta, with whom he corresponded on these matters, he once described himself as an atheist, holding only to a belief in human sympathy or love.[82] But he seems to have shifted easily back to the type of theism that was common among Unitarians, and which for reasons of heart as well as head he was anxious to defend. His wife spoke of 'a deep religious feeling at the bottom of his nature which made the materialist tone of the day as alien to him'.[83] The heart reveals itself, as would be expected, when personal recourse to philosophy has to be made. Some features of Mill's religious belief have been traced to the sense of loss he felt after his wife's death. Similarly with Jevons: writing to a friend in 1878 to sympathise with a death in his family, Jevons recalled the death of his brother.

If any one has had cause to doubt the benevolent government of human affairs, it is I and my brothers and sisters; and yet nothing can eradicate from my mind the belief there must be a brighter side to things, and that we do not see all. It may be very unscientific, and 'exact thinkers' like Mill may have proved the opposite. In that case I must consent to remain among the unscientific.[84]

---

[79] *Pure logic*, p. 294.
[80] In addition to the pages from this treatise published by his wife, there are extensive notes on the theme of 'human nature and development' in the Jevons Papers, JA6/36/1–86. They consist of notes on Darwin's two main works, Tylor's early history of mankind, Herschel's physical geography, Helmholtz on conservation of force, George Lewes, Max Müller on language, Froude, and George Eliot's *Felix Holt*.
[81] See PC, I, pp. 66, 133, 158, 180.   [82] See *Ibid.*, pp. 99, 154–7, 258, 325–7, 379.
[83] *Letters and journal*, p. 451; see also the testimony of his granddaughter, R. Könekamp, biographical introduction to PC, I, p. 52.
[84] Letter to Broadfield, 7 April 1878, PC, IV, p. 250.

As we have seen, Jevons was far from consenting to this description of himself. Proving that Mill was unscientific was a way of dispelling what was chilling in his religion of humanity and preserving what was comforting in Spencer's. Mill's 'evil' was to have slighted one of the basic tenets by which Jevons had always conducted his private life, and to have failed to recognise the inspiriting public moral Jevons read into Spencer's philosophy. Heart and head could be reconciled.

PART III

Free exchange and economic socialism

Fig. 5. Sir Louis Mallet. Photograph of a
drawing by Philip Homan Miller
published in 1896.

Fig. 6. Henry Sidgwick. Photograph *c.* 1860
when he was 52.

7

Louis Mallet and the philosophy of free exchange

I do not believe that . . . there is any happiness to be compared to that of the intercourse between a master who finds a pupil worthy of him and a pupil who finds a master worthy of him. But in such intercourse it is absurd to assign to the disciple a passive part. What the disciple afterwards gives out as the faith of the master is really a joint product of their two minds, and their two individualities.

I

In the letter that provides my epigraph, the diplomat Robert Morier, a fellow disciple of Cobden, had credited Louis Mallet with having upheld 'more perfectly and completely than Cobden did himself, the higher and more ideal side of the Cobdenic creed'.[1] Although Mallet denied this, Morier was right in thinking that Mallet's version of Cobdenism represented the creed in one of its least pragmatic forms. By the time this was revealed to a larger public in 1891 as a result of the posthumous publication of *Free exchange*, a collection of Mallet's published and unpublished writings, it was obvious that he spoke for a version of Cobdenism that had been in retreat for two decades or more.[2] It was retreating in the face of two main threats, one against which Cobdenites had long fought under banners that bore either 'non-intervention' or 'peace and retrenchment', the other arising from extensions of the suffrage that were shifting

[1] Letter from Morier to Mallet, quoted in Bernard Mallet, *Sir Louis Mallet: a record of public service and political ideals* (London: J. Nisbet, 1905), p. 36. This biography by his eldest son, who also wrote the original DNB entry on his father, has not been superseded. It quotes many letters without giving their dates and authors. Where possible I have supplemented the son's evidence by consulting the collections referred to in later notes.
[2] *Free exchange: papers on political and economical subjects including chapters on the law of value and the unearned increment by the late Right Honourable Sir Louis Mallet, CB* edited by Bernard Mallet (London: Kegan Paul, 1891).

political initiatives towards more interventionist interpretations of the proper role of the state. The first of these was a recrudescence of expansionist versions of the imperial idea, symbolised by the events leading up to the occupation of Egypt in 1882 and by rising levels of expenditure on armaments. It had merely acquired a new name, 'jingoism', a word that replaced Cobden's 'panic mongering'. On that well-rehearsed topic, Mallet, by the end of his official career, could speak with the authority of someone who had experience of administering the imperial system from its Indian pinnacle, a vantage point that also required him to take a position on the Russian menace, real, or as he believed, one capable of being appeased by collaboration.

Mallet had no hesitation in labelling the second threat as 'socialism'. While this could refer to self-avowed socialist ideas, for Mallet it chiefly described something more threatening: what was happening within the Liberal party and on the 'progressive' wing of British politics. By the 1880s the Cobden Club had also become infected. Its most obvious recent manifestations were the Irish Land Act of 1881, which interfered in the contractual relations of landlord and tenant, and the radical 'unauthorised programme' published by Joseph Chamberlain in 1885. Jingoism and socialism, on Mallet's reading of these signs of the times, were both predictable outcomes of the revival of those retrograde nationalist and protectionist forces against which Cobden had struggled with some success in the 1850s and 60s. Belief that he had survived into a world in which these forces were jeopardising the prospects of progressing towards the Cobdenite millennium lends an embattled quality to Mallet's correspondence and the writings he tried to complete during the final years of his life. They reflect a mood of mounting despair, not merely that the true version of the creed was no longer understood by the younger generation, but that it was being actively betrayed.

There can be few qualms about appropriating the religious overtones of faith, creed, and even millennial hopes to describe Mallet's identification with Cobdenism. He shared with Cobden a profound conviction that there was a 'perfect harmony of moral and economical laws'. Bringing the understanding of such natural laws to bear on a corrupted world required taking a stand on the 'rock of God's providence' rather than on the 'quicksand of human invention'. Drawing on family memories, the experience of his grandfather, Jacques Mallet du Pan, a Huguenot refugee from the first French revolution of 1789, Mallet attributed the failure of the revolution to a denial of this truth: a belief that personal liberty and the right to private property were the creation of man-made law rather than a divinely inspired prerequisite of any just system of law.[3] Close rapport between master and pupil had been established while Mallet was acting as Cobden's lieutenant on the home front during the negotiations that led up to the Anglo-French trade treaty in 1860. As Cobden wrote to a long-standing friend and ally at the time, 'I never met with any one who more completely shared our opinions, and our animus.'[4] Devotion to Cobden's memory, defence of his opinions, and animosity towards opponents of the creed were to provide the keynote of Mallet's career as a civil servant in the Board of Trade, as leader of trade missions to Berlin, Paris, Turin, and Vienna, and finally, and more incongruously for someone who fully endorsed Cobden's misgivings about Britain's eastern empire, as Permanent Under-Secretary of State for India from 1874 to 1883.

As one of Cobden's closest collaborators during the final years of Cobden's life, Mallet was widely recognised as keeper of the Cobdenite conscience. Two years after Cobden's death in 1865 he wrote an account of Cobden's political opinions that reached a larger audience when reissued by the newly founded Cobden Club.[5] It was part summary of achievements, part statement of unfinished business. He also recruited John Morley and then actively assisted (monitored might be a better description) the composition of what became the standard *Life of Richard Cobden*.[6] Regrettably from Mallet's point of view, these memorialising successes were accompanied by a string of Whitehall reverses when the policy of achieving multilateral free trade via bilateral trade treaties with European nations, using the most-favoured-nation clause, was repudiated in favour of the more rigidly unilateralist policy adopted by Robert Lowe as Gladstone's Chancellor of the Exchequer. Mallet was left to conduct a largely unavailing rearguard action in support of the treaty alternative from a Board of Trade that had seen the transfer to the Foreign Office of the commercial division he had headed. Although the transfer had Mallet's blessing, Foreign Office resistance to granting commercial expertise any

---

[3] *Free exchange*, pp. 13–14.

[4] Letter from Cobden to Hargreaves, 26 December 1861, Cobden Papers, West Sussex Record Office.

[5] 'The political opinions of Richard Cobden' appeared in the *North British Review*, March 1867, and then as an introductory essay to the *Political writings of Cobden*. The version cited here is that reprinted in *Free exchange*, pp. 3–71.

[6] As Morley said in the preface to the second edition (1881): 'It was [Mallet] who first induced me to undertake a piece of work which he had much at heart, and he has followed it with an attention, and interest, and a readiness in counsel and information, of which I cannot but fear that the final product gives a very inadequate idea.' See too a letter from Mallet to Gladstone, 26 January 1875. Cobden Papers, West Sussex Record Office, vouching for Morley's suitability as a biographer, despite political differences.

standing beside the more traditional aristocratic concerns of ordinary diplomacy ensured that he was not part of it. He was forced to watch the treaty policy crumble from a distance, fuming at the incompetent and ineffective efforts of the Foreign Office to combat what he could only regard as a policy of 'isolation', a failure on the part of Lowe's 'school of English chauvinism' to build on the pan-European initiatives he had pioneered with Cobden in the 1860s.[7]

While these battles within the civil service for control over the direction of Britain's trade policy occupied much of Mallet's energies when he was at the Board of Trade, he was also keen, especially after his retirement, to campaign against those members of a wider intellectual community whom he judged to be guilty of lending support to forces antagonistic to Cobden's goals.[8] In practice this meant that he considered it essential to conduct a counter-offensive against the 'English' school of political economy, chiefly as represented by Mill and his followers. Here too Mallet's discipular contribution had some markedly individual – indeed, individualistic – characteristics. Whatever political economy he may have learned from his father, John Lewis Mallet, a founder member of the Political Economy Club, was consolidated at the Board of Trade when that department was at the heart of the early moves towards freer trade. Mallet also found it necessary to examine more closely and critically those trends in professional economic thinking – increasingly taking place within universities – that only became manifest in the decades after Cobden's death. As a member of the Political Economy Club from 1870 onwards, and as an examiner of the prize essay competitions sponsored by the Cobden Club in the 1880s, he was in a good position to take the intellectual temperature of a body of knowledge that he regarded as essential to all sound statesmanship.[9] Though practical realities and hard economic facts were part of his daily existence, Mallet's chief interest lay in fundamental principles. Sound economic theorising was what mattered and 'empiric' became a term of abuse in his vocabulary, somewhat akin to opportunism.

---

[7] See Mallet's letter to T. B. Potter, 17 March 1879 on 'Reciprocity', as reprinted in *Free exchange*, p. 132.

[8] A sample of Mallet's views can be found in the essays on commercial treaties and reciprocity in *Free exchange*.

[9] 'It is the fashion with "practical men" to distrust principles, but there is no government worthy of the name without them, and for my own part every year's experience only convinces me more and more of what I have held from a boy that there can be no statesmanship without a foundation of economical knowledge.' Cited in *Sir Louis Mallet*, p. 152 without identifying the source.

II

Unlike most of his peers in a remarkable generation of senior civil servants, Mallet did not enjoy the advantages of a public school and university education.[10] Self-education could well have been a source of personal sympathy between him and Cobden. University qualifications, often supplemented by membership of the Bar, were increasingly important in the world heralded by the Northcote–Trevelyan reforms, even though patronage was still the main route into what later became the administrative class.[11] Like his father before him, Mallet entered the service as a junior clerk in the Board of Audit at the age of sixteen. When he took up his Indian duties he may have been the first person to complete the journey from junior clerk to Permanent Under-Secretary.[12] In doing so he succeeded his cousin, Herman Merivale, whose contrasting career illustrates the meritocratic advantages conferred by a brilliant university beginning. Merivale obtained a first in classics at Oriel College, Oxford and was elected to a fellowship at Balliol. After being called to the Bar he was elected to the Drummond Chair of Political Economy; he entered the civil service as successor to Sir James Stephen as Permanent Under-Secretary at the Colonial Office on the strength of these qualifications and the publication of his Oxford lectures on colonies and colonisation. He was offered the job at a salary of £1,500 p.a. without interview.[13]

Mallet was a late convert to the Cobdenite cause. Unlike Bagehot, for example, he was not excited by the extra-parliamentary campaign against the Corn Laws conducted by Cobden and Bright during the 1840s; and it was some time before he came to regard free trade as anything better than a palliative for inequality and social injustice.[14] There are hints of a personal tendency towards socialism which may have been averted by an early encounter with Frédéric Bastiat's *Harmonies économiques*, an attack on a combined target of French protectionism and socialism provoked by

---

[10] As an indication of the relevant peer group, the following civil servants became members of the Political Economy Club alongside Mallet: Herman Merivale, Edwin Chadwick, George Cornewall Lewis, Henry Thring, Stafford Northcote, and Thomas H. Farrer.

[11] See Henry Parris, *Constitutional bureaucracy: the development of British central administration since the eighteenth century* (London: Allen and Unwin, 1969).

[12] This was the claim of Bernard Mallet (*Sir Louis Mallet*, p. 104) who achieved his own senior status as a civil servant via the more conventional route of Balliol.

[13] The appointment has been judged to be 'an extreme case of appointment by merit alone'; see Parris, *Constitutional bureaucracy*, p. 74.

[14] Mallet appreciated the League's activities better when dealing with Cobden's record in retrospect than he did at the time. Compare remarks cited in *Sir Louis Mallet*, pp. 19–22 with *Free exchange*, pp. 5, 12, 21–2, 27–31.

manifestations of both of these during the 1848 revolution. Mallet's first statement of approval of Cobden's position was one of agreement with the stance he took in opposing the Crimean war, temporarily losing his seat in parliament as a result. Full conversion did not occur until Mallet was given an opportunity to work with Cobden on the Anglo-French trade treaty.[15] Their collaboration proved highly successful. While Cobden was in Paris Mallet kept him informed about potential threats to the negotiations coming from the Treasury and the Foreign Office, handled much of the detail on tariff schedules, reported on the reactions of chambers of commerce throughout the country, fed the press with items that would keep the subject in the public eye, and was determined that Cobden should receive sole credit for the outcome.[16] Cobden was an exception to the ordinary run of politicians Mallet had encountered; he was 'one who fully realised the noblest ideal of a statesman, a man of perfect honesty, courage, independence, and consistency, guided by a rare combination of wisdom and benevolence'.[17] Such a tribute may appear to have ritual features, but its sincerity is confirmed when read alongside Mallet's frequent private complaints about the low standards of public life in Britain – complaints from which he exempted Peel but not, significantly, Gladstone.[18]

Mallet claimed that his French ancestry distinguished him from the ordinary flag-waving patriots who sneered at Cobdenites as 'peace at any price men':

I am a French Protestant by blood, and should be unworthy of my father, if I were not ready to shake the dust off my feet and leave my country on one side, if it trampled down great principles of human freedom in the pursuit of selfish

---

[15] The above is based on the meagre evidence assembled by Bernard Mallet (see *Sir Louis Mallet*, pp. 19–32). His father left no connected account of the steps he took towards conversion, and the son was unable to establish whether his father encountered Bastiat's writings before or after his collaboration with Cobden, a fact that could be of some significance to his adherence to the Cobdenite cause, as will be clear from what is said later.

[16] See the frequent letters exchanged by Cobden and Mallet during the negotiations in the Cobden Papers at the West Sussex Record Office and the British Library, and in the Mallet Papers, Balliol College. On 5 December 1860, for example, Mallet wrote that 'I shall be very jealous of any appropriation by [Gladstone], or any one else, of the merit of the Treaty. The credit is Richard Cobden's alone.'

[17] *Sir Louis Mallet*, p. 35, quoting a letter written after Cobden's death.

[18] During the treaty negotiations Mallet regarded Gladstone with almost as much suspicion as he did Palmerston; see letters written on 27 April 1862 and 2 February 1865, Cobden Papers, West Sussex Record Office. See too his letter to Grant Duff, 11 April 1868, stating that '[Gladstone] has not I think *originated* any great fiscal principle. He has merely carried on Peel's policy.' Papers of Grant Duff, India Office Select Materials, British Library, MSS Eur F234/37. On the complexities of the relationship between Gladstone and Cobdenism, see Anthony Howe, 'Gladstone and Cobden', in D. Bebbington and R. Swift (eds.), *Gladstone centenary essays* (Liverpool: Liverpool University Press, 2000), pp. 114–32.

aims. I love my country, not because I happen to have been born a cockney, which seems to me to be the stupidest form of patriotism, but because on the whole she seems to me to have done more for the human race so far than any other with whose history I am acquainted, and because I see the possibility of achievements far higher than any she has yet to record.[19]

Such high-flown sentiments feature a great deal in Mallet's writings, including, as in the above case, letters to friends, though on this occasion the tone may have been affected by the knowledge that Morley hoped to publish the exchanges between Mallet and Morier in the *Fortnightly Review*. The conviction that Britain was destined to accomplish even greater things if it pursued the internationalist ideals of Cobden amounted to a bid for a higher kind of disinterested or cosmopolitan patriotism. As we shall see, it diverged sharply from the patriotic sentiments cultivated by the new generation of historical economists.[20]

On a less exalted plane, there can be no doubt that Mallet's Anglo-French credentials played a part in giving his version of the Cobdenite creed a more explicit theoretical or doctrinal basis. Cobden's friendship with Bastiat, the leading publicist for free trade in France, allowed Mallet to assemble and embellish a credo based on a composite figure:

These two men were necessary to each other. Without Cobden, Bastiat would have lost the powerful stimulant of practical example, and the wide range of fact which the movement in England supplied, and from which he drew much of his inspiration. Without Bastiat, Cobden's policy would not have been elaborated into a system, and beyond his own immediate coadjutors and disciples would probably have been imperfectly understood on the Continent of Europe.[21]

Another result of his reading of Bastiat was Mallet's construction of a Manichean narrative of economic thinking in which all that was good resided with a 'French' school of economic theorists that could be traced back to Condillac, and all that was evil could be traced to an 'English' school that began promisingly, if not entirely securely, with Adam Smith and had degenerated badly in the hands of Ricardo, Mill, and their followers. Smith had remained Cobden's favourite economic authority. Despite the centrality of the Corn Laws to Ricardo's restatement of the Smithian position, his writings played little or no part in the thinking and

---

[19] Mallet to Morier, 26 January 1878, Morier Papers, Balliol College.
[20] See pp. 266–7 below.
[21] *Free exchange*, p. 23. How Morley intended to handle the relationship between Cobden and Bastiat was one of the issues in which Mallet took a special interest; see Morley's letters to Mallet, 2 March, 16 and 17 May 1880, Cobden Papers, British Library.

propaganda of Cobden and the Manchester school generally. Not only was the *Wealth of nations* a more approachable work than anything written by Ricardo, it came without a law of rent which suggested that any gains to other income recipients from free trade in foodstuffs would be at the expense of the landowning interest. For a movement that was often deeply antagonistic to the landed aristocracy on social and political grounds, but sought to prove that all classes and nations would benefit from the end of protection, this was not an acceptable emphasis. The Ricardian case for free trade also depended on a link between wages and the price of food that appeared to confirm the 'cheap labour' charges brought by the Anti-Corn Law League's opponents, and had to be avoided on those grounds alone.[22]

Much of the criticism of Ricardo on the part of Christian political economists earlier in the century, beginning with Malthus, had centred on Ricardo's conflictual interpretation of the law of rent.[23] Cobden's friend, the phrenologist George Combe, supplied the Christian providentialist teaching noted in the Prologue. A similar message could be found in Bastiat, and together they supplied an evangelical dimension lacking in the writings of secular political economists: a faith in the naturally harmonious world created by God which it was the duty of his servants to establish on earth by removing the adventitious evils of feudal privilege and protectionism. Mallet's narrative adopted this position as its starting point, adding socialism as the most recent example of a selfish, class-based, protectionist mentality. Smith's English followers were criticised for losing sight of the necessary connection between 'the dry facts of science and the great social laws which alone give them life and meaning'; they lacked 'a belief in the steady natural gravitation of all the interests of our race towards order and moral progress'.[24] This separation of economic facts from their 'correlative moral consequences' accounted for their failure to achieve political results. As we shall see here and in the following essay, it was also to be the single most important reason for the unbridgeable gap that opened up between Mallet and many of the economists who practised their profession within an academic setting.

---

[22] On these differences between Ricardians and the Manchester School, see M. Blaug, *Ricardian economics* (New Haven: Yale University Press, 1958), pp. 204–9.

[23] See my *Riches and poverty* (Cambridge, Cambridge University Press, 1996), pp. 352–4, 377–85.

[24] *Free exchange*, p. 16. Cobden had expressed similar sentiments when he complained that political economists had lost sight of the 'benign truths of Adam Smith'; see letter to Bright, 5 November 1855, British Library, Add. MS 43650, fos. 154–5. The letter will be printed in volume III of *The letters of Richard Cobden*, ed. Anthony Howe (Oxford University Press).

III

As the story was developed in the uncompleted parts of *Free exchange* on the 'law of value and unearned increment', the parts that occupied Mallet during his retirement, it took on dimensions that went well beyond the original reservations of the Manchester school towards the Ricardian case for free trade. The diagnosis turned on the rift that had arisen between an English school that had followed an ambiguous Smith and those who pursued the stricter and more enlightened logic of the 'French' school of *libre échange*, according to which exchange values depended on utility rather than labour inputs or costs of production. We incur costs when the products of labour, land, and capital possess utility and hence value to us in meeting our needs as consumers, the ultimate arbiter of public interest. Wages, rent, and profits are therefore the effect rather than the cause of value, and are subject to uniform causal processes that had been obscured by the separate theories advanced by Ricardians to explain these prices or rewards. Land, being nature's gift, may be free to all, but it only acquires value when it becomes private property and through human agency provides a 'service' to others. The term 'service' embraces both the labour effort required to produce something and the labour it saves others. Exclusive property creates natural monopolies which are justified when they provide a valued service and when, as a result, the scarcity price induces us to tailor use to need. An economy is a system, in Bastiat's phrase, that generates *'services pour services'*, and it operates in an optimal fashion when not subject to restrictions. A regime of free exchange allows us to meet our needs with the least labour possible, and in the course of doing so generates just rewards to the contributing factors of production. It harnesses material interests that are capable, when not impeded by war, excessive taxation, and artificial monopoly, of delivering indefinite improvement in the condition of the working classes and eliminating all unnecessary forms of inequality. If one adds development of the world's resources in the interests of a community of nations at peace with one another, the lineaments of the Bastiat–Cobden millennium are in place.

In Mallet's hands the above position was pursued by extensive criticism of the Ricardian view of exchange value as it had been articulated by Mill. In addition to Mill's confusion of cost with value, Mallet was anxious to draw attention to specific ways in which Mill had aided 'the formation and diffusion of a popular opinion favourable to arbitrary and artificial methods of social regeneration'.[25] Although Mill had been a member of the Cobden Club committee since the club's inception, Mallet suspected him of being a lukewarm advocate of free trade. This could readily be documented by Mill's support for the principle of a temporary tariff based on 'infant industry' considerations, a position often cited by those seeking to justify resort to tariffs in Germany, the United States, Canada, and Australia.[26] Mallet was the source of the anecdote that Cobden, on his deathbed, had said that Mill had 'done more harm by his sentence about the fostering of infant industries, than he had done good by the whole of the rest of his writings'.[27] But what Mallet chiefly had in mind when speaking about 'artificial modes of social regeneration' was Mill's endorsement of the policy of taxing the 'unearned increment' in land values as part of the programme of the Land Tenure Reform Association issued in 1871. Useful Cobdenite proposals for abolishing 'feudal' restrictions on the freedom to trade in land were being sacrificed in the interests of 'communism'. For this offence Mallet boasted that he had been able to move that Mill's name be dropped from the Cobden Club committee. In a letter to Thorold Rogers, justifying his action, Mallet averred that 'between Feudalists and Communists, there is no chance for Freedom'.[28]

Mill's error could be traced to his failure to accept Bastiat's lessons on the irrefrangible connection between exchange and private property. By attributing value to labour, and by noting that the cost of production in agricultural pursuits varied according to the quality of the soil or location, Mill had concluded that part of the reward going to landownership was due not to nature 'but to the labour and efforts of the community at large'. This had led him to mount an attack on private property in the case of land, and to favour 'collective appropriation, in the name of science and on the pleas of social expediency'.[29] In levelling such charges Mallet was joining those who believed that a long line of socialists – Louis Blanc, Vidal, Considérant, Proudhon, Marx, and Lassalle – had 'drawn their deadliest weapons from Ricardo's armoury', with the land national-isers and Henry George following suit in the 1880s.[30] What Ricardians

[25] *Free exchange*, p. 228.
[26] On the infant industry case, see Mill's *Principles of political economy*, CW, III, pp. 918–19.
[27] See M. E. Grant Duff, *Notes from a diary, 1889–1891*, 2 vols. (London: John Murray, 1901), I, pp. 99–100.
[28] Mallet to Thorold Rogers, 24 March 1873, Bodleian Library, Oxford, Rogers Papers.
[29] *Free exchange*, pp. 240–1.   [30] *Ibid.*, p. 233.

had confined to the special properties of land, socialists had extended to all non-labour or property incomes.

Mallet's move to exclude Mill from the deliberations of the Cobden Club occurred a few weeks before Mill's death and therefore provoked no reaction.[31] Although Mill would have rejected the grounds given for his exclusion, it is doubtful if he would have been greatly disturbed by the event; his membership of the committee had become a formality, and he was critical, in private, of the club's political priorities.[32] As a faithful Ricardian campaigner for abolition of the Corn Laws from his youth, Mill had been active in the cause of free trade for much longer than most Cobdenites. But after the victory of the Anti-Corn Law League in 1846 he had other goals in view, including those that were to bring him into conflict with Mallet and the Cobden Club. His own projections of the long-term benefits of abolition of the Corn Laws had always been less euphoric, mainly because the law of diminishing returns in agriculture played a larger part in his thinking, and he laid more stress on the continuing threat to working-class living standards posed by Malthusian pressures.[33] Mill, as Bagehot had noted with sympathy, was also critical of 'non-interventionism' as a guide to British foreign policy and explicitly opposed to the Cobdenite policy of protecting the shipping of neutrals during war.[34]

The Indian land revenue system was to be another bone of doctrinal contention between Mill and Mallet. As noted in an earlier essay (3), Mill followed his father's use of Ricardian logic in supporting the *ryotwari* as opposed to the *zemindari* system.[35] This entailed an assumption that the government was the ultimate landowner, and that its revenue needs could best be met by a direct rental levy on the peasant cultivator rather than

---

[31] Indeed, the minutes of the Cobden Club simply record that Mill's name was among several that it was resolved should be struck off on grounds that they had not been able to attend; see minute, 7 March 1873, Cobden Papers, West Sussex Record Office. Unusually, for a prominent founding member of the club, no notice was taken of Mill's death.

[32] Evidence for this has to be sought in his *Correspondence*; see CW, XVI, pp. 1037, 1350; and XVII, p. 1658.

[33] Writing after repeal, Mill was anxious to maintain that any rise in wages that could be achieved by the measure, or through improvements in agricultural technology, could be eroded 'unless during this interval of prosperity the standard of comfort regarded as indispensable by the class, is permanently raised'. See *Principles*, CW, III, pp. 349, 850.

[34] See especially his 1859 article 'A few words on non-intervention', CW, XXI, pp. 109–24. For comment on the larger issues raised by this disagreement, see Bernard Semmel, *John Stuart Mill and the pursuit of virtue* (New Haven: Yale University Press, 1986), pp. 107–10; and Stefan Collini, *Public moralists* (Oxford: Oxford University Press, 1991), pp. 147–8.

[35] See p. 77 above.

through the intermediary of the *zemindari*, or landowning/tax-collecting class. Given his objections to the underlying theory, it was inevitable that Mallet should join those members of the Indian administration who sought to shift a rent-based revenue system towards one based on permanent settlement and taxation of all sources of income. In 1872 Mallet had been rescued from his dead-end post at the Board of Trade by an invitation from the Duke of Argyll to serve as a member of the India Council when he took office as Secretary of State. Argyll and Mallet had collaborated on Cobden Club affairs, and in a publication that appeared under the club's auspices Argyll had justified rental incomes and the 'improving' role of the private landowner on impeccable commercial, as opposed to 'feudal', principles.[36] Not surprisingly, while having responsibility for Indian affairs he opposed the concept of state landownership.[37] Mallet supported this position by maintaining that 'the function of rent is to restrain the undue pressure of population on the soil'. Rent operated as a providential device in checking, through rising rental values, the growth of population. It also served as a spur to force the land-hungry to emigrate and protected the 'higher wants of society' from being overwhelmed by mere subsistence needs.[38] Using rent rather than taxes as the source of government income was part of the 'inheritance of Oriental despotism'; it nullified the beneficial workings of the market by removing the only effective restraint on the main cause of pauperisation in India.

I do not agree with Mr Mill that because land is limited it is not a fit subject for appropriation by individuals, but should be considered as the common property of all. On the contrary, the fact that land is limited affords the strongest possible reason for its appropriation by individuals as the only method, consistent with personal liberty, by which the population can be kept in due proportion to the means of subsistence.[39]

Mallet also called upon the testimony of Henry Maine, another Anglo-Indian expert serving on the India Council, to show that land had never been adequately cultivated except under conditions in which the family was the largest unit of ownership.[40]

---

[36] See an *Essay on the commercial principles applicable to contracts for the hire of land* (London: Cobden Club, 1877).
[37] See his defence of this in the course of an attack on Henry George in 'The prophet of San Francisco', *The Nineteenth Century*, 86 (1884), pp. 555–7.
[38] See *Free exchange*, pp. 98–100, and the entire chapter on unearned increment on pp. 300–52.
[39] *Sir Louis Mallet*, p. 117; and *Free exchange*, note on pp. 326–7.
[40] *Sir Louis Mallet*, pp. 116–17; and letter to Sidgwick, 14 July 1887, Sidgwick Papers, Trinity College, Cambridge.

It followed too that Mallet was opposed to the prevailing 'public works' school of administration in India. He wanted to preserve greater scope for private investment and pointed out that many irrigation and railway projects undertaken at public expense were unlikely to be remunerative in a poor country like India. The same considerations applied in a rich country like Britain: if profits could be made on such projects, it was better for them to be returned to private monopolists rather than distributed to the community at large by a state monopoly, either as non-remunerative services or as a source of relief from other taxes. The natural forces that created private monopolies could control them. The powers associated with public monopolies, being arbitrary, the result of human artifice, were more likely to be abused by a growing army of functionaries, or by politicians seeking visible popular outcomes without regard to their fatal though hidden drawbacks.[41]

IV

All of this was unadulterated Bastiat, a libertarian or free market philosophy applied with equal force to European and Indian conditions. It was based on a critique of Mill's political economy that was fundamentalist in several respects, theoretical, political, and ultimately religious. It turned on one of the most basic of propositions in the science of political economy, the theory of value, where it called for rejection of the labour or cost-of-production approach to exchange value in favour of one based on utilities and the operation of supply and demand. It took a thorough-going 'individualist' view of the danger to personal independence posed by state interference in contractual relationships, one that was far more dogmatically pro-*laissez-faire* than anything to be found in authors such as Adam Smith or Mill. And its politico-economic vision was suffused with the notion of a divinely organised world, the full potentialities of which could only be realised if the diseases of feudal privilege, protectionism and socialism were eliminated.

Looking for signs that this philosophy was making headway in the academic world in the 1870s, Mallet could discern only one bright spot: Jevons's *Theory of political economy*, with its attack on the Ricardo–Mill school and its blunt announcement: 'The truth is with the French School.'[42]

[41] *Sir Louis Mallet*, pp. 119–26; and 'Free trade and free enterprise' and the 'Note on state railways', in *Free exchange*, pp. 95–108.
[42] *Theory of political economy*, 2nd edn (London: Macmillan, 1879), p. xlix.

Jevons had delivered a mathematical demonstration of Bastiat's virtuous circle of 'wants, satisfactions, efforts', and Mallet was therefore prepared to adopt his concept of 'final utility' as the best statement of the theory of exchange.[43] This was far more heartening than the attacks on orthodox political economy coming from such Comtean and inductivist critics as J. K. Ingram and T. E. Cliffe Leslie. What they offered amounted to a rejection of the deductive verities of the science. It was an alternative to orthodoxy that came with the unacceptable nationalist or anti-cosmopolitan dimensions imparted by its affiliates within the German historical school. It could only result in 'a period of purely empirical legislation, and a series of reactionary economical experiments, which could not fail seriously to retard the progress of civilization'.[44]

Although there is little direct evidence on the subject, it seems likely that Jevons proved to be a disappointment to Mallet. Jevons's consumer-centred version of the theory of utility did not eventuate in a crusade in favour of the sanctity of private property and a minimal state. Indeed, when Jevons's *State in relation to labour* appeared in 1882, it revealed that he took a pragmatic position on the subject of state intervention in economic affairs, uncommitted to any set of a priori principles, whether pro- or anti-*laissez-faire*. In other writings he showed what Mallet might have regarded as a disquieting willingness to countenance municipal efforts to use local taxes to supply public amenities.[45] Given his admiration for Jevons, Mallet was also saddened to learn that he could obtain no support from him on the subject of bimetallism, another of the causes he was active in promoting during the final decade of his life. The only signs of the philosophy of free exchange being recognised by British economists could be found in the work of H. D. Macleod, whose self-promoting eccentricities ensured that all academic openings were closed to him.[46]

As we shall see more clearly in the next essay, the revolution Jevons had called for in British economics did not result in any dramatic rupture with the past as far as the basic approach to state intervention was concerned. Nor did it lead to *rapprochement* with Bastiat and the 'French'

---

[43] See p. 150 above. For Mallet's adoption of Jevons's position, see *Free exchange*, pp. 238–9, 261, 300. See too a letter to Farrer dated 26 February 1886: 'I think Jevons's definition of Final utility as the regulator of Value is perhaps the best'; Farrer Papers, Surrey Record Office.

[44] *Free exchange*, pp. 242–4

[45] For Jevons's views on state intervention and municipal initiatives, see pp. 164–5 above. Only on the question of railway nationalisation did he pursue a line that conformed with Mallet's.

[46] On Macleod and his peculiarities, see J. Maloney, *Marshall, orthodoxy and the professionalisation of economics* (Cambridge: Cambridge University Press, 1985), pp. 120–33.

school within the academic community. From Mallet's point of view, this meant that Mill's influence on the teachers of economics in the universities remained the dominant one. Mill's theoretical abstractions may have been misbegotten but they were far from being innocuous.

They are responsible to a great degree for the false direction in which the minds of the present generation have of late been moving. They have diverted interest and energy from the agencies of international progress. They have overturned confidence in the great principles of private property and free exchange, and given a new impetus to schemes of social regeneration by false and artificial methods. They have brought into an unnatural and sinister alliance the teachings of the English universities, and of Proudhon and Karl Marx.[47]

Although this was plainly an over-reaction, Mallet's belief that Mill had made the *laissez-faire* principle vulnerable to attack on some issues, notably those connected with landownership and state control over bequests, would have commanded much wider support. There is no doubt too that Mill's *Principles* was responsible for blocking or sidelining other developments associated with the ideas of Jevons and Bastiat, though Mill mainly relied on his orthodox disciple, John Elliot Cairnes, to defend the position they shared from the attacks mounted by these two authors. Cairnes had good reason to believe that he was speaking for Mill as well as himself in responding to them: his answers involved an appeal to methodological precepts adumbrated in Mill's *Logic* as well as the more substantive doctrines on the theory of value expounded in his *Principles*.[48] When reviewing Jevons's *Theory* Cairnes noted that it was based on 'a conception of the law of value at bottom the same with that propounded by Bastiat in his "Harmonies Economiques"' – a work he had recently subjected to severe criticism in an article planned with the help of Mill and approved by him.[49]

Cairnes's critique of Bastiat's system of optimism reveals some important assumptions he shared with Mill. The first of these related to the basic architecture of the abstract science of political economy, the

<hr />

[47] *Free Exchange*, pp. 350–1.
[48] See Mill's letter to Cairnes, 5 December 1871, written when Cairnes was reviewing Jevons (CW, XVII, pp. 1862–3). For a dissection of the methodological and other reasons why Mill and Cairnes rejected Jevons and marginalism, see N. de Marchi, 'Mill and Cairnes and the emergence of marginalism in England', in R. D. C. Black *et al.* (eds.), *The marginal revolution in economics: interpretation and evaluation* (Durham, NC: Duke University Press, 1973), pp. 78–97. For an interpretation that places more emphasis on the political reasons for the failure of Mill and Cairnes to forsake the Ricardo–Mill version of the science, see J. Lipkes, *Politics, religion and classical political economy in Britain: John Stuart Mill and his followers* (London: Macmillan, 1999).
[49] PC, VII, p. 148.

structural features of the economic world that it chose to highlight. Mill had explicitly rejected any identification of the science with catallactics, the science of exchanges: that was 'too confined' in scope and gave too much prominence to exchange when compared with the two other main branches of political economy concerned with production and distribution. Mill underlined these priorities by postponing the treatment of exchange value to Book II, and by connecting exchange with distribution rather than with production. The laws of production, being based on physical laws, did not depend on exchange. Nor was exchange vital to distribution:

Even in the present system of industrial life, in which employments are minutely sub-divided, and all concerned in production depend for their remuneration on the price of a particular commodity, exchange is not the fundamental law of the distribution of the produce, no more than roads and carriages are the essential laws of motion, but merely a part of the machinery for effecting it.

Exchange was not 'in the nature of things' but a matter of 'temporary accidents arising from the existing constitution of society'.[50]

The second set of assumptions shared by Mill and Cairnes concerned the status of the *laissez-faire* principle and any general presumption of harmony in economic affairs. When writing on the grounds and limits of the principle, beyond those 'necessary' functions which were an integral part of the responsibilities of the state, Mill had placed the onus of proof on those who recommended government interference: '*Laisser-faire*, in short, should be the general practice: every departure from it, unless required by some great good, is a certain evil.'[51] But he had followed this with a long list of exceptions that showed under what circumstances and according to what principles public good would be served by optional forms of intervention. In other words, *laissez-faire* was simply a maxim or practical rule of thumb that needed to be subjected to a test of expediency that would vary with circumstances. To the existing category of such 'public' goods as defence, police, education, bridges, and harbours were added the new public utilities of the mid- and late-Victorian period, chiefly water and gas. Here natural monopolies or the vagaries of competition between a limited number of suppliers made public (state or municipal)

---

[50] *Principles*, CW, II, pp. 455–6. Mill did not attack Bastiat frontally, but he withdrew a reference to Bastiat as 'a high authority among French political economists' in later editions of the *Principles*, and argued at length that Henry Carey, the source of Bastiat's defence of property in land, had failed to dent the Ricardian theory. See *ibid.*, pp. 299, 424–8.

[51] *Principles*, CW, III, p. 945.

participation, regulation, or ownership necessary for purposes of consumer protection. Mill provided guidance on such matters in his *Principles* as well as by appearing as an expert witness in the case of London's water supply.[52]

Cairnes went one stage further in his inaugural lecture on the subject at UCL in 1870. In the interests of the ongoing relevance of the science, especially in the eyes of those who now sought 'positive and reconstructive' reforms, he felt it essential to repudiate the idea that political economy was little more than 'a sort of scientific rendering of this [*laissez-faire*] maxim'. This 'mere handy rule of practice' had no scientific basis. The science was neutral with respect to 'particular systems of social and industrial existence'; it was concerned with the causes of a specific range of events rather than with the moral and political choices which individuals or whole societies should be making: 'It has nothing to do with *laissez-faire* any more than communism.' Bastiat and the free trade movement exemplified the first of these rejected alternatives. Cairnes maintained that Bastiat's 'plausible optimist falsities' confused the idea that *human* interests were harmonious with the statement that *class* interests were as well. Bastiat and his followers overlooked the powerful part played by 'passion, prejudice, custom, *ésprit de corps*, class interest' in human affairs, all those forces that led interested parties to confuse their interests with the public good.[53] In his *Sophismes économiques* Bastiat had displayed considerable forensic skills when responding to protectionists, but in the later work, when facing up to the 'grim visage' of socialism in France after 1848, he had attempted to recast the foundations of political economy in order to answer the new threat. The science cultivated by English authors could not satisfy Bastiat's polemical needs:

> What he aimed at supplying was, not a positive science, not a body of doctrines which should simply *explain* the facts of wealth, but one which, while explaining, should also *justify* those facts – should justify them, that is to say, as manifested in the results of those fundamental institutions of modern society, private property, freedom of industry, of contract, and of exchange.[54]

It was not so much an example of open-ended scientific inquiry as an attempt to prove that left to themselves there was a providential order in economic affairs. Fact and natural right were merged in a manner that, to Cairnes, represented a reversion to a French style of thinking that had

---

[52] *Principles*, CW, II, pp. 141–2; III, pp. 955–6; and *Essays on economics and society*, CW, V, pp. 431–7.
[53] See 'Political economy and laissez-faire', in Cairnes's *Essays on political economy* (London: Macmillan, 1873), p. 246.
[54] 'Bastiat', *Essays*, p. 318.

been prominent during the second half of the eighteenth century, with Rousseau's *Social contract* and the Declaration of the Rights of Man as its best examples. He cited Mill's *Logic* for its criticism of theories of politics based on abstract right, and charged Bastiat with having confused is and ought by exploiting the linguistic ambiguities of key terms in the economic vocabulary such as value, worth, and service. He saw too the connection with land tenure reform: if Bastiat was right, what he and Mill had argued with respect to the need for state intervention in dealing with the unearned increment in the income of landowners was invalid.

Mill offered advice on French economists and lent Cairnes some of the books he needed to mount what began as an attack on Comte's dismissal of political economy and went on to encompass Bastiat. On this subject Mill's opinions had not changed since he had corresponded with the Saint-Simonians and Tocqueville in the 1830s.[55] He agreed in general that 'French philosophic writers seem to me decidedly inferior in closeness and precision of thought to the best English, and more in the habit of paying themselves with phrases and abstractions'. He singled out Louis Reybaud and Michel Chevalier for criticism, the latter having been Cobden's opposite number during the Anglo-French trade negotiations during the 1850s; they were 'unfavourable specimens of French economists as to close thinking', Reybaud being guilty of belonging to 'a narrow and prejudiced school'.[56] Mill appreciated Bastiat's qualities as a 'dialectician' on free trade, but regarded his posthumous work, *Harmonies économiques*, as marred 'with a *parti pris* of explaining away all the evils which are the strongholds of Socialists'. French economists were divided between Malthusians and anti-Malthusians, and between utilitarians and anti-utilitarians as well: 'This last distinction extends even to political economy, in consequence of the prevailing French habit of appealing to intuitive principles of *droit* even on economic subjects.' Mill wanted Cairnes to pursue his critique one stage further:

Some other time perhaps you might find it useful to carry on the examination of Bastiat's doctrines to the social, or practical, point of view, and shew how far from the truth it is that the economic phenomena of society as at present constituted always arrange themselves spontaneously in the way which is most for the common good or that the interests of all classes are fundamentally the same.[57]

---

[55] See p. 40 above.
[56] There was an element of tit for tat in this: Reybaud had devoted a chapter to Mill in his *Economistes modernes* (Paris, 1862) criticising him for the sympathetic treatment he had given to French socialism after the 1848 revolution.
[57] 16 November 1869, CW, XVII, pp. 1664–5; and 15 September 1870, p. 1764.

Among the many things that Mill and Cairnes had in common, therefore, was rejection of any assumption that the 'invisible hand' of the market was endowed with providential properties for harmonising human activities.

Cairnes was far too much of a professed Millian for his attack on Bastiat to carry any weight with Mallet. He could see nothing in Cairnes beyond a 'stupid' rehash of Mill's mistakes in separating the science from the one set of moral conclusions that gave the science its central role in understanding human affairs.[58] As will be seen in the following essay, Mallet's relationships with academic economists did little to convince him that the dangers of socialism, as he saw them, were likely to meet much resistance from other professors of the science.

v

Mallet belonged to a long line of Board of Trade officials committed to free trade and to a *laissez-faire* position on the role of the state.[59] Espousal of the bilateral treaty route towards freer trade was, from this point of view, merely a controversial extension of the idea that the state's chief responsibility was to bring order and stability to the private transactions of merchants and manufacturers, giving due attention to the claims of exporters as well as importers. Defence of these policies through non-official publications, while still in office, often using the Cobden Club as the vehicle, was not unusual; the practice was carried on by Mallet's contemporaries and successors at the Board of Trade, T. H. Farrer and W. H. Gatrell.[60] Bernard Mallet went to some trouble to show that his father's political convictions did not infringe civil service proprieties; he did not exercise his parliamentary vote before retirement, and free trade was a bipartisan commitment during his career: 'No suspicion of indiscretion could attach to the championship of doctrines of unquestioned orthodoxy, and, as a matter of fact, Sir Louis Mallet found in later years quite as much (or as little) sympathy for his ideas on one side of politics as

---

[58] For his views on Cairnes, see *Free exchange*, pp. 229n, 249, 261, 270–1, 273–4, 283n, 285–6, 288–9. In correspondence with Farrer he described Cairnes's attack on Bastiat as 'one of the most discreditable in economic controversy – and *so stupid*. I mean in want of subtlety. He misses all the fine points.' Letter, 28 December 1886, Farrer Papers, Surrey Record Office.

[59] For his predecessors, see Lucy Brown, *The Board of Trade and the free trade movement* (Oxford: Oxford University Press, 1958).

[60] Farrer's *State in relation to trade* was followed by Gatrell, his successor, in *Our trade in relation to foreign competition* (1897). See D. C. M. Platt, *Finance, trade and politics* (Oxford: Oxford University Press, 1968), pp. xxx–xxxix.

on the other.'[61] The second part of this sentence takes a little away from its opening, but Mallet's most outspoken statements, it could be argued, were published after he had retired. When Bernard Mallet published his biography in 1905 he regarded the problem as having been solved by the passage of time: his father's opinions were of historical interest only and could no longer offend party susceptibilities. There was some truth in his admission, rueful though it may have been, that 'they will certainly not, as a whole, appeal to any existing body of political opinion'.[62]

Inter-departmental politics was another matter. Mallet fought his corner fiercely against the Treasury and Foreign Office, inserting news items, sent to him in confidence by Cobden, in tame press outlets, and later becoming such a persistent spokesman for a proactive approach to free trade that he effectively ruled himself out as a candidate to run the new commercial division in the Foreign Office, though he was patently the best qualified person to do so. It is significant that Morier, an aspiring diplomat, chose to describe himself simply as 'A disciple of Richard Cobden' when his hard-hitting anti-Lowe *Letters on commercial treaties, free trade and internationalism* appeared under Cobden Club auspices in 1870. There are more prominent contemporary examples of the use of newspapers and other forms of publication by civil servants to further political and departmental ends, the best known being those of Charles Trevelyan and Edwin Chadwick. The Board of Trade had a tradition of its own in such matters well before Mallet took up his duties there in 1847.[63]

The Cobden Club, founded as a memorial to an esteemed statesman, untainted by office, and as an ostensibly non-partisan body with international affiliations, capable of acting as the sponsor of quasi-academic as well as more obviously topical publications, proved its value here. It was as successful in its chosen sphere as the Anti-Corn Law League had been when the cause had to be fought by rougher, more populist methods.[64] The club provided as respectable a cover for the political activities of civil servants like Mallet and Morier as it did for academics such as Thorold Rogers and Cliffe Leslie, who also used it for this purpose. By the 1880s the club, partly as a result of the catholicity of its membership, found

---

[61] *Sir Louis Mallet*, pp. 38–9.   [62] *Ibid.*, p. viii.

[63] See G. Kitson Clark, '"Statesmen in disguise": reflexions on the history of the neutrality of the civil service', *Historical Journal*, 2 (1959), 19–39.

[64] On the composition and activities of the club, see Anthony Howe, *Free trade and liberal England* (Oxford: Oxford University Press, 1997), ch. 4.

itself increasingly divided over the role of the state in domestic affairs.[65] Coming on top of the Irish Land Act, Home Rule threatened to allow Ireland to follow other self-governing colonies in adopting infant industry protectionist measures. Mallet found himself among a minority of old-style Cobdenite liberals facing a majority leaning more towards the interventionism of Chamberlain's radical programme and the collectivist attractions of what became known as 'New Liberalism'.

Taxation of the unearned increment in urban ground rents was part of what Mallet described as 'the new radical or reactionary programme', an 'economical heresy' that alongside other measures designed to control natural monopolies was utterly incompatible with remaining a free trader: 'men must choose between the two: they cannot support or connive at such measures as have been signalised, and at the same time stand forward, when it is convenient to do so, as the champions of Free Trade, without exposing themselves to the charge either of stupidity or dishonesty'.[66] Unsurprisingly, many other members of the club refused to accept the imperatives built into this binary choice, with the result that by 1886 Mallet was complaining to Farrer that the club had become 'a set of windbags whose heads are full of socialism, particularism, suspicion etc., and who do everything with a party purpose'.[67] It was no longer a suitable vehicle for advancing the universal truths of the free exchange philosophy.

Some of the leaders of another body founded in the 1880s, the Liberty and Property Defence League, were prepared to make Mallet's message part of their own. *Free exchange* joined a small collection of works by the Duke of Argyll, Wordsworth Donisthorpe and Macleod favoured by the League, all of them dedicated to the free exchange interpretation of the scope and meaning of economics. Their writings provided weapons that could be used to defend private property against movements like those associated with Henry George and the Fabians as well as those associated with the 'new' trade unions, municipal socialism, and the trend towards collectivist and paternalistic legislation being pursued by Liberal and Conservative governments. Ideologically, one could say that a marriage had been arranged between the followers of Mallet's composite Cobden–Bastiat version of economics and those committed to the ultra-individualistic ideas embodied in Herbert Spencer's *Man versus the state*.

Thomas Mackay, a retired wine merchant with legal training, had devoted his retirement to the affairs of the Charity Organisation Society

---

[65] *Ibid.*, pp. 133–41, 191–2   [66] *Free exchange*, pp. 329–32.
[67] Letter to Farrer, 25 January 1886, Farrer Papers, Surrey Record Office.

and to writings on the Poor Law that took the 1834 Amendment Act as the acme of all correct thinking on the subject of the dependent poor and outdoor relief.[68] Mackay's combination of dogmatic Malthusianism, Spencerian individualism, and the theories of free exchange expounded by Mallet and Macleod made him an ideal candidate for editing the publications of the League. In opposition to what he described as 'the eclectic empiricism which is current in the doctrines of the official teachers of the science', Mackay took *Free exchange* to be a warning against 'a popular misconception that Cobden confined his advocacy of Free Trade to matters of international commerce. Rightly understood, the creed of Richard Cobden applied to the whole economic organisation of society.' Whether this made Cobden 'the anticipator, as it were, of the political philosophy of Mr Spencer' was something that could be floated but not inquired into too closely.[69]

The League answered the appearance of *Fabian essays* in 1891 with *A plea for liberty: an argument against socialism and socialistic legislation* edited by Mackay, with an introduction by Spencer. This was followed in 1894 by another work under the same editorship entitled *A policy of free exchange* in which Macleod supplied the opening theoretical chapter showing the connections between the science of economics and free exchange in a manner reminiscent of Mallet's story of how economic thinking in England had taken the wrong turn. The same collection contains essays by Bernard Mallet and St Loe Strachey, the latter having been rescued from socialism through his conversion to the free exchange position by the younger Mallet when they were both undergraduates at Balliol in the seventies. Conversations with the father confirmed what the son had taught.[70]

The reception given to *Free exchange* outside the above camp treated it as the work of the last of the Manchester Romans. James Bonar pointed out, as Cairnes had done over twenty years before, that the negative programme for removing restrictions on economic freedoms, reducing

---

[68] See J. W. Mason, 'Thomas Mackay: the anti-socialist philosophy of the Charity Organisation Society', in K. D. Brown (ed.), *Essays in anti-labour history* (London: Macmillan, 1974), pp. 290–316.
[69] See 'Empiricism in politics', *National Review*, 25 (1895), 793. Mackay reviewed Mallet's book alongside works by Whately, Macleod, Arthur Latham Perry, and the Duke of Argyll in 'The revolt against orthodox economics', *Quarterly Review*, 199 (1901), 346–71, reprinted as chapter 7 in his *Dangers of democracy: studies in the economic questions of the day* (London: John Murray, 1913).
[70] J. St Loe Strachey, *The adventure of living: a subjective autobiography* (London: Hodder and Stoughton, 1922), pp. 158–163. Strachey went on to be editor of the *Cornhill Magazine* and then proprietor and editor of *Spectator*, the leading Unionist journal. Bernard Mallet included part of Strachey's testimony in *Sir Louis Mallet*, pp. 41–2.

military expenditure, and abolishing all indirect taxes was not likely to do much to rectify the unequal distribution of wealth in Britain. He judged Mallet to be out of step with the more positive philosophies of politics that excited the present generation, which 'consciously or unconsciously has gone beyond a conception of the State as a kind of corporation separate from the people and in treaty with it to receive a certain payment and render a *quid pro quo*'.[71] R. R. Marett, an Oxford philosopher and anthropologist, who reviewed it for the Christian Social Union journal, the *Economic Review*, praised Mallet for representing Cobdenism whole, including its international dimension and opposition to territorial aggrandisement. But he noted that whereas Cobden had spoken 'with victory before his eyes', Mallet was 'colder and more despondent, as befits the champion of a lost cause'. He illustrated this by drawing attention to one of the conclusions of the book on the subject of the poor: 'When the limits of production have been reached, any additional population must migrate to other lands, or perish, unless they can be supported by charity. If they perish, the responsibility must rest with those who call into life beings for whom there is no means of support; and this is how it should be.'[72] Was this not the mark of 'a dismal, not to say immoral, Utopia'? For Marett brighter alternatives lay in the expansion of England abroad, in America and Australia; but his observation points to another peculiarity of Mallet's thinking.

Perfectibilism and pessimism, like the stark contrast Mallet made between freedom and slavery, were placed in a knife-edge balance. Mallet thought that Mill's welcome to a stationary state in which economic growth would cease to be a major preoccupation was evidence of a 'morbid habit of mind'.[73] Compared with the optimistic projections of Bastiat on the possibilities of 'permanent abundance', it may have merited such a description. But Mallet's optimism was also tempered by an emphasis on the immediacy of the Malthusian dilemma that lost none of its pessimistic features by being treated as a problem that contained its own providential solution. Here was Mr Podsnap dressed in black, an example of the kind of thinking that Mill condemned as 'complacent optimism, which represents the evils of life as desirable things, because they call forth qualities adapted to combat with evils'. It was an idea that went along with a Victorian concept of 'character' and its formation through trial. Mill's interest in ethology also centred on character formation; and he was no less convinced than any dedicated individualist

---

[71] Book review in *EJ*, 1 (1897), 761–5.   [72] *Free exchange*, p. 205.   [73] *Ibid.*, p. 350.

by the view that performance of various political and economic roles was essential to the development of moral autonomy and strength of character. But by contrast with Mallet he believed that it was part of our duties 'to free human life from as many as possible of its difficulties, and not to keep up a stock of them as hunters preserve game, for the exercise of pursuing it'.[74]

By the final decades of the nineteenth century, much to his vexation, Mallet's was not the only version of the Cobden creed on offer. If he had lived to see Chamberlain's tariff reform campaign he might have taken it as confirmation of his opinion that it was impossible to be in favour of free trade *and* domestic measures that defied the ruthless logic of free exchange. In that respect Mallet might have said that while Chamberlain was wicked he was neither stupid nor dishonest. Tariff reform was also embroiled in the post-Boer war soul-searching, a war that had been an instance of what Cobden would have regarded as imperial panic-mongering on a grand scale. Some of the academics Mallet mistrusted volunteered for service in the cause of free trade during the tariff reform campaign, using weaponry he might have deemed suspect. The forms of Cobdenism that survived well into the twentieth century were often precisely those 'New Liberal' and Labour ones that attempted to reconcile the peace aims and internationalism of free trade with socialistic remedies at home.[75] One of the essays in Part V of this book deals with a leading figure in 'New Liberalism', J. A. Hobson, whose anti-imperialism and Cobdenite sympathies had to be reconciled with a radical diagnosis of capitalism's failings and an active programme of income redistribution through an embryonic welfare state. It was the kind of diagnosis that would have appalled Mallet: he might, therefore, have taken some pleasure in observing some of the intellectual difficulties Hobson experienced in steering a straight course by his chosen lights.

---

[74] *Principles*, CW, III, p. 943.
[75] For the continuities between Cobdenism and 'New Liberalism', and the survival of key elements in the Cobden creed over a longer period, see the final chapter of Howe, *Free trade and liberal England*.

8

Henry Sidgwick and economic socialism

... though Mill had concealed from us the extent of his Socialism, we were all, I think, conscious of having received from him a certain impulse in the Socialistic direction: we have at any rate ceased to regard the science of Political Economy as opposing a hard and fast barrier against the Socialistic conception of the ideal goal of economic progress.   'The economic lessons of socialism', *EJ*, 1895[1]

I

When the above opinion was published Henry Sidgwick was writing in reminiscence mode. A considerable part of his work as a political economist over the previous two decades had been devoted to an exploration of the new relationship between political economy and socialism opened up by Mill. Most readers of the professional journal in which the article appeared would have known this, and many would have been more personally enthusiastic about socialism as a political goal than Sidgwick ever found it possible to be. As was noted in an earlier essay (3), the founders of the Fabian Society, Sidney Webb and Bernard Shaw, were especially interested in the lessons socialists could learn from Mill's political economy and other recent developments associated with Jevons's theory of value.[2] Sidgwick, on the other hand, was inquiring into what political economy had learnt from socialism.

Expressions of apprehension in the face of the revival of socialism can be gleaned from Sidgwick's journal and letters, but he also accepted that there was an 'unmistakable drift towards Socialism in Western Europe'. For someone who took his public duties as philosopher and professor as seriously as Sidgwick did, this meant he was obliged to go as far as current

---

[1] As reprinted in Henry Sidgwick, *Miscellaneous essays and addresses* (London: Macmillan, 1904), p. 242.
[2] See p. 86 above.

knowledge allowed in deciding the best means of accommodating the inevitable. It says something more about his attitude towards this development that if any country was to become the locus of the first experiment in state socialism, he hoped, with a sly reference to assumptions he thought he shared with his audience, that 'we shall all agree to yield the post of honour to Germany'.[3] A few years earlier he had feared this task would fall to Britain.[4]

Sidgwick was typical of those who were, to adapt Bagehot's phrase, post-Mill adherents of political economy. Mill's writings had been crucial in helping him make the transition from his studies as a classicist towards becoming a moral philosopher whose sphere of competence, in imitation of Mill, extended beyond ethics to include the sciences of political economy and politics. It was natural for Sidgwick to seek Mill's advice on the first question of public conscience he faced: whether to resign his fellowship at Trinity College on grounds of his inability to subscribe to the Church of England's Thirty-nine Articles.[5] Sidgwick proved to be a consistent disciple of Mill on several matters of practical ethics, including one of the more controversial ones, higher education for women. He belonged to that generation of Cambridge students who began with an interest in Mill's *Logic* and then moved on to his *Principles of political economy* and other political writings, inspired by Mill's mounting reputation as a public moralist.

But Sidgwick's intimate knowledge of Mill's writings had not prepared him for the posthumous disclosure of how far Mill was prepared to go towards accepting some co-operative version of socialism as the legitimate successor to the 'provisional' arrangements embodied in current economic institutions based on private property, competition, and the self-interest principle. Defence of these arrangements during the 1880s and beyond was increasingly labelled 'individualistic' to distinguish it from the various 'socialistic' alternatives. The statement in the *Autobiography* that Mill and his wife's 'ideal of ultimate improvement' went beyond democracy 'and would class us decidedly under the general designation of Socialists' seemed to take commitment to this goal beyond the measured sympathy meted out to socialism in the third and subsequent editions of Mill's *Principles* and the posthumous 'Chapters on Socialism'. Sidgwick

---

[3] 'Economic lessons', in *Miscellaneous essays*, p. 235.
[4] Diary entry for 17 March, 1886, in *Memoir*, p. 442.
[5] See letters to Mill, 3 August and 26 November 1867, in *Additional letters*, CW, XXXII, pp. 180–1, 185.

quoted the following sentence from Mill's *Autobiography* and italicised the part that perturbed him: 'I look forward to a time when the rule that they who do not work shall not eat will be applied not to paupers only, but impartially to all; and when the division of the produce of labour, instead of depending, in so great a degree as it now does, on the accident of birth *will be made by concert on an acknowledged principle of justice.*' Speaking on behalf of those who had been brought up on Mill's writings, Sidgwick claimed they were 'as much surprised as the "general reader" to learn that our master, the author of a much-admired treatise "On Liberty" had been all the while looking forward to a time when the division of the produce of labour should be "made by concert"'.[6]

Mill's autobiographical admission jarred with Sidgwick's understanding of the English mainstream in political economy, a tradition that since the writings of Nassau Senior and Mill on the methodology of the science in the 1830s, if not before, had been careful to separate the ideal from the actual, the scientific analysis of the processes by which wealth was produced and distributed, assuming no interference on the part of government, from the practical and normative question of whether *laissez-faire* or some alternative regime, mercantilistic or socialistic, generated the best attainable result. Sidgwick criticised those who confused *laissez-faire*, treated as an assumption useful for the purposes of forming hypotheses, with a prescription. Earlier socialistic criticism of the distribution of incomes in capitalist societies had confirmed the wisdom of this separation: more definite things could be said about how an increased production of material wealth could be achieved than about the justice of the system by which incomes and wealth were distributed.

As a moral philosopher who was chiefly interested in practical ethics, Sidgwick was drawn to subjects that offered scope for what he called 'reflective analysis of general facts which common experience has already made familiar'.[7] He wanted to show how a common-sense perspective could bring linguistic clarity to the various issues raised by state intervention. Since many people still understood 'principles of political economy' to mean an inquiry into what practical rules of conduct should be followed by individuals and governments, he wanted to build on and modify rather than legislate against ordinary linguistic usage. He was not interested in confining discussion to scientific issues by enforcing a rigid distinction between positive and normative propositions. His aim was to

---

[6] 'Economic lessons', in *Miscellaneous essays*, p. 241.
[7] *Principles of political economy*, 2nd edn (London: Macmillan, 1887), p. 31.

find ways of following and then guiding public discussion back and forth across the boundary between is and ought questions, science and art, without confusion, recognising that some propositions were more likely to enjoy consensual support than others.

Neither Sidgwick's personal misgivings nor his reservations about Mill's socialistic aspirations prevented him from engaging with the phenomenon to which he had earlier given the useful label, 'economic socialism', a blanket term that covered the expanding agenda of state action in matters social and economic during the final quarter of the nineteenth century, as well as speculative blueprints for more ambitious versions of state socialism. His aim in dealing with this phenomenon was 'to reduce to its proper limits the supposed opposition between orthodox political economy and what is vaguely called socialist, or semi-socialistic, legislation'.[8] Bringing conceptual clarity and a modicum of philosophic calm to the discussion of these subjects became a Sidgwick speciality, one that he pursued in articles, addresses, and his *Principles of political economy*, returning to it in the *Elements of politics* in the 1890s. The third and concluding book of his *Principles* was devoted to the 'art' of political economy defined as the 'general theory of practice'; and it was there that he updated Mill's treatment of exceptions to *laissez-faire* in the light of new empirical evidence, but along lines that Mill would have recognised and possibly approved. Sidgwick gave a scrupulously fair hearing to various forms of intervention in the workings of the market, actual or conceivable. It lacked only the warmth that his more radical mentor, unencumbered by academic duties, brought to these topics. Indirectly, then, charting a course that avoided the excesses of dogmatic *laissez-faire* on one side and wholesale socialistic rejection of the status quo on the other, describes the direction in which Sidgwick attempted to take Mill's inheritance. Instead of doing this by finding some average between extremes, he claimed to be showing why those who advocated extreme solutions were arguing along erroneous lines.

There was a national, if not a nationalist, dimension to all this. As we have seen in the case of Jevons and Mallet, the English tradition was under attack from those who maintained that on a fundamental issue, the theory of value, wisdom lay with an alternative French tradition of utility theorising. While Sidgwick thought that Jevons's *Theory of political economy* was 'the most important contribution to economic theory that has been

---

[8] 'Economic socialism', originally published in the *Contemporary Review*, November 1886, as reprinted in *Miscellaneous essays*, p. 200.

made in England for a generation', he cannot be described as an enthusiastic, certainly not as a proselytising convert:

I accept Jevons's doctrine of 'final utility' as in the main true and as an important addition to the older theory; but I am not prepared to say that the modifications thus introduced into the theory of value as expounded (e.g.) by Mill is enough to make me regard Jevons doctrine as a new basis. But I am quite content to be described as a follower of Jevons.[9]

Jevons's attacks on the English tradition had the qualities least appreciated by a man of Sidgwick's cautious temperament: they were 'exaggerated and violent', and 'entirely false and misleading' where Mill was concerned. Mill was still the model for his own work, and while he conceded that Jevons had been right in giving more prominence to consumption, he followed Mill in confining himself to production, distribution, and exchange as the more important economic activities that the science had to explain.[10] Sidgwick adopted the language of utilities gained and lost, total or final; he also expanded the notion of wealth to include 'transient utilities' (services) and even those unmeasurable 'unpurchased utilities' that made estimates of material wealth difficult to calculate. But he did so in the manner of a utilitarian who had never deserted the Benthamite fold rather than as someone who had been newly enfranchised by Jevons. After all, if he had been so inclined, he could have pointed out that as the author of *Methods of ethics*, his first and best-known work published in 1874, a work praised by Jevons for introducing 'a precision of thought and nomenclature which was previously wanting', he could hardly be accused of being unaware of the strengths and weaknesses of utilitarianism as the basis for moral conduct.[11]

In common with Mill and Cairnes, Sidgwick was keen to distinguish his version of the science from the approach adopted by Bastiat and his admirers.[12] An introductory chapter in his *Principles* dealing with the scope of political economy noted the 'great interval' that existed between the practice of Smith's English followers and those who 'completely fused' questions of science and art.[13] Hence the 'marked difference between the

[9] See *Principles*, p. 9; and for the credo see his letter to Foxwell, 27 November 1886, Sidgwick Papers, Trinity College, Cambridge, now included on the CD version of Sidgwick's works, InteLex Corporation, 1992.

[10] *Principles*, pp. 9, 26–7.

[11] For Jevons's view of *Methods of ethics*, see Jevons's article on 'utilitarianism' in 'John Stuart Mill's philosophy tested', as reprinted in *Pure logic and other minor works*, edited by Robert Adamson and Harriet A. Jevons (London: Macmillan, 1890), p. 288.

[12] *Principles*, p. 400.   [13] *Ibid.*, pp. 20–1.

general tone of English political economists and the general tone of the leading continental advocates of laissez-faire, of whom Bastiat may be taken as a type'.[14] Conflating the benefits of natural liberty with natural justice was attributed more to the Physiocrats than to Smith: 'natural' for Smith often connoted 'actual' rather than 'beneficial'. Smith's English followers had never maintained that existing inequalities could be justified, merely that interfering with distribution 'must tend to impair aggregate production more than it could increase the utility of the produce by a better distribution'. English economists now agreed that governments had some responsibility for promoting production, and they had 'rarely ventured on [the] daring flights of optimistic demonstration' that would be needed to prove that the existing distribution of wealth granted every worker his or her just deserts.[15]

One of the central philosophical features of the Bastiat position was an appeal to natural rights thinking of a kind that had been anathema to utilitarians since Bentham's attack on it as 'nonsense on stilts'. As Sidgwick put it when speaking of the individualistic and anti-étatist arguments of Herbert Spencer as well as Bastiat, 'this whole discussion of natural rights is one from which, as a mere empirical utilitarian, I should prefer to stand aloof'.[16] Other contemporary intellectual developments provoked the same reaction, but circumstances did not permit aloofness: Sidgwick found himself engaged in holding an 'orthodox' line on the methods appropriate to political economy and an 'English' line against the fusion of normative and positive questions. One of Mill's legacies was to have promoted issues of distribution over those of production:

> in the latter half of the century – largely through the influence of Mill's remarkably persuasive work – the original predominance of production over distribution, in the current view of the art of political economy, has been almost inverted, and the aim of improving distribution has become continually more prominent in the minds of those who study political economy with a practical object.[17]

Questions of fairness and distributive justice were not merely given greater prominence; they could not be evaded on purely scientific grounds: 'For the conclusions of economic science have always been supposed to relate ultimately . . . to actual human beings; and actual human beings

---

[14] 'Economic socialism', in *Miscellaneous essays*, p. 204. For other remarks directed against Bastiat, see *Principles*, pp. 23–4.

[15] 'Economic socialism', in *Miscellaneous essays*, p. 204.   [16] *Ibid.*, p. 211.

[17] See Sidgwick's article on 'Political economy: method', in *Dictionary of political economy*, ed. R. H. I. Palgrave, 3 vols. (London: Macmillan, 1899), III, p. 137.

will not permanently acquiesce in a social order that common moral opinion condemns as unjust'.[18] Here too there was a problem of finding a path between extremes: between those who held that *laissez-faire* achieved justice through free exchange and those who regarded private property as theft. In several important respects, then, Sidgwick remained faithful to arguments derived from Mill – arguments that survived the apparent endorsement of socialism in the latter's *Autobiography* and the acceptance of newer approaches to the theory of value.

II

Before considering more closely Sidgwick's views on 'economic socialism' it may be helpful to revert to the opinions of Cairnes, an even closer follower of Mill, whose ringing declaration of the independence of the science of political economy from *laissez-faire* conclusions was discussed in the preceding essay (7). For purposes of symmetry Cairnes had added that the science had nothing to do with communism either, though since *laissez-faire* was still widely accepted as a shorthand description of an outlook on economic policy that had been highly influential in Britain, while communism existed mainly in the realm of speculation and small-scale experiment, symmetry might appear to be merely verbal. Although Cairnes had far less to say about communism, he made some cryptic remarks about socialism at the end of an inaugural lecture given in November 1870 that would have been anything but cryptic to his auditors. In September Napoleon III's armies had been defeated at Sedan, and the siege of Paris had begun, a siege that was to lead to the establishment of the Paris Commune in the following spring. Cairnes invited his audience to agree that only the 'spectre of socialism, that rank growth of economic ignorance' could explain why France had surrendered her liberties to a Louis Bonaparte, the person responsible for declaring war on Prussia and hence for 'the terrible catastrophe which we now witness and deplore'.[19]

Equating socialism with economic ignorance does not sound like an unbiased inquiry into the subject, but as Cairnes was later to point out, as far as communism, the most extreme version of socialism, was concerned, the controversy had been effectively disposed of by Mill's examination of the subject – 'an examination not less remarkable for its thoroughness than for the candour, and even tenderness towards those whose opinions

---

[18] *Principles*, p. 501. [19] *Essays in political economy* (London: Macmillan, 1873), p. 264.

he opposes'.[20] Cairnes wished to keep his distance from what he took to be the essential characteristic of modern socialism, the use of the power of the state to redistribute wealth. Here Cairnes anticipated Sidgwick's misgivings by registering disagreement with Mill's approval of socialism in his *Autobiography*. He quoted the same sentence that troubled Sidgwick before making the following protest: 'I cannot but regret that a philosophy of social life with which I so deeply sympathize should be prejudiced by verbal associations fitted, as it seems to me, only to mislead.' An ideal state of affairs that might arise 'when the character of human beings and the conditions of human life are widely different from what they now are' was being confused with 'the employment of the powers of the State for the instant accomplishment of ideal schemes, which is the invariable attribute of all projects generally regarded as Socialistic'.[21] By setting up the wrong 'verbal associations' a crucial distinction between aspiration and feasibility was being blurred. A proclamation of allegiance to socialism, however vaguely future-oriented, cast doubt on one of Cairnes's last claims on Mill's behalf. In his obituary assessment he had said that Mill was responsible for a vital lesson in emancipation:

[Mill] was the first, if not to perceive, at least to enforce the lesson, that, just because [political economy] is a science, its conclusions carried with them no obligatory force with reference to human conduct. As a science it tells us that certain modes of action lead to certain results; but it remains for each man to judge of the value of the results thus brought about, and to decide whether or not it is worth while to adopt the means necessary for their attainment . . . It is not for political economy or for any science to say what are the ends most worthy of being pursued by human beings.[22]

If we judge these things by later distinctions between 'classical' and 'neo-classical' standpoints, Cairnes and Sidgwick occupied different theoretical camps. For unlike Sidgwick, Cairnes was not prepared, even lukewarmly, to be added to the list of converts to the utility approach to consumer demand. Although he enjoyed good personal relations with Jevons, he reviewed the *Theory of political economy* without much understanding, charging that it was merely a tautologous exercise in verbal and mathematical dexterity.[23] He had good reason to believe that in levelling such charges he was speaking for Mill as well as for himself. Defending the

---

[20] *Some leading principles of political economy newly expounded* (London: Macmillan, 1874), p. 323.
[21] *Ibid.*, p. 316n.
[22] 'Mill's political economy', first published in *The Examiner*, 1873, and then reprinted as an appendix to Alexander Bain, *John Stuart Mill: a criticism* (London: Longmans, 1882), p. 201.
[23] For Cairnes's review of Jevons, see PC, VII, pp. 146–52.

body of knowledge Mill had created from internal and external attack had been a central theme of Cairnes's professional existence ever since he published his lectures as Whately Professor of Political Economy at Trinity College, Dublin, on the *Character and logical method of political economy* in 1857. An updated version of this impeccable defence of Mill's methodological stance in upholding the legitimacy of abstract deductive methods, the hypothetical findings of which could subsequently be verified by inductive evidence, was issued in 1875, the year of Cairnes's own death. The reissue was conceived as a response to Jevons's claims that political economy had to be a mathematical science because it dealt with quantitative phenomena. Since Cairnes believed that political economy rested on axioms derived from a combination of physical and mental science, and since he did not believe that 'mental feelings admit of being expressed in precise quantitative forms', it had become necessary once more to defend orthodoxy from the most recent threat.[24]

In what proved to be his last substantive contribution to political economy, *Some leading principles of political economy newly expounded*, published a year after Mill's death, Cairnes found other matters beside socialism on which he was no longer in harmony with his master. In addition to an exposition of his own ideas on the relationship between costs of production and value, Cairnes resisted the misunderstandings arising from Mill's – as Cairnes thought, unnecessary and over-generous – concessions to critics of the fixed or predetermined version of the wage-fund theory. In making these concessions Mill thought he had carried Cairnes with him much further than proved to be the case.[25] Mill's almost casual recantation of the doctrine in a review of William Thornton's *On labour* in 1869 came as a blow to those who were keen to preserve the integrity of the established version of the science. Sidgwick described it as an 'unexpected shock' and dated the end of the 'halcyon days' of the science from its appearance.[26] Cairnes criticised Mill for carelessness and for giving too much comfort to those who were looking for flaws in the scientific edifice. His reservations on this matter went well beyond anything he had signalled to Mill when writing the book.[27] It was to be his

---

[24] See the preface to the second edition of *The character and logical method of political economy* (London: Macmillan, 1875), posthumously reissued, 1888, pp. iv–v.
[25] See Mill's letters to Cairnes on his review of Thornton's book and on Cairnes's projected work, CW, XVII, pp. 1587, 1616, 1894, 1909, especially his statement that: 'You may imagine how gratifying it is to me that you give so complete an adhesion to the view I take of the wages fund' (p. 1616).
[26] *Principles*, pp. 4–5.
[27] Cairnes's last statement to Mill on the subject certainly gave the impression that he was happier with Mill's position than later proved to be the case: 'All that you have said on the subject of the

last act in defence of orthodoxy, a defence on this occasion against the errors of his mentor. Like his peremptory dismissal of Jevons's theoretical innovations, it misfired badly in the eyes of other members of the political economy guild. Instead of binding up wounds, the captious manner in which he criticised Mill lent credence to Jevons's charge that Mill had left a 'shattered' science rather than an organised body of knowledge. The performance was regarded by Sidgwick as an ungenerous one that had further 'contributed to impair the unique prestige which Mill's exposition had enjoyed for nearly half a generation'. It was one of the signs that 'the waves of disputation are in danger of submerging the really sound and valuable results of previous thought'. Believing that the new ideas of both Cairnes and Jevons 'admit of being stated in a form less hostile to the older doctrines than their authors suppose' was one of the justifications Sidgwick gave for writing his *Principles*.[28]

III

Sidgwick first began to take an interest in political economy in the mid-1860s; he found it a congenial intellectual exercise because it was 'just in the right stage of scientific progress', with 'not too many facts to be got up'.[29] He began lecturing on the subject as part of the Moral Sciences tripos at Cambridge in 1873; and publications followed a few years later, assisted initially by an invitation from John Morley to contribute to the *Fortnightly Review*. The themes Sidgwick chose for his first three articles were not exactly popular ones – the method appropriate to economic inquiry, the definition of money, and the wage-fund theory – but each of them addressed issues that had been the subject of serious public debate during the previous decade.[30] The articles enabled Sidgwick to rehearse positions he would later embody in his *Principles* and to illustrate the claims for the methodology outlined in the first of them.

   Entering the lists in the late 1870s, during the aftermath of the disputes that coincided with the celebrations of the centenary of the *Wealth of*

"wages-fund" seems to me excellent. The conception, as now delineated, is, so far as I can see, invulnerable; while it retains all that is required to serve as a basis for a theory of wages.' Since it seems unlikely that politeness had become deceit, we must conclude that Cairnes's convictions hardened against any concessions to critics of the wage-fund theory as his book proceeded to a conclusion.
[28] *Principles*, p. 7.
[29] See letter to Oscar Browning, 27 September 1865, as cited in *Memoir*, p. 131.
[30] *Fortnightly Review*, 16 (1879), February, April, and July.

nations, it was impossible to avoid taking a stand on the questions debated by Robert Lowe, J. K. Ingram, T. E. Cliffe Leslie, and Walter Bagehot.[31] Sidgwick initially refused to regard Ingram's Comte-inspired manifesto for absorbing political economy within sociology or Leslie's historico-inductive programme as posing a fundamental challenge: it was 'merely a disagreement as to the mode of using the old method, the range of application of the old principles, the degree of emphasis laid on considerations of which all admit the relevancy and importance'.[32] Declaring neither of the extreme positions to be capable of carrying the day, he maintained that 'the most important progress in theoretical economics has been and will be derived from an exercise of thought which is not strictly deductive or inductive, as these terms are commonly used'. What he proposed instead was reflective analysis or interpretation of facts, 'that is the application to concrete facts of such general conceptions . . . as may fix the most important characteristics of the facts, and present them permanently to the mind in their true relations'.[33] Analysis entailed bringing greater linguistic precision to bear on the concepts in common use for apprehending economic realities – a modest and suitably philosophical agenda, but one for which Sidgwick made ambitious claims when it came to offering worldly advice. Few practical questions could be settled by reason alone, but

abstract reasoning may supply a systematic view of the general occasions for Governmental interference, the different possible modes of such interference, and the general reasons for and against each of them, which may aid practical men both in finding and in estimating the decisive considerations in particular cases. Thus it may show, on the one hand, under what circumstances the inevitable drawbacks of Governmental management are likely to be least, and by what methods they may be minimised; and where, on the other hand, private enterprise is likely to fail in supplying a social need – as where an undertaking socially useful is likely for various reasons to be unremunerative to the undertakers – or where private interests are liable to be markedly opposed to those of the public, as is generally the case with businesses that tend to become monopolies.[34]

This was the programme Sidgwick was to follow when devoting an entire book in the *Principles of political economy* to 'art'. He later chose *Elements of politics* as the title for his companion work, rather than political philosophy

---

[31] See pp. 134–42 above. As noted there, Sidgwick registered a fuller judgement on Bagehot's solution in the 1890s; see pp. 146–7 above.

[32] 'Economic method', *Fortnightly Review*, 16 (1879), February, p. 305.   [33] *Ibid.*, p. 308.

[34] 'The scope and method of economic science', in *Miscellaneous essays*, p. 176.

or political science, because it underlined his commitment to 'determining the rules for governmental action'.[35]

The practical side of Sidgwick's political economy was also reflected in the campaign he conducted against the proponents of the larger sociological, historicist, and evolutionary guides to the future on offer from Comte, Spencer, and social Darwinists such as Benjamin Kidd, whose 'intellectual force and industry' was offset by their 'fatuous self-confidence'.[36] Although he used more diplomatic language in public, he judged these rival methods of studying social phenomena to be incapable in their present provisional state of supplanting economics as a guide to legislative or other kinds of action. Sidgwick became as well known for his attempts to deflate the claims of the opposition as he did for his defence of the orthodox method in economics against its critics. One of the conclusions of his most extensive treatment of the subject, his presidential address to Section F of the British Association in 1885, was that 'our historical friends make no attempt to set before us the new economic pudding which their large phrases seemed to promise. It is only the old pudding with a little more ethical sauce and a little more garnish of historical illustrations.'[37] For a sceptical ethicist of Sidgwick's standing, there was something peculiarly arrogant in the almost theological confidence with which some contemporary sociologists pronounced on morals.[38] It also gave him some pleasure to point out that when authors such as Cliffe Leslie wanted to prove some point about the incidence of taxation they employed the usual a priori assumptions of economics rather than engaging in appeals to historical or inductive evidence.

Part of the attraction to Sidgwick of occupying the stance of the empirical utilitarian lay in its pragmatic and piecemeal qualities; it held out possibilities for gradual adaptation of policies to trends that could never be predicted accurately. It fitted the constructive conservatism and sceptical tendency of his basic outlook, what he described in his journal as 'scepticism of a humble, empirical, and more or less hopeful kind'.[39] The usable currency of political economy could be contrasted with the grandiose promissory notes being issued by the evolutionary sociologists. Sidgwick could discern no consensus emerging from the various moral and economic end-states being prophesied, though there was a suspiciously

---

[35] *Philosophy, its scope and relations* (London: Macmillan, 1902), p. 26.
[36] *Memoir*, p. 421.   [37] 'Scope and method', in *Miscellaneous essays*, p. 188.
[38] For the broader aspects of Sidgwick's attack, see 'Political prophecy and sociology' and 'The relation of ethics to sociology', reprinted in *Miscellaneous essays*.
[39] *Memoir*, p. 417.

close relationship between them and the political and ethical preferences of the sociologist in question. Some prophetic statements by Comte were already looking rather foolish. Sidgwick was not proud of his labours in exposing Comte's extravagances, but felt them necessary in view of the publicity being given to Comtist conclusions when Ingram's article on political economy appeared in the *Encyclopaedia Britannica*. The summary of his address that he confided to his journal says it all: 'I charge the Sociologists with mistaking the statement of the problem for its solution, and deluding themselves into the belief that they know the *laws* of evolution of society, because they have a clear conception of the *general fact* of social evolution.'[40]

As far as the main theme of this essay is concerned, however, it is not difficult to detect a bias in favour of the work Sidgwick chose to represent the socialist version of the evolutionary perspective, Albert Schäffle's *Bau und Leben des Sozialen Körpers* (1875–8). The 'carefully guarded and elaborated socialism of Schäffle' contrasted favourably with the 'naïve and unqualified individualism of Spencer'. Schäffle's account of industrial society under capitalism, rendered summarily into Sidgwick's English, supplied the empirical challenge that Spencer had failed to confront:

The tendency of free competition to annihilate itself, and give birth to monopolies exercised against the common interest for the private advantage of the monopolists; the crushing inequality of industrial opportunities, which the legal equality and freedom of modern society have no apparent tendency to correct; the impossibility of remunerating by private sale of commodities some most important services to the community; the unforeseen fluctuations of supply and demand which a world-wide organisation of industry brings with it, liable to inflict, to an increasing extent, undeserved economic ruin upon large groups of industrious workers; the waste incident to the competitive system, through profuse and ostentatious advertisements, needless multiplications of middlemen, inevitable non-employment, or half-employment, of many competitors; the demoralisation, worse than waste, due to the reckless or fraudulent promotion of joint-stock companies, and to the gambling rife in the great markets, and tending more and more to spread over the whole area of production – such points as these are unnoticed in the broad view which our English sociologist takes of the modern industrial society gradually emancipating itself from militancy; it never enters his head that they can have anything to do with causing the movement towards socialism to which his German *confrère* has yielded.[41]

Although Sidgwick did not believe that economic science owed anything to socialist authors, he sympathised with the agenda for political

---

[40] *Ibid.*, p. 421.   [41] 'Scope and method', in *Miscellaneous essays*, pp. 195–6.

economy summarised in this passage: monopoly, instability, and the waste associated with modern forms of advertising and retailing figure in his own economic writings. Though he found Schäffle's book 'remarkable', he did not regard it as science. But he was prepared to consider it as 'a careful definition of the ground on which science may some day be built'.[42] It is also significant that, in contrast to Mill's Francophone tendencies, Sidgwick chose German socialism as the modern benchmark, while believing that Marxism, for all its claims to be scientific and to have no connection with the earlier socialism of Robert Owen and Saint-Simon, was merely an updated version in which 'the older ideas have gained in precision, articulation and coherence, by being brought into closer relation to the reasonings of Political Economy'.[43]

The dialogue between German socialism and political economy had resulted in recognition of an important truth: it arose from the collision of two muddles, with the truth landing 'substantially on the Socialists' side'. The muddle on the political economy side centred on the idea that capitalists needed to be rewarded for their abstinence in creating capital; on the socialist side (and here Marx was assigned the blame) it centred on the idea that 'the labourers naturally and properly should divide up the whole produce of labour among themselves'. English socialists – one presumes he chiefly meant the Fabians – were giving the second of these muddles a wide berth. It was now recognised that capital and the reward to capitalists could be separated, with the result that while a socialist state would have to exercise abstinence in order to create capital goods, it would not have to reward anyone for doing so. Sidgwick admitted too that Mill's emphasis on saving as the condition for capital accumulation had glossed over the equally important role of technical innovation and industrial skill in creating the need for it.

Sidgwick apologised for not paying as much attention to socialist experiments as economists had done in the past. The co-operative movement, though a success, had not taught what socialists hoped it would teach; it had demonstrated why competition among retailers entailed waste and did not always serve the interests of poor consumers, but not that capitalists and private employers could be dispensed with.[44] To judge from advice he sought from J. M. Ludlow, a Christian socialist with considerable knowledge of socialist literature and experiments, Sidgwick was interested personally in making what would later be called an 'ethical'

[42] *Memoir*, p. 421.   [43] 'Economic lessons', in *Miscellaneous essays*, p. 238.
[44] See the note on this in *Elements of politics*, 2nd edn (London: Macmillan, 1897), p. 149.

investment in co-operative productive enterprises, presumably, in Mill's fashion, as a solution to the problem of conflict between capital and labour.[45] But the main reason for bypassing these voluntary experiments in his writings was his assessment that Europe had entered the era of state socialism.

When he had an opportunity to observe working-class socialists, as he did when he attended the Industrial Remuneration Conference in 1885, Sidgwick could take a native Yorkshireman's view of men from the North: 'I do not think the acrid declamatory Socialism which has its home in London will go down with the people of Lancashire and Yorkshire. No doubt they have now inclinations towards wild panaceas as regards land; but I think they have a practical turn of mind, and will not be led far astray.' This seems to have been as reassuring to Sidgwick as the observation with which he linked it, namely that the spokesman for the Liberty and Property Defence League at the conference, the law lord and zealous libertarian proponent of *laissez-faire*, Lord Bramwell, was 'a complete failure. Individualism of the extreme kind has clearly had its day'.[46]

IV

One of the non-working-class speakers Sidgwick probably heard at the conference was his ex-pupil and brother-in-law, the future Conservative prime minister, Arthur James Balfour, who spoke on 'Land, land reformers, and the nation'.[47] Balfour was contributing to the theme of the third day of the conference: 'Would the more general distribution of capital or land, or the state management of capital or land, promote or impair the production of wealth and the welfare of the community?' Henry George's ideas on land tenure reform occupied the attention of many of the speakers, and they were Balfour's main target. Speaking as a Conservative MP, as a wealthy landowner, and as the nephew of the third Marquess of Salisbury, Balfour managed something of a rhetorical coup by stating that on grounds of 'intellectual force' he would have found it more satisfying to be dealing with Marx than George. Unfortunately,

---

[45] See letters from Ludlow 13 July 1869 in Sidgwick Papers, Trinity College, Cambridge, Add. MS c 94/91 advising on German socialist literature and co-operative enterprises in Rochdale, Leicester, and Wolverhampton. Sidgwick appears to have been thinking of making an investment of as much as £2,000.
[46] *Memoir*, p. 399.
[47] See *Industrial remuneration conference: report of the proceedings and papers read in Prince's Hall, Piccadilly under the presidency of the Rt. Hon. Sir Charles W. Dilke* (London: Cassell, 1885), pp. 336–68.

whereas 'Marx is but little read in this country, Mr George has been read a great deal' for a reason that Balfour had addressed earlier in his speech. He had begun by contrasting English and continental debates on socialism. In England, 'where socialism has never as yet taken profound root, political events and economic theories have combined to turn the attention of would-be social reformers in the direction of land rather than of capital'. The more profound political and social division was between an urban manufacturing population that was Whig or radical in its political sympathies, and a landed interest now presumed to be both aristocratic and Tory. Defining moments in nineteenth-century party-political strife in England, illustrated by events such as the first Reform Act and repeal of the Corn Laws, were posed as conflicts between town and country rather than between capital and labour or even rich and poor.

Balfour also drew attention to the reinforcement given to this tendency by 'the language of theoretical economists', which treated the share going to landowners as liable to increase without 'expenditure or exertion on [their] part'. He did not question the legitimacy of such theorising for 'scientific purposes': his aim was rather to show 'how economic theory has accidentally given scientific form to any floating jealousy there may be, or rather must be, of a species of wealth, which, from obvious causes, con-stantly tends to appear larger than it is, and which influences the imagi-nation to a degree out of all proportion to its magnitude, as compared with that of riches accumulated in other and less obvious forms'.[48] Although George was the main target, Mill was implicated implicitly when referring to the unearned element in landed incomes, and explicitly when commenting on those 'who have built schemes of social reform on the somewhat frail foundation of a peasant proprietary'.[49] Balfour also thought that agricultural depression, the fact that with falling agricultural prices and rents land had become 'an almost unsaleable commodity', now made it possible to discuss land tenure 'in a spirit of scientific impartiality'.

If he heard or read it, Sidgwick left no record of his reaction to his brother-in-law's speech; but he could not avoid dealing with land tenure reform and the doctrine of the unearned increment as part of contem-porary economic socialism. After all, even the practical men of the North were capable of being attracted to 'wild panaceas as regards land'. As Balfour had implied, it was very much an English speciality, and in the 1880s it occupied a central place in radical politics. The successors to Mill's Land Tenure Reform Association were the Land Nationalisation

---

[48] *Ibid.*, p. 339.   [49] *Ibid.*, p. 341.

Society led by Alfred Russel Wallace, who followed Balfour on the Industrial Remuneration platform, and the Land Restoration Leagues inspired by George's teachings on the merits of the 'single tax'. The ideas of land reformers thrived in the era of 'democratic' politics inaugurated by the third Reform Act of 1884, which admitted rural working-class males to the electorate. Chamberlain's 'unauthorised programme' led the way in 1885, and land reforms of one kind or another later became a standard component in the Liberal and Labour party programmes. By 1889, at the more theoretical or intellectual end of British politics, the 'law of rent' had been officially enshrined as 'the very corner-stone of collectivist economy' by the Fabians. Sidgwick had heard this from Bernard Shaw at the meetings of Section F in the previous year, when he also learned that attention had shifted from the 'agricultural landlord-drone' to urban ground rents that would have to be taxed 'to meet the ever-growing necessity of providing work and wages for the unemployed'.[50]

Sidgwick had been prepared by Mill's teachings on land tenure reform to think that land nationalisation, though not advocated by Mill, 'looms, if I may say so, on the horizon'.[51] But he regarded Mill's thinking as unrepresentative: most economists were not in favour of expropriating landlords.[52] More surprising, perhaps, is what Sidgwick thought was an acceptable alternative, the 'doctrine of ransom' or 'reparative justice', whereby the poor, those excluded from 'their original share in the spontaneous bounties of Nature', should be eligible for compensation by the rich. Though difficult to arrange, the compensation should aim to give the poor 'a fuller share than they could acquire unaided of the more communicable advantages of social progress, and a fairer start in the inevitable race for the less communicable advantages'.[53] This reparative idea is a diluted version of Mill's more radical position on the severely qualified nature of property rights in land, rights that were 'the original inheritance of the whole species'.[54] It has more in common with another long-standing

---

[50] See the sympathetic report of Shaw's speech in *Memoir*, p. 497.

[51] 'Economic lessons', in *Miscellaneous essays*, p. 243.

[52] On land he speaks of Mill as an 'important exception', whose 'orthodoxy on questions of this kind is somewhat dubious'; see 'Economic socialism', in *Miscellaneous essays*, p. 213n.

[53] *Ibid.*, p. 213. Sidgwick was still toying with novel ways of implementing this idea when he returned to the subject in the second edition of the *Elements of politics* (1897), but the type of expenditure remained broadly educational, either to improve 'the efficiency and mobility of labour' or to extend to the working classes 'some share of the culture which we agree in regarding as the most valuable result of civilisation'; see pp. 72–3, 163.

[54] See Essay 3 above, p. 76.

moral and political tradition connecting the right of the poor to relief on grounds of their exclusion from a common patrimony.[55]

Landed wealth was something with which Sidgwick was personally as well as professionally well acquainted both as a fellow of one of the richest Cambridge colleges and as the husband of a member of the Balfour family with all its Salisbury connections. As a young man he was not inclined to interfere with rental incomes as long as this was compatible with agricultural improvement. Indeed, he favoured use of Ricardian rent as a means of maintaining an aristocracy of talent, and was to retain a concern for the damage greater equality of income and wealth could have on high culture.[56] Sympathy for the plight of Irish landlords, if left to the mercies of their tenants, was Sidgwick's chief reason for deserting the Liberals for Liberal Unionism over Home Rule.[57] While enjoying a house party at Whittingehame, his brother-in-law's Scottish estate, he confided some mildly disloyal reflections of a non-analytical kind to his journal. Although he could not support any of the radical measures for breaking up large estates, he mentioned two of the modernising forces acting on the landed aristocracy that he regarded as healthy:

the cheapness of corn which is driving them all to look into ways and means as any man of business would; and the extension of the franchise which is obliging them to argue before their labourers as an advocate before his jury. Every day they are becoming more genuinely members of a free industrial community. But they do not like the transition, and I am not impolite enough to tell them that it is good for them.[58]

When dealing with the unearned increment under the heading of 'distributive justice' in his *Principles*, Sidgwick accepted the 'abstract validity' of the case for communal appropriation. Since some future unearned increment was already embodied in the purchase price of land, the case was confined to unforeseen increases, which might be difficult to distinguish from earned increments. He also recognised the problem to which Balfour had alluded when speaking about the effect of agricultural depression: compensation for 'undeserved decrement'. In evidence to the Royal Commission on Local Taxation given in 1897 he revealed a willingness to support measures of relief that acknowledged the change in circumstances surrounding land ownership since the repeal of the Corn

---

[55] See Thomas A. Horne, *Property rights and poverty: political argument in Britain, 1605–1834* (Chapel Hill: University of North Carolina Press, 1990).
[56] See *Memoir*, p. 132, and p. 222 below. [57] *Ibid.*, p. 524; see also p. 439.
[58] Diary entry, 29 August 1885, *Memoir*, pp. 422–3. Final sentence in CD version.

Laws: 'the recent fall in the annual value of land consequent on the cheapness of agricultural products caused by free importation, affords a good opportunity for at least reducing the burden' of local taxes on land. On these equitable grounds he gave his blessing to the scheme of partial relief from local rates that had been implemented by the Conservative government in the previous year, when falling rental revenues attributable to the depression had been the chief justification.[59] But if public ownership was part of any socialistic ideal, nationalisation with full compensation might be the only way of proceeding, though it would involve massive public borrowing. There was also the danger of 'inertness or jobbery incident to public ownership', an objection that might be amended as standards of public management improved. Returning to the subject when writing his *Elements of politics*, Sidgwick reached the conclusion that best fitted his cautious temperament; he thought the redistributional advantages that could be attained via communal ownership were outweighed by the economic disadvantages 'at the present stage of social and political development'.[60]

V

The various land reform alternatives had been thoroughly rehearsed in Britain; there was also a large literature on land tenure systems throughout Europe. But if land could be nationalised or brought under public control in some way, the next question for any socialist state would be why other forms of capital should not be subject to public ownership. It was often via the better known route of land that the wider question of nationalisation of industry was raised. This was less well-known territory, and in the absence of examples of communities that had taken this step Sidgwick found it necessary to exercise his imagination by supposing what might happen if production could be placed in the hands of a state seeking to distribute the social dividend according to socialist principles.[61] Here the

---

[59] See Report of the Royal Commission on Local Taxation, 1899, C 9528, answers by Sidgwick, pp. 99–112, quotation p. 112; and for comment on this support for a controversial concession by the Conservatives to their landowning supporters, see Stefan Collini, 'My roles and their duties: Sidgwick as philosopher, professor, and public moralist', in Ross Harrison (ed.), *Henry Sidgwick*, Proceedings of the British Academy, 109 (Oxford: Oxford University Press 2001), pp. 35–6.

[60] *Elements of politics*, pp. 147–8n.

[61] The chapters in Sidgwick's *Principles of political economy* (London: Macmillan, 1883; 2nd edn, 1887) that deal with these issues are chapters 3–7 in Book III, especially the last two entitled 'The principles of distributive justice' and 'Economic distribution'. Sidgwick returned to these subjects in the *Elements of politics*; see especially chapters 4–5, 10–11. Chapter 10 is entitled 'Socialistic interference'.

'abstinence' issue mentioned earlier, and the distinction between interest or profit on capital and the wages of management became relevant, especially when higher returns could be attributed to skill and enterprise rather than combination or monopoly.

The earnings of skilled and professional labour also contained elements of scarcity or monopoly return. The differentials attributable to this could be diminished by free or cheaper education at community expense: here the 'reparative' argument could be called upon. But was the payment of interest on capital a 'removable cause of inequality of opportunities'? In principle Sidgwick thought it was: the socialists were right in maintaining that 'the social accumulation of instruments might conceivably be carried on by the community and without any payment of interest'.[62] He could not regard the problems of making the transition to this kind of society as any greater than those involved, say, in the abolition of slavery or feudal serfdom. One possible reason he could treat this issue with historical equanimity was that he felt the main objection to socialism lay elsewhere, where it had always lain for English followers of Smith: 'I object to Socialism not because it would divide the produce of industry badly, but because it would have so much less to divide.'[63]

In these circumstances economic considerations prevailed over abstract justice, which is why Sidgwick used '*economic* distribution' as the title of the next chapter in his *Principles*. The subject could be opened up via Bentham's dictum on the diminishing utility associated with additions to wealth, leading to the conclusion that 'the more any society approximates to equality in the distribution of wealth among its members, the greater on the whole is the aggregate of satisfactions which the society in question derives from the wealth that it possesses'.[64] But this was true only if the total wealth to be divided did not fall, population did not rise, and there was no impediment to the happiness derived from non-economic sources. Superfluous wealth when redistributed might simply lead to a greater preference for leisure, an increased population, and diminished powers of accumulation and risk-taking. The need for a governing class might be met by salaried officials, but the same solution would not take care of the community's need for knowledge and culture. The case for scientific knowledge with short-term technological benefits might survive the equalisation of incomes, but that for scholarship and culture could suffer. Ever anxious to be fair to all sides, however, Sidgwick conceded that

---

[62] *Principles*, p. 516.   [63] *Ibid.*, p. 517.   [64] *Ibid.*, p. 520.

arguments in favour of existing inequalities were mostly arguments against sudden and sweeping changes rather than 'mild and gentle steps'.[65]

If a communistic solution could be achieved without impairing production or increasing population, the proposition that it would produce more happiness than the present system was 'a very plausible one'.[66] If governmental administration proved more efficient than private competitive management, of course, the state could pay for the conversion of all economic assets into public property from increased proceeds. Taken in conjunction with the effect of free education in reducing the scarcity value of higher forms of labour, '[w]e should have arrived at something very like the ideal of economic distribution which German Socialists have put forward, without any sudden shock to the expectations formed by the present system of private property'.[67] Sidgwick had already established that 'unqualified laisser faire' could not be defended 'as tending to realize the most economical production any more than the best possible distribution of wealth'. And the conclusion for the future that he drew was, for once, more categorical than anything uttered by Mill: 'it seems to me quite possible that a considerable extension of the industrial functions of government might be on the whole advantageous, without any Utopian degree of moral or political improvement in human society'.[68]

VI

There was one existing English institution that, almost by definition, did not presuppose any utopian assumptions about moral improvement: the Poor Law system inaugurated in 1834, which confirmed the legal right of paupers to relief, but only under the deterrent conditions summarised as 'less eligibility'. Since 1871 Sidgwick had been active in what he described as 'quasi-philanthropic work'. This took the form of founding and administering the affairs of the Cambridge branch of the Charity Organisation Society (COS), acting as its chairman and as a member of the executive until the 1890s.[69] The COS had been founded in 1869 as a locally organised voluntary organisation seeking solutions based on 'desert' and operating in parallel with the 'indoor' assistance granted to meet basic 'needs' as of right by the Poor Law. It offered discretionary 'outdoor' charitable assistance on the basis of expert case-work assessments designed to separate deserving cases of accidental and remediable pauperism from

---

[65] *Ibid.*, p. 530.   [66] *Ibid.*, p. 527.   [67] *Ibid.*, p. 529.   [68] *Ibid.*, p. 530.
[69] See *Memoir*, pp. 341–2.

undeserving ones. As Sidgwick noted when dealing with this as part of the
art of political economy in his *Principles*, the plight of those who had
fallen into indigence through no fault that could be foreseen underlined
the 'moral necessity of supplementing [the English poor law] by private
almsgiving'.[70] Equipped by experience of these institutions, and fortified
by what was becoming known about alternative systems of support
abroad, especially in France and the experiments in social insurance being
pioneered in Bismarck's Germany, Sidgwick felt it was possible to go well
beyond mere imagination in discussing the effect of communistic proposals such as a guaranteed minimum wage and its likely partner, an
unqualified 'right to labour'. As on other matters, his opinions ranged
from envisaging possible future circumstances which would make it
feasible to live with such entitlements to expressing anxieties about the
direction in which change was actually occurring.

Sidgwick considered the English poor law to be a form of intervention
that might appear to be designed merely to protect health and life but
was in fact, though not intention, 'communistic in its effects'. Unearned
income was being granted to paupers at the expense of a compulsory levy
on non-paupers, with the usual disincentive or 'moral hazard' effects as
far as thrift and exertion were concerned on the part of those at or near
the minimum standard being guaranteed to paupers. The effect on
recipients of aid was modified only by expecting work to be performed
'under somewhat disagreeable conditions'. Although the English system,
combining the Poor Law with COS activities, did little to improve the
capacity of inmates to deal with the realities of the job market after leaving
the workhouse, Sidgwick seems to have thought that it made the best of
a bad job under present English conditions. What he feared was that its
unpopularity in trade union or working-class circles would lead to 'socialistic degradation' as democratic pressures on a system that was already
communistic eroded the remaining individualistic safeguards.[71] He was
attracted by William Blackley's proposals to finance old-age pensions by
means of compulsory insurance arrangements paid, once and for all,
in youth, but thought they were not a practical proposition in British
political conditions. The German system of compulsory social insurance,
financed by a mixture of contributions from employers, the employed,
and the state, also avoided the communistic outcome, whereby assistance

---

[70] *Ibid.*, p. 536.
[71] These fears were expressed in an unpublished lecture, possibly to the Charity Organisation Society.
The text of the lecture can be found on the CD of Sidgwick's works.

was granted regardless of any prior contribution to the fund from which assistance was drawn. Some combination of French, English, and German approaches, involving 'regulated [outdoor] private almsgiving, public relief [via the workhouse], and compulsory insurance', was probably the best solution.[72]

Most of the other cases to which Sidgwick gave prominence in his treatment of the art of political economy pointed in a more collectivist or socialistic direction. This was true both of his decision to reopen Mill's infant industry argument for tariffs and his extension of Mill's list of exceptions to the *laissez-faire* principle. Other advanced nations had persistently failed to follow Britain's lead in confining tariffs to those used for revenue purposes. If 'the common sense of this civilized world has pronounced in favour of Protection' it was the duty of the reflective analyst to seek an explanation rather than dismiss it as mere folly or knavery. A temporary infant industry tariff was a good example of the way in which governments were often called upon to promote production; and it could be justified on grounds of abstract theory even if the gains were 'more than counterbalanced by the general bad effects of encouraging producers and traders to look to Government for aid in industrial crises and dangers, instead of relying on their own foresight, ingenuity and energy'.[73] It was no longer sufficient to condemn protection of native industry on static free trade grounds. Once acquired, trade advantages could become permanent, an argument that might be comforting to a 'patriotic Englishman' but troubling to a 'patriotic foreigner'.[74] Sidgwick took Mill's case one step further by showing that a temporary tariff might be justified from a cosmopolitan standpoint on grounds of the positive benefits attached to industrial development, with the savings on the transport costs involved in international trade being part of the gains.[75]

The sentence in Mill that Cobden had condemned on his deathbed had grown into an elaborate chapter to which Sidgwick gave greater publicity by using it as an illustration in his presidential address to Section F.[76] He wanted to show that the decisive arguments against infant industry tariffs were political rather than economic: no actual government

---

[72] *Elements of politics*, p. 166. See too his preface to the translation of Aschrott's *English poor law system* (London: Knight, 1888).
[73] *Elements of politics*, p. 489.   [74] 'Scope and method', in *Miscellaneous essays*, p. 178.
[75] Sidgwick's chapter on the infant industry tariff (Book III, chapter 5) is an application of the theory of international values he had set out earlier (Book II, chapter 3) in which distance and transport costs were the main feature of his attempt to improve on Mill's exposition.
[76] 'Scope and method', in *Miscellaneous essays*, pp. 177–80.

possessed the wisdom 'to keep their protective interference within due limits' or was capable of carrying out the delicate task involved in maintaining an artificial system of industrial encouragement.[77] But one feature of protection that seems to have been attractive to Sidgwick was its use in reducing the fluctuations in earnings and employment associated with global trade, one of the points noted in his summary of Schäffle's position. The mature conclusion, after a good deal of see-sawing around the problem, was that in 'extreme cases', 'a civilized community ought to be always prepared to give effective aid, through its Government, in any case of acute and widespread distress caused to any section of its members by changes in industry or trade'.[78] Potentially, that opened up a very wide class of problems for which intervention might be justified, with only the sign marked 'extreme cases' (no criteria attached) to discourage allcomers from applying.

Sidgwick's treatment of economic exceptions to *laissez-faire* was elaborately taxonomic, though – bearing in mind his claims for conceptual analysis – never *merely* taxonomic. Paternalistic intervention was based on the absence of those ideal conditions assumed by economic theory when agents were judged not to be capable of taking sufficient care of their private economic interests. The education of children and the protection and promotion of health, morality, and culture fell into this category. On the other hand there was that large non-paternalistic category of forms of intervention 'which it is the more direct business of economic theory to analyse and systematize'. Into this category fell those arguments for intervention that arose 'even in a society composed – solely or mainly – of "economic men" ' acting under competitive conditions, but where the outcome had 'no tendency to realise the beneficent results claimed for it'.[79] Cairnes had been mistaken in dismissing *laissez-faire* solely as a practical maxim: by giving full weight to it as a hypothesis it was possible to locate more precisely the reasons why intervention might be justified.[80] Use of this insight allowed Sidgwick scope for dealing with a wide range of other situations in which market incentives would not produce adequate solutions. It included the accepted range of public goods such as lighthouses, bridges, and harbours, and went on to deal with other topics

---

[77] *Principles*, pp. 488–9.
[78] *Ibid.*, p. 509: 'From this point of view we must admit that there is some force in what has been urged by Protectionists as regards the tendency of Protection to keep the conditions of production more stable, and prevent the great fluctuations in local demands for labour which the changes of widely extended trade are liable to cause.'
[79] *Principles*, p. 403   [80] See the comment on Cairnes in *ibid.*, p. 403n

that would furnish the heartland of what later became known as 'welfare economics', those examples of market failure attributable to externalities, neighbourhood effects, and indivisibilities. Prominent among the examples chosen by Sidgwick were those connected with the natural environment (afforestation and flood or disease control); conservation (regulation of fishing and hunting where voluntary agreement was likely to break down), and public utilities (natural monopolies, activities that promised only long-term social returns but were unremunerative to private agencies); and cases such as roads where collection of tolls could detract from their utility to the public. Government intervention was not appropriate in all cases where market provision failed or fell short of what it promised, but the conclusion of Sidgwick's extended treatment of divergences between private and social returns was that it should lead us to accept 'governmental interference as not merely a temporary resource, but not improbably a normal element of the organization of industry'.[81]

VII

When distancing his own 'English' approach to political economy from the 'French' alternative, Sidgwick had referred opaquely and pejoratively to the British admirers of Bastiat as 'subordinate members of the "Manchester School"'.[82] Louis Mallet, a fellow member of the Political Economy Club, fitted this unflattering description. Minus discipleship to Bastiat, so did T. H. Farrer, Mallet's former Board of Trade colleague, who was also a member of the Cobden and Political Economy clubs. In his *Principles* Sidgwick singled out Farrer's book on *Free trade versus fair trade* (1881) as an example of the kind of closed Euclidian mentality that was no longer appropriate to these questions; it was couched in a 'fanatic' language that reflected the 'old belief in the harmony of the interest of each industrial class with the interest of the whole community', a language that had lost its hold on 'the mind of our age'.[83] None of this boded well for good relations when Mallet and Farrer were appointed external examiners for the Cobden Club prize at Cambridge in 1885/6, with Sidgwick and Alfred Marshall serving as the internal examiners. It provided an opportunity for a frank exchange of views that did much to confirm the stereotypes held by both sides.

---

[81] *Ibid.*, p. 414.   [82] *Ibid.*, p. 400.
[83] Farrer, in his *Free trade versus fair trade* (London: Cobden Club, 1881), had said that, in defending free trade, he felt as though he was being asked to prove the self-evident axioms of Euclid; for Sidgwick's comment, see *Principles*, p. 487.

Surviving correspondence chiefly centres on how far Sidgwick and Marshall were prepared to go in endorsing the more radical views of Mill or in qualifying or rejecting free trade and *laissez-faire*. Mallet questioned Marshall on the soundness of Mill on such matters as the unearned increment and the theory of value, and received answers that could only confirm his suspicions of the hold Mill still exerted. Marshall conceded that the theory of unearned increment was 'logically the worst thing [Mill] ever did in Political Economy', but was not prepared to go beyond this.[84] What concerned the ex-civil servants was the effect academic publications could have in undermining the public commitment to free trade. Was it not better, Farrer inquired, for these subjects to be 'thrashed out in private by those who will do it coolly and argumentatively' rather than allow 'theoretical objections, not going to the root of the matter or demanding a change of policy' to be used 'by platform orators, and having weight as coming from philosophers and out of "Academe"'?[85] Since publishing the first edition of his *Principles* in 1883 Sidgwick had presented his views on exceptions to free trade privately to the Political Economy Club; but as we have noted he had also included them in his presidential address to Section F.

In writing to Sidgwick, Farrer professed to be open-minded about academic treatments of exceptions, but it is also clear that he had his correspondent in view as much as those unnamed academic economists he cited as illustrations of the dangers involved:

I am very glad you agree about the general question. It is quite possible that an exhaustive statement of the possible, or rather ideal, cases in which protection is defensible, coupled with a comparison of such cases with the actual facts of protection in the world might do good to the cause of Free Trade. My own mind is so constituted as to be asphyxiated in the abstractions of many of our great teachers. I am always asking 'Possibly true in some abstract Heaven (or Hell), but how about the work-a-day world.'

Sidgwick was in many ways the very model of an academic, much given to the use of conditional statements and hypothetical imperatives that impatient readers could mistake for genuine ones. It must also be

---

[84] 'I am sorry that there is no chance of our agreeing about Mill. I think even the passages you quote, though badly expressed, are defensible in the sense in which he seems to me to have meant them. But while holding that Jevons was really more in agreement with Mill than he thought, I do not say the same of McCleod [*sic*]. I believe I agree substantially with both Mill and Jevons, but not with McCleod.' See letters from Marshall, 8 June and 17 November 1886, Mallet Papers, Balliol College.

[85] Farrer to Sidgwick, 28 May 1887 in Sidgwick Papers, Trinity College, Cambridge. See too a letter dated 9 June giving a rapid-fire dismissal of the infant industry case.

admitted that some of his taxonomic abstractions could be asphyxiating. But his defence of the role of 'abstract reasoning' shows that he would not have accepted Farrer's charge of living in an unreal world. Practical statesmen as well as undergraduates could benefit from the exercises in common-sense reasoning contained in Sidgwick's textbooks.

In the letters that passed between Farrer and Mallet comparing notes on their encounters with the academics the language was stronger, particularly from Mallet, who could see no point in discussing matters that had been settled long ago by Bastiat. He found Farrer's attitude far too accommodating. Of Farrer's book on the *State in relation to trade*, he predicted that it would do little to stem the tide running in favour of the 'evils of government interference': 'I do not indeed believe that this will be done, until men have the courage to aver the conviction that this is not an open question. Of course, until Mill and Cairnes and the rest of that fatal school are finally discredited, it is useless to look for any rational change. The demoralization is universal.' Why had Farrer conceded that there was no a priori objection to the state as trader? 'Of course if this were true it would be useless to continue the controversy. Sidgwick and the Socialists can always say that until their system has been tried for a few hundred years, it would be impossible to say whether it is better or worse than what he calls the "individualistic" system'.[86]

Responding to Sidgwick's request for suggestions for improvements in the second edition of his *Principles*, Mallet took particular exception to Sidgwick's speculative exercises on the possible shape of a socialist future. He bombarded him with questions centring on the consequences of state ownership and management of industry, and socialist criteria for achieving distributive justice. How would the profits of state-run enterprises be distributed to the populace at large? If used to relieve taxes, wage-fund objections were relevant: would there not be an increase of population without any accompanying increase in the stock of capital? How would Sidgwick distinguish between the idle and the industrious? Those private capitalists who had been bought out would continue to live on the income from interest at home or seek more profitable outlets abroad. What motive would anyone have to save, and what alternative to the profit motive would get the business of society performed in as efficient a manner as the service currently provided by such private captains of industry as Commodore Vanderbilt? Anyone with extensive experience of government would know how few public officials worked for the sake of duty alone;

---

[86] Mallet to Farrer, 24 December 1886, Farrer Papers, Surrey Record Office.

they would demand high salaries, thereby perpetuating the inequalities Sidgwick was seeking to remove. Government involvement with industry had always proved to be corrupt and inefficient. Even the Post Office and the telegraph services would be better and more cheaply run if left in private hands. Henry Maine was right in saying that there were only two ways of getting the world's business done, slavery and coercion on the one side, and competitive industry on the other. Was it not the height of irresponsibility for economists to be burdening government with responsibilities in the field of distribution, and encouraging the poor to look to government for their salvation?[87]

Sidgwick's arguments on the question of distributive justice aroused little sympathy from Mallet: 'I do not myself think this is in itself important or even desirable. On the contrary I believe that inequality of fortune affords one of the strongest motives for productive energy, but however this may be, the poor are getting richer quite as fast as the rich.'[88] Robert Giffen's evidence of an improvement in the living standards of the poor was all that Mallet needed to counter Sidgwick's concern with reducing income inequalities, though Sidgwick was surely right to respond by pointing out that:

What [Giffen] attempted to prove was that the income of manual labourers *in the aggregate*, or on the average has increased in the last fifty years more than the incomes of other classes: but he does not, so far as I know, attempt to prove this of the poorest class of manual labourers: and I should say that there was a 'growing inequality' in distribution if the difference between the highest and the lowest class was increasing. And this no one, so far as I know has disputed.[89]

Sidgwick protested that Mallet had exaggerated the extent of their disagreement: he had conceded many of Mallet's points as empirical issues, and was not making definite proposals for implementation. From what we know about Sidgwick's political inclinations at this time (those of a Liberal Unionist who was worried about becoming a Tory), it must have required restraint or irony for him to point out that 'your arguments appear to me to be *chiefly* directed against a view that is more definitely socialistic than mine'.[90] It is certainly not surprising that the normally

[87] Letters to Sidgwick, 8 April and 16 September 1886, and 14 July and 5 December 1887, Sidgwick Papers, Trinity College, Cambridge. The Maine reference was to his book on *Popular government*, which Sidgwick, let alone Mallet, regarded as 'the best anti-democratic writing we have had'; see *Memoir*, p. 392

[88] Mallet to Sidgwick, 14 July 1887, Sidgwick Papers, Trinity College, Cambridge.

[89] Sidgwick to Mallet, 23 July 1887, Sidgwick Papers, Trinity College, Cambridge.

[90] Sidgwick to Mallet, 20 August 1887, Sidgwick Papers, Trinity College, Cambridge.

scrupulous Sidgwick did not mention Mallet as one of those who had helped him revise his book. The gulf between the two economic mentalities had not been bridged at any point. In Mallet's book, published after their exchanges, Sidgwick was dismissed simply as Mill's 'latent apologist'.[91]

VIII

Sidgwick was, of course, a great deal more than that, though it is easy to see why Mallet came to that conclusion. The confrontation between Mallet and Sidgwick, minor though it might seem, illustrates some central features of the dispute between Individualists and Socialists that was at the heart of public debate from the 1880s up to the First World War. Sidgwick, along with many of his contemporaries, could use the capital letters without wishing to signal the need to proclaim exclusive allegiance to either of the ways of thinking so described. By contrast, although Mallet clearly disliked being pigeon-holed as 'individualistic' by his opponent, he had all the qualities needed to qualify as an extreme example of the species. Sidgwick, for his part, regarded Mallet, along with Farrer, Spencer, and the Liberty and Property Defence League as anachronisms whose demise was to be welcomed, not because they opposed socialism but because they gave a bad name to the essential core of individualism to which Sidgwick was still firmly attached. Conceptual clarity required distinctions to be made between socialistic arguments that were merely individualistic ones in disguise, and vice versa. On the one hand, revealing that some forms of intervention had individualistic credentials was a useful calming strategy: nothing essentially novel was being proposed. On the other, drawing attention to what was genuinely socialistic could act as a stronger warning against bureaucracy and corruption, particularly in the 'democratic' world of party competition for votes opened up by the third Reform Act of 1884.

Attachment to the individualistic virtues and priorities of Mill's *On liberty* underlies Sidgwick's concern about Mill's possible apostasy. And yet continuities with Mill remained strong. Sidgwick did not make as much noise on the subject of the Malthusian problem, but it was still one that required attention: population pressure remained a constraint on improvements to working-class living standards. Though artificial methods of contraception were not openly canvassed, Mill's other favoured solution,

---

[91] One of only two references to Sidgwick in *Free exchange*. see p. 356. The other (p. 170) disputes his treatment of national debt.

state-supported emigration to colonies of settlement along Wakefield lines, was still on Sidgwick's agenda in the 1880s.[92] Mill's acceptance of the principles of 1834, with its rigid separation between 'needs' met by a public agency on a deterrent basis, and the activities of private charitable agencies making judgements based on 'desert', was no longer such a straightforward issue to Sidgwick, with all his experience of COS activities. Collaboration ('intimate mutual acquaintance') between official Poor Law guardians and those working for the COS was now essential.[93]

Friedrich Hayek paid Sidgwick the compliment of saying that his *Elements of politics* was 'the last comprehensive attempt to restate the principles of a free society'. But he took back more than he gave by adding: 'Though in many ways an admirable work, it scarcely represents what must be regarded as the British liberal tradition and is already strongly tainted with that rationalist utilitarianism which led to socialism.'[94] This says more about a particular mid to late twentieth-century variant on Mallet's individualism than it does about Sidgwick's actual intellectual relationship with socialism. Yet Sidgwick was plainly some kind of rationalist utilitarian, albeit of a pragmatic variety. In this respect it would be hard to distinguish him from Mill or Jevons: each of them was an empirical utilitarian, unwilling to believe in the existence of fixed *axiomata media* in making judgements about policy.[95] But there is always room for questions of degree when making judgements about the wisdom of increasing the role of the state. Mill's opinion that state or municipal management was still insufficiently efficient to be trusted with land nationalisation, a measure he thought might otherwise be workable, has been noted.[96] For all his admiration of Spencer, Jevons was not impressed by the evolutionists' attempt to substitute maximum liberty of action for happiness as the social maximand:

So intricate are the ways, industrial, sanitary, or political, in which one class or section of the people affect other classes or sections, that there is hardly any limit to the interference of the legislator. . . . It is impossible, in short, that we can have the constant multiplication of institutions and instruments of civilisation which evolution is producing, without a growing complication of relations, and a consequent growth of social regulations.[97]

---

[92] See *Principles*, pp. 467–75.
[93] Cf. Mill on the Poor Law in *Principles*, CW, III, pp. 961–2 and Sidgwick's preface to Aschrott, *English poor law system*, p. ix.
[94] See *Constitution of liberty* (London: Routledge, 1960), p. 419n.
[95] See p. 164 above on Jevons and Mill.   [96] See Essay 3, note 70 above.
[97] *State in relation to labour*, 3rd edn (London: Macmillan, 1894), pp. 14–15.

More significantly, despite his acknowledgement of the contribution made by Bastiat and the French school, and a general antagonism to socialism, Jevons was well disposed towards a wide range of public goods: 'There can be little doubt that, as civilisation progresses and the political organisation of peoples is gradually developed and perfected, the public expenditure in works of utility will increase to the average advantage of everybody.'[98] Sidgwick too, as we have seen, had become more convinced that Britain's urban and industrial civilisation might require more extensive powers on the part of government. Mill might have been prepared to recognise the need for such powers on a case-by-case basis, but Sidgwick saw them as historical trends pointing in one direction only. His students and readers were being prepared, however reluctantly, for a new world in which government was likely to be a larger and more permanent presence in social and economic life. The two junior colleagues of Sidgwick who feature prominently in the next part of this book took this as a starting point for their own, initially more radical, approaches.

[98] *Principles of economics* (London: Macmillan, 1905), p. 41.

PART IV

Foxwell and Marshall

Fig. 7. Herbert Somerton Foxwell. Photographs showing him as a young man
in 1878 aged 29 and as an old man in 1936 aged 87.

Fig. 8. Alfred Marshall. Photographs showing him as a young man
in 1865 aged 23 and as an old man in his eighties.

9

The old generation of political economists and the new

> Of course I should soften down what you say as to the discontinuity between the old and the new school of economists even in the matter of laissez-faire. But bar this, I agree heartily.
>
> Letter from Marshall to Foxwell, 10 March 1884[1]

I

Marshall was commenting appreciatively on the syllabus of a lecture Herbert Somerton Foxwell had just given to working-class audiences in Yorkshire as part of the Cambridge University extension scheme. The initial 'of course' indicates a disagreement they had failed to resolve, whether as teacher and pupil, their relationship during the late 1860s, or as fellow lecturers teaching parts of the Moral Sciences tripos over which Sidgwick presided in the following decades. Foxwell had associated the older generation of political economists with 'a very dismal and ungenerous dogmatism' on the subject of *laissez-faire*, contrasting this with the new generation's practical reformist sympathies: 'It is true that the new political economy does not dogmatise as to the best form of social policy. But few will study it long without forming some general views as to the direction of future progress.' He offered 'a sketch of a social ideal which is democratic without being uneconomic' that spoke of achieving equity in the distribution of wealth; of education and sanitary laws designed to help those who lacked advantages in the 'competitive struggle'; and of public control of industry 'to secure the health and decent subsistence of those employed'. Profit-sharing schemes were countenanced alongside state and municipal undertakings. Monopolies would be controlled and the public given a chance of sharing in 'unearned accessions of wealth'. Fraudulent speculation would be curbed through publicity, and middlemen would

---

[1] *Correspondence*, I, p. 172

somehow be 'economised'. Security in the face of industrial change was promised through insurance and 'measures adapted to steady prices', a veiled reference to Foxwell's interest in bimetallism as a means of arresting the fall in the general price level. Finally, perhaps to give assurance that the proposals, though radical, did not entail state socialism, it was anticipated that social capital would continue to be amassed through private philanthropy; and that voluntary associations would remain the means of removing 'the worst effects of individualism'.[2]

With most of this Marshall could heartily agree, partly because he may have helped to form Foxwell's opinions on some of these matters. Foxwell's syllabus and subsequent forays into the same field concurred with the general aim if not detailed content of Marshall's own efforts when addressing working-class audiences during the 1880s; they shared a belief in the importance of demonstrating that as far as remedies to the 'social question' were concerned, economists were on the 'progressive' wing of British politics. Marshall later described his opinions and activities during this period as embodying a 'tendency to socialism' which he attributed to his inquiries into inequalities of income and his conclusion that many of them were remediable. Mill's chapter on the future of the labouring classes and his posthumously published articles on socialism had fortified this predisposition.[3] For reasons that will soon become obvious, it is unlikely that Mill played a positive part in Foxwell's formation. That the latter exhibited a similar tendency, however, can be illustrated from a casual observation made in a letter he wrote to Jevons in anticipation of receipt of his book on the *State in relation to labour*:

I hope to find that you have taken up – well I wont say a Socialistic position, because some dislike the word: but at all events a position from which you recognize the obligation of the individual to society, and the necessity for some control, in the public interest, of his endeavours to secure his private gain. The more I read about the condition of labour, the more convinced I am of the necessity and advantage of organization and control. It vexes me to hear the authority of P[olitical] E[conomy] always appealed to by the selfish rich on the other side. I don't think it will be so much longer, from what I see of the younger generation of economists.[4]

---

[2] Syllabus of Cambridge University extension lecture on 'Political economy and democracy' delivered at Heckmondwike and Dewsbury, 5 and 6 March 1884. Printed by Darley Terry, Dewsbury and Normanton.
[3] See *Industry and trade* (London: Macmillan, 1919), p. vii.
[4] Letter to Jevons, 10 April 1882, PC, V, p. 186.

Foxwell's stance can be characterised as leaning in a socialistic direction while being careful to maintain some distance from avowed socialists. The conclusion of an address he gave to the British Association in 1888 was that 'if the State does not become social reformer, it inevitably will become Socialist', an outcome that neither he nor Marshall would have welcomed.[5] The syllabus of his lecture contained a Darwin-influenced warning against bureaucratic methods as a check on the ' "tendency to variation" which is the source of all development', a warning that, as we shall see, could equally have come from Marshall in just that form.

At this stage in their relationship, then, it was chiefly Foxwell's stark disjunction between the moral outlook of the old and new generation of economists to which Marshall objected. Compared with the subject on which they were later to be in public disagreement, the merits of tariff reform as opposed to free trade – the subject responsible, or so Foxwell thought, for Marshall's antagonism to his candidacy for the chair Marshall vacated in 1908 – their running dispute over how the history of the discipline should be depicted might seem a matter of pedagogic pedantry at best. Yet the dispute proved symptomatic of deeper disagreements that increasingly began to reveal themselves as the two men made their separate but unavoidable journeys from being spokesmen for the young and what was new to becoming, willy-nilly, representatives of the old and outdated.

The contrast between new and old was central to the way in which both men chose to hold and expound their respective positions during the last two decades of the century. Both were writing in the shadow of the supposed conflict between economists and human beings, with Foxwell believing that the economists of the previous generation deserved to be condemned while Marshall took a far more forgiving line. The contrast between economists' thinking on wages, now and then, featured in Marshall's lectures on Henry George's theme of progress and poverty in 1883, and in his addresses to the Co-operative Wholesale Society and the Industrial Remuneration Conference in 1885. These were the first occasions on which he made use of the theory of distribution on which he had been working since he published an early version of it in the popular textbook he wrote with his wife, Mary Paley Marshall, in 1879, the *Economics of industry*. Unusually for the ever-cautious Marshall, the addresses were written 'in two days at white heat', and our informant, his

---

[5] *Papers on currency and finance* (London: Macmillan, 1919), p. 277.

wife, considered them to be some of the best things he ever wrote.[6] On these occasions he was anxious to explain the wage-fund doctrine and defend the older generation from the accusation of hostility to the interests of labour. The contrast between old and new reappeared in his Cambridge inaugural lecture on 'the present position of economics'; and it became an integral part of his chapters on the growth of economic science and its methods in the first edition of his *Principles of economics* in 1890. In the same year he returned to the subject in his presidential address to Section F of the British Association on 'Some aspects of competition'; and he made it the leitmotif of an address delivered to the Cambridge Economic Club in 1897.[7] In other words, it had become his favourite mode of presenting his ideas.

Likewise with Foxwell, who expanded on the hints in his Yorkshire lectures in a short monograph on *Irregularity of employment and fluctuations of prices* based on three lectures given in 1886, his contribution to the topics opened up by the Industrial Remuneration Conference. It provided the organising principle of the survey of 'the economic movement in England' which he wrote for an American audience in the following year.[8] An introduction to a translation of Anton Menger's *The right to the whole produce of labour* furnished an excuse to return to the subject in 1899 against a background of concern with socialism, especially the newer German or revolutionary forms of it. Three decades later, in his eightieth year, Foxwell was still preoccupied with the subject. When nominated as president of the Royal Economic Society, the first serving academic to hold the post since the society was founded in 1890, he planned to speak at its annual general meeting in 1930 on 'some of the unfortunate effects of the influence of the Ricardians'. For a society that had recently committed itself to a project for publishing a complete edition of Ricardo's works and correspondence it was an eccentric choice. Foxwell's failure to carry out his plan says something about illness and old age, a record of difficulty in completing projects, and a possible late attack of discretion for which his well-earned reputation for trenchancy had not prepared those who had had dealings with him earlier. The episode is testimony to what had become a life-long obsession with the

---

[6] See the notes on Marshall that she compiled for Maynard Keynes's use in writing his obituary of Marshall, Keynes Papers, Archive Centre, King's College, Cambridge, E3/6/8.
[7] For the first and third of these, see *Memorials*. For the second, see *PE*, Book I, chapters 4–8. These were removed to Appendices B, C, and D in the fifth edition, 1907.
[8] 'The economic movement in England', *Quarterly Journal of Economics*, 2 (1887), 84–103.

sins of an earlier generation of British economists, and with those of Ricardo in particular.

II

Marshall and Foxwell owed a good deal to Sidgwick as mentor and patron of the tripos within which political economy occupied an important if subordinate position. Marshall was generous in acknowledging this debt when Sidgwick died in 1900, but he had shown the fabled ingratitude of the (middle-aged?) young when he returned to Cambridge in 1885, aged 43, to take up the chair of political economy left vacant by Henry Fawcett's death. Sidgwick, only four years older than Marshall, had been idolised by him as the doyen of young university reformers in the 1860s and 70s. In the following decade, however, he became an obstacle to Marshall's ambitions to create a spacious separate home for the new science of economics he was in the process of building. This ambition was finally realised in 1903, with some help from Foxwell, when an Economics tripos was established that had only a strategic alliance with 'associated branches of political science' and none with the other parts of the Moral Sciences tripos. There were many sources of friction between Sidgwick and Marshall on the way to this goal, and there was also some direct rivalry on economic questions. Marshall had by then pledged himself solely to economics, rather than to psychology, the discipline that had chiefly interested him earlier. But he could still be worried by potential competition from Sidgwick in his chosen speciality: he feared that some of the ideas with which he hoped to adorn his *Principles* might be prematurely incorporated into Sidgwick's textbook on the basis of notes taken by his former students, Foxwell and John Neville Keynes, who were now assisting Sidgwick.[9] He was prepared to concede that the third book of Sidgwick's *Principles* on the functions of government merited special praise, even going so far as to say that it was 'by common consent, far the best thing of its kind in any language'.[10] But when writing his own *Principles* Marshall chose to speak of pure and applied science rather than about science and art, giving the following reason why he would not be following Sidgwick's example: 'It seems better to regard the science as pursuing its inquiries with more or less direct reference to certain practical issues, and as pointing the way

---

[9] See letter to J. N. Keynes, 8 February 1881, *Correspondence*, I, p. 131.
[10] Speech about Sidgwick, 22 November 1900, *Correspondence*, II, p. 442.

towards solutions of them, than to make pretension to the authority of an Art, complete and self-contained, and responsible for the entire direction of conduct in certain matters.'[11] Sidgwick's approach was being politely consigned to a back shelf.

One reason for this difference of intellectual styles can be found in Sidgwick's greater confidence in straightforward economic applications of the principle of the greatest happiness of the greatest number to define public good. Marshall, on the other hand, was anxious to play down the static hedonistic implications of any equation of economics with standard versions of utilitarianism as an ethical creed. 'Hedonics' was the pejorative term he employed to distance himself from more wholehearted forms of the doctrine. Commenting on Edgeworth's *New and old methods of ethics* he expressed his doubts as follows: 'As to the interpretation of the dogma, I think you have made a great advance: but I have still a hankering after a mode of exposition in which the dynamical character of the problem is made more obvious, which may in fact represent the central notion of happiness as a process rather than a statical condition'. In a follow-up letter he added: 'I think there is room for question whether the utilitarians are right in assuming that the end of action is the sum of the happiness of individuals rather than the vigorous life of the whole'. This is a sign of those Hegelian hankerings after the collective that occasionally surface in the introductory chapters of the *Principles*.[12]

Evolutionism showed how static forms of utilitarianism might be capable of becoming a stage in the dynamic process of moving to a higher ethical stage.[13] Marshall was heavily committed to the search for an evolutionary form of ethics, and entertained several different accounts of social evolution, from the biological ones associated with Darwin and Herbert Spencer to others allied with Henry Maine's historical jurisprudence, Comte's dynamics, Hegel's philosophy of history, and Marx's variation on Hegelian themes. We have seen that Sidgwick was sceptical about the ethical claims of the evolutionists. As he said in a puzzled letter to Marshall at a fairly early stage in their relationship:

As for Evolution, I quite understood the view you expressed last term, but I do not think I agree with you and I am quite sure I do not with Karl Marx . . . I say

---

[11] *PE*, II, p. 154.
[12] See letters to Edgeworth, 8 February and 28 March 1880, *Correspondence*, I, pp. 124–5; see too *PE*, I, p. 25.
[13] See, for example, his short speech to the British Economic Association on 'Economics and ethics', *EJ*, 3 (1893), 388–90.

I do not quite know if I agree with you: for I do not know whether you mean more than to insist on the *limitations* of Benthamism and the need of supplementing it with some historical sociology. But I certainly do not think it the *special* function of the Philosophy of Jurisprudence to develop dynamical conceptions. On the contrary I feel as if a grasp of the method of determining rules had been of the greatest value to myself, and how few MP's have really got it any critical debate will indicate. It seems to me that the tendency just now, owing to the positivists, is rather over-historical than otherwise.[14]

Marshall was no keener than Sidgwick to see economics cede territory to Comte's putative sociology, but he regarded organic growth and the rise of a new historical consciousness as the most important advance made by the new generation.[15] It entailed recognition of the relativity of laws to specific stages of development, and a general acceptance of the proposition that 'the laws of the science must have a development corresponding to that of the things of which they treat'. The disparate shades of Goethe, Hegel, and Comte could be invoked as testimony to the way in which the insights of the biological sciences were being extended to the sciences concerned with 'the development of the inner character and outward institutions of man'.[16] Unlike Foxwell, as we shall see, Marshall was not prepared to endorse the most common criticism of the old generation, that they ignored history and other types of inductive evidence: Marshall believed they were practical men steeped in the facts relevant to their concerns. Their error lay in neglect of 'a method of studying facts that we now see to be of primary importance'; they were insensitive to the variety and pliability of human institutions and motives revealed by comparative-historical studies: 'The same bent of mind, that led our lawyers to impose English civil law on the Hindoos, led our economists to work out their theories on the tacit supposition that the world was made up of city men.'[17]

It would not have been difficult for Marshall and Foxwell to agree that Sidgwick, though not a typical representative of the older generation, lacked qualities that would mark him out as a member of their own. On a Cambridge map he stood much closer to them than Fawcett, whom Foxwell dismissed as 'a mere inferior reproducer of Mill', but he was distant from them in other respects. Foxwell organised his account of the emerging state of economic enlightenment in England under three headings: it was 'the joint product of theoretic criticism, historical

---

[14] Letter from Sidgwick to Marshall, July or August 1871, *Correspondence*, I, p. 13; see also p. 214 above for Sidgwick's opposition to Comtists and Spencer.
[15] For Marshall's rejection of the Comtist programme, see *PE*, I, pp. 770–1 and *Memorials*, pp. 163–4.
[16] *Memorials*, p. 154.   [17] *Ibid.*, p. 155

method, and humanistic feeling'.[18] The first of these he associated with
the use of mathematics in articulating the new ideas on value and distribution connected with utility. Here Jevons was the leader, an opinion
Foxwell maintained before and after Marshall's *Principles* was published.
Sidgwick, as we have seen, was not an enthusiastic follower of Jevons. He
had encouraged Marshall's earliest mathematical work by distributing
copies of chapters from an unfinished book on foreign trade and domestic
values, but was content to follow Mill's literary or philosophical model in
his own.

The historical or 'realistic' method, for Foxwell, included statistical
inquiry and historical research as well as 'grasp of the idea of social
evolution'. Sidgwick had originally been attracted to political economy
because it did *not* involve mastering a large number of facts.[19] Nor was
economic history ever a prominent feature of his writings. Although he
and Marshall shared the same tutor in Dresden when learning German,
initially in both cases so they could read Kant in the original, Sidgwick did
not acquire Marshall's taste for Hegel's *Philosophy of history* and the
writings of the German historical school, a taste that manifested itself in
the chapters on economic history in the early editions of Marshall's
Principles and the enthusiastic endorsement he gave to the contribution of
the school to the formation of the new generation's point of view. The
teaching of nineteenth-century economic history as well as the history of
money and banking were part of Foxwell's duties under Marshall's pro-
fessorship; and while they later disagreed about the weight to be attached
to history within the new Economics tripos, it was a disagreement over
balance rather than principle.[20] Judged according to a distinction that
Marshall imported from chemistry, Sidgwick might be said to belong to
the literary and qualitative stage of the discipline's history. His short-
coming in the eyes of Marshall and Foxwell was that he showed no sign of
moving, as progress now required, to the scientific and quantitative stage.

What Foxwell meant by 'humanistic feeling' will require more attention later: for the moment it is enough to say that he had fewer qualms
than Sidgwick or Marshall about attributing lack of this feeling to the
older generation. Marshall was prepared to concede that as a result of
failure 'to see how liable to change are the habits and institutions of

---

[18] 'Economic movement', p. 87.   [19] See p. 212 above.
[20] It was part of the emerging disagreement that Marshall began to think that there was too much
history on offer in the Economics tripos: see letters to Foxwell, 8 and 12 February 1906, *Correspondence*, III, pp. 123–7.

industry', they lacked 'the faith that modern economists have in the possibility of vast improvement in the condition of the working classes'.[21]

This type of moral earnestness became the hallmark of Marshall's pronouncements on future prospects, and it united him with Foxwell on some of the key issues on the progressive agenda of the 1880s. Sidgwick's brand of cautious scepticism did not lend itself to such pronouncements. Lack of willingness to exercise moral leadership was one of the charges Marshall levelled at Sidgwick when he arrived from Oxford to take up the Cambridge chair in 1885. In Sidgwick's words: '[Marshall] contrasted my lecture-room, in which a handful of men are taking down what they regard as useful for examination, with that of [T. H.] Green, in which a hundred men – half of them BAs – ignoring examinations, were wont to hang on the lips of the man who was sincerely anxious to teach them the truth about the universe and human life.' Sidgwick could allow himself a little irony in reporting the immodesty of Marshall's account of Green's message, but he was frank in conceding that he had no uplifting moral or political message of his own to propagate.[22]

Marshall was keen to make a number of strategic linguistic innovations in his version of the science (for example, to substitute 'satisfaction' for 'pleasure' to reduce the possibility of confusing economics with ethics), but Sidgwick's method of 'reflective analysis', a philosopher's approach pursued via a study of ordinary language, ran counter to Marshall's anxiety to attract 'trained scientific minds', schooled in the habits of mathematical or natural scientific thinking, to economics. As Marshall made clear in his inaugural lecture, such minds could be deterred by the metaphysical parts of the Moral Sciences tripos. He also suggested that the tripos encouraged 'an attitude of philosophic indifference to wealth and all its concerns' that inhibited engagement with the material causes of poverty. The cap did not fit Sidgwick in all respects (he had a double first in mathematics and classics and could hardly have written anything on political economy without taking an interest in poverty); but he was right to sense that Marshall's inaugural lecture was a 'threatened declaration of war'.[23]

III

Sidgwick and Marshall were *not* at war when it came to rejecting Jevons's revolutionary interpretation of the history of British economic thinking, his claim that it was essential to make a radical break with the

---

[21] 'Present position', *Memorials*, p. 155   [22] *Memoir*, pp. 394–6.   [23] See *Memoir*, p. 402.

Ricardo–Mill tradition on the theory of value and distribution. It was partly with this in mind that Sidgwick sought to calm the 'waves of disputation that are in danger of submerging the really sound and valuable results of previous thought'.[24] Marshall had similar irenic aims. Although he had extensive plans for modernising the science (more extensive than Sidgwick or Jevons could conceive), he was, as a matter of temperament and principle, committed to doing so in a manner that stressed continuity with the past. Marshall appears to have held a sophisticated impersonal version of the fat oxen fallacy: if discontinuities were absent from economic nature, they should also be absent from the history of the discipline studying that nature. He genuinely believed that one of the features of the new historical consciousness was hermeneutic advance 'in the skill with which the partial thoughts of economists of earlier times are interpreted':

> We have learnt that most of them were true seers, with careful habits of observation and that what they meant to say was for the greater part true within its limits; though what they said does not always fully suggest to us what was in their own minds until we have supplied the latent premises which they instinctively took for granted.[25]

Supplying these 'latent premises' accounted for much of Marshall's work as an original economic theorist and historian of economics; there was no distinction between the two pursuits in this respect. His earliest theoretical innovations were made as a result of translating Mill's verbal theorems into differential equations to extend their generality and precision and then rendering them into geometry for ease of exposition and understanding.[26] The book he wrote with his wife billed itself conservatively as an attempt 'to construct on the lines laid down in Mill's *Political Economy* a theory of Value, Wages and Profits, which shall include the chief results of the work of the present generation of Economists'.[27] One justification for the twenty-year-long process of gestation which preceded publication of the *Principles of economics* is that Marshall wanted to be sure he had written something that continued to meet this specification while being as comprehensive as the work by Mill he aimed to replace. Given the Ricardian origins of the main theoretical apparatus in Mill's *Principles*, it followed that Ricardo was owed the same degree of charity as

---

[24] See p. 212 above. [25] 'The old generation of economists and the new', *Memorials*, p. 533.
[26] For his reasons for choosing this approach, see p. 278 below.
[27] Alfred Marshall and Mary Paley Marshall, *The economics of industry*, 2nd edn (London: Macmillan, 1881), preface to first edition.

Mill – indeed more in view of his originality as a thinker and awkwardness as an expositor.

Contemporary critics noted the extraordinary lengths to which Marshall was prepared to go in providing generous reinterpretations of the doctrines expounded by Ricardo and Mill designed to minimise theoretical discontinuities between past and present thinking. It became a common criticism that he had either over-generously 'rehabilitated' Ricardo (at the expense of historical truth), or that his modifications to Ricardo's theory had not gone far enough, resulting in unresolved conflict with other parts of his statement of the conclusions of modern economics.[28] Examples of failure, weakness, or error in the work of the older generation were either excused by reference to the peculiarities of British historical circumstances at the time of writing, or dismissed as mere careless uses of language. 'Shallow and dogmatic hangers-on' were held responsible for much of the misunderstanding and disinformation: 'I think it most important to make clear that the narrowness charged against economists is to be found almost exclusively in the writings of people who were not economists, but who had dabbled in economic literature enough to be able to quote without their context passages that wd serve them a good turn [towards] their own dirty ends by their own mean and cruel manoeuvres.'[29] While Foxwell was telling working-class audiences that they were right to suspect and reject the heartless teachings of the older generation of economists, Marshall was informing them that 'nearly all the greatest economists have been earnest and fearless friends of the working classes'. On the vexed question of the wage-fund doctrine, Marshall maintained that when placed in context it still made a lot of sense:

Almost everything that was ever said by the great economists of the first half of the century is true now if properly understood. Much of it will remain true for ever . . . There has been a great change; but it has not been in the theory itself, it has been in understanding how it is to be applied, and how it is not to be applied.[30]

To serious students of the science Marshall was prepared to go further in acknowledging that there was some justice in the charges levelled

---

[28] See W. J. Ashley, 'The rehabilitation of Ricardo', *EJ*, 1 (1891), 474–89; Frank A. Fetter, 'The passing of the old rent concept', *Quarterly Journal of Economics*, 15 (1901), 416–55; and Edwin Cannan, *A review of economic theory* (London: P. and S. King, 1929), pp. 317–29.

[29] Letter to J. N. Keynes, 17 November 1889, *Correspondence*, I, p. 305.

[30] 'Theories and facts about wages', *Co-operative Wholesale Societies' Annual*, 1885, as reprinted in *Industrial remuneration conference: report of the proceedings and papers read in Prince's Hall, Piccadilly under the presidency of the Rt. Hon. Sir Charles W. Dilke* (London: Cassell, 1885), pp. 186–99.

against the older generation. Collective endeavour had not been given as much attention as individual action, and 'they exaggerated the strength of competition and its rapidity of action'. The forces of demand and supply were treated as more mechanical in their operation (outside the city and foreign trade) than they were in reality. There was even 'some ground, though a very slight one, for the charge that their work is marred by a certain hardness of outline and even harshness of temper'.[31] Bentham rather than Ricardo was held responsible for this defect; though Bentham was admired by Marshall on other grounds, notably for his understanding of the importance of measuring the strength of motives, an aspect of economics that gave it the best chance among the moral sciences of achieving advanced scientific status. As we shall see in the succeeding essay, Marshall entertained high hopes that his theoretical innovations would serve as a bridge carrying the science from qualitative economics towards its quantitative destiny as a branch of knowledge with important practical and ethical bearings.

With regard to Mill, whose *Principles* had 'in a great measure deter-mined the attitude [that nearly all the older living economists in England] take with regard to social questions', a generalisation that was certainly true of Marshall himself and Sidgwick, Marshall was prepared to make some concessions to critics.[32] In a conciliatory gesture to Jevons he had admitted 'that Mill was not a constructive genius of the first order, and that, generally the most important benefits he has conferred on the science are due rather to his character than to his intellect'. But he stuck to the view that what seemed like fallacies in Mill's work were merely 'incomplete truths'.[33] A decade later he was still employing the same arguments in his unsuccessful attempts to discourage Foxwell from con-tinuing to let the side down in public.[34] Within Marshall's pantheon, however, there could be less compromise over Ricardo's standing: he remained a 'masterful genius' possessed of an uncanny 'power of threading his way without slip through intricate paths to new and unexpected results'.[35] Perhaps he was guilty of excessive use of abstract reason, of

---

[31] *PE*, I, p. 760.   [32] *PE*, II, p. 759: a defensive remark about Mill's *Principles*.
[33] Letter to Jevons, 4 February 1875, *Correspondence*, I, p. 32.
[34] Marshall agreed that '[Mill] is literary; and therefore full of error. But I think that he and Ricardo contain the kernel of truth'; letter to Foxwell, 8 August 1883, *Correspondence*, I, p. 168. Earlier he had written: 'Only do not vilify Mill. I believe that some of the modern extravagent [*sic*] school, by exaggerating his faults instead of bringing out his virtues, as was their duty, have done more harm to economic science than a hundred open enemies like George could do'; letter to Foxwell, 22 July 1883, *Correspondence*, I, p. 166.
[35] *PE*, I, pp. 761–2.

thinking of man as a constant quantity, but Marshall joined Bagehot in attributing Ricardo's virtues and vices in this respect to his semitic origins ('no English economist has had a mind similar to his').[36] As we shall see, none of this cut any ice with Foxwell.

Marshall's presentations of the work of the old generation were set against the background of what can only be described as a Whig economic history of Britain. It was a history in which the experience of widespread misery and pain was genuine, a real test of the character of the English race. If anything, Marshall was inclined to exaggerate the storminess of the seas through which the nation had had to navigate (another favourite image): it lent courage to the efforts of those who tried to do so and went some way towards explaining their failures. The legacy of the Napoleonic wars in the form of inflated food prices, taxation, and public debt was stressed. Maladministration of the Poor Law prior to 1834 led to circumstances in which the worst survived at the expense of the best: Marshall estimated that this factor alone explained half of extreme misery and poverty. Economists understood the population pressures that lay behind all this and explained why 'as bread grew dearer, cultivation was creeping up the hillsides'. In making so much of the law of diminishing returns while technology remained as it was, the economists could explain rising rents and falling wages; but the 'other-things-being-equal' clause that went with the law was often overlooked because it had no practical relevance to their circumstances. Economists also understood the benefits of free trade and gaining access to the cheaper imported food and raw materials, but they 'had no hope that the landed interests which then ruled the country could be made to allow it'. This diverted attention to the one ameliorating factor that could be controlled: capital accumulation. But it also led to 'a slovenly way of talking' about the way in which the total amount available for wages was fixed by the stock of capital, a mistake no longer committed by the new generation:

the younger economists do not speak of wages as limited by capital. But they say that every increase of capital raises wages, because it increases the productiveness of industry; it increases the competition of the capitalist for the aid of labour, and thus lowers the rate of interest and increases that part of the total produce which capital is compelled to resign to labour.[37]

---

[36] 'Present position', *Memorials*, p. 153.
[37] 'Theories and facts', *Cooperative Wholesale Societies' Annual*, 1885, as reprinted in *Industrial remuneration conference*, p. 192.

Diminishing returns had to do a good deal of work in Marshall's version of British economic history, and he was sometimes guilty of stretching the point in the direction required to make his apology felt. Addressing a popular audience he could say that 'when Mill wrote, the English labourer was suffering from bad Poor Laws, Corn Laws, and other misfortunes', a remark that was vulnerable to a simple rejoinder from the pedantic that when Mill wrote his *Principles* the Poor Law had been amended and the Corn Laws recently abolished.[38]

IV

Foxwell's contrasting hostility towards the older generation of economists acquired additional features over time, but it began as a reflection of the views of two non-Cambridge figures, Jevons and Toynbee, with whom he had established close personal friendships before their premature deaths in 1882 and 1883 respectively. By adopting a mixture of their opinions on Ricardo and Mill, Foxwell was immunised against Marshall's over-generous hermeneutic principles. Indeed, Foxwell's broad historical judgements were registered on the basis of far less close textual analysis than was characteristic of other historians who were critical of orthodoxy during this period.[39] Although differences of opinion between Foxwell and Marshall were acknowledged privately, they did not become public until Foxwell wrote a letter to *The Times* in 1903 questioning a manifesto that Marshall and thirteen other economists had signed that was critical of Chamberlain's tariff reform proposals. Foxwell's survey of the British academic scene in 1887 gave due recognition to Marshall's contribution in raising the general level of economic instruction and in training half the holders of chairs of economics in Britain. A few years later, however, after publication of Marshall's *Principles*, Foxwell confessed to John Neville Keynes, his fellow lieutenant under Marshall, that he disagreed 'very profoundly with Marshall on many points, especially in regard to Ricardo, Mill, economic method, and Consumption'.[40] These topics were closely interrelated and point to Foxwell's enduring loyalty to Jevons's memory and achievements.

---

[38] 'Three lectures on progress and poverty', as reprinted in *Journal of Law and Economics*, 12 (1969), 181–226.
[39] The contrast is sharpest with W. J. Ashley and Edwin Cannan; see D. Winch, 'Foxwell, Rae, and Adam Smith', *Adam Smith Review*, 3 (2007), 15–36.
[40] Letter to J. N. Keynes, 25 January 1891, Marshall Papers, Marshall Library, University of Cambridge.

With regard to economic method it was Jevons's 'realistic' statistical work on cyclical and long-term price movements that Foxwell most appreciated. He had edited Jevons's *Investigations in currency and finance* in 1884, and in his own work on *Irregularity of employment* he spoke of Jevons as 'the most brilliant economist of his time', modestly describing his own use of time-series evidence as 'little more than [an] attempt to place before you in a simple form the bearing of Jevons' research on the problem before us'.[41] This was contrasted with the 'sterile logomachy and academic hair-splitting' of the immediate post-Ricardian era. Ricardo had none of Jevons's virtues: he had 'adopted what was intended to be a rigorously abstract and deductive manner, but without any of those formal aids to precision and clearness which scientific, and especially mathematical method provides'.[42]

Foxwell's reference to 'consumption' was shorthand for the central point at issue between Jevons and Marshall on the theory of value. Foxwell was not prepared to accept Marshall's 'blades-of-a-pair-of-scissors' approach to supply and demand, his treatment of market value as the outcome of a process of mutual determination, with consumption and the cost of production playing more or less active or passive roles depending on the time available for adjustment and other circumstances. To Foxwell, Jevons's principle of final or marginal utility underlying consumption was 'universal and fundamental', whereas the other side of the account relating to costs was 'special and accidental'. The principle applied to markets for pre-existing resources, non-reproducible goods such as rare pictures and books, and almost all commodities in the short run. On this view of things Marshall was perpetuating the mischief Ricardo had created by concentrating on costs of production, where the harm was most evident in the field that was Foxwell's speciality, money and banking: 'I think I may say that no writer who was subject to this particular Ricardian influence has ever adequately or scientifically treated monetary problems.'[43] Marshall

---

[41] *Irregularity of employment and fluctuations of prices* (Edinburgh: Co-operative Printing Company, 1886), p. 17.

[42] Introduction to Anton Menger, *The right to the whole produce of labour* (London: Macmillan, 1899), p. lxxii; and the historical school 'oppose arrogant and universal dogmatism resting upon crude reasoning and limited basis of observation'; see 'Economic movement', pp. 89–90.

[43] Letter to J. N. Keynes, 24 January 1901, Foxwell Collection, Baker Library, Harvard Business School. He spelled out his position on money in an unpublished part of a review of a work by the Duke of Argyll: 'the school of Mill, who thought Demand could affect the temporary fluctuations of value not its normal level, were thus rendered entirely unable to give an adequate explanation of questions involving the value of money. For here, owing to the mass of the existing stocks, the influence of cost of production is a minimum while in consequence of the sway of custom and legislation, the influence of demand is a maximum.'

took a diametrically opposed position on where the mischief lay: 'Ricardo's theory of cost of production in relation to value occupies so important a place in the history of economics that any misunderstanding as to its real character must necessarily be very mischievous.' Ricardo was fully aware of the role of demand, but since 'he regarded its action as less obscure than that of cost of production', had passed it 'lightly over'.[44] As we shall see, this helps to account for the lower status Marshall assigned to 'wants' and demand when compared with 'activities' and supply. It also helps to explain his sympathetic approach to the Ricardian theory of rent 'properly understood'.[45]

Many of the accusations Foxwell levelled at the old political economy were more moral than methodological. He charged that it was 'strongly materialistic, sacrificing national welfare to the accumulation of individual wealth'; that it was 'distinctly unmoral . . . inasmuch as it claimed that economic action was subject to a mechanical system of law, of a positive character, independent of and superior to any laws of the moral world'.[46] According to the Foxwell version of history, this monolithic dispensation had been forced to give way to one that was more aware of its limitations, more healthily eclectic in its combined use of theory, history, and other forms of inductive evidence. A fatalistic period of *laissez-faire* individualism had yielded to a more optimistic era of 'corporate action and public control'.[47] Moral territory lost since the Middle Ages as a result of disastrous changes associated with the industrial revolution was being regained through trade union activity, government regulation, and some evolutionary tendencies that favoured a more altruistic outlook – the kinds of things he held out as pledges to his Yorkshire audiences.[48]

Foxwell's main charge was that political economy had mirrored rather than countered the period of industrial anarchy that reigned during the 'painful chapter' describing British industrialisation between 1760 and 1850. Foxwell's pessimistic narrative contained elements that parallel Toynbee's catastrophist interpretation of the industrial revolution, though in his hands a Whig story acquired a Tory twist. Although the effects of unleashing the forces of competition had been beneficial to some, it was destructive to many. The rise of manufacturing was accompanied by

---

[44] See *PE*, I, pp. 503, 525, the opening chapter of Book VI, and Appendix I.
[45] See pp. 272–3 and 285–6 below.   [46] 'Economic movement', p. 85.
[47] This theme dominates the historical parts of *Irregularity of employment*; see especially pp. 12–14.
[48] *Ibid.*, p. 58. In outlining his proposals for reforms designed to deal with unstable prices and irregular employment, Foxwell spoke of the need for a 'moral tonic' capable of restoring social order and justice.

disruption of the old paternalist and protective institutions and corporative organisations. The period had zero-sum features that were not those currently being stressed by Henry George:

> The very same industrial changes which raised the wages of those who could secure employment, made the position of the majority more precarious and their prospects more indefinite. Thus while wealth increased rapidly, population and destitution advanced with almost equal strides. This is the real explanation of the observed connection of Progress and Poverty.[49]

Foxwell's most individual contribution to this historical diagnosis consisted in superimposing on it a monetary interpretation of the crucial turning points, the most important of which in recent decades coincided with the demonetisation of silver after 1873. As an enthusiastic bimetallist, keen to stabilise prices and employment by reinstating silver alongside gold as a monetary metal, he regarded this as the most significant date in recent economic history. It had ushered in a prolonged period of downward pressure on the wholesale prices of commodities and exerted a deflationary brake upon the helter-skelter period of economic growth that preceded it. He also made it serve as a moral dividing line between an uncaring period in the history of economic opinion and a more serious concern with mitigating the insecurities of the labour market caused by the blind operation of market forces and those 'pulsations of industry' generated by credit cycles and secular waves of depreciation and appreciation in the value of money. One could describe Foxwell's position as an amalgam of Toynbee's condemnation of the failures of earlier policies to deal with the human costs of industrialisation with Jevons's interest in long-term cyclical movements in the prices of primary products.

v

Toynbee's life and death impinged on the lives of Marshall and Foxwell in significant ways. His death enabled Marshall to move from Bristol University College, where his duties as Principal had already proved onerous and damaging to his health and morale, to take up those vacated by Toynbee at Benjamin Jowett's Balliol, chiefly the teaching of political economy to Indian civil service candidates. During his final illness Toynbee had expressed the wish that Foxwell would correct the versions of his lectures on the industrial revolution which had appeared in the press,

---

[49] *Irregularity of employment*, p. 13.

though in the end this task fell to Alfred Milner with help from a more orthodox product of the Oxford history degree, W. J. Ashley.[50] When giving an account of his first library, Foxwell said that the material he had collected on the industrial revolution for the period 1760 to 1860 was for Toynbee's use.[51] As we have seen, Foxwell fully shared Toynbee's sympathies and preferences when writing on economic history and the history of economics. These were cognate fields that owed their modern origins to the way in which, when cultivated together, as they were by members of the German historical school and their Anglo-Irish sympathisers, they could be used to support relativistic conclusions with regard to the progressive properties, or rather perhaps lack of them, of economic science.

The early arrangements for dealing with Toynbee's legacy found Marshall and Foxwell acting in concert, on the surface at least. Marshall was offered, but refused, the chairmanship of the Toynbee Trust, the body that nurtured work in the East End of London at Toynbee Hall, mainly in the form of lectures to working-class audiences. Foxwell, a member of the trust, invited Marshall to write an introduction to a report by Langford Lovell Price on industrial peace in 1887, most of which was devoted to an exposition of Marshall's views on the meaning of a 'fair rate of wages'. But it was preceded by an appreciation of Toynbee that gave Marshall an opportunity to place his own interpretation on the legacy. Toynbee, Marshall recognised, was 'impatient with the attitude of passionless observation which he thought many of the older economists took'; he wanted something more engaged, something that registered directly the sufferings of those oppressed by poverty and adverse economic forces. The word 'thought' here plants a seed of doubt, and Marshall proceeded to water it by adding:

> But as time went on he somewhat changed his attitude towards the earlier economists. He learned to understand their difficulties better to see what led them at times to make assumptions which at first sight appear perversely unreal; and he got to distinguish their own opinions from those which are attributed to them by people who want to quote economic authority for partisan purposes.[52]

In this way, one might say, Marshall contrived to replace Foxwell's Toynbee with a figure more congenial to his own position.

---

[50] See Alon Kadish, *Apostle Arnold: the life and death of Arnold Toynbee, 1852–1883* (Durham, NC: Duke University Press, 1986), pp. 215–16.

[51] See 'Economic libraries', in H. Higgs (ed.), *Palgrave's dictionary of economics*, 3 vols. (London: Macmillan, 1926), I, p. 870.

[52] 'On Arnold Toynbee', introduced and edited by John K. Whitaker, *Marshall Studies Bulletin*, 6 (1996), 45–48.

Fig. 9. Arnold Toynbee. Photograph probably taken a few years before his death, aged 31, in 1883.

In his survey of the state of economics Foxwell had cited Toynbee as a prime example of 'the moral and humanistic criticism of our economic life and institutions', illustrated by the abolition of slavery, factory legislation, attempts to reverse the new Poor Law of 1834, and the Christian socialism of Kingsley, Maurice, and Hughes. These were illustrations of what Toynbee had described as 'Tory socialism', protection of the poor by the rich.[53] For his American audience Foxwell painted a portrait of Toynbee as a saint-like character:

Sensitive, intensely sympathetic, altruistic almost to asceticism, his intellectual being seemed to rest, like a thin transparent crust, upon a deep suppressed sea of emotion; and at times, when his usually pale, chiselled features were lit up with a flash of insight or an eager, eloquently expressed conviction, he seemed like one inspired, and he certainly inspired in no ordinary degree those with whom he came in contact.[54]

Less elegiacally Marshall too had spoken of Toynbee as 'the ideal modern representative of the medieval saint', the St Francis *de nos jours*. But in saying that 'the leading controlling strain of his character was emotional' he was also indicating that Toynbee belonged to a different breed from those who combined their warm hearts with cool Cambridge heads.

Foxwell cited Ruskin as another example of humanistic feeling, as an illustration of the way in which art had had 'its effect in recalling men from commercialism to consider the simple, eternal ends of life and the ideal conditions of healthy existence'.[55] Ruskin was also linked with William

---

[53] *Lectures on the industrial revolution of the eighteenth century in England*, 1884 (London: Longmans Green, 1923) p. 84.
[54] 'Economic movement', p. 98.   [55] *Ibid.*, p. 100.

Morris as another example of 'the socialistic leaning of the artistic temperament'. They were, of course, the obvious examples to choose, but it is not surprising to learn that Foxwell had been the only Cambridge economist to sign a congratulatory telegram to Ruskin on his birthday in 1885.[56] Marshall had met Ruskin in Oxford during the latter's tenure of the Slade chair. It seems significant that at no point did he find it necessary or convenient to give a direct answer to Ruskin's critique of the science he was in the process of turning into a serious professional pursuit, especially when *Unto this last* was enjoying renewed interest in the 80s and 90s.

Ruskin is cited only twice in the *Principles of economics* and on both occasions in tandem with Carlyle, with William Morris added in one of these instances.[57] If the older economists had been clearer in stating that material wealth was not the main aim of human effort, Marshall claimed,

they would have escaped many grievous misrepresentations; and the splendid teachings of Carlyle and Ruskin as to the right aims of human endeavour and the right uses of wealth, would not then have been marred by bitter attacks on economics, based on the mistaken belief that the science had no concern with any motives except the selfish desire for wealth, or even that it inculcated a policy of sordid selfishness.[58]

He later coupled Carlyle and Ruskin when making a double distinction: first, between the views of earlier economists and those 'harsh employers and politicians, defending exclusive class privileges early in the last century'; and secondly, between Carlyle and Ruskin and their followers. While the leaders were credited with 'brilliant and ennobling poetical visions' the followers were guilty of holding 'the great economists responsible for sayings and deeds to which they were really averse'. 'As the imitators of Michael Angelo copied only his faults, so Carlyle, Ruskin and Morris find today ready imitators, who lack their fine inspirations and intuitions.'[59] One has to be careful when reading this kind of thing in Marshall: 'poetical' takes away some of the emphasis on 'splendid' or 'brilliant and ennobling'. 'Fine inspirations and intuitions' is also double-edged when one remembers Marshall's commitment to what he called 'hard thinking'. Marshall praised Morris's *News from nowhere* as a stimulus to 'aspiration', as being 'a joy for ever': but it embodied 'unmixed good' precisely because it did not 'profess to be practical.'[60]

---

[56] See n. 73 on p. 115 above.   [57] *PE*, I, p. 61; II, p. 386.   [58] *PE*, I, p. 22.
[59] *Ibid.*, p. 47; see too p. 789n.
[60] 'Social possibilities of economic chivalry', as reprinted in *Memorials*, p. 329

VI

Another sign of convergence between Foxwell's opinions and those of Toynbee is the emphasis he placed on Ricardo's culpability. In his lectures on the industrial revolution Toynbee had become fixated on Ricardo, whom he maintained had established complete hegemony over political economy from 1817 to 1848. Beyond this he had 'revolutionized opinion [in parliament] on economic subjects'. Overcoming this malign influence was essential to the victory of human beings over the economists, a victory that Toynbee, like Foxwell, believed to have taken place somewhere in the 1870s and 80s.[61] Ricardo's crime, for both of them, was a dogmatic attachment to deductive theories that were, in Toynbee's words, 'at once the great prop of the middle classes, and their most terrible menace; the latter because from it have directly sprung two great text-books of Socialism, *Das Kapital* of Karl Marx, and the *Progress and poverty* of Mr Henry George'. Or as Foxwell put it: 'by a singular irony of fate, it happened that Ricardo, by this imperfect presentation of economic doctrine, did more than any intentionally socialist writer to sap the foundations of that form of society which he was trying to explain, and which he believed to be the typical and natural, if not, indeed, the ideal social state'.[62] Foxwell coined the term 'Ricardian socialism' to describe the school of English socialist thought that had anticipated Marx's class-based analysis of the evils of capitalism. Ricardo's chief error lay in an 'unscientific use of hypothesis' centring on a labour theory of value that was open to the interpretation (by ninety-nine readers out of one hundred, Foxwell estimated) that wealth was exclusively due to labour and therefore that 'unearned' elements could be found in the rewards going to land and capital.

Foxwell's reputation as an economist came to rest less on publications under his own name than on his compulsive activities as the collector of two of the largest libraries of economic classics. Bibliophilia, of course, carries no obligation to admire authors or their ideas. On the inside cover of his copy of Ricardo's *Principles*, Foxwell wrote: 'The first edition of this disastrous book, which gave us Marxian socialism and the Class War. Deductive playthings of this type, completely divorced from realities, make very dangerous literature for the half-educated. It is like giving a child a razor to play with.'[63] By coincidence Marshall employed the same

---

[61] See *Lectures on the industrial revolution*, p. 140.
[62] Introduction to Menger, *Right of labour*, pp. xli–xlii.
[63] Copy in Foxwell Collection, Baker Library, Harvard Business School.

image of danger from sharp objects in his defence of Ricardo ('his thoughts are like sharp chisels with which it is specially easy to cut one's fingers'), but the danger arose from 'awkward handles' and inappropriate use rather than anything intrinsic to the chisels. By supplying Ricardo's 'latent premises' Marshall thought he could enable the chisels to remain safe and serviceable.[64]

With little apparent success Marshall had urged Foxwell not to 'vilify' Mill. Foxwell granted that Mill may have been an exception to the tendency to worship the 'economic Baal', but he was hobbled by his earlier education and could only put 'new wine in old bottles to the irreparable injury of his logical reputation' (a Jevonsian conclusion).[65] Mill fared no better in Foxwell's version of the history of English socialism: he had been side-tracked into admiration for the 'romantic utopias of Fourier and Owen, or the academic industrialism of St Simon and Comte', with the result that he overlooked the more important revolutionary challenge coming from Marx, Engels, and Lassalle. He was unable 'to appreciate really original or profound conceptions, either in metaphysics or sociology' and therefore 'his influence on the whole was distinctly soporific'.[66]

Foxwell's early appreciation of the importance of Marx was the source of some pride later. He might judge Marx's reputation to be exploded, to be '*very* Early Victorian' as he once put it, but there was still kudos to be had from bearing early witness to the challenge his writings posed. Foxwell wrote a couple of short articles on Marx for the *Pall Mall Gazette* when the English translation of *Capital* appeared in 1887, and claimed that he would have written more if his interest in socialism had not been discouraged by Marshall.[67] The articles focused on the fallacies of Marx's theory of value and exploitation. After citing the refutation of this theory by Philip Wicksteed, the performance that had led to the conversion of Bernard Shaw and other Fabians to the Jevons position on value earlier in the decade, Foxwell concluded that: 'In this all economists agree, though they have followed different methods in their analysis of scarcity. No single proposition of this analysis, as it may be found in the works of writers like Jevons, Mr Marshall, and Dr Sidgwick, is shaken by Marx's criticism.'[68]

---

[64] *PE*, I, p. 777.   [65] 'Economic movement', p. 85.
[66] Introduction to Menger, *Right of labour*, p. lxxviii.
[67] See letter to F. Macmillan, 27 July 1919, Macmillan Archive, British Library. With pardonable exaggeration, perhaps, Keynes maintained that Foxwell was 'the first English economist to appreciate [Marx's] importance', *Essays in biography*, JMK, X, p. 271.
[68] 'The textbook of modern socialism', *Pall Mall Gazette*, 6 and 13 May 1887, pp. 5–6, 4–5.

What moved Foxwell to praise was Marx's description of the 'economic evolution of society':

His highly coloured descriptions of capitalism will in due time be displaced by impartial history. But his vivid perception and portrayal of the immense social significance of industrial development will be long studied for the sake of the strong stimulus it gives to the economic imagination; a stimulus greatly needed in this country.[69]

There is almost a sense of regret that Marx's obvious talents should 'lean towards catastrophism rather than evolution', though it was in that direction that Foxwell's own account of the industrial revolution leaned. To his American readers Foxwell could report that while a tinge of Marxism could be detected in some recent trade union documents, 'the imported socialism of a certain class of London and semi-foreign labour does not seem to have taken any great hold on the abler and more responsible artisan leaders'. It was only among a dilettante middle-class audience that the ideas of Henry George and Marx had acquired cult status.[70]

Marshall may well have discouraged Foxwell from teaching courses on the German socialists in general and Marx and Lassalle in particular, but it was certainly not because he was indifferent to their writings. He had read *Das Kapital* in 1870, a year after the first volume appeared, and could give an account of what he had learned, even when, as in the following example, he chose not to name the author:

It is from German writers, some of whom have been of Jewish origin, that the world has received the greater part of the most thoroughgoing of recent propositions for utilizing the property of the world for the benefit of the community with but little reference to the existing incidents of ownership. It is true that on closer investigation their work turns out to be less original as well as less profound than at first sight appears; but it derives great power from its dialectic ingenuity, its brilliant style, and in some cases from its wide-reaching though distorted historical learning.[71]

He credited Marx with having opened his eyes to some historical features of capitalism at a time when they were not widely understood.[72]

Marshall was, of course, familiar with Marx's theory of value, and having read Menger's study in its original did not need Foxwell's

[69] *Ibid.*, p. 4.   [70] 'Economic movement', pp. 98–9.   [71] *PE*, I, p. 769
[72] Letter to unknown correspondent, 20 October 1889, Marshall Papers, Marshall Library, University of Cambridge. '. . . I owe much to him. I read his book in 1870, and his extracts from English blue books – garbled though many of them are – were of great service to me. Now everyone knows about the state of factory labour early in the century; in 1870 very few people had given their attention to it.'

introduction to the English translation to appreciate its argument that Marx and other revolutionary socialists had borrowed from English sources.[73] When the translation appeared he politely said that he looked forward to reading the introduction, if not to what he could easily predict it would have to say about Ricardo. He probably thought of Foxwell as having been misled by his animus against Ricardo into accepting Marx's interpretation of him as a pure quantity-of-labour theorist of value, as someone who had lent support to the erroneous idea that labour is the sole source of the surplus from which the reward to capital derives. As he stated in his *Principles*: 'Rodbertus and Marx do indeed boldly claim the authority of Ricardo for their premiss; but it is really as opposed to his explicit statement and the general tenor of his theory of value, as it is to common sense.'[74] Marshall would not feel enthusiastic about a colleague continuing to teach what he regarded as a disingenuous half truth, though notions of *Lehrfreiheit* would prevent him from interfering with the content of Foxwell's lectures and classes. Hence perhaps the indirect method of dissuasion Marshall seems to have employed: he said that he would give his blessing to a special subject on Marx and German socialism, but only on condition that the required reading included the second and third volumes of *Capital*. Since these were only available in German, a language he knew Foxwell did not command, the result could well be described as discouragement.[75]

VII

The 'socialistic' emphasis Foxwell hoped to find in Jevons's work on the labour question consisted of a programme designed to curb unscrupulous competition and compensate the victims of economic insecurity and change, a programme he referred to in summary fashion as involving 'organisation and publicity'. During the 1880s and 90s most of his practical efforts on this front were taken up by the campaign in favour of bimetallism. Winning Marshall over to this cause would have been a major coup, and Foxwell advised his friends within the Bimetallic League on the best way of doing so.[76] Their arguments failed to satisfy Marshall's scruples, and since he could not adopt 'the excrescences which the League

---

[73] See the reference to the German version of Menger's work in an early edition of *PE*, II, p. 632n.
[74] *PE*, I, pp. 503, 587–8, 816.
[75] Letter to Foxwell, 12 February 1906, *Correspondence*, III, p. 127.
[76] See P. D. Groenewegen, *A soaring eagle: Alfred Marshall, 1842–1924* (Aldershot: Edward Elgar, 1995), pp. 351–2.

has borrowed from the US silver men' he preferred to stick with his own schemes for creating monetary stability which involved indexation (a tabular standard) and what he called 'modified bimetallism'.

One of the things Foxwell was most proud to claim in retrospect was to have been 'perhaps the first English-speaking economist to put in a word in defence of business combinations'.[77] He had followed up his lectures on the consequences of and remedies for unemployment with an address given to the British Association in 1888 on 'the growth of monopoly, and its bearing on the functions of the state' in which he adopted a position akin to those who analysed the trust movement in the United States from an institutionalist perspective.[78] His chief argument was that competition was a transitional stage on the road to monopoly, and that monopolies possessed social advantages based on their superior efficiency and capacity to bring greater stability to production and employment. Marshall mentioned this work as indicative of the attitude of 'younger English economists' in his presidential address to the British Association in 1890 on 'Some aspects of competition'.[79]

Foxwell also had a soft spot for guilds and their modern equivalents, trade associations and trade unions:

The cheap and immediate satisfaction of every unreasonable whim of the consumer is not the sole purpose of our economic organisation. The old gilds had their faults; but one of their merits was, that they made rapid changes in the amount and kind of employment less practicable. And the trade unions have done much to grapple with this difficulty, in the organised trades, by their regulations in regard to apprenticeship.[80]

What Foxwell appears to have favoured was a form of privately sponsored corporatism moderated by public regulation and the pressure of 'civilised' public opinion acting as a 'moral tonic' to restore what had been destroyed by a century of unbridled individualism. Here too there was an echo of Toynbee in the notion that competition was neither good nor bad, but something that had to be regulated in a pragmatic way without recourse to dangerous experiments of the state socialist kind.[81]

[77] See 'The nature of the industrial struggle', in *Papers on current finance* (London: Macmillan, 1919), p. 88.
[78] See Philip L. Williams, 'The attitudes of the economics profession in Britain and the United States to the trust movement, 1890–1914', in John D. Hey and Donald Winch (eds.), *A century of economics: one hundred years of the Royal Economic Society and the Economic Journal* (Oxford: Blackwell, 1990), p. 97.
[79] *Memorials*, p. 276n.   [80] *Irregularity of employment*, pp. 56–7.
[81] *Lectures on the industrial revolution*, pp. 67, 157–8.

In correspondence with Bernard Shaw, in which the Fabian programme of land nationalisation was a central topic, Foxwell admitted that the measures he was advocating were 'unheroic', and that 'on a prima facie theoretical view' the advocates of nationalisation had some justification. As a practical proposal, however, he thought there was little to be said in its favour: 'Are we for instance quite certain that land in the hands of such public bodies as we are likely to get under purely democratic election would be better managed than it now is by good landlords, or even that the rent proceeds would on the whole be spent to greater advantage, taking a broad view of the total expenditure of the landlord class?' Foxwell's alternative was to give the existing system a fair trial:

I see in it, when properly developed and subject to the control of all the humanizing and moralising agents in modern civilization, immense capacities for social good. To secure these it seems to me we only want to develop and assist, with our eyes open, tendencies already blindly operating... People are apt to overlook the voluntary nationalisation which goes on under the present system, and which in my opinion far exceeds the total net profit that would arise under any conceivable communistic system.[82]

With regard to the issue that would divide Foxwell and Marshall more publicly in 1903, Chamberlain's tariff reform campaign, both men had opportunities for learning which way the other was likely to move if the issue ever became a matter of public debate. In 1875 Marshall had made a special trip to the United States to study, among other things, the results of what he flatteringly described as 'enlightened protectionism'. In his contribution to the Industrial Remuneration Conference, when dealing with remediable causes of inconstancy of employment, he had made it plain that he thought that for a country in Britain's situation protection would do more harm than good.[83] Similarly, in reverse, Marshall could easily have picked up hints of Foxwell's likely stance. Foxwell had reported to his American readers in 1887 that depression had shaken confidence in free trade, that belief in it was now 'somewhat less confident and rigid'. The Fair Trade League's activities had also been aided by what he described as 'the remarkable growth of English national feeling'.

---

[82] Letter to G. B. Shaw, 16 November 1886, Shaw Papers, British Library, Add. MS 50511.

[83] 'though I have heard many able arguments for Protection in countries whose chief exports are of raw produce, I have never read any arguments for Protection in England that seems to me even plausible. I believe it would be as foolish, though not quite as mischievous, as the plan sometimes proposed, to try to raise wages by curtailing production all round'; see 'How far do remediable causes influence prejudicially (a) the continuity of employment, (b) the rates of wages?', *Industrial remuneration conference*, p. 181.

Imperial federation was now on the agenda of both political parties; and he added gnomically (but with a hint of approval) that 'whether or not nationalism will leave its mark on our tariffs, we cannot doubt that it will influence our legislation and foreign policy'.[84] Privately, he was more frank about his sympathies: in a letter to John Neville Keynes he described himself as '*in theory* a confirmed and convinced Fair Trader. It is only my disbelief in the self control and intelligence of the democracy which prevents my openly attacking the clumsy but comparatively simple principle of Free Trade'.[85]

Though clearly tempted, Foxwell did not feel able to take as active a part in support of tariff reform as he had on bimetallism, partly because he now had less time to devote to such things, partly because he did not feel confident about the people with whom he would have to co-operate. He quickly learned that the non-signatories to the manifesto in favour of free trade, those he referred to anonymously in his letter to *The Times* as 'the historical group of English economists', Hewins, Ashley, Cunningham, Price, and himself, could not agree on a counter-manifesto. Hewins wanted something much stronger than the rest could accept. In any event, Foxwell acknowledged that this was not a wise move when the other side could muster a larger team not merely in numbers but 'probably in the weight of the names' as well. He contented himself with advising the Prime Minister, Balfour, the only political figure to whom he was prepared to offer unconditional support over this issue, though he said that he would plump for Chamberlain if forced to do so.[86] He was no more attached to free trade than he had been to *laissez-faire*: 'A man will not secure his interest without fighting for it; there is nothing in a system of laisser faire that automatically guarantees individual interest. The same is true of a nation.'[87]

Marshall's relish for a fight, especially as he grew older, was much less highly developed than Foxwell's. Or rather it may be more accurate to say that his desire for victory in an important public argument was qualified by regard for professional propriety, his own and that of the science to which he had dedicated his life. Wounded by the public ridicule directed

[84] 'Economic movement', p. 96

[85] Letter to J. N. Keynes, 2 April 1885, Marshall Papers, Marshall Library, University of Cambridge.

[86] 'If I were forced to vote on the practical question I should vote unreservedly for Balfour, and if forced to Yes or No, then Yes for Chamberlain.' See letter to J. Bonar, 22 November 1903, Foxwell Collection, Baker Library, Harvard Business School.

[87] See letter to A. J. Balfour, 17 August 1903, commenting on the free trade manifesto and 'Economic notes on insular free trade' in Balfour Papers, British Library, Add. MS 49855, fos. 160–1, 162–5.

at the manifesto he had been persuaded to sign as an example of academics meddling in politics, he drafted a preface to the memorandum on fiscal policy he was asked to provide that was designed to explain his motives. Although he normally followed the rule of not 'taking part in the discussion of a burning political question, even if it contains a large economic element', he had made an exception in this case because 'the [political] leaders on either side have formally accepted certain distinctly economic statements and arguments as a part – not the whole – of the basis of their positions'. He mentioned here Balfour's 'Economic notes on insular free trade' and the 'economic utterances' of Chamberlain and the Tariff Reform League which had been circulated by the million 'among people who have had no scientific training'. Since some of the economic propositions in these documents were invalid, economists (and here he took it for granted that the signatories of the manifesto represented the majority within the profession) were bound 'to contradict these statements'. He added in conclusion that as a human being with his own 'affections and enthusiasms', he had a 'passion for Anglo Saxon ideals', an oblique way of signalling his own form of patriotism by saying that he set more store by keeping the Anglo-American relationship in good repair than he did by improving the relationship of Britain to its former colonies through imperial preference.[88] Marshall's private admission in 1900, in the context of the Boer war, in which his sympathies were decidedly anti-jingo and pro-Boer, that Chamberlain was 'the only eminent public man whom I have ever thoroughly distrusted' undoubtedly contributed to his opposition to him in 1903. Indeed, 'distrusted' replaced what he had at first written, 'hated and loathed'.[89]

The *Memorandum on fiscal policy of international trade* that Marshall wrote in response to a request from Charles Ritchie, the free-trade-minded Conservative Chancellor of the Exchequer, and T. H. Elliot, his senior civil servant, was much better suited to his professional style. It resembled one of those broad initial statements of position that key witnesses often submitted to Royal Commissions prior to being cross-examined on the detail. By 1903 Marshall had considerable experience of this mode of proceeding, having given evidence to several official inquiries and served as a member of the Royal Commission on Labour in 1894. The format allowed him to speak as 'a student of economics rather than an advocate of any particular policy' without forsaking freedom to comment on the

---

[88] The draft is preserved in the Marshall Papers and has been printed in *Correspondence*, III, pp. 60–1.
[89] Letter to N. G. Pierson, 6 April 1900, *Correspondence*, II, p. 275.

ethical and political issues aroused by protection. The memorandum was a consistently argued statement of the case for maintaining the status quo by someone who could genuinely claim to have studied the empirical evidence closely for over thirty years. True to his reading of the work of members of the German historical school, and that of Friedrich List, whom he admired, Marshall gave full recognition to the case in Germany and other industrialising countries for infant industry or 'educative' tariffs. This was, of course, the position hinted at by Mill and further developed by Sidgwick, but Marshall's treatment of the case had the added weight that came from the empirical evidence he commanded.

Arthur Cecil Pigou had been employed in Cambridge since 1900 on funds provided by Marshall and later by the Girdlers' Company; he had taken over much of Marshall's teaching in advanced economics. Though still in his twenties Pigou not only signed the free trade manifesto but took an active speaking and writing role on the subject, obtaining praise from Edgeworth for his masterly handling of the theoretical questions involved. Predictably, Foxwell disliked what he called the 'smart fencing with abstract principles *à la* Pigou' that he found in the literature defending free trade.[90] It would have been more difficult for him to speak about Marshall's memorandum in that fashion. Marshall had made a concession to the case for retaliatory tariffs by Britain, but Foxwell might still have felt the memorandum was insufficiently alive to the dangers to which British trade was subject in a protectionist world where tariffs were being used as the means of advancing national interests. The memorandum was only made available to a wider public five years after it had been written. By then Foxwell had acquired a more personal grievance against Marshall for the part he had played in ensuring that Pigou would be chosen as his successor. Foxwell believed that Marshall had never forgiven him for his letter to *The Times* in 1903, drawing attention to something Marshall found embarrassing: his signature of a manifesto that was the subject of public ridicule. Pigou had other qualities that would have commended his candidacy to Marshall in 1908, not least of them being youth (he was barely thirty to Foxwell's nearly sixty). Inevitably, however, where each of the two main candidates stood on tariff reform has become part of the post-mortem on the direction taken by Cambridge economics after 1908.[91]

[90] See letter to J. Bonar, 22 November 1903.
[91] See the literature on the filling of Marshall's chair in the Bibliographical Notes.

Foxwell continued to live in Cambridge (a few doors away from the Keynes family in Harvey Road) and act as director of studies for St John's, but he withdrew from all teaching on the ground that he could never 'have the assurance to address a Cambridge audience again, with the stamp of incompetency so publicly branded upon me by a body of experts'.[92] Although Marshall made one or two guilt-driven overtures towards him, they were rejected. Tariff reform continued to feature in their lives. Having given up the idea of writing a second volume of *Principles*, Marshall decided to write a book on *National industry and international trade*, initially on the expectation that tariff reform would soon again be on the public agenda.[93] This proved wrong, and when the book emerged as *Industry and trade* in 1919 the issue was given only marginal treatment. As public interest faded, Foxwell seems to have become more firmly convinced of the rectitude of the Balfour–Chamberlain position, though he wanted a broader policy than one based simply on tariffs. As he wrote to Hewins in 1917 'where you say Tariff Reform, I would rather say a National Trade policy'.[94] At much the same time he was attracted to Henry Page Croft's National Party, a right-wing splinter group from within the Conservative and Unionist Party which had tariff reform, imperial unity, and strong national defence as the main planks in its platform.[95] Foxwell's Cambridge colleague, William Cunningham, became president of the Cambridge branch of the National Party, and Foxwell attended the 1919 party conference as a delegate, having admired Cunningham's presidential address, a 'masterly statement of the general European situation and England's duty in regard to it'.

When Cunningham died in the same year Foxwell pronounced him to be 'a great National Economist, the modern representative of an old English tradition, unfortunately interrupted by the atomism and premature cosmopolitanism of the laissez-faire age'. Cunningham wasn't like those 'modern intellectuals, who think patriotism vulgar, and affect to be the friends of every country but their own'.[96] His was the corporatism of a pre-individualistic age in which the importance of the little platoons

---

[92] Letter to Marshall, 1 June 1908, *Correspondence*, III, p. 191.
[93] See letter to S. A. Armitage-Smith, 27 June 1908, *Correspondence*, III, p. 195.
[94] Letter to W. A. S. Hewins, 14 September 1917, Hewins Papers, Sheffield University.
[95] William D. Rubinstein, 'Henry Page Croft and the National Party, 1917–22', *Journal of Contemporary History*, 9 (1974), 139.
[96] 'Archdeacon Cunningham', *EJ*, 29 (1919), 382–95.

composing the nation was properly appreciated. In the past Foxwell had not shared Cunningham's suspicions about economic theory: the example of Jevons showed that it was possible to combine theory with economic realism: 'But on further consideration I have not only learnt to understand Cunningham's mistrust of economic theory, but find myself more and more inclined to move in his direction.' Foxwell's verdict on Cunningham's attitude to tariff reform sounds like the one he would have wanted to have passed on his own position:

I have come across nothing in his works, nor in converse with him, that would justify Protection in the sense many Tariff Reformers use the term. His position was essentially that of the National Economist, whose supreme aim is not temporary cheapness, but the permanent increase of the productive power and general welfare of his country; of his country first, then of Britons overseas, and next of his country's friends.[97]

One man's patriotism is often another's xenophobia. The programme of the National Party called for immigration control, internment of enemy aliens, punishment for pacifist propaganda, and the eradication of German and pro-German influences, where this entailed sacking any civil servants who had been enemy subjects before the war. The anti-pacifist clause imparted another twist to the Pigou–Foxwell story when Foxwell and Cunningham appealed (not once but three times) against the Cambridge recruitment board's decision to accept Pigou's plea for exemption as a conscientious objector. Foxwell volunteered to take over Pigou's teaching duties if this would enable him to be drafted rather than continue with a combination of teaching, part-time work for the Board of Trade, and ambulance work in France during the vacations. Once again, Pigou was occupying a political position close to that of Marshall, whose interventions in the press during the war earned him a reputation for being pro-German.[98] Attacks by Croft on 'cosmopolitan finance' and 'international moneylenders' lent a strong whiff of anti-semitism to the National Party programme, and this was compounded by the attention drawn to the number of Russian communists who were Jews, those 'semi-foreign' socialists Foxwell had alluded to earlier. In his mid-sixties, Foxwell's Unionist allegiances were put to the ultimate test by Irish Home Rule. His daughter reported that 'as a keen politician he was ready to back

---

[97] *Ibid.*, 389.
[98] For an account of this episode, see Stuart Wallace, *War and the image of Germany: British academics 1914–1918* (Edinburgh: Donald, 1988), pp. 13, 144–7, 169–70, 177–8.

up Lord Carson and the Irish loyalists, not only with his money but with a rifle if necessary'.[99]

Judged by correspondence and the notes for the lectures on socialism that he gave after the war, as Foxwell became older the keen politician in him seems to have become increasingly incensed by the direction taken by politico-economic events and policies. In the 1880s and 90s he was a 'progressive' Conservative who could be friendly not merely to Shaw, but to the Fabian programme, which 'though genuinely socialistic in its ulterior aims, appears from its latest manifesto to have adopted a policy of gradual and detailed reform, so practical and opportunist that it can hardly be called socialistic in the sense here given to that term'.[100] Reports of his lectures on competition at UCL could deceive H. M. Hyndman into thinking there was a chance he might support the programme of the Marxist Social Democratic Federation, an impression that was quickly and rather vehemently scotched.[101] Foxwell was antagonistic to the 'people's budget' in 1909, which he considered to be yet more evidence of Ricardo's disastrously radical legacy. It was the 'worst and crudest budget of modern times – worthy of the shallow and rhetorical Henry George, whom our Chancellor, his namesake, Lloyd George, much resembles'.[102] Foxwell was alarmed by the further leftward moves of the Liberals, the rise of the Labour party, and the emergence of more militant types of trade unionism during and after the war. During the immediate post-war period he thought that British politics was characterised by a pervasive kind of 'Bolshevist bitterness'.[103]

In his obituary of Cunningham that same year he identified himself with another of his subject's beliefs:

With Carlyle, he did not believe any society ever had existed, or could or should exist, based on the 'Cash Nexus' alone. The most important practical questions depend at every point on the complicated reactions of human nature and human motive. The live issues of today turn ultimately on points of character and personality. They require treatment, not on the lines of mathematical physics, so much as of ethics and psychology.[104]

[99] Audrey G. D. Foxwell, *Herbert Somerton Foxwell: a portrait*, Kress Library of Business and Economics, publication no. 1, (Boston, 1939), p. 15.

[100] Introduction to Menger, *Right of labour*, p. ciii.

[101] Hyndman initiated the correspondence in October 1882. It continued until Foxwell attacked the social democratic programme root and branch in a letter of 18 December, a copy of which he kept. The letters are part of the Freeman collection.

[102] Letter to E. R. A. Seligman, 23 June 1909, Seligman Papers, Special Collections, Columbia University Library.

[103] Letter to F. Macmillan, 27 July 1919, Macmillan Archive, British Library.

[104] 'Archdeacon Cunningham', 388.

The financial crisis that overtook the second Labour government in 1930 prompted Foxwell to consider a further aspect of Carlyle's inheritance, a proper regard for heroes: 'There is a splendid opportunity for a really strong man in England.'[105] With Carlyle mentally lurking in the wings, it is little wonder that Foxwell regarded Mill's performances as 'distinctly soporific'.

[105] See letter to W. R. Scott, 15 April 1930, Foxwell Collection, Baker Library, Harvard Business School.

10

Wealth, well-being, and the academic economist

> . . . the spirit of the age induces a closer attention to the question whether our increasing wealth may not be made to go further than it does in promoting the general wellbeing; and this again compels us to examine how far the exchange value of any element of wealth, whether in collective or individual use, represents accurately the addition which it makes to happiness and wellbeing.
>
> *Principles of economics*[1]

> Such work as this belongs to the academic economist. For he has no class or personal interests to make him afraid of any conclusion which the figures, when carefully interpreted, may indicate; he accepts the premises of the working classes that the wellbeing of the many is more important than that of the few. He is specially trained to detect the falsity of the mirage which is caused by the fact that the comfort of a few rich men sometimes has a higher bidding power in the market than more urgent needs of many poor, and will outbid them in the market. Being thus fortified by the consciousness of his own rectitude, the economist, in the coming generation even more than in the past, must dare when occasion arises to oppose the multitude for their own good.
>
> 'The old generation of economists and the new', address to Cambridge Economic Club, 1897.[2]

I

Marshall was always confident in his capacity to discern what demands the spirit of the age was likely to make on the academic economic experts of the future. It usually made strenuous calls on both intellect and character, with a bias towards practical tools that would facilitate public understanding and decision-making. A further crusading element came from a desire to give voice to the unvocal and unorganised consuming many at the expense of the vocal few who had the resources and incentive

[1] *PE*, I, p. 85.   [2] As reprinted in *Memorials*, p. 305.

to speak on behalf of any specific producing interest. As the final remark in the epigraph attests, however, the earnest yet objective academic economist was also expected to expose short-sighted clamour on the part of the multitude. It amounted to an ambitious didactic programme involving thorough permeation of public life by those economic ways of thinking capable of improving the well-being of the many. Marshall's most famous pupil, John Maynard Keynes, recorded a Bloomsbury verdict on this Victorian dimension of his mentor's mentality in the 1920s when he said that Marshall was 'too anxious to do good', holding that this was 'the defect of that other great quality of his which always touched his pupils – his immense disinterestedness and public spirit'.[3]

There is a direct connection between the two statements that form the epigraph to this essay. The 'figures' needing the economist's interpretation in the second quotation were those required to estimate improvements in real income over long periods of time. In the case Marshall was using as an illustration it was the increase in real income wage-earners now enjoyed as a result of the introduction of steam engines and improved iron manufacture during the previous half century. This was meant to show that wage-earners were not merely consumers of food, clothing, and housing but beneficiaries of the capital equipment and technology that had fostered the growth of wealth over time. But the figures in question could equally have been those statistics of consumption that Marshall believed to be capable of collection and organisation around a concept he considered to be of great potential importance to well-being. It was a concept that would enable the academic economist and the practical decision-maker to estimate the size of the gap between well-being and wealth produced by a wide range of policy choices, the challenge outlined in the first quotation. Marshall originally labelled this concept 'consumers' rent' because it had properties analogous to agricultural rent, a producers' surplus payable to landowners over and above what tenant farmers required to cover their costs of production. Later he decided to call it simply 'consumers' surplus'.

The idea made its earliest appearance in a work on the theory of foreign trade and domestic values which Marshall began in 1873 and abandoned in 1877 when he started work with his wife on *The economics of industry*, a popular introductory work that he later much regretted writing. The unfinished chapters of the discarded book contained several of his most significant innovations as an economic theorist: external economies,

---

[3] 'Alfred Marshall' in *Essays in biography*, in JMK, X, pp. 200–1.

increasing returns, quasi-rent, and consumers' surplus. In its original setting the last of these was meant to provide an economic measure of the indirect effects on consumer satisfaction of customs duties and other taxes, a measure of the incidental destruction of satisfaction that could not be offset by the revenue from the duty or tax.[4] The burden of a tax on consumers was underestimated if it was confined to the pecuniary loss involved in the increased price paid. The tax deterred them from consuming as much as they did before the tax was levied, and there is a loss of consumers' surplus on all these forgone units. The idea was based on a simple inference based on the law of diminishing utility which suggested that we derive more satisfaction from the earliest units of any good or service we consume than the later ones. The price we pay measures the satisfaction we anticipate from the last or extra unit we can just be induced to purchase. It does not tell us what satisfaction we derive from the previous units we have purchased. We derive additional satisfaction from being able to consume goods and services at lower market prices than those we would be prepared to pay rather than go without them entirely, something that is obvious in the case of cheap necessities but extends to all goods in some degree.

In the language of utility theory, if consumers' surplus could be made manifest, it would tell us something about total utility as opposed to the marginal utility measured by price. In judging any particular situation we would be able to gauge how much more well-being than wealth was available, and whether well-being could be increased by policies such as the imposition of a tax or the granting of a bounty that shifted the demand and supply schedules in a direction that increased the amount of surplus available. In an older language, consumers' surplus was a measure of the difference between exchange value (on which calculations of wealth *are* based) and value in use (on which calculations of well-being *could* be based). Either way, as we have seen, it was possible to resolve such puzzles as the water/diamond paradox more satisfactorily and provide an answer to Ruskin's question why it was possible for pornographic prints to fetch a higher price or exchange value than 'priceless' Tintorettos.[5]

We noted in the previous essay how keen Marshall was to endow Ricardo with an understanding of the role of demand in determining value, while recognising that he could have been a little more attentive.[6] Marshall was not going to follow Jevons in bending the rod the other way: he gave a decidedly downbeat treatment to what Jevons had believed

---

[4] EEW, II, pp. 77–8, 212–25, 279–83.   [5] See p. 108 above.   [6] See pp. 251–2 above.

to be liberating discoveries or rediscoveries. The older generation of British economists had said little about consumer demand because 'they really had not much to say that was not the common property of all sensible people'. The recent revival of interest could be attributed to 'mathematical habits of thought' and the new possibilities for making use of statistical evidence on consumption 'to throw light on difficult questions of great importance to public wellbeing'.[7] But Marshall wanted to keep the demand for final goods, those generated by consumer wants, in proper perspective. The demand that mattered from an economic and ethical standpoint was that connected with the factors of production and hence the distribution of incomes. The new marginal theory provided a way of showing that the earnings of any agent of production depended on the value of the products made by their participation. But once more it was on the supply side of the market for factors that Marshall was keen to place his emphasis.

Despite devoting Book III of his *Principles* to 'wants and their satisfaction', then, Marshall diminished the centrality of the subject by stressing that wants ruled life only in the animal or lower stages of existence. In more civilised states they played a dependent role when compared with 'efforts and activities', those relations into which people enter in the course of their working or productive lives and by which their 'characters' were formed, for good or ill. The adjustment of wants to activities and the creation of new wants as a result of new activities was the foundation on which he wished to build his own scientific edifice rather than on any theory of consumption alone. Character formation as a result of quasi-Darwinian processes of adaptation to changes in the work environment lay at the centre of Marshall's contribution to a subject to which he would *not* have wished to be described as contributing: sociology.[8] Jevons had recognised the need for a form of evolutionary sociology to complement economics, but left it for others to achieve. Marshall was altogether more ambitious in the inclusiveness of his conception of what he called the 'economic organon': his preference was to be regarded as someone who had redrawn the boundaries of economics sufficiently generously to make these larger 'organic' ('biological' as opposed to 'mechanical') themes part of the most advanced of the social sciences. Hence, of course, his long-term goal ('The Mecca of the economist

---

[7] See *PE*, I, pp. 84–5.
[8] The seminal articles on Marshall *qua* sociologist were written by Talcott Parsons and later incorporated into his *Structure of social action* (New York: McGraw-Hill, 1937).

lies in economic biology rather than in economic dynamics') and his belief that economics would arrive at Mecca within the next one hundred years (i.e. by 2024).[9]

II

In staking out the territory for which his concept of consumers' surplus was designed, Marshall was also keen to bypass the total versus marginal utility version of surplus outlined above. Failure to do this had been Jevons's 'great error'; he had treated the curve representing the diminution of 'final' utility as quantity increased as though it was a demand curve relating price and quantity.[10] This had added to the tendency to confuse 'hedonics' with economics and had embroiled economics in ethical controversies that the science had neither the means nor the need to resolve.[11] Nor was Marshall interested in building on the simple psychology underlying the notion of an individual's consumer surplus. This had no operational significance: the demand curves for individual consumers would always remain hypothetical and could shed no light on any important public issue. The most interesting cases related to aggregate consumers' surplus as roughly measured in money terms via statistics of market demand. It was here that Marshall's hopes rested, though he did not expect to have data for drawing a demand curve throughout its length, covering the whole range of possible prices. The best he could expect was information on the demand curve in the immediate vicinity of current market price, which he thought would be good enough for many of the purposes he had in mind. Expressed in the language of diagrams that Marshall favoured for exposition and comprehension, consumers' surplus was measured by the size of the triangles formed beneath what would later be characterised as a partial equilibrium demand curve, the ones sitting on top of the rectangle marked out by price and quantity before and after a posited change such as a tax or subsidy ($P'RP$ in Figure 10).

Marshall veered sharply from bluff confidence to caution and back again when expounding the conclusions that could be drawn from his analysis of consumers' surplus. One of his criticisms of Jevons was that he

---

[9] *PE*, I, p. xiv. The prediction was made in conversations with his wife; see the notes she compiled for Keynes's use when writing his biographical essay in the Keynes Papers, Archive Centre, King's College, Cambridge.

[10] He was guilty of 'applying to utility propositions that are only true of price'; see letters to J. N. Keynes, 26 November and 2 December 1889, while Keynes was writing the article on 'consumers' rent' for Palgrave's *Dictionary of political economy;* see *Correspondence,* I, pp. 306, 308–9.

[11] *PE*, I, pp. 17n, 101n.

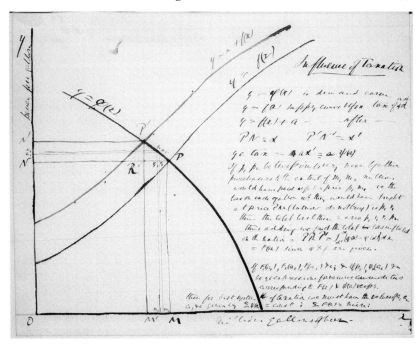

Fig. 10. Marshall diagram. Taken from a notebook which Marshall kept (1867–72) and headed 'Influence of Taxation', it appears in EEW, II, pp. 279–80. The *x* axis represents 'million gallons of beer' and the *y* axis 'pence per gallon'. The annotation reads:

$y = \Phi(x)$ is demand curve
$y = f(x)$ is supply curve before tax of a pence
$y = f(x) + a$ is supply curve after tax of a pence
$PN = \alpha$; $P'N' = \alpha'$

The tax [revenue] = $a\alpha' \equiv \psi(a)$. If p_1, p_2 be two points very near together, purchasers to the extent of $m_1 m_2$ millions would have paid up to price $p_1 m_1$ i.e. the loss on each gallon which they would have bought at price PM (but now do not buy) is $p_1 r_1$. Thus the total loss to them equals the area $p_1 r_1 r_2 p_2$. Thus adding up we find the total loss inflicted on the nation $= PRP' =$

$$\int_{a'}^{a} \{\Phi(x) - \Phi(a)\}dx = F(a)$$

since Φ and f are given.

If $F_1(a_1)$, $F_2(a_2)$, $F_3(a_3)$ etc. and $\psi_1(a_1)$, $\psi_2(a_2)$, $\psi_3(a_3)$ etc. be the expressions for various commodities, corresponding to F(a) and ψ(a) respectively, then for the best system of taxation we must have the values of a_1, a_2, a_3 etc. given by $\sum \psi(a) = $ constant and $\sum F(a) = $ minimum.

had attempted to draw inferences about well-being from his utility curves without realising, or informing his readers at least, that it was necessary to know 'whether the commodity taxed is one consumed by the rich by the poor or by all classes alike'. It was also necessary to assume that the marginal utility of money remained more or less constant, a condition that could be met if the goods in question occupied only a small proportion of the consumer's total budget. Under these circumstances changes in the price did not have troublesome effects upon the income of consumers and hence the demand for all goods. Marshall was always careful to point out that the satisfaction sacrificed by a rich man would be much less than that experienced by a poor man for whom an additional pound represented command over greater potential sources of satisfaction.

Marshall also maintained that many things about inter-personal comparisons of states of well-being that might trouble those with philosophical scruples would come out, so to speak, in the statistical wash. He could defend the legitimacy of making such comparisons in terms that were both strong and broad:

By far the greater number of the events with which economics deals affect in about equal proportions all the different classes of society; so that if the money measures of the happiness caused by two events are equal, it is reasonable and in accordance with common usage to regard the amounts of the happiness in the two cases as equivalent. And, further, as money is likely to be turned to the higher uses of life in about equal proportions, by any two large groups of people taken without special bias from any two parts of the western world, there is even some *prima facie* probability that equal additions to their material resources will make about equal additions to the fullness of life, and true progress of the human race.[12]

Marshall could also sound impatient when faced with doubt about such measurements. Inaccuracies of measurement, being definite, were corrigible; and 'it is useless to say that various gains and losses are incommensurable, and cannot be weighed against one another. For they must be, and in fact they are, weighed against one another before any deliberate decision is or can be reached on any issue.'[13] Marshall made the plea of incommensurability sound like moral evasion: it was the duty of the academic economist to grapple with the heterogeneity of the types of evidence needed to assess the relative weights that people did in fact assign to their physical, mental, and moral well-being. In such matters, once again, he proved bolder than Jevons – a more fully paid-up utilitarian – had found it possible to be.[14]

---

[12] *Ibid.*, I, p. 20, repeated in modified form on p. 131. For the earliest statement of the assumption, see EEW, II, p. 215.

[13] *Memorials*, p. 302.

[14] For Jevons, '[e]very mind is . . . inscrutable to every other mind, and no common denominator of feeling seems to be possible'; see *Theory of political economy*, 2nd edn (London: Macmillan, 1879), p. 15.

The chief emerging characteristic of modern economic life for Marshall was 'deliberateness' rather than selfishness or competitiveness, the deliberate exercise of choice on the basis of careful analysis and forethought.[15] Deliberateness required measurement as a means of weighing alternatives, and while markets furnished plenty of evidence for this purpose in the case of private economic gain, the lack of a social equivalent often meant that the public case was not given its due. Even if a class of great administrators could be trained, with 'instincts with regard to public interests which able business men have with regard to their own affairs', it was always necessary in a democracy for such administrators to have ways of demonstrating the advantages of public undertakings to the larger community. There was a need to equip the public official with a means of assessing the consequences of public action that could stand comparison with those in regular use by private capitalists. There was also a need to give voice to the interests of the 'silent many' and thereby help protect the unorganised consumer against the better-organised battalions serving capital and labour.[16]

It is worth underlining the professed collectivist purpose Marshall had in mind and the hopes he attached to his diagrams:

The rapid growth of collective interests, and the increasing tendency towards collective action in economic affairs, make it every day more important that we should know what quantitative measure of public interests are most needed and what statistics are required for them, and that we should set ourselves to obtain these statistics.

It is perhaps not unreasonable to hope that as time goes on, the statistics of consumption will be so organized as to afford demand schedules sufficiently trustworthy, to show in diagrams that will appeal to the eye, the quantities of consumers' surplus that will result from different courses of public and private action. By the study of these pictures the mind may be gradually trained to get juster notions of the relative magnitudes of the interests which the community has in various schemes of public and private enterprise; and sounder doctrines may replace those traditions of an earlier generation, which had perhaps a wholesome influence in their time, but which damped social enthusiasm by throwing suspicion on all projects for undertakings by the public on its own behalf which would not show a balance of direct pecuniary profit.[17]

---

[15] *PE*, I, pp. 5–6.

[16] *PE*, I, pp. 491–2. The problem was how to deal with the 'pushing and clamorous few in an economic controversy'; they were usually 'a group of producers who can put their case well, and who show great energy and resource in making themselves heard. Hence has arisen the tradition that the economist is generally on the side of the consumer as against the producer: he aims at protecting the unvocal many who consume the products of a particular trade, against the vocal few who speak on behalf of the trade'; see 'The old generation of economists and the new', in *Memorials*, p. 303.

[17] *PE*, I, p. 493.

While much of this would, in principle, be unsurprising to someone like Sidgwick or even Mill, the statement contains several features exclusive to Marshall. The belief in 'diagrams that will appeal to the eye', indeed the whole idea of mental pictures as a guide to relative magnitudes, highlights the intuitive basis of his preference for geometric devices that enjoyed the supposed advantage of being connected with statistics.[18] What this statement also makes plain is the intended connection between consumers' surplus and 'collective interests' pursued via 'collective action'. In addition to piecemeal fiscal interventions of the tax-bounty kind the latter could typically include the actions of a publicly regulated monopoly capable of supplementing its ordinary revenue calculations with an assessment of the gain or loss to consumers' surplus of pursuing different pricing strategies. 'Social enthusiasm' for public ventures could be rekindled and rearmed to make it the ally of that general 'tendency to socialism' mentioned in the previous essay. What later became mere 'blackboard economics' of the kind that dominated the microeconomic textbooks of the mid to late twentieth century was initiated by Marshall with a regard for the actual scale of the forces at work, say, on a typical local gas company's revenues. Acquiring a sense of these magnitudes was an essential feature of Marshall's teaching. The illustrative examples he used in his *Principles* were to be a preliminary to a concrete study of 'the Protean shapes' now assumed by trusts and modern trade combinations and monopolies.[19] *Industry and trade*, published in Marshall's old age, made good this promise, in part at least.

III

But having, with a hint of swagger, supplied the decision-maker with what he claimed would become a serviceable measuring device in keeping with the spirit of the times, a way of balancing gains against losses to public well-being from various policies and business practices, Marshall proceeded to take a markedly cautious line on the feasibility and desirability of state intervention in the industrial field. The interventionist scheme for taxing the products of decreasing return industries and

---

[18] As he explained to Edgeworth: 'When tackling a new problem, I generally use analysis, because it is handier . . . But – partly because curves require no special training, partly because they bear more obviously on the science of Statistics – I intend never to use analysis when I can use geometry'; see letter, 28 March 1880, *Correspondence*, I, p. 125.
[19] *PE*, I, p. 477.

subsidising those enjoying increasing returns, a feature of the book he had left on one side in 1877, resurfaced boldly in his *Principles* along with the claims we have examined so far. But it came with the following list of 'semi-ethical' considerations that would have to be met by anyone attempting to implement the scheme:

> They would have to reckon up the direct and indirect costs of collecting a tax and administering a bounty; the difficulty of securing that the burdens of the tax and the benefits were equitably distributed; the openings for fraud and corruption; and the danger that in the trade which got a bounty and in other trades which hoped to get one, people would divert their energies from managing their own businesses to managing those persons who control the bounties.[20]

Such thoughts were not, in essence, different from those Adam Smith might have penned with the corrupt governments of his day in mind. Marshall, however, acknowledged the advances that had taken place in the competence and probity of governments during the nineteenth century, the 'general movement towards higher ethical standards, which has been steadily cleansing Parliament, and invigorating Governmental departments'.[21] This did not prevent him from issuing warnings against allowing the dead hand of bureaucracy to stifle industry. It was partly a matter of race and character: what might be acceptable to submissive Germans was not likely to work in the more vigorous and enterprising Anglo-Saxon world.[22] Marshall had sufficient faith in the formative influence of the Darwinian struggle to believe that businessmen's capacities had been finely honed by competition. The contrast here was with the mentality of the public official, dulled by routine, wary of innovation:

> His competence to decide on . . . business problems is therefore likely to be inferior to that of a man of equal natural ability and energy, who has given his whole time and strength to the thoughts and the actions that relate to the same business problems; and who has tested his judgement by applying it to many various risks which appertain to them, and which he has borne on his own shoulders.[23]

It was a very different state of mind from the one he assumed in the *Principles* when speaking of 'great administrators' armed with a sense of

---

[20] *Ibid.*, pp. 473, 470, 475.

[21] 'Memorandum on fiscal policy', in *Official papers by Alfred Marshall* (London: Macmillan for the Royal Economic Society, 1926), p. 395.

[22] 'bureaucratic management is less suitable for Anglo-Saxons than for other races who are more patient and more easily contented, more submissive and less full of initiative, who like to take things easily and to spread their work out rather thinly over long hours'; 'Some aspects of competition', in *Memorials*, p. 275.

[23] *Industry and trade* (London: Macmillan, 1919), p. 666.

the magnitude of the consumers' surpluses that could be garnered or protected by appropriate intervention, and prepared to expound their proposals in democratic settings. The extension of the sphere of government into industry risked setting on foot a process of mutual contamination: 'when proposals for large changes in the field of economics are prompted partly by political motives then they are likely to bring about results which will not be satisfactory from the economic point of view, and will perhaps introduce morbid elements into politics'.[24]

The clinching argument deployed by Marshall in his memorandum on fiscal policy in 1903 had been a political one, and it rested partly on his observations of the effects of protectionism on American politics. There was an irresistible tendency for protective policies to become ever more intricate and in the process corrupt. The 'moral harm' this had done to American political life outweighed any benefits that might have been conferred by tariffs on American industry. Hence Marshall's conclusion in favour of retaining the status quo in Britain: free trade was worth preserving in spite of changed economic conditions precisely 'because it is *not* a device, but the absence of any device'.[25] He drew special attention to the way in which British trade unions, excellent though they were in other respects, would be tempted under a protectionist regime to use their strength to promote the interests of particular groups of workers; they could become a corrupt force in British politics comparable to that exercised by landowners before the Corn Laws were abolished.[26]

The strongest of these warnings was expressed in *Industry and trade*, a work that appeared in 1919 when Marshall was seventy-seven. The tendency to socialism had worn thin: 'no socialistic scheme, yet advanced, seems to make adequate provision for the maintenance of high enterprise, and individual strength of character'.[27] Far more galling, perhaps, was the following undated private admission to his nephew:

He told me on one occasion that a major disappointment in his life was the recognition, which gradually forced itself on him, that his concept of consumers' surplus was devoid of important practical application, because it was not capable of being quantified in a meaningful way. At the outset he had high hopes that it could have practical applications, and for many years he had

---

[24] *Ibid.*, p. 496: 'the heavy hand of Government tends to slacken progress in whatever matter it touches', and 'business influences are apt to corrupt politics; and political influences are apt to corrupt business' (p. 672).
[25] *Official papers*, p. 394.   [26] *Ibid.*, p. 396.   [27] *Industry and trade*, p. viii.

wrestled with it, but had finally reached the conclusion that it was a theoretical and not a practical tool in the economists' workbox.[28]

As a theoretical tool the concept continued to serve one useful purpose. It demonstrated that there were no grounds for believing that the outputs and prices generated under a system of competitive markets represented a position of 'maximum satisfaction'. There were several ways in which enlightened governments could turn 'the economic actions of individuals into those channels in which they will add the most to the sum total of happiness'.[29] Marshall understandably chose Bastiat as the typical exponent of the harmonistic doctrine, and while Bastiat himself could be dismissed in a footnote this does not disguise the importance Marshall attached to denying the claims of this entire school of thought.[30] Bastiat, 'a lucid writer but not a profound thinker', was one of those popular economists whose influence with the general public Marshall felt it necessary to combat. The idea that 'the natural organization of society under the influence of competition is the best not only that can be practically effected, but even that can be theoretically conceived' embodied an attitude of complacency towards economic outcomes which he consistently opposed. Apart from the ways in which consumers' surpluses could be manipulated to public advantage, it ignored the basic truth contained in the idea that the satisfactions attached to an additional increment in the income or expenditure of the poor were greater than those of the rich.[31]

In spirit Marshall's reasons for rejecting the Bastiat position do not differ from those given earlier by Mill and Cairnes.[32] But use of the surplus concept provided a more precise way of demonstrating that the market price of goods did not always represent the best outcome when viewed from the standpoint of public well-being. Whereas the maximum satisfaction school made equity seem like the automatic outcome of any solution that guaranteed efficiency, Marshall regarded equity, the distribution of consumers' and producers' incomes, as something that always needed to be considered separately yet alongside economic efficiency. Cairnes had argued that conflicts between private and public interests were legion in economic life. Marshall had hoped to equip academic

[28] Claude W. Guillebaud, 'Some personal reminiscences of Alfred Marshall', *History of Political Economy*, 3 (1971), 6.

[29] *PE*, I, p. 475.

[30] See *PE*, II, p. 759; see also I, p. 763n. The main argument against the doctrine is in I, pp. 470–5.

[31] *PE*, I, pp. 17–19, 130–1, 171, 474, 851–2.   [32] See pp. 194–7 above.

economists with a useful piece of mental apparatus that would enable them to play a role in arbitrating in such conflicts. Disappointment centred on the fact that the role proved more theoretical than practical.

IV

Bastiat had died in 1850, but his reputation had been kept alive by individual disciples such as Louis Mallet and H. D. Macleod, and by the Cobden Club, who distributed his writings, especially *Economic harmonies*, in large quantities from the 1860s onwards. In the 1880s the popular author who was reaching the largest audiences was a figure at the other end of the political spectrum, Henry George, whose *Progress and poverty* sold 100,000 copies in the three years after its first appearance in 1879, and whose speaking campaign on the merits of radical land reform and the 'single tax' drew large audiences throughout Britain. This alone might have been enough to overcome Marshall's dislike of public controversy, but there were other reasons at work as well.

As we have noted in connection with his participation in the debate on tariff reform, Marshall's personal line on professional engagement in controversy was a high one. It was best left to those who possessed 'sound digestions'; his own priorities lay in establishing the 'causes of causes' rather than 'proximate causes and their effects'; it was more important 'to establish truth than to confute error'. But in his forties, at least, Marshall was not averse to some fisticuffs in the process of confuting error, and his Cambridge friends, Sidgwick and Foxwell, clearly expected the rising star of the new economics profession, with the first volume of his *Principles* maturing in his study, to pronounce on George's errors. This he did in three public lectures in Bristol in 1883, followed a year later by a direct confrontation in Oxford, while still maintaining that he 'would rather put in one brick just where it should be in the slowly rising edifice than plant a hundred brickbats with the utmost dexterity exactly between the eyes of Mr George'.[33]

Marshall set a patronising tone from the outset by describing George as being 'by nature a poet, not a scientific thinker. The real value of his work does not lie in his treatment of questions that require hard study and clear thought, but in the freshness and earnestness of his views of

---

[33] *Official papers*, p. 368; and a letter to Foxwell, 22 July 1883, *Correspondence*, I, pp. 163–6. The lectures were given 19 and 26 February and 3 March, and the face-to-face meeting took place in Oxford, 15 March 1884.

life.'[34] After rehearsing the evidence of rising real wages (he thought they had tripled during the nineteenth century) Marshall concluded that wealth and want were not moving in opposite directions; that if progress was driving a wedge into the distribution of incomes, it was, contrary to George's contention, forcing the bulk of working-class incomes upwards. It was only pressing down on a pauper class, the residuum, those who were 'physically, mentally, or morally incapable of doing a good day's work with which to earn a good day's wage', a class that was of grave concern, though it was now a smaller proportion of the population than it had been before reforms in the Poor Law were introduced in 1834. For this class Marshall favoured a dose of German-style discipline as a way of preventing it from infecting the normal workforce.[35]

Marshall then went on to show how many of the products consumed by the working classes were the outputs of industries that had benefited from technological and other innovations; they obeyed the laws of increasing return and were the kinds of industries which his consumers' surplus analysis had suggested should be expanded at the expense of diminishing-return industries. George had lampooned the cruder versions of the wage-fund theory and Marshall responded with a potted version of the new marginal product theory of distribution: 'the great law of distribution is that the more useful one factor of production is, and the scarcer it is, the higher will be the rate at which its services are paid'. Implicitly, then, Marshall was announcing that Mill had been proved wrong and the steam-whistlers right in placing faith in the benefits of technology. At the same time, Marshall's account of how delayed marriage (but not, significantly, birth control, for post-Darwinian reasons connected with the worldwide competition between races) and education had helped increase the scarcity of labour and the capacity of the working classes to take control of their own destiny was perfectly in line with Mill's prognostications for the labouring classes.[36]

Marshall's third lecture tackled what lay at the heart of George's proposals: the doctrine of rent and the English land tenure system. Before dealing with its economics, however, he set aside matters with which the

---

[34] 'Three lectures on progress and poverty', *Journal of Law and Economics*, 12 (1969), 186.

[35] *PE*, I, pp. 714–17; see Gareth Stedman Jones, *Outcast London: a study in the relationship between classes in Victorian society* (Penguin Books, 1971), pp. 287, 301–7 on Marshall's part in forming the new attitude to the residuum.

[36] See pp. 48–53 above. 'My remedy for poverty, therefore, is to increase the competition of capital and of the upper classes of industry for the aid of the lower classes'; see Three lectures on progress and poverty', 209.

subject had been confused and on which modern economists no longer
claimed to have special expertise, those questions of 'historical fact and of
moral obligation, which are the subject of heated political controversy'.
These were contrasted with 'economic reasonings which have the authority
and precision of science'.[37] Given the central role played by ideas of
historic dispossession in the land reform movement, this was a bold
simplification. It allowed Marshall to suggest that errors of jurisprudence,
compounded by pardonable defects in the writings of the older generation of economists, should not be treated as though they were errors
attributable to modern economic science. Having listed the three main
charges brought against private landlordism in England – tyrannical
influence, imperfect tenant security, and the inferiority of wage labour
to peasant proprietorship – Marshall proceeded to mount a 'moderate'
defence based on Britain's unparalleled record as a pioneer in making
agricultural improvements, capped by the following back-of-an-envelope
empirical observation: 'It requires as much capital to buy twenty acres as
it does to farm a hundred.' Rich landlords who were willing to take a low
rate of return on their capital, possibly for sentimental or status reasons,
performed a useful function: they left the tenant farmer to employ his
more limited capital and greater agricultural skills to best account. On
peasant proprietorship Marshall accused its defenders, Mill and Cliffe
Leslie, of having drawn 'sweeping inferences from exceptional cases'.
Since they had written, the position of peasant proprietors had deteriorated, while that of the English rural wage labourer had improved greatly.

Marshall was prepared to make a couple of concessions to the land
reformers, if not to the schemes of land nationalisation being advocated
by George and Wallace. The first damns with faint praise. Easing the sale
of land had some potential benefits: a small plot of land, bought 'not
as a commercial investment, but as one of affection, like the purchase of
a dog, often has a healthy influence on character'.[38] The second concession is more significant: he accepted in the case of new countries that sales
of land should be confined to the usufruct only for a hundred years, with
the land reverting to the state for no compensation at the end of the
period. In old countries a modified version of this could be enacted: taxation of rental incomes could be remitted in the case of land transferred
to the state. Marshall regretted that land had been granted to railways in
perpetuity, rather than, as in France, for a limited period.

[37] *Ibid.*, 200.   [38] *Ibid.*, 204.

As we shall see in the following section, Marshall was to make use of other opportunities to comment on land and other taxes in the coming years. He was also to find himself the target of criticisms from a fellow critic of George who occupied a position at the opposite end of the politico-economic spectrum, George Douglas Campbell, the eighth Duke of Argyll. The Duke was a Peelite turned Cobdenite turned Liberal Unionist, who had broken with Gladstone over the second of the Irish Land Acts. He had defended the regulation of rental contracts according to strict commercial principles (natural economic laws) in a Cobden Club publication, and was a lively opponent of George's schemes during the 80s.[39] Like his fellow *libre échangiste*, Louis Mallet, Argyll was determined to expose the deficiencies of the Ricardian theory of rent. He was also dissatisfied with Marshall's efforts to mend defects in the 'shattered science', a phrase associated with Jevons's attack on Ricardo and Mill. These conclusions were expounded in an imposing work published in 1893 entitled *Unseen foundations of society: an examination of the fallacies and failures of economic science due to neglected elements* in which 'exclusive possession' emerged as a neglected factor of production alongside 'mind' and 'ability', terms meant to describe the enterprise and initiative of landowners such as the author in investing in agricultural improvements which gave them a just title to the rents they received. That the owner of a very large chunk of Scotland was prepared to write a sustained apology for landlordism is hardly surprising. That he did so by constructing the apology according to strict free market principles lends additional interest to the exercise.[40]

Some of the writings of the *libre échangistes* were reviewed in the pages of the *Economic Journal*, the organ of the newly formed British Economic Association (the Royal Economic Society after 1902). But the only one of them to receive anything like a full response was *Unseen foundations*. It also seems fitting that Marshall should have given that response, though since he had been attacked in the book and Argyll had become one of the honorary vice-presidents of the association, perhaps it was almost a duty. Marshall distinguished 'Ricardian dogma' from those developments of Ricardian ideas that were a legitimate part of 'modern analysis'.[41] As in his *Principles*, Marshall stressed that rent was 'the leading species of a large

---

[39] See an *Essay on the commercial principles applicable to contracts for the hire of land* (London: Cobden Club, 1877).
[40] See John W. Mason, 'The Duke of Argyll and the land question in late nineteenth-century Britain', *Victorian Studies*, 21 (1977–8), 149–70.
[41] 'On rent', *EJ*, 3 (1893), 74–5.

genus'. It did not differ from the 'producer's surplus' or the 'quasi-rents' that could be earned on pre-existing capital assets (physical or human) whenever revenues exceeded variable costs over the short term. Marshall's concessions, however, were limited. Rent on land was still the *leading* species, and 'it has peculiarities of its own which are vital from the point of view of theory as well as practice'. The earnings of owner-occupiers in new countries were more in the nature of profits or quasi-rent than rent proper. Even so, 'a far-seeing statesman will feel a greater responsibility to future generations when legislating as to land than as to other forms of wealth; and even there land must be regarded as a thing by itself from the economic as well as from the ethical point of view'.[42] Just as nature conferred advantages on agriculture that were independent of the actions of landowners, so urban land often derived 'true rents' from the advantages of situation. Significantly, Marshall added that 'a special tax on these would not much affect production directly', thereby endorsing the legitimacy of the original Ricardian principle in the form it had been applied to *ryots* in India by the Mills, father and son.[43] The main thrust of Marshall's reply is defensive of Ricardo's view of the part costs of production play in determining value, and even of the doctrine that, under some circumstances, Ricardo was right to state that rent does not enter into the costs of production. It allowed Marshall to conclude – with a sly dig at Argyll's lack of appreciation of these academic subtleties – that 'the analysis of which Ricardo was the chief builder, has firm if often unseen foundations'.[44]

V

On questions of taxation, as on other matters, Marshall took Mill as his point of departure and gradually modified his position as he became more comfortable in drawing conclusions from his own theory of distribution. He was also responsive to empirical evidence on the incidence of taxation and the broader political changes in what was becoming acceptable fiscally, notably in the case of the changes introduced by the 'people's budget' of 1909. Mill had condemned the snobbish aspirations of the English middle classes and had therefore refused to recognise them in his scheme of proportional income taxation: each person or family, regardless of class or income, was to be given the same untaxable allowance to cover

---

[42] 'On rent', 77. Marshall refers the reader to Book V, chapter 9 of *PE* for a fuller defence of this position.
[43] See p. 77 above.   [44] 'On rent', 90.

'the requisites of life and health, and with protection against habitual bodily suffering, but not with any indulgence'.[45] This reflected his refusal to accept any psychological law sanctioning inter-personal comparisons of enjoyment and thereby progressive income taxation of the rich, though he advocated a steep form of progressive tax on inheritances and would have wished to tax the other form of unearned income derived from rising land values. Marshall, by contrast, accepted the implications of the law of diminishing marginal utility as applied to incomes and recognised that 'necessary' expenditures could vary with economic occupation. Some necessaries were essential to the maintenance of 'efficiency' as opposed to mere subsistence; he also recognised a category of consumption goods that could be regarded as 'conventionally necessary'.[46]

As a further move away from the Ricardian view of taxation, in his evidence to the Royal Commission on Local Taxation in 1897 Marshall made an opening announcement to the effect that 'taxes are paid by persons, not things'; and that in consequence the inquiry should not relate to 'the distribution of the burden of taxation between different kinds of property, but to the distribution of the burden between different classes of person with special reference to their interests in different kinds of property'.[47] In simpler language, tax equity was not a matter of what kind of property the taxpayer owned, but how rich or poor that property made him or her. This took some heat off landowning as a special plutocratic form of income, and it was reinforced by other Marshall *obiter dicta* announcing that the law of diminishing returns was temporarily in abeyance and that 'the ownership of land is not a monopoly'.[48] It is noticeable, however, that he considered the Ricardian foundations still to be sufficiently firm for him to recommend a tax on 'that part of the (annual) value of land which arises from its position, its extension, its yearly income of sunlight and heat and rain and air', all those influences which gave it a 'public value' greater than the 'private value' derived from the outlay of landowners.[49] Site values in cities could legitimately be subject to a 'fresh air' rate designed to defray local costs of providing gardens, playgrounds, and wider streets.[50]

---

[45] See *Principles*, CW, III, pp. 808–11.　　[46] See *PE*, I, pp. 68–70.

[47] See *Official papers*, p. 492.

[48] *Official papers*, p. 340. For the temporary suspension of the law of diminishing returns see 'Social possibilities of economic chivalry', in *Memorials*, p. 326.

[49] *Official papers*, p. 341.

[50] *Ibid.*, pp. 360–1. He stood by this proposal ten years later; see letter to *The Times*, 13 November 1909, *Correspondence*, III, pp. 235–6.

Access to fresh air and light, and the value 'of being able to stroll amid beautiful and varied scenery' was one of Marshall's most persistent hobby-horses.[51] He welcomed the movement of population to the new suburbs and supported 'garden cities'. One of the voluntary associations that succeeded in bringing Marshall and Foxwell together was the Society for Promoting Industrial Villages, a scheme launched in 1885 with the object of creating healthy workshop employment in rural settings as a remedy for unemployment and overcrowding in cities. The aim conformed to Marshall's proposals for housing the London poor and his desire to see further rural immigration into cities reversed. He regarded expenditure on parks and playgrounds in large cities as one of the most important uses of private and public money – more important, he once claimed, than old-age pensions.[52] On this subject Marshall came closest to expressing his own version of the environmental ethic Mill had endorsed when speculating about a zero-growth society – or, rather more realistically, when supporting the Commons Preservation Society.

Marshall's willingness to make inter-personal comparisons meant that he could be forthright on the justice of redistributing income and wealth through progressive taxation and estate duties. While he objected to the deadening bureaucratic effect of what he described as 'administrative' socialism, he was not prepared entirely to condemn its cousin, 'financial' or redistributive socialism. As he pointed out in answer to an inquiry about his views on the 'people's budget', while some of its tax measures might be predatory, 'A cautious movement towards enriching the poor at the expense of the rich seems to me not to be cease to beneficial, merely because Socialists say it is a step in their direction.'[53] He also retracted his earlier opposition to taxes, such as death duties, which might retrench on capital, and he did so on grounds that Mill would certainly have recognised: given Britain's capacity to accumulate and export capital a 'small check to its growth would but postpone a little the day when most of her new accumulations are exported'. He was consistent in this because he altered his view again when contemplating the much higher tax burdens

---

[51] *PE*, I, p. 166.
[52] See *ibid.*, I, pp. 199–200; see also pp. 320–1, 718, 803. For other evidence of his concern, see 'Where to house the London poor', in *Memorials*, pp. 142–51, and a letter to Horsfall, 8 March 1900, *Correspondence*, II, p. 270: 'The fresh air and bright sunshine strengthen and stimulate, and at the same time soothe their nervous systems; and the beauty of ever changing nature offers an initiation to reverent and religious feeling, whether it be precipitated in theological forms or not.'
[53] Letters to Lord Reay, 12 and 15 November 1909, *Correspondence*, III, pp. 231–5, 237–8.

left by the First World War, when renewal of capital at home was a more important consideration.[54]

VI

There had long been a tradition of arguing that the economist, in his academic or professional capacity, did not comment on the moral worth of differing human wants or on what consumers chose to buy. Bagehot had expressed this provocatively when he said that a pot of beer and a religious book could both be wealth and hence of equal regard.[55] Jevons upheld the neutral or a-moral stance towards goods and the lifestyles they supported more piously by acknowledging that economics only dealt with 'the lowest rank of feelings': it had nothing to say about the 'higher calculus of moral right and wrong' that 'would be needed to show how [man] may best employ that wealth for the good of others as well as himself'.[56] Or as he expressed the limitation in his *Principles of economics*: 'It belongs to other branches of the moral and social sciences to investigate the ultimate effects of actions. In economics we treat only of proximate effects. A revolver is a means of attaining both good and evil, but we have only to consider whether it is wanted, and, if wanted, how it may be obtained with the least cost of labour.' For a mixture of what might be described as professional reasons, then, the traditional approach to consumer behaviour was exactly what Jevons said it was, an inquiry into 'the *mechanics* of utility and self-interest'.[57]

On the basis of the law of diminishing marginal utility economists could say something about the satiability of wants, those belonging to the lower rank at least, and could take an interest in the stock-flow problems posed by durable and perishable consumer goods. Jevons has interesting things to say about utilisation over time, about the effects of fashion and luxury, and about the recycling of discarded goods and waste by-products.[58] Nor was the self-denying ordinance rigid: after repeating the mantra that 'the economist must take the nature of the man or the woman as he finds it', he confessed that he could not 'resist pointing out how slight an alteration of wants and tastes would often result in a great

---

[54] See 'National taxation after the war', in W. H. Dawson (ed.), *After war problems* (London: Allen and Unwin, 1917), pp. 313–45.
[55] See pp. 135–6 above.
[56] The quotations come from the *Theory of political economy*, pp. 8, 13–15, 29.
[57] See p. 150 above.
[58] See the opening seven chapters on utility, wealth, and consumption in his *Principles*.

increase of wealth'.[59] In addition to believing that the English prejudice against non-white breads was harmful to working-class budgets and health, he had strong views on the degrading enjoyments of urban industrial workers. Bagehot's pot of beer, taken in quantity, could not be regarded with moral equanimity by the economist.

Marshall would certainly have agreed and was less willing to make any sharp distinctions or self-denying ordinances. It also seems unlikely that he would have been amused by Bagehot's frivolity. An important feature of his self-appointed mission was to overcome the conflict between ethics and economics, or rather, perhaps, construct a *via media* between them along which economics (and hence economists) could enjoy privileged access. Modesty required him to argue that economics was the servant of ethics, but it was one of its busiest and most useful servants, and as ethics 'gave herself mainly to the higher problems of the ultimate basis of duty' so economics needed to find new ways of serving these higher ideals.[60]

Marshall made several distancing moves away from the 'hedonic' emphasis imparted by the Jevonsian version of the science. Mention has been made of the way in which 'satisfaction' was substituted for 'pleasure', but the most simple and effective of Marshall's moves consisted of replacing Mill's 'economic man' and, more especially Bagehot's 'man, the money-making animal', with 'man in the ordinary business of life'. Economics dealt with the whole man, while concentrating on certain aspects of that whole. This provided another way of blurring the distinction between selfish and altruistic behaviour. It is a sign of Marshall's sensitivity to all currents of opinion that he denied that in the process of getting and spending there was any point in distinguishing between what was selfish and what was altruistic. As in all such matters, whether we think of the continuous functions of calculus or the continuities of Darwinian evolution, there was an unbroken spectrum between self-regarding and social concerns, leaving us free, as our aspirations and moral capacities rose, to move upwards along the spectrum to the altruistic end.

It will be abundantly clear by now that Marshall considered it part of his professional duty to pronounce on a wide range of human behaviours. Indeed, in his effort to convince his late-Victorian public that economics had much to contribute to the attainment of 'noble' ends, he not only

---

[59] *Principles of economics: a fragment of a treatise on the industrial mechanism of society and other papers*, with a preface by H. Higgs (London, Macmillan, 1905), p. 32, citing his support for the Bread Reform League.
[60] 'On economics and ethics', *EJ*, 3 (1893), 389.

refused to concede territory to critics of conventional economics such as Ruskin, but gave strong signs of wishing to take over Ruskin's role as an arbiter of public taste. A good example of this can be found in a chapter on industrial training in the *Principles* that was designed to answer Ruskinian exaggeration of the defects of present days. We were apt to underestimate the 'solid qualities of the modern machine-tending artisan', the intelligence, 'self-mastery', and transferability of the skills acquired in the higher forms of manual work, when compared with 'the lighter virtues of the medieval handicraftsman'. The chapter included a section contrasting the laxity of art education with the character-forming 'hard thinking' of science.[61] Marshall dealt only with those arts that appeal to the eye, as opposed to literature and music, to which he assigned superior qualities in contributing to the 'fullness of life' because they involve 'manufacture' and the skill of 'artisans' or practitioners. Neither Ruskin nor Morris was mentioned here, but there is a side-glance towards them surely in the remark that the European artisan in the Middle Ages, like that of Eastern countries today, has 'obtained credit for more originality than he has really possessed'. There is no variety, merely repetition, in their ideas. Nowadays, fashion and changes in technology enable the artisan to innovate, relying on his own resources, but with 'no slowly matured public criticism to guide him'.[62] Modern artisans are more apt to be occupied in the management of machinery, developing solid faculties, but not those likely to 'contribute directly towards the progress of art'. World markets lead to the 'hasty and hurried efforts of the designer by compelling him to be always watching the world movements of the supply of and demand for art products' – a position close to Ruskin's. The artisan does not have these skills: he follows but does not lead. Morris was praised for deriving an inspiration from oriental designs that had placed English fabrics and decorative products in the world's first rank. While technical education could not add directly to the production of genius, then, it was able to 'save much natural artistic genius from running to waste', thereby compensating for the fact that the older handicrafts could not be revived on a large scale. This last remark can be read as an implicit, perhaps explicit, rejection of the aims of Morris and Co. in their hopes of creating a mass market for their work.

Marshall could be as disdainful as Ruskin in his condemnation of those lifestyles that did not reflect station and economic roles.[63] He was free with his opinions on the uses and misuses of wealth by rich and poor

[61] Book IV, chapter 6.   [62] *PE*, I, p. 213.   [63] See *ibid.*, pp. 134–7, 720.

consumers alike. Activities were superior to mere wants, and while the earning of incomes was character-forming, the spending of them frequently was not. Much of it took the form of 'display' rather than expenditure on goods that yielded 'solid, unostentatious pleasure of a wholesome kind'. Nor was he afraid to employ terms that were earlier more closely associated with the 'feudal' position, as is clear from the title he gave to an important lecture in 1907, 'Social possibilities of economic chivalry'. Indeed, this represented Marshall's version of Ruskin's programme for a moral revitalisation of the behaviour of the 'captains of industry', a phrase taken from Carlyle. They were enjoined to take 'a delight in doing noble and difficult things because they are noble and difficult'. For a post-Darwinian thinker such as Marshall, what might otherwise seem like pious hope could be fortified by the idea that the path towards this goal had already been smoothed by those evolutionary processes associated with modern forms of competition and technological innovation. It was now necessary to redirect these latent talents within the business community towards chivalric or charitable goals – an art collection that could be left to the public or a park open to all. Voluntary activities of this kind would make it less necessary to call upon and risk increasing the powers of an official bureaucracy, or those 'iron bonds of mechanical symmetry' which Marxists postulated as being necessary to their project. The spirit of the times had assigned a missionary role to economists that called for 'steady, searching analysis, and for a laborious study of actual conditions'. It required establishing a persistent linkage between 'economic studies and chivalrous effort' in 'our own minds and those of others'.[64] Marshall could not be accused of failing to lead by example, even if the moralising embarrassed those, like Keynes, who were disposed to admire him, and exasperated those, like Tawney, who were not so disposed and thought Marshall's praise for businessmen would delay the overthrow of the 'economic oligarchy'.[65]

VII

Marshall's interest in character, in this case the character of his ideal student of social problems as well as that of the new businessman, places him squarely amid the Victorian moralists. Since he sometimes plied this

[64] 'Social possibilities', in *Memorials*, p. 346.
[65] *R. H. Tawney's commonplace book*, ed. J. M. Winter and D. M. Joslin (Cambridge: Cambridge University Press, 1972), p. 11.

trade in the public media as well as lecture halls and scientific publications there is a temptation to think of him as part of the earlier tradition of public moralists, as someone worthy of being placed in the same category as Mill, the person who provided the youthful Marshall with inspiration and a scientific base-line. But there are reasons why this description is no longer helpful when applied to a late nineteenth-century academic with Marshall's ambitions to be the leader of a professional scientific community with international affiliations. In part at least the primary audience he hoped to impress was an academic or scientific one, and as the final essay in this book will illustrate, that required publications that were more specialist than the kinds of general periodicals, newspapers, and magazines in which Mill's work appeared. During the first phase of his career Marshall wrote for the *Academy*, the *Fortnightly Review*, and the *Contemporary Review*, as well as journals such as *Bee-Hive*, which had strong connections with the trade unions and the labour movement. But after 1887 everything he wrote that was connected with serious economics either appeared between two of Macmillan and Company's stout green covers or in articles in the new specialised learned journals. The only exceptions were letters to *The Times*, notably during the period in which he was arguing for his Economics tripos.

Reverting to a subject that arose in the preceding essay, it should be noted that by the time he was elected to Marshall's chair, Pigou (whose first book, on *Robert Browning as a religious teacher*, was hardly that of a narrow-minded economic specialist) had published ten articles in the *Economic Journal*, two more than Marshall achieved throughout his whole career. Foxwell, who had done far more than Marshall or anybody else to get the journal and its sponsoring association off the ground, could only ever muster a few reviews, bibliographic notes, and reports on current economic affairs. Marshall's publishing career straddled the old and new worlds. Pigou was almost entirely immersed in the new world in which economists spoke to fellow-economists, except on those occasions on which they chose to take part in a larger public debate, as he had done over tariff reform. This was partly a simple matter of age and the dates when the new professional outlets became available. But it was also a matter of personal temperament. Maynard Keynes, a Cambridge neighbour since childhood who came to know Foxwell well, reported that he was against writing books 'except for grave cause'. Foxwell's daughter confirmed this by saying that her father disapproved of the Germanic trend in favour of research and publication, believing that teaching was the main duty of university teachers. Keynes gave a less flattering reason: '[Foxwell]

was for ever occupied with all manner of details, and never left himself
the opportunity for concentration on a continuous piece of work'.[66]

These observations are all perfectly understandable within the context
of the process known as professionalisation, a process occurring in a
number of disciplines at this time, and one in which Marshall has rightly
been accorded a crucial role on behalf of economics. But having made
such observations there are still elements that cannot readily be assimilated into that kind of story. Marshall also had a longing to have his
Principles and other serious works read by businessmen and other opinion-
leaders. That is why he hid the mathematics which enabled him to reach
his conclusions, and why the student audience for his *Principles*, ostensibly an advanced textbook, could not fail to be aware that the author was
often speaking over their shoulders to another ghostly audience. They
could not complain of being talked down to: rather the challenge was
how to become sufficiently elevated in their understanding, sentiments,
and aspirations (in a word, their character) to earn the inner rewards of
belonging to the 'we' being addressed throughout. Faced with Marshall's
list of questions that lay 'outside the range of economic science, yet
supply a chief motive in the background to the work of the economist',
it would be hard not to feel that one was being recruited into an ethical
crusade.[67] In 1923, a year before he died, hard though it is to credit,
Marshall wished that he had devoted his life to psychology rather than
economics, on the ground that it would have given him more scope to
talk about 'ideals'. What prevented him from saying more on this subject
was the imagined incomprehension of the businessmen in his imagined
audience.[68] Here is yet another example of Marshall's acquisitive instincts
hiding as reticence, his persistent attempts to enjoy all the safety and
dignity of the austere and modest professional concerned only with the
causes of causes, while not losing any chance to pontificate on the higher
ethical goals at which 'we' should be aiming.

---

[66] See *Essays in biography*, in JMK, X, p. 278. For the daughter's remark, see Audrey G. D. Foxwell,
Herbert Somerton Foxwell: a portrait, Kress Library of Business and Economics, publication no. 1
(Boston, 1939), p. 12.

[67] *PE*, I, pp. 41–2

[68] Mary Paley Marshall's notes for Keynes's biographical memoir, Keynes Papers, Archive Centre,
King's College, Cambridge.

PART V

Heretics and professionals

Fig. 11. John Atkinson Hobson.

'A composition of successive heresies': the case of J. A. Hobson

... I cannot claim for myself an objectivity and disinterestedness which I have denied to others. Indeed, the biographic details in which I have indulged ought to help to explain not only the steps along which my economic thinking has proceeded, but the slipperiness of these very steps, and the likelihood, perhaps certainty, that my economic humanism, a composition of successive heresies, is defective when regarded as a whole.

Confessions of an economic heretic[1]

I

Such modest self-reflections are one of the attractive features of Hobson's *Confessions*, written near the end of a life that was more influential in 'progressive' circles in Britain and the United States than perhaps he realised. Modesty came from the knowledge that he could be judged as he had judged other social actors and authors, often as semi-conscious victims of their circumstances. Hobson had launched a number of circumstantial explanations of a conspiratorial kind. The most famous of these connected capitalism with imperialism and both with certain types of parasitic investment activity, a theory expounded in *Imperialism: a study* published in 1902, for which, as a result of Lenin's uses of it, he is still best known in some circles. As we shall see in the succeeding essay Hobson was also prone to use such explanations when contemplating the science of economics and those who held the academic posts from which his heresies had excluded him. 'Victorious capitalism' had exerted, he maintained, a potent influence 'to impress the justice and utility of its procedure upon the dawning science of economics and to exclude from consideration all

---

[1] *Confessions of an economic heretic: the autobiography of John A. Hobson* (1938), ed. M. Freeden (Brighton: Harvester Press, 1976), p. 90.

attempts to challenge its intellectual domination'.[2] In 1938, when this was written, it could have been read as a self-promoting observation designed to dramatise his own challenges to that domination, the earliest of which, oversaving as the clue to depression, had recently been rehabilitated, though not endorsed, by Keynes's *General theory of employment, interest and money* in 1936. But Hobson's self-examination was candid enough to recognise that 'the break-away disposition is not necessarily the free play of a reasonable mind'; that heresy carried with it the risk of 'dogmatic overconfidence'.

In developing what he described as his 'economic humanism' Hobson had closely associated himself with Ruskin, and more will need to be said below about the ways in which Hobson developed Ruskin's social vision for his own purposes. But since Hobson took the initial steps in his career as an economic heretic before he decided to pay special attention to Ruskin's life and writings, something must first be said about his relationship with orthodox versions of the science. This was unmediated by Ruskin at the outset and only given partial colouring by his influence later. Although Hobson retained his suspicions of orthodox economics, and frequently gave vent to them, he overestimated the monolithic qualities of the orthodoxy he faced and exaggerated his own independence of mind. Friends and figures whom he admired – a fairly diverse gathering if Cobden, Ruskin, L. T. Hobhouse, Tawney, and Thorstein Veblen are taken as representative – could be duly praised. But when speaking about economists, especially British ones, Hobson was given to sly innuendo in his popular works, with the borrowings he made in his more academic writings being marked by minimal acknowledgement and maximum emphasis on any divergence.

The steps he took towards a coherent position of his own were indeed slippery, and the biographical narrative he assembled did not provide an accurate guide to the various twists and turns he took during a half-century of prolific writing that resulted in the publication of more than a book a year and a great deal of ephemeral journalism along the way. The journalism required rapid powers of assimilation and provided ample opportunities for expressing firm opinions that were at odds with those he held, equally firmly, in later writings. Keeping track of such a career was difficult for the author, let alone his readers, and Hobson was less interested in supplying a chronicle than in tracing the 'causal and casual occurrences' that had shaped his thinking. Despite acute awareness of the

---

[2] *Confessions*, pp. 24–25n.

dangers of autobiography, Hobson was also prone to the ordinary pitfalls of memory lapse. While his account of events and ideas needs to be treated with caution, one of the reasons he gave for his exclusion from the fledgling academic world of professional economics contains an unmistakable ring of truth.

II

Hobson first became acquainted with political economy as a schoolboy through a moralised and mildly reformist university extension course on the subject given in his home town, Derby, in the 1870s. The course he took used Mill's *Principles* and Mrs Fawcett's primer based on her husband's simplified version of Mill as its textbooks, often known, through an American pun on the lady's name, as the 'milk and water' offering.[3] Despite Mill's interest in socialist alternatives, it was here that Hobson later claimed he had partially glimpsed the lesson about the potent influence of 'victorious capitalism', and had found the idea of wages being paid out of a fund based on past savings unacceptable. This was before he went up to Lincoln College, Oxford, where he obtained a third-class degree in *Literae Humaniores* in 1880 – a degree that condemned him to a spell as a schoolteacher of classics. In 1887 he embarked on a less secure occupation as a peripatetic lecturer on the university extension circuit, specialising in English literature and economics, publishing some articles in the new professional journals, and beginning a career as journalist and freelance author. The more regular academic livelihood Hobson sought in the nineties, though less urgently after he inherited a share of his father's local newspaper fortune in 1897, was initially denied him on grounds of his first act of heresy in a book he wrote with a businessman, Alfred Mummery, in 1889, *Physiology of industry: being an exposure of certain fallacies in existing theories of economics.*

By joining Mummery in this enterprise Hobson attached his name to a theory purporting to show that 'an undue exercise of the habit of saving is possible, and that such undue exercise impoverishes the community, throws labourers out of work, drives down wages, and spreads that gloom and prostration through the commercial world which is known as depression in trade'.[4] This amounted to a denial of an orthodox

---

[3] Hobson's bare account of this can now be supplemented by the research of Alon Kadish on the tutor involved, the Rev. William Moore Ede, later Dean of Worcester; see his 'Rewriting the *Confessions*: Hobson and the extension movement', in M. Freeden (ed.), *Reappraising J. A. Hobson: humanism and welfare* (London: Unwin Hyman, 1990), pp. 137–40.
[4] *Physiology of industry* (London: John Murray, 1889), p. iv.

macroeconomic doctrine ruling out the possibility of general as opposed to partial overproduction, except as the result of acute monetary disorder – an exception the authors discounted. Their conclusions clashed too with conventional wisdom on the straightforward connection between capital accumulation and economic growth, and with the moral imperatives that linked individual thrift with prudent self-help. With Mummery leading the way, Hobson had joined a long line of underconsumptionists, those who had maintained, on various grounds, that there were chronic tendencies at work in capitalism generating breakdown and depression. According to the terminology later worked out to classify different theories of economic crisis or cyclical disorder, Hobson was an underconsumptionist of the oversaving variety, with the main fault being attributed to 'real' as opposed to monetary factors. As Hobson developed the case, when left to his own devices, these 'real' factors encompassed many features of late-Victorian society which occupied the attention of students of the 'social question': urban poverty, unemployment, unequal bargaining power as between rich and poor, the competitive build-up of large capital concentrations, and a consequent maldistribution of income as between savers and spenders which favoured the former at the expense of the purchasing power needed to sustain full employment.

Towards the end of the 1890s and during the Boer war Hobson extended the scope of his thesis of chronic oversaving to explain the emergence of new and more aggressive types of jingoistic imperialism. This ensured that underconsumption featured, on and off, in several of Hobson's publications before the outbreak of the First World War. But it was the special emphasis he placed on the 'unearned', 'forced', or non-functional element in incomes that was to become Hobson's trademark as an economic theorist and policy advocate, a role he continued to occupy, self-consciously, long after he had become the spokesman for a theory of economic welfare of a kind that could be described as economic humanism. It also survived his emergence as the proponent of an organic version of social science based on a collectivist version of the doctrines of social evolution associated with Herbert Spencer, with new elements being supplied by related debates on sex and eugenics inaugurated by Darwin's cousin, Francis Galton, that were later to be further embellished by Freudian ideas.

The Mummery/Hobson team had more limited objectives in view in 1889: they were mounting a theoretical diagnosis of the causes of the prolonged depression that began in the early 1870s. One of the supporting arguments in *Physiology* that was to play an important role in Hobson's later analyses of the defects of capitalism concerned the divergence between the individual and social interest in the supply of capital, with competition acting as a wedge driving them further apart during depressions. The argument was based on a distinction between 'makers' and 'traders' that could be illustrated by what had happened during the boom that preceded the 1873 slump. They connected the boom with the public-debt-financed Franco-Prussian war, which had had the effect of increasing wholesale prices and the profits earned by a Europe-wide community of producers or makers. This had led to an increase in investment that was left high and dry by the subsequent collapse of demand for final goods. Depression reversed the previous relationship between makers and traders, giving the latter an opportunity to dictate terms to the former, and inducing a shift in productive resources towards selling activities that was not accompanied by a proportionate fall in the price of retail goods. Competition between traders took the form of larger numbers of retail outlets, with 'quality' rather than price being the means by which competitors sought to retain a hold on shrinking markets. Many of the qualitative improvements on offer were bogus, based on the ignorance of consumers; they took the apparent shape of 'conveniences of neighbourhood, affability, shop front, advertisements etc', beneath which adulteration and other forms of chicanery could take place. In other words, 'the law of competition no longer applies', or as a later generation of economists would express it, a situation called 'monopolistic competition' arises, bringing with it excess capacity.[5] Mummery and Hobson were able to cite a long list of orthodox economists from Mill through to Sidgwick and Marshall who had observed the greater stickiness of retail compared to wholesale prices.[6] What they added to this was, first, an explanation of why this was a symptom of depression, and, secondly, a degree of moral indignation that makes one wonder what exactly happened to Mummery's business. They conceded that the rise of traders at the expense of makers *could* represent something more positive by way of service to consumers, but there is no doubt about the moral preference of the authors for the disciplined activity of 'making' when compared with the unhealthy laxity of 'trading'. It entailed a shift from more to less productive activities from the point of view of society; and the unhealthy growth of retailing was a form of 'waste' that should be added to that other source of social waste associated with depression, unemployed labour.[7]

---

[5] *Physiology*, pp. 149–50.
[6] For Sidgwick's concern with this feature of modern capitalism, see pp. 215–16 above.
[7] *Physiology*, p. 157.

What Hobson later described as his 'narrower heresy' had a history that could be traced to Lauderdale, Malthus, Sismondi, Chalmers, Rodbertus, and, in some moods, Marx. In Hobson's own day others had revived it. Thus by 1896, when he repeated his heresy in the *Problem of the unemployed: an enquiry and an economic policy*, he could cite the examples of Lauderdale and Malthus together with the work of Uriel Crocker in the United States and that of a friend and fellow rationalist or anti-religionist, the future Liberal MP, J. M. Robertson, entitled the *Fallacy of saving*. More tellingly, perhaps, he could also cite the conclusions of the majority and minority reports of the Royal Commission on the Depression of Trade in 1886, the former of which, while denying the existence of general overproduction, recognised that excess capacity had played a major part in reducing prices and profits to depression levels.[8] As he made plain in later exchanges with his critics, Hobson did not regard himself as reviving an ancient heresy so much as building on the insights of a new generation that was no longer writing under the influence of the wage-fund doctrine.[9] He was familiar with the standard responses of opponents of undercon-sumptionist explanations for depression: Adam Smith's argument that 'saving is spending'; Mill's dictum that 'a demand for capital is not a demand for labour'; and the orthodoxy embodied in Say's law of markets, which provided the basis for the assumption that aggregate production always generated enough income to sustain an equivalent level of aggre-gate consumption, though not necessarily at existing prices, profits, and interest rates. Ricardo, Mill, and their orthodox post-marginalist succes-sors upheld the law, with varying stress being placed on the circumstances that might lead to its suspension. As a further complication, Hobson himself upheld Say's law.[10] As was true in the case of Marx, he needed it, for expositional purposes at least, to show how the capitalist system *might* operate when contrasted with the pathological states to which it was prone as a result of inequality in the distribution of incomes. Say's law was to define the version of macroeconomics that Keynes, in his own challenge to it, was later to describe as the 'classical' theory, the theory that needed to be overthrown to make way for his explanation for unemployment in the inter-war period. Having reached this conclusion Keynes could pay

---

[8] *Problem of the unemployed* (London: Methuen, 1896), pp. ix, 61–2. For a detailed study of the context surrounding the Mummery/Hobson book, see A. Kadish, 'The non-canonical context of the *Physiology of industry*', in J. Pheby (ed.), *J. A. Hobson after fifty years* (Basingstoke: Macmillan, 1994), pp. 53–77.
[9] See his reply to A. W. Flux's criticisms, in 'Saving and spending', *Economic Review*, 9 (1899), 186–96.
[10] See p. 327 below.

Hobson the backhanded compliment of being part of that underground group of authors who, 'following their intuitions, have preferred to see the truth obscurely and imperfectly rather than to maintain error'.[11]

In 1889, then, Hobson was thought to be guilty of reviving a time-honoured fallacy. The unsympathetic reception given to *Physiology* by those who had sufficiently well-established positions to justify their role in making discretionary appointments undoubtedly created difficulty for Hobson in obtaining a regular position as a teacher of economics. Edgeworth's dismissive review of the book in a journal read by extension lecturers must have been damaging, though he was not responsible for orchestrating the moves that temporarily excluded Hobson from giving extension courses in economics in London. Foxwell took the lead in this, citing the support of James Bonar for his opinion that Hobson was 'a man only notorious for a very fallacious attempt to prove that thrift is morally and socially a vice'. Hobson was able to identify Foxwell as the person responsible for his exclusion and duly sent him a plea that admitted to rashness and stated that he was not irrevocably committed to the under-consumptionist position, a plea designed to answer an unspoken charge of political bias: 'I have no special "sympathies" which would make me cleave obstinately to a position taken on purely intellectual grounds.'[12] Foxwell was unmoved, despite the fact that neither he nor Bonar could be described as slavish upholders of orthodoxy. Dissidents are often especially sensitive to forms of dissent that risk giving the very idea of dissent a bad name. The issues surrounding the possibility of general overproduction had been sufficiently well rehearsed throughout the nineteenth century for them to seem *vieux jeu*. Foxwell's study of 'irregularity of employment' in 1886 had attacked 'the fatalistic, crude, anti-social doctrine of *laissez-faire*' in terms that would have done credit to Ruskin, let alone Hobson. But Foxwell's emphasis fell on those monetary causes for irregularity that Mummery and Hobson had dismissed.[13]

III

Even if Hobson had not decided, after wavering, to cleave obstinately to his oversaving thesis there were other reasons why he was likely to be

---

[11] *General theory of employment, interest and money*, in JMK, VII, p. 371.
[12] See letter to Foxwell, 12 January 1892, cited in Kadish, 'Rewriting the *Confessions*', pp. 146–7.
[13] See H. S. Foxwell, *Irregularity of employment and fluctuations of prices* (Edinburgh: Cooperative Printing Company, 1886), p. 77; and the chapter on 'Scarcity of gold as an economic factor', in *Physiology*, pp. 186–201.

treated as suspect by the new professionals. His lack of respectable academic credentials in any of the fields then thought to be useful as
preparation for specialisation in economics and economic history mattered in the meritocratic world of competitive examinations and early
professionalisation. Francis Ysidro Edgeworth, for example, had also
obtained an Oxford degree in classics; but it came with first-class honours
attached and was then supplemented by a self-taught command of
mathematics and statistics that allowed him to place his personal stamp
on economics. Oxford was to supply more than its fair share of economic
dissidents during the final quarter of the century. Unlike Hobson, many
of these emerged from the school of modern history in which economics
occupied a more prominent place than in the *Lit. Hum.* alternative.
Hobson may have heard Ruskin lecture at Oxford, but he missed that
other seminal influence on Oxford dissidents in the early 1880s, Arnold
Toynbee, and was not attracted by the historicist or inductivist critique of
economic theorising that many of them favoured.

Although Hobson could, on occasion, sound like other ethical critics of
the English science in its abstract form, an opponent of its narrow
'economic man' assumptions and its unwillingness to embrace normative
as well as positive propositions as part of a science contributing to the 'art
of social progress', he was more sympathetic to the deductivists (as long
as they did not use mathematics) than he was to those who based their
critique on economic history. In the first major work he wrote after
Physiology, his *Evolution of modern capitalism*, he practised a form of *histoire économique raisonnée* on the industrial revolution in Britain, basing
himself on existing secondary sources. But his main allegiance in this and
other writings was to something more Spencerian, something he called
'scientific history', the discovery and application of those 'laws of the
movement of industrial forces' that underlay organic evolution. In this
sense the book, as he admitted, belonged more 'to economic science rather
than to industrial history'.[14] The evolutionary perspective was deliberately
teleological and future-oriented, yielding prophecies, if not precise predictions, of the kind Hobson assigned to his final chapter on 'civilisation
and industrial development'. It was here that he charted the imperfect
adjustment of structure to environment and the ways in which rational
intervention could speed up organic processes and remedy the failings of
earlier attempts to deal with the consequences of the industrial revolution.

---

[14] *Evolution of modern capitalism* (London: Walter Scott, 1894), p. 2.

Organicism was later to lead Hobson to espouse the cause of sociology and criticise economists, such as Marshall, for dismissing the idea that economics could be absorbed within sociology.[15] But whatever Hobson may have learned from other social sciences, and especially from the sociological writings of his friend, Hobhouse, he also recognised that he had entered 'the sphere of sociology through the portals of economic theory'.[16] His criticisms of what he took to be orthodox economics were primarily theoretical and ideological rather than methodological. He could defend the need for abstraction with as much fervour as any orthodox theorist. Indeed, Cairnes became the authority he cited on the necessity for hypotheses in a science that had limited possibilities for direct experiment.[17]

The notion that a social science capable of yielding an art of social progress can be formed upon inductive lines by setting a number of persons to study facts, and then by ordering these facts and extracting their common measures in laws and tendencies, is the futile product of an incapacity to think clearly upon the conditions of science. The laws or principles needed for the selection, the ordering, and the interpretation of concrete facts of history cannot be got out of these facts themselves, but must be imposed by a process which, at any rate relatively to these facts, is *a priori*.[18]

Speaking of the much-vaunted 'historic spirit', he once described its factual inquiries as 'dull monuments of patience' with 'no appreciable value, either theoretic or practical'.[19]

It is one of the ironies surrounding Hobson's relationship with orthodox economics that the nearest equivalent to this position within the academic community can be found in Marshall, one of its dominant spirits. Although Marshall was more respectful towards the work of economic historians, he too had Spencerian longings and preferred an evolutionary approach based on the 'reasoned history of man' to more particularistic versions of political and economic history.[20] Indeed, we find Hobson making use of one of Marshall's favourite mottos to defend this view: 'The study of facts always discloses "the many", never "the one"; yet, if there is to be a "science of history", it will consist in this very discovery of the "one", the "unity", the "laws" of action, which induction alone is

---

[15] See criticism of Marshall, 'whose hankerings after humanity continually break the rigour of his mathematical proclivities', in *Social problem: life and work* (London: J. Nisbet, 1901), pp. 58–60.
[16] *Confessions*, p. 79.   [17] *Evolution of modern capitalism*, p. 8.   [18] *Social problem*, pp. 281–2.
[19] 'The academic spirit in education', *Contemporary Review*, 63 (1893), 242.
[20] The quoted phrase comes from 'The old generation of economists and the new', as reprinted in *Memorials*, p. 299.

impotent to disclose.' He shared too Marshall's belief that rationality, or as Marshall called it, 'deliberateness', was the mark of the evolving form of civilisation associated with industrial economic development. Deliberateness enabled modern man to make predictive calculations that took him beyond his immediate interests; and it allowed rich nations, again as Marshall had argued, to make sacrifices of present material comfort for future, more altruistic, goals.[21]

Where Hobson decisively parted company with Marshall was in rejecting the latter's other favourite motto: *Natura non facit saltum*. For Marshall this summarised a lesson about change being gradual and continuous that could be reinforced by analogy with modern physics and post-Darwinian biology. Hobson objected strongly to the former analogy, to the idea that economic variables could be treated as continuous and infinitely divisible, the assumption that licensed use of differential calculus to pose economic problems as ones of maximisation or minimisation. Although the marginal buyer or seller played a crucial part in Hobson's theory of unequal bargaining, 'marginalism' became a term of abuse, and in the eyes of Marshall, the target of much of Hobson's criticism of marginal 'doses', this consigned him to the category of 'a vigorous and suggestive writer on the realistic and social sides of economics' who was 'apt to underrate the difficulty of the problems which he discusses'. Decoding Marshall's polite prose, this meant that Hobson was an amateur in matters of theory who did not understand calculus and was more attracted to the drama of 'convulsive' as opposed to continuous change. Instances of convulsive change had to be recognised, but they 'throw no true light on the processes of normal steady evolution'.[22] Edgeworth had also weighed in on this matter by arguing that Hobson's failure to grasp the issue amounted to mathematical ignorance: 'Imagine an analogous application of the differential calculus in physics...an objector substituting x wherever a mathematician had used dx or Δx.'[23] Many academic economists shared Hobson's mixture of suspicion,

---

[21] See *Social problem*, pp. 282–4.
[22] See *PE*, I, p. 409. This was in response to Hobson's attack in the *Economics of distribution* (London: Macmillan, 1900), pp. 144–9. For some acute remarks on the issues at stake in this dispute, see J. Maloney, *Marshall, orthodoxy and the professionalisation of economics* (Cambridge: Cambridge University Press, 1985), pp. 44–6.
[23] 'The theory of distribution', *Quarterly Journal of Economics*, 18 (1904), 167. Edgeworth also responded to Hobson's later attack ('Marginal units in the theory of distribution', *Journal of Political Economy*, 12 (1904), 449–72) in 'Application of the differential calculus to economics', *Scientia*, 7 (1910), 80–103, taking in Hobson's latest statement of his criticisms in *The Industrial System* (London: Longmans, 1909), p. 110.

antagonism, and incomprehension when faced with the use of mathematics to express economic relationships, but none of them took quite such a fundamentalist line in thinking that discontinuity and indivisibility were essential features of modern economic life.

At this point we encounter another paradox. Whatever Hobson might say about the deficiencies of marginalism, every step in his arguments on the economics of pricing and distribution presupposed the work of pre- and post-marginalist economic ideas, classical and, what he was one of the first to criticise as, neo-classical economics. He acquired a knowledge of economic literature as a result of having to prepare extension courses based on the seminal works of the older generation of economists, including Marx, to which he added recent professional writings in his chosen fields of interest, chiefly those on post-Jevonsian value theory with special reference to the theory of distribution, and post-Marshallian welfare economics.[24] The pre-marginalist inspiration could be found in the Ricardian theory of rent as fortified by Mill's doctrine of the 'unearned increment'. As both Jevons and Marshall had demonstrated, the rent theory was one aspect of the classical approach that could readily be rendered in the new marginalist language. Hobson granted that this theory was 'the one genuinely revolutionary element in the older economic teaching', an exception, therefore, to his usual charges of conservatism and class bias in favour of *laissez-faire*.[25] He could not fail to be aware of the prominent role played by the theory of rent in Sidney Webb's thinking and in Bernard Shaw's contribution to *Fabian essays*, first published in 1889, with a significant contribution by William Clarke, a friend whose writings on jingoism and empire Hobson later edited.[26] Hobson differed from the Fabians on many public issues, including empire, but his failure to mention parallels between his own theory and that employed by the Fabians could either be a sign of his desire to maintain political distance,

---

[24] The content of his courses can be gauged from the summer course he gave on 'The growth of economic theory from Adam Smith' in 1895 under the auspices of the Oxford University extension system. It covered the entire field, including Marx, Marshall, 'recent Austrian theory', and concluded with 'the efforts of thinkers like Comte, Owen, and Ruskin to broaden and "humanise" Economics'.

[25] *Social problem*, p. 23. One sign of memory lapse in the *Confessions* is the extraordinary sentence with which he opens chapter 2: 'In my early approaches towards economic study it had struck me as odd that the private ownership of land and the receipt of rent seemed a matter of no importance to our political economists.'

[26] See *William Clarke, a collection of his writings*, ed. by H. Burrows and J. A. Hobson (London: Swan Sonnenschein, 1908).

or of the subjective claims to originality he was keen to register for his own, as he thought, more general theory of pricing and distribution.

As in the case of the Fabians, Hobson's thesis depended a great deal on the absorption of post-marginalist writings. For reasons that, paradoxically perhaps, become clearer as soon as Ruskin enters the picture, Hobson had a soft spot for Jevons's programmatic statement of the goal of economic science.[27] But the post-marginalist authors who appear most frequently in Hobson's economic writings in the 1890s and beyond are Marshall and Böhm-Bawerk, the latter made known to him through William Smart's translations. Böhm-Bawerk eschewed mathematics in favour of arithmetic based on a kind of Robinson Crusoe economics that was more congenial to Hobson's tastes in matters of theory.[28] Hobson had employed the Marshalls' *Economics of industry* as a textbook for his extension courses, and was to add the *Principles of economics* to his personal reading not long after its publication in 1890. It was, as he said, 'the leading English textbook of today', and in that work he would have encountered various distinctively Marshallian tools of analysis, notably the concept of elasticity of demand; the principle of limited substitution between factors of production; the distinction between industries characterised by increasing or diminishing returns to scale; an emphasis on time through the distinction between short- and long-run adjustment to market price; and the extension of the concept of rent to all factors of production in the form of 'quasi-rent'. Hobson would also have encountered Marshall's concept of consumers' and producers' surplus. Hobson makes use of all these tools while at the same time suggesting that they support more radical conclusions than Marshall was prepared to draw from them. Unlike his friend Hobhouse, who also employed Marshall's notions of quasi-rent and surplus in his earliest and most Fabian work, *The labour movement*, Hobson emphasises his departures rather than his borrowings from Marshall.[29]

---

[27] See pp. 314–15 below.
[28] Böhm-Bawerk's horse-trading illustration provides the heart of Hobson's argument on 'The economics of bargaining', *Economic Review*, 9 (1899), 20–41; and he is cited on the same theme in the *Economics of distribution*, pp. 11–24, 64–7. Marshall is in the background throughout this work; his criticism of the one-sided approach to value through utility in demand is endorsed (pp. 68–70), but Jevons's claim to be the founder of the subjective utility approach is praised (pp. 91–2). The preference for illustrations based on barter also underlined the way in which Hobson preferred to treat money as a veil or mere distraction from underlying economic realities.
[29] 'In what follows I am guided mainly by Prof. Marshall, whose account is the most comprehensive'; see L. T. Hobhouse, *The labour movement* (London: Unwin, 1893), pp. 56n, 67, 87. See also S. Collini, *Liberalism and sociology: L. T. Hobhouse and political argument in England, 1880–1914* (Cambridge: Cambridge University Press, 1979), pp. 62–6.

Whereas Marshall wanted to show the precise limits within which his surplus concepts were valid, Hobson stressed their pervasiveness. By adding other elements derived from the older classical vocabulary, notably a distinction between 'productive' and 'unproductive' surpluses, he gave the concept further normative purchase in advancing what he described as his 'most destructive heresy'. It was destructive because it cast doubt on the legitimacy of large parts of the income enjoyed by the property-owning classes.

Assuming, as Hobson was wont to do when dealing with orthodox economics, that its spokesmen were committed to a general demonstration of the efficiency and equity of free enterprise capitalism, an assumption that could be verified in only a few cases, the destructive part of the heresy consisted in a thorough-going rejection of market price as the measure of and instrument for achieving economic efficiency and social justice. Although economists were united in exposing and opposing monopoly powers, Hobson believed that even under competitive conditions there was always a zone of indeterminacy where skill, cunning, or some other advantage in bargaining played a part in shifting the balance of gain in favour of one of the parties. Böhm-Bawerk's contribution to this analysis lay in his demonstration that differential gains arise from the subjective evaluations of buyers and sellers, how keen they were to buy or sell being unknown to the other parties to the exchange. On Hobson's reading this meant that market dealings involved a degree of force, fraud, and cunning. How pervasive such practices were under current economic conditions tended to vary in his estimation. As we shall see later, on occasion, when dealing with the issues raised by international trade, Hobson could be as conventional in his account of the benefits of free exchange and the international division of labour as any orthodox economist.

'On occasion' is the crucial phrase here, because the macroeconomic implications of Hobson's theory of underconsumption pointed in a direction that was not always favourable to free trade in goods, persons, and capital. The strong version of Hobson's position also depended on the teleology of the organic processes under investigation, not so much on what was, but on what was becoming. Hobson held that the concentration of capital would increase as a result of natural processes of industrial evolution, unless these were checked by 'rational' forms of regulation that included nationalisation of those industries supplying standardised goods and services. Greater prevalence was sustained by adding to the conventional condemnation of monopoly a concern with the 'waste' associated with excessive competition, the distended overgrowth of selling activities at the expense of those involved in making goods which was part of his underconsumptionist explanation for depression.[30] This was the contribution of the 'narrower' heresy to the broader 'destructive' one. In return, the destructive heresy contributed to the narrower one a belief that the responsibility for oversaving came from those classes who 'possess certain elements of income which are not earned by effort, and which are therefore not required to satisfy any present legitimate wants'.[31] Consumption without any prior act of production offended Hobson's most general ethical maxim on such matters – 'from each according to his powers, to each according to his needs' – a maxim that was his guide to the requirements of any healthy form of economic democracy.[32] And since part of the various surpluses or rents earned by property-owners had a 'social' origin that could not be justified by the economic services provided, they could be redistributed to labour through higher wages or appropriated by the state through taxation without inflicting harm or discontinuity in the performance of necessary functions. At a later stage, Hobson linked these surpluses with his oversaving diagnosis, thereby bringing micro- and macroeconomics together. Those capable of earning surplus incomes were responsible for the effortless saving that led to underconsumption. Redistribution through taxation would achieve two goals simultaneously: public consumption could be financed, and the tendencies to oversaving prevented.

One of the ways in which Hobson introduced an idealistic element into his economic reasoning was to attach moral value to the form and size of income received and spent. He reversed an earlier assumption that landowners were idle spendthrifts by treating them, in common with all other recipients of 'forced' or surplus incomes, as savers by virtue of the difficulty they had in slaking their appetites by luxury expenditure alone. What came without effort went into savings, willy-nilly. In this way Hobson gave new life to the 'classical' distinction between productive and unproductive uses of surplus. The moral dimension also entered the macroeconomic diagnosis in the form of dislike of retailing.

---

[30] 'it is commonly by superiority in the arts of competition, which do not necessarily involve superiority of production, that the modern business firm is able to get business'; see *Problem of the unemployed*, p. 84.

[31] *Ibid.*, p. 88.

[32] See *The crisis of liberalism*, with an introduction by Peter Clarke (Hassocks, Sussex: Harvester Press, 1974), p. 81.

IV

From the middle of the 1890s onwards Hobson was engaged on two parallel lines of inquiry. First, he needed to complete his economic theory of distribution and connect it with his oversaving thesis in a manner that would enable him to decide what kind of policy regime would best support the economic and moral case for shifting the balance of economic power in favour of spenders rather than savers. Secondly, he had begun the work on Ruskin that would eventuate in *John Ruskin, social reformer* and make Ruskin the patron saint of a system of 'social economics', or economic humanism, that Hobson hoped to develop. In the *Confessions* he stated that he had not, by then, made much progress in bringing together 'the definitely humanist and ethical trend of my Ruskinian thought with this analysis of the economic processes of distribution'.[33] The latter did not derive from the former, and was not to be fully reconciled with it while Hobson was preoccupied, as he was during the next decade, with the more pressing political issues connected with the political economy of empire and tariff reform. Ruskinian threads run through the *Social problem* (1901) and reappear in *Imperialism* (1902), both of them highly-combative works; but the most comprehensive attempt to assemble the different strands of Hobson's thinking, *Work and wealth: a human evaluation*, did not appear until 1914, and by then Ruskin had been thoroughly assimilated and, in the process, Hobsonised.

The account Hobson gives of how he came to write his biography of Ruskin in the *Confessions* suggests, initially at least, that it was not a natural choice of subject. The initiative came from friends in the London Ethical Society who thought he would benefit from a diversion of his energies 'from the physics to the ethics of industry'.[34] Ethical imperatives of the a priori or emergent variety were never absent from Hobson's economics, but the engagement with Ruskin imparted a new 'human' dimension to it. Earlier references to Ruskin confirm the opinion expressed in the *Confessions* that he regarded *Unto this last* more as 'passionate rebellion than as a critical and constructive work'. When writing in 1891, for example, Hobson had linked Ruskin with Carlyle as prophets who had slighted the economic causes of the shift towards industrial society and had nothing to contribute to the

---

[33] *Confessions*, p. 48. Although the *Economics of distribution* was first published in 1900, two years after the biography of Ruskin, it was based on articles published in 1891–2 and lectures given in 1897.
[34] See J. H. Muirhead, *Reflections by a journeyman in philosophy* (London: Allen and Unwin, 1942), p. 97.

understanding of urban poverty.[35] Hobson had also completed the *Evolution of modern capitalism*, a work that had 'a study of machine production' as its sub-title. This accounts for his other reservations before he undertook a detailed examination of the work of the author of *Unto this last*: 'The violence of its assault upon modern processes and the demand for "captains of industry" to dominate economic life repelled me.'[36] Although Hobson clearly overcame this repulsion, he did not abandon these opinions. Whatever ills he might associate with machinery under existing social arrangements, and however much he might sympathise with a return to agrarian, artistic, more self-sufficient and self-fulfilling styles of life, he was in little doubt that technology, when placed under 'rational' social control, had a positive part to play in improving the quality of life.

Nevertheless, those friends who commissioned the book were right to sense that there were affinities between author and subject, a minor one being based on the fact that both men lived on rentier incomes and may have felt freer to depart from conservative parental guidance when their fathers died. Hobson could identify with Ruskin's defence of his practice of living on interest payments while believing them to be morally wrong.[37] They both had a profound disbelief in the justice of a society constructed along *laissez-faire* lines, and Hobson's interest in the various forms of 'waste' associated with competitive capitalism fitted well with some of Ruskin's concerns. In common with other extension lecturers Hobson had included Ruskin in his courses on English literature and modern thinkers.[38] The subject appealed to Hobson's literary instincts and interests, allowing him to show skills in dealing with Ruskin's prose and temperament that are rarely displayed in his economic writings. What Hobson found in his remarkably thorough study (undertaken while Ruskin was still alive, but before the Cook and Wedderburn edition was available) was a good deal more than the muddle and romantic moral protest he had anticipated on the basis of his earlier reading. Indeed, the account of Ruskin as reformer begins with a defence of *Unto this last* and

---

[35] *Poverty: an inquiry into the industrial condition of the poor* (London: Methuen, 1891), p. 33.

[36] *Confessions*, p. 38.

[37] 'There is no more convincing testimony of the inherent incapacity for reasoning in the average sensual man than the charge of "inconsistency" brought against a Socialist on the ground that he does not attempt to cure a social evil by an individual remedy'; see *ibid.*, p. 152.

[38] On Hobson's teaching in this field, see Lawrence Goldman, 'Ruskin, Oxford, and the British labour movement, 1880–1914', in D. Birch (ed.), *Ruskin and the dawn of the modern* (Oxford: Oxford University Press, 1999), pp. 64–73. One of Hobson's moves in the biography, as in his earlier courses on literature, was to place Ruskin within a literary tradition that included Carlyle, Tolstoy, Emerson, Browning, Arnold, Whitman, and Ibsen.

Munera pulveris as evidence of Ruskin's impeccable scientific credentials and achievements.[39]

As will be clear from what has been said about Hobson's engagement with economics, he brought to his task something Ruskin lacked, an understanding of the historical development of the science, and, more importantly, knowledge of recent theoretical work on value, utility, and costs. This also meant that Hobson's attempt to construct a theory of humanist economics along Ruskinian lines incorporated some significant additives and correctives derived from sources that were not part of Ruskin's scattered reading on the subject. Knowledge of current economic thinking enabled Hobson to give a more systematic account of Ruskin's ideas couched in a language that facilitated comparison with the emerging orthodoxy – a comparison that Hobson saw as being almost entirely to the advantage of Ruskin. In marked contrast to his fellow-disciple Smart at this stage, he was not convinced that marginalist economics had answers to the problems of value and distribution that were superior to those advanced by Ruskin.[40] Economics was still too close to what Ruskin had caricatured as a mere 'commercial' or 'covetous' science based on the separate treatment of self-seeking behaviour, and too strongly wedded to measures of economic well-being that were capable of being quantified in monetary terms. Neither of these could provide a genuine basis for a more humane conception of economic life. The commercial and mechanical interpretation of wealth lacked the organic or holistic approach to the relationship of work to life that Ruskin had called for and Hobson was beginning to think he could supply.

By 1898 it was impossible for Hobson to overlook Marshall's abandonment of the 'economic man' assumption and his attempt to include non-pecuniary motives, in so far as they influenced the getting and spending of incomes at least. But the inclusion of non-material goods in estimates of wealth was taken by Hobson to be one of those revealing psychological moments when doubt or guilt enters the picture: 'The actual and increasing transgressions made by political economists outside the limits laid down by their own definition was a most convincing, because an unconscious testimony to the uncertainty of their position.'[41]

---

[39] 'Alike in possession of material facts, in command of language, and in trained capacity of argument, he was quite competent to discuss economic problems with Senior, Fawcett, and J. S. Mill'; *John Ruskin social reformer*, 3rd edn (London: James Nisbet, 1904), pp. 61–2.

[40] Cf. pp. 117–18 above.

[41] *John Ruskin*, pp. 72–3. Hobson allowed himself some sarcasm on this in his next book, where he described the economists' attempt to humanise economics as 'half-humorous, half-pathetic', akin

Ruskin's political economy was twice removed from this by virtue of his stress on 'organic unity' of production and consumption, and his substitution of a 'vital' or life-sustaining measure of wealth for one based on money valuation alone. The all-embracing qualities of this vision could be liberating, but it also carried risks that Hobson recognised more clearly after he had gone a little further towards his own conception of the economics of welfare. Even in a work designed to celebrate Ruskin's achievement Hobson had to moderate some of his subject's more sweeping claims and chart a middle course between his teachings and those of the new economic orthodoxy Hobson had been criticising during the previous decade.[42]

One sign of this can be found in Hobson's use of Jevons's summary statement of the aims of a pure science of political economy as a point of reference: 'Given, a certain population, with various needs and powers of production, in possession of certain lands and other sources of material; required, the mode of employing their labour which will maximise the utility of the produce.'[43] Here was a conception of political economy based on subjective utility that, in 'a single rhetorical flight', contained a partial anticipation of Hobson's aims in prescribing 'social utility' as the proper goal of any humane version of the science. The Hobson version shows the influence Ruskin had in redefining the goal, a goal that corresponded with that of Ruskin's Xenophonic master of a self-sufficient household.[44] It re-emerged in *Social problem* as: 'Given a number of human beings, with a certain development of physical and mental faculties and of social institutions, in command of given natural resources, how can they best utilize these powers for the attainment of the most complete satisfaction.'[45]

Jevons had failed to carry through with the enterprise for a number of reasons. As was characteristic of most economists, he had confined his attention to 'the actual desires of men as reflected in their industrial conduct'; he had refused to go beyond 'what is' to consider 'what ought to be'; and he had adopted a simple aggregative (non-organic) view of

---

to 'the successful retired trader who buys pictures, grows orchids, subscribes to the hunt, and does other polite and public-spirited things to make himself agreeable'; see *Social problem*, p. 38.

[42] Hence the shrewdness of Colin Matthew's remark that: 'Perhaps to his surprise Hobson found himself, vis-à-vis Ruskin, a conservative rather than the dangerous radical he seemed to his friends to be becoming'; see H. C. G. Matthew, 'Hobson, Ruskin and Cobden', in Freeden (ed.), *Reappraising J. A. Hobson*, p. 16.

[43] *Theory of political economy*, 2nd edn (London: Macmillan, 1879), p. 00.

[44] See p. 107 above. [45] *Social problem*, p. 7.

what constituted social utility.[46] Although Ruskin was superior to the hedonistic utilitarians in all these respects, Hobson still wanted to maintain that 'so far as his conception of the end is concerned' Ruskin could 'not unaptly be classed as a utilitarian'.[47] Organic evolution served as a means of correcting both Jevons and Ruskin. It pointed to the need for 'higher' standards in judging future wants, and eliminated Ruskin's most serious defect, a belief in the immutability of values. The economists were right in assuming that utilities varied with quantity. Those who had fully absorbed Spencerian ideas on organic evolution were right and Ruskin wrong in thinking that wants could not be improved qualitatively over time.[48]

Hobson was shifting Ruskin towards some popular forms of 'idealism' that played a formative part in 'New Liberalism', and associating him with recent biological ideas on evolutionary sociology. This allowed Hobson to join hands with Patrick Geddes and appropriate his idea of a Ruskinian 'calorimeter' as a means of measuring the 'intrinsic value' or 'absolute power of anything to support life'.[49] Ruskin may not have advanced to this degree of understanding, but he could still be recognised as a pioneer in this field. What Hobson wanted was a more thorough-going 'subjectivisation' of objective economic quantities as the only way in which political economy could be given practical purchase on public goals. A concept of social utility that went beyond existing needs and tastes had not merely to be proclaimed in Ruskin's manner but given operational significance. Through his stress on the organic relationship between work and life, between production and consumption, Ruskin had also shed light on the human dimension to the costs of production, bringing the 'costs', 'value', and 'utility' of ordinary economists into more fruitful relation with one another.[50]

At this point, however, Hobson introduced a criticism that was to remain a permanent feature of his later assessments. While Ruskin had enlightened the world on what constituted real human utility, in common with Jevons he had not fully applied the doctrine of intrinsic value to the cost side of the problem, to the subjective losses imposed on those of differing ability, race, sex, and age by the intense, dangerous, and monotonous work required by the modern industrial system. This failure had 'injured [Ruskin's] reputation as an economic thinker'. A more organic inquiry into the connection between effort and satisfaction was to set the agenda for Hobson's later work.[51] But Ruskin's most serious

---

[46] *John Ruskin*, pp. 79–81.   [47] *Ibid.*, p. 85.   [48] *Ibid.*, pp. 101–3.
[49] *Ibid.*, pp. 87–9; on Geddes, see pp. 115–16 above.   [50] *John Ruskin*, p. 93.   [51] *Ibid.*, pp. 97–9.

defect, *pace* Geddes, lay in his lack of understanding of Darwin, Wallace, Huxley, and Spencer, with the result that his social vision contained no 'sense of continuous development'.[52] In place of a progressive dimension to human aspirations all Ruskin could offer was stasis. His 'strong love of order' had led him 'to conceive social reform as a work of restoration, a realisation of definite principles of social good in a pattern common-wealth, where peace and contentment would prevail, and when stable and rational authority would be subject to no disturbing influence'.[53] By recoiling from any inquiry into the reaction of organicism to environ-ment and vice versa, by rejecting the emerging biological sciences, Ruskin had lost an opportunity to strengthen his ethical message.

V

Hobson thought he could find some support for the oversaving aspect of his heresy in Ruskin's criticisms of Mill's doctrine of 'the social utility of unlimited saving'.[54] Ruskin had certainly deployed some irony at Mill's expense when dealing with the distinction between productive and unproductive consumption, though whether this amounted to an over-saving diagnosis of depressions is to be doubted on the basis of other evidence.[55] On some central features of Ruskin's creed, however, Hobson found it necessary to temper Ruskin's charges against political economy. For example, in Hobson's own field of interest within economics he found himself having to dilute some of Ruskin's more extreme pro-nouncements on the evils and waste associated with competition. Ruskin had painted too dark a picture of modern commerce and exaggerated the degree of chicanery involved in competitive pursuits, especially where large numbers of buyers and sellers were involved. The idea that equity in exchange should depend on equality of time or strength expended, an idea Ruskin borrowed from Adam Smith, was also rejected in favour of the views of Sidney and Beatrice Webb on the national minimum.[56] But Ruskin's 'most disputable doctrines' were his denial that there could be any legitimate profit on exchange, that there could be no increase in use value as a result of exchange, such that where advantages accrued they had

[52] *Ibid.*, p. 101. [53] *Ibid.*, p. 106. [54] *Ibid.*, pp. 111, 121–4, 127.
[55] Although Hobson could not have known this, Ruskin had endorsed Mill's rejection of Sismondi's theory of underconsumption in his marginal comments on Book III, chapter 14 of Mill's *Prin-ciples*, 'Of excess supply': 'An admirable chapter in general aim of overthrowing Sismondi's monstrous idea.'
[56] *John Ruskin*, pp. 134–7.

to be attributed to cheating. Even in unequal exchanges the weaker party gains something. Ruskin's failure to distinguish 'interest' from 'usury' amounted to a denial of the productivity of capital.[57] Correction of these points was essential to remove those parts of his system that made it vulnerable to hostile critics.

With regard to the true ordering of society Hobson was sympathetic to Ruskin's idea that the state should have extensive powers in the fields of marriage and education. Although Ruskin had been prudish in his unwillingness to enter into details on the subject of population control, Hobson professed to see, beneath the stringent requirements Ruskin had laid down on the subject of marriage, a recognition of modern eugenicist concerns: 'the prohibition of definitely anti-social marriages, the refusal to allow epileptics, criminals, or the victims of serious hereditary evil, to increase and multiply at an incalculable cost to society, is one of the plainest demands of social welfare'. Hobson could not accept Ruskin's romanticised vision of the woman's role as one in which they needed to be protected from the arduous pursuits that take place outside the home. When writing on women in modern industry in the *Evolution of modern capitalism* Hobson had concluded that the tendency of machine-industry to take women away from home 'must be looked upon as a tendency antagonistic to civilisation'.[58] He did not stress, but neither did he exclude lower intelligence as one of the factors explaining women's lower prod-uctivity and wages. But Ruskin's denial that women should engage in intellectual as opposed to emotional and artistic activities came too close to an argument for their subordination for Hobson. Women were entitled to their share in the benefits of the movement towards equality that men had long enjoyed. Hobson did not range himself behind all the 'belligerent advocates of women's rights', but he was closer to Mill than to Ruskin on this question.[59]

On the reordering of industry, however, Hobson found Ruskin guilty of 'a new feudalism, in which class distinctions are to be strictly pre-served'. Too much reading of Plato and a 'fanatical abhorrence' of radical doctrines of natural equality, plus some ideas condoning slavery derived from Carlyle, were responsible for this error.[60] Ruskin had not realised how far his unconscious acceptance of advanced liberal ideas had carried him from the anti-democratic views of Carlyle.[61] The 'tempered feudalism' of his scheme for vesting control in the hands of an established class of

---

[57] *Ibid.*, pp. 140, 145–52.   [58] *Evolution of modern capitalism*, p. 320.   [59] *John Ruskin*, pp. 266–76.
[60] *Ibid.*, pp. 156–9.   [61] *Ibid.*, p. 190.

landowners was inadequate; and he had wavered between voluntary action through guild membership and state action to regulate industry. Reliance on the moral conversion of the upper classes, the captains of industry, was another weak link: these were the very classes which, according to Ruskin's own analysis, had been corrupted by their current role in the system. State agency was required to undertake what re-moralised private economic agents in positions of authority could never accomplish by means of their control over minor parts of the system.[62]

By now Hobson was speaking of Ruskin's refusal to accept democracy and his reliance on the voluntary conversion of the upper classes as 'a radical defect in his social thinking' that rested 'as all such errors must, upon moral obliquity'.[63] Ruskin's indignation when faced with the dehumanising aspects of machine production and the debasement of modern taste by cheap goods was justified. It did not make him a complete Luddite on machinery, but he had a 'sentimental' attachment to handicraft and peasant cultivation that was inappropriate to modern circumstances. Ruskin's lack of personal experience of physical labour had led him to advocate such work as part of everybody's life. This was admirable, but it also explained Ruskin's underestimation of the benefits of machinery in lightening the physical burden and increasing the chances of leisure.[64]

Considered as the means by which Ruskin's ideas were conveyed to a new generation, *John Ruskin, social reformer* deserved and enjoyed a far longer life than other end-of-century assessments by Smart, Geddes, and others.[65] Over its extended life the book attracted readers who might have found Hobson's economic writings unpalatable. It became the medium through which many early twentieth-century students of Ruskin, especially those holding left-of-centre opinions, learned how Ruskinian ideals could be made to serve modern purposes.[66] Hobson's admiration for Ruskin's pioneering contribution to 'social economics' remained undimmed, but he could only overlook its defects by making it part of his own heterodox form of economics and by adding an assortment of advanced liberal ideas that a 'violent Tory' of Ruskin's mettle would have condemned. A sympathetic early reviewer summed up the matter admirably: 'We have here not only "John Ruskin, Social Reformer", but also J. A. Hobson, Social Reformer of a later generation. We are face to face not only with a single work but with a double personality, and the

---

[62] *Ibid.*, pp. 196–8   [63] *Ibid.*, p. 204.   [64] *Ibid.*, p. 213.   [65] See pp. 115–20 above.
[66] For studies of the part played by Hobson and others in disseminating Ruskin's ideas, see the essays by Jose Harris and Lawrence Goldman in Birch (ed.), *Ruskin and the dawn of the modern.*

interest of the work gains enormously by that fact.'[67] By attaching Ruskin firmly to one of the fashionable contemporary variations on the socialist theme Hobson also helped to declare open season for others to do so.

As one might expect, Ruskin figures in the first book Hobson wrote after completing the biography and in his more academic study of the economics of distribution, the latest points reached on each of his parallel lines of inquiry. He does so as one of the 'enlightened teachers of humanity' alongside Carlyle, Emerson, and Tolstoy, and, less comfortably, amid such 'great representative thinkers' as Bentham, Owen, Comte, J. S. Mill, Mazzini, and Spencer.[68] The 'illth' associated with vicious and vulgar items of consumption is recognised, though it comes alongside the earlier criticism of Ruskin's error in making value 'a permanent immutable property': 'low-class' books could be 'a genuine means of enlightenment to a people living at a lower level'.[69] The attempt to achieve reform through the voluntary action of 'captains of industry' is bluntly dismissed as 'fatuity', though Ruskin's emphasis on art and artistry as the supreme goal of work is praised.[70] In *Imperialism* there are some Ruskinian elements, notably in the condemnation of the trade in some tropical products as illth. But, despite a final chapter entitled 'The human interpretation of industry', Ruskin does not feature in *Industrial system: an inquiry into earned and unearned income* (1909), Hobson's most serious pre-war treatment of the issues he had made his own. There is a warm tribute to Ruskin at the beginning of *Work and wealth*, but it also contains sharper criticism of his failure to analyse the costs of labour in 'vital' terms, with the result that: 'From a Pisgah height his mind's eye swept in quick penetrative glances over the promised land, but he did not occupy it, or furnish any clear survey.' Hobson hoped to finish the job, but to do so along more manageable lines.

It was one thing to attack political economy for ignoring human values, but it was another to:

insist that the barrier between political economy and other social sciences and arts should be torn down, and that all phenomena of vital import should become the objects of its study. Had Ruskin been able to keep to the narrower scope, doubtless he would not have been Ruskin, but his attack on current economic theory and practice would have been vastly more effective.

---

[67] E. A. Barnett's review in *Economic Review*, 9 (1899), 131. [68] *Social problem*, pp. 2, 227.
[69] *Ibid.*, pp. 17–9. [70] *Ibid.*, pp. 136, 227, 244.

This clearly reveals Hobson's new strategy: he was now going to 'accept the ordinary definition of the boundaries of economic studies', and 'seek to make our human survey and apply our human valuation within these limits'.[71] It was a retreat from the elaborate demonstration in the *Social problem* of the inherent incapacity of economics, operating within its present limits, to mount an attack on any of the serious ethical questions facing society. But as we shall see it accords with Hobson's re-immersion in the economic theory needed to deal with the problems of empire and international trade during the intervening period. Although there was to be no abatement of his criticisms of economics, Hobson had returned to the boundaries of economics recognised by economists. He also accepted the distinction between the science and art of welfare, something he had initially denied when faced with J. N. Keynes's restatement of the distinction between positive and normative propositions in his *Scope and method of political economy*.[72]

For Hobson the biography of Ruskin was to prove a staging post from which he could advance towards a 'science and art of social utility' constructed according to evolutionary principles that would resolve the demands of work and life, and reconcile individualism with socialism. Only a thoroughgoing substitution of a subjectively based notion of social utility for present monetary measures of wealth would suffice, beginning with present individual valuations and then moving on to 'harmonise the good of the individual with the good of the society'.[73] While the criticism that domestic goods were constantly passing into commercial ones, and vice versa, was a valid comment on monetary estimates of national wealth, Hobson went further in suggesting that it was impossible to place a valuation on public roads and other amenities.[74] While it is true that there were no uncontroversial methods of converting the costs and utilities into 'true' human or subjective costs, methods of estimating the public utility of public assets such as bridges had been part of the professional literature since Jules Dupuit's writings in the 1840s. As we have seen, Marshall had made an independent attempt to mobilise the concept of consumers' surplus for the same purposes.

As a result of Hobson's later attempts to give operational significance to Ruskin's goals, he was able to state some of the difficulties that lay in

---

[71] *Work and wealth* (New York: Macmillan, 1914), pp. 10–12.
[72] Compare remarks on Keynes in *Social problem*, pp. 68–9, 75 with 'Economic art and social welfare', *Journal of Philosophical Studies*, 1 (1926), 472.
[73] *Social problem*, p. 39.   [74] See *ibid.*, p. 41.

the path. How could one differentiate the satisfactions derived from economic goods from those 'vital goods and ills which lie outside this economic ambit' without fusing 'economic with other vital processes so as to disable them for separate study'? How far was it possible to modify current satisfactions and dissatisfactions by reference to intrinsic values? And, finally, there was the problem of how far the 'pleasures and pains of one man can be compared with those of another'. These are the classic problems for any theory of economic welfare of the kind tackled by Marshall, Edgeworth, Pigou, and others. How too could a social consensus be formed that was not an aggregation of existing evaluations? It is here that the organic nature of society plays its part; this made it possible for Hobson to envisage a future form of society in which individuals gladly act in accordance with a shared conception of social need, sacrificing their 'passing caprices and desires to a fuller sense of the part which it is capable of bearing in the fulfilment of the larger social process'. For this Hobson called upon Rousseau's notion of a 'general will', an answer to a similar problem, and coupled it with the hope that diversity could still be retained on quasi-Darwinian grounds.

VI

It followed from Hobson's normative priorities that economics, supplemented by evolutionary projections, should be judged by the assistance it gave in clarifying or justifying certain policies or programmes of social reform. Taxation of the element in incomes that could be traced, via the notion of unearned income or forced gains, to 'social' causes rather than economic function, and associated policies of redistribution in favour of wage-earner/consumers, whether as wages, old-age pensions, or as public services, were a stable element in Hobson's thinking. They went alongside nationalisation of certain industries and a comprehensive welfare state that by the inter-war period had come to include a large measure of state economic planning of industry as well. Here there was a natural progression from curbing maldistribution of income and wealth towards greater state intervention. The same cannot be said of other policies equally strongly connected with the theories Hobson espoused.

In his earliest work, *Physiology*, 'practical considerations' were merely sketched, ostensibly because anything more would detract from the theory being advanced, but possibly too because he and Mummery could not present a united front on remedies. Mummery's death in a climbing accident in 1895 deprived us of an opportunity to learn how he would have

developed the underconsumptionist thesis. In 1889 the partners could
agree that taxes should penalise saving rather than consumption, and that
measures that maintained wages, increased the number engaged in wage-
earning employments, and shortened hours of work were beneficial during
conditions of depression. Whether such measures should be reversed in
conditions of 'full demand' was not made clear. Distinguishing between
cyclical downturn and chronic breakdown was a perennial problem for
underconsumptionists: if a particular disease is endemic why should it
manifest itself only sporadically or cyclically? This could explain why
Hobson was more active on this front in foul-weather conditions of large-
scale unemployment, when it was not necessary to prove the existence of
disease. Support for trade unionism as a cure for underconsumption via
the increased share of national income going to labour was to remain a
prominent part of Hobson's policy agenda, though his ardour for trade
unions cooled when he joined the Labour Party and observed the influence
of union paymasters on its deliberations.[75] Shorter hours of work also
acquired a humanist dimension when they were seen as the basis for
increased leisure.

   More controversially, the Mummery/Hobson team also endorsed the
instinct that had led the American and Australian labour movements to
oppose the immigration of foreign labour.[76] Hobson was to expand on his
fears of foreign immigration in his book on poverty, making use of
Beatrice Potter's studies of the Jewish community in East London to
underscore a similarly hostile racial stereotype.[77] The immigrant Jew was
the archetypal 'economic man', fulfilling the assumptions of Ricardo
(characterised by Potter as 'the Hebrew economist') by exploiting the
possibilities opened up by supplies of labour available at bare subsistence
levels. Foreign Jews, according to Hobson, were 'steady, industrious,
quiet, sober, thrifty, quick to learn, and tolerably honest'; they were not
'quarrelsome and law-breaking, like the low-class Italians who swarm into
America'. But these virtues were also their chief defects from a national
point of view:

Admirable in domestic morality, and an orderly citizen, he is almost void of
social morality. No compunction or consideration for his fellow-worker will keep
him from underselling and overreaching them; he acquires a thorough mastery of
all the dishonourable tricks of trade which are difficult to restrain by law; the

---

[75] See *Confessions*, p. 126.   [76] *Physiology*, pp. 212–13.
[77] B. Potter, 'The Jewish community', in C. Booth (ed.), *Labour and life of the people in London*,
   17 vols. (London: Macmillan, 1892), I, p. 590.

superior calculating intellect, which is a national heritage, is used unsparingly to enable him to take advantage of every weakness, folly, and vice of the society in which he lives.

Foreign Jews were engaged in producing articles of commerce which could be produced by native workers under better industrial conditions; they possessed a natural aptitude for organising 'sweated trades': 'Independence and mastery are conditions which have a market value for all men, but especially for the timid and often down-trodden Jew. Most men will contentedly receive less as master than as servant, but especially the Jew.'[78]

If immigration had its dangers for the native workforce, emigration often removed, at the bottom of the cycle, just those skilled artisans who were needed at home when recovery came. British interest lay in assisting the emigration of 'large bodies of the lowest and least competent workers', a preference which also led Hobson to endorse Charles Booth's 'drainage scheme' (a close relative of Marshall's solutions for the problems of the 'residuum'): the removal of the surplus of 'cheap and inefficient labour' to industrial colonies under government supervision.[79] When Hobson had formulated his policies for income and wealth redistribution, such measures were relegated to the category of palliatives. Although he was one of the sharpest critics of the 'monadic' or individualistic and moralising philosophy that lay behind the attitudes of the Charity Organisation Society to social reform, his environmentalist or organic alternative left plenty of scope for a racialist and eugenicist treatment of 'character'. Eugenics was an interest he shared with many 'New Liberal' allies as well as with his orthodox contemporaries within the economics profession.[80] Though Hobson's anti-semitism may not have been racist it was certainly racialist, leaving open inquiry into whether the observed characteristics of individuals should be attributed to Lamarckian processes of acquisition through environmental and cultural formation rather than genetic inheritance. This made sense when dealing with the occupations of poor Jews, but it is more difficult to discern any such discrimination in Hobson's treatment of the rich Jews whom he believed to have created in Johannesburg an essentially Jewish town, and when he suggested that the Boer war was being fought to protect the stranglehold an international

---

[78] *Poverty*, pp. 59–60, 62–3, 98–9. On Hobson's anti-semitism, see C. Holmes, 'J. A. Hobson and the Jews', in C. Holmes (ed.), *Immigrants and minorities in British society* (London: Allen and Unwin, 1978).

[79] *Poverty*, pp. 138–41.

[80] See 'The social philosophy of charity organisation', *Contemporary Review*, 70 (1896), 710–27.

oligarchy of Jewish financiers had managed to establish over South African natural resources.[81]

Hobson later disclaimed any policy of curbing immigration as part of a free trade heritage that he wished to uphold, and the racial proclivities of Jews are not given prominence in his later writings. On the civil rights of the American Negro his attitudes remained impeccably liberal in both contemporary and modern senses of the term; and he went to a good deal of trouble in *Imperialism* to discredit the teachings of those who argued for aggressive imperialism on grounds of superior racial fitness and the need to maintain the struggle between 'higher' and 'lower' races. But these two phrases did not always appear in quotation marks in Hobson's texts: he recognised the distinction and the responsibilities that went with it. What he wanted to stress was the failure of the white races to live up to their ideals by ruling over subject peoples in ways that were designed to raise them in the scale of civilisation. Just as in domestic policy he believed that it was the responsibility of governments to prevent breeding by inferior beings, so on the international level he could envisage a form of 'stirpiculture' aimed at producing an optimum blend of racial characteristics.

VII

In 1889 Mummery and Hobson rejected the 'charge of commercial imbecility, so freely launched by orthodox economics against our American cousins and other protectionist communities'. While the traditional case for free trade was sound under normal conditions, in a 'diseased state of commerce', they suggested, 'it by no means follows that a protective system will have . . . noxious results'.[82] Protection could remedy an unhealthy aspect of depression, the social waste associated with a distended system of retailing and advertising. If it merely had the effect of boosting the making of goods at the expense of such selling activities, it followed that 'protective measures do not inflict the damage which orthodox free traders assign to them'. We do not know if the youthful Hobson experienced any sense of conflict between the orthodox case for multilateral free trade, with the idealistic overtones that appealed to the cosmopolitan sympathies he later revealed, especially in his biography *Richard Cobden: the international man* (1918), and the policy conclusions

---

[81] See *The War in South Africa* (London: J. Nisbet, 1900), pp. 11–12, 189–97.
[82] *Physiology*, pp. ix, 207.

suggested by an underconsumptionist diagnosis of the ills of capitalism. In 1889, concerned as he was with cyclical depression, he might have regarded protection as a movable feast, a counter-cyclical device.

Other issues could trigger similar concerns and potential conflict. In the 1890s he became increasingly apprehensive about the threats to British prosperity coming from her protectionist competitors. As early as 1891, for example, he had speculated about the possibility of greater restrictions on international labour migration inducing increased capital outflow to cheap labour countries such as China and India. The resulting loss of trade would lead to Britain embracing protection, a regime that would have to be accompanied by 'a policy of prohibitive taxation on exported capital'.[83] Hobson was warning about rather than welcoming these developments, but his fears on this score grew when 'fair trade' campaigns gave way to arguments for full-blooded tariff reform along imperial lines, and when coercive policies ostensibly designed to open up China and Africa to British goods were adopted. Instead of simple market-driven capital flight in pursuit of low-wage labour and higher profits, he now saw the new forms of imperialism as part of a competitive scramble for outlets for surplus capital, with investors conspiring with governments to obtain political and military assistance in achieving goals that served their interests rather than those of the nation.[84] In countering this Hobson was keen to minimise the benefits of external expansion accruing to the few by stressing those gains to the people at large that would result from 'internal social and industrial reforms' that realised the potential of the home market.[85]

Hobson had become convinced that the era of free trade in Britain was rapidly coming to an end: it no longer commanded the support of the powerful interest groupings at home, and it ran counter to the rise of economic nationalism abroad. In 1902 he was pessimistic about the prospects for 'a new and unexpected rally' behind 'Manchesterism', a word to which Hobson could attach both positive and negative connotations. It could be a pejorative label for *laissez-faire* economics or it could

[83] 'Can England keep her trade?', *The National Review*, 17 (1891), 1–11.
[84] See 'Free trade and foreign policy', *Contemporary Review*, 72 (1898), 167–80. This article is now seen as Hobson's first attempt to put forward an economic theory of imperialism. See B. Porter, *Critics of empire: British radical attitudes to colonialism in Africa* (London: Macmillan, 1968), pp. 194–5; and P. J. Cain, *Hobson and imperialism: radicalism, new liberalism, and finance, 1887–1938* (Oxford: Oxford University Press, 2002), pp. 68–78.
[85] 'Free trade and foreign policy', 179. In doing so, however, he overplayed his hand by downgrading the actual benefits that Britain derived from foreign trade, as was pointed out by Leonard Courtney when the arguments were repeated in *Imperialism*; see 'What is the advantage of foreign trade?', *The Nineteenth Century*, 53 (1903), 806–12.

be misunderstood shorthand for those pacific internationalist ideals he associated with Cobden. But he also saw chinks of light amid the gathering gloom. He was prepared to take comfort from the fact that the rise of protectionism could reverse the decay of British agriculture which was 'directly attributable in large measure to the industrial specialisation of a free trade policy' and 'has long been a matter of regret, not only among sentimental and artistic folk, but among the few thinkers who concern themselves with the roots of a sound national life'. Getting back to the 'sturdy yeoman stock of yore' was a solution to the problems of 'deterioration of the physique of the race' and would not be without benefit to a great military nation.[86] Looking backwards, dependence on foreign trade under the illiberal institutions of mid- and late-Victorian England had led to an unbalanced growth in manufacturing.[87] Looking forwards, Hobson believed that a law of the decreasing significance of foreign trade was in operation as demand shifted towards non-tradable goods with a higher component of skill and less dependence on the cruder manufacturing processes that used imported raw materials.[88]

When Chamberlain's campaign for tariff reform got under way, however, Hobson was quick to lend his pen to the opposition, especially to those who stressed the effect on wage-earners' living standards. In little under a year since his last speculations on the threat to British living standards posed by foreign competition, he was arguing that as a result of free trade the volume and per capita value of British trade had increased, and that the evidence of income-tax returns and savings bank deposits showed that 'money wages and real wages have risen largely for almost all classes of worker'.[89] The growing excess of imports over exports was not a source of concern when the invisible exports associated with shipping and insurance services and the interest and profits on foreign investments were taken into account. Protectionists maintained that the diversion of production and consumption that would result from their measures was painless: 'Does our tariff reformer assume that a vast quantity of capital and labour lies permanently idle in expectation of this new employment?' In other words, since Britain enjoyed full employment any diversion of

---

[86] See 'The approaching abandonment of free trade', *Fortnightly Review*, 77 (1902), 443–4. Agrarian reforms that would reduce Britain's dependence on foreign food had been advocated by Hobson in 'The decay of English agriculture', *Commonwealth*, 1 (1896), 85–8.
[87] See *Imperialism: a study* (London: J. Nisbet, 1902), p. 89.
[88] See 'Occupations of the people', *Contemporary Review*, 78 (1905), 188–202.
[89] See 'Protection as a working-class policy' in H. W. Massingham (ed.), *Labour and protection: a series of studies* (London: T. Fisher Unwin, 1903), p. 54.

resources from the most efficient uses indicated by free exchange would entail displacement from more to less productive employments, reducing the aggregate wealth of the empire in the process.[90] The various forms of social waste from unemployment and misemployment that had dominated his writings on inequality and poverty in the 1890s were forgotten – or, at least, not mentioned. The inequities that generated underconsumption now provided arguments in favour of free trade. As the examples of America and Canada showed, protectionist regimes benefited the profits of 'landlords, railroads, land-speculators, mortgagors, and middlemen'. Why were British workmen being invited to accept taxes on their food for the benefit of such classes? The interests of the consumer/ worker would be sacrificed to those of manufacturers who had the political muscle to make their interests count. British political life would be subject to the 'general corruption and debasement' that was 'the inevitable result of protection under democratic forms of government'.[91] The 'progressive' developments associated with trade unionism, municipal socialism, and factory legislation were threatened by protectionism. Free trade was the only regime capable of providing the setting within which the required redistribution of income from savers to spenders could occur.

A year later Hobson brought out a book *International trade* that carries a subtitle 'an application of economic theory', which shows how easily he could vary the way in which he presented himself to the public. On this occasion he was plying the trade of theorist in a manner that would have done credit to the most conventional of economists, bringing established theory to bear on emotive issues and purporting to conduct a judicious survey of the respective merits of free trade and protection. Say's law and even the 'invisible hand' of the market play the role assigned to them in the most complacent forms of orthodox economics, though they now feature harmoniously alongside oversaving explanations for unemployment. Protection gains plausibility as a result of the underuse of existing capital and labour (the position adopted in *Physiology*), and provides a valid argument in the case of specific industries suffering from what Say's law enthusiasts would call a case of partial glut. But a general protective tariff directed against dumping by foreign monopolies adds to the power of domestic monopolies to raise prices and gives discretionary powers to officials to regulate imports. Large emergencies might justify such powers, but in lesser cases 'it would assuredly be safer to bear the blow than to put the clumsy and ineffectual weapons of import duties into the

[90] *Ibid.*, pp. 57 61.   [91] *Ibid.*, pp. 78–89.

hands of imperfectly wise officials'. It was difficult to distinguish between industries experiencing long-term structural decline and those experiencing temporary difficulties. Cheap foreign goods, whether or not they fell into the category of dumped goods, benefited British consumers. The resulting damage to British trade should be accepted 'in the same spirit in which we should accept imports which undersold our products by superior use of machinery or better natural resources'.[92] Hobson managed to combine an underconsumptionist diagnosis with free trade by presenting protection as both an unwarranted intervention in the operation of normal markets and, alongside its partner, imperialism, as 'a class policy, instinctively devised in order to break and divide . . . the blind, ill-directed forces of social reform which are groping after the establishment of a juster economic order'.[93]

Having found a way of reconciling radical economics with Cobdenite sympathies, Hobson went on to write an up-tempo survey of the prospects for, and the benefits to be derived from, international capital flows, employing the traditional arguments connecting such investments with the maintenance of domestic employment levels and export markets. The policy conclusion was that control over such investment would not benefit British industry, and that free movement of labour internationally was an essential accompaniment: 'legal restrictions upon free immigration sharply contravene the economy of modern financial capitalism'.[94] Capital that could not be absorbed at home was going abroad in search of profit: 'In proportion as this function is skilfully fulfilled the wealth of the world is increased', and while the primary object of investors was to raise their own incomes and share prices, 'they are usually compelled by competition to communicate a good deal of the gain of their proceedings, through normal processes of markets, to other people in their capacity of consumers or producers'.[95] How else could 'the natural and human resources of relatively backward countries' be exploited to the benefit of both parties? All nations gained from the expansion of international markets: 'The process of competition is subordinate to cooperation.'[96] Underconsumption appears in the pages of the survey, but foreign investment was the natural response to its existence, and future improvements in wage levels would make for greater stability.[97] When accompanied by

---

[92] *International trade: an application of economic theory* (London: Methuen, 1904), pp. 140–1.
[93] *Ibid.*, p. 181.
[94] *An economic interpretation of investment* (London: *The Financial Review of Reviews*, 1911), p. 139.
[95] *Ibid.*, pp. 19–20.   [96] *Ibid.*, pp. 94–5.   [97] *Ibid.*, pp. 37, 85, 143.

imperialist expansion, as in the notorious case of South Africa, a 'bellicose interpretation of investments' could endanger Cobdenite hopes for international harmony. Though Cobden was too optimistic on this score, he was right in thinking that a large and regular trade between nations acted as an agency 'for peace and good government in proportion as the finance grows more distinctively international'.[98]

Volte-face is not too strong a description of the change in Hobson's views on immigration control and protection as anti-depression policies. But these, one could argue, had been advocated in 1889 and everybody is allowed to change their opinions over a couple of decades. More remarkable are the rapid shifts in position, tone, and style over the period 1902–11, from the slashing attack on international finance capitalism in *Imperialism* to the docile acceptance of it in *An economic interpretation of investment*; from the predictions about the declining importance of foreign trade, involving a mixture of relief and anxiety, to the enthusiastic endorsement of Cobden's desire for an expansion of international commerce in all forms. Journalistic opportunities played some part in this (*Economic interpretation* was written for a monthly journal read by investors), as did the turn of political events and discussion.[99] The initial threat posed by Chamberlain called for one response and the unexpected rally in favour of Manchesterism when the electorate rejected tariff reform in 1906 called for another. Attacks on the 'people's budget' of 1909 from those who maintained that its punitive taxation of property incomes would compound the tendency for British capital to be invested abroad rather than at home could bring Hobson into the field in support of the government, on this occasion joined by a youthful Keynes who was beginning his own career as a politico-economic commentator.[100] Hobson had so thoroughly adjusted to the shifting demands of his journalistic calling that he did not think it worth mentioning any of these changes in his position in the *Confessions*.

Reverting to a thread in earlier essays in this book may help to place Hobson's twists and turns in longer perspective. During the Boer war

---

[98] *Ibid.*, pp. 110, 118.

[99] For a consideration of the political context, see Avner Offer, 'Empire and social reform: British overseas investment and domestic politics, 1908–1914', *Historical Journal*, 26 (1983), 119–38. Offer defends Hobson from accusations of inconsistency on the grounds (a) that the ambiguity was present in his earlier writings, and (b) that 'his overriding preoccupations were moral and not economic' (128). Peter Cain, on the other hand, has reinforced his earlier critique in his latest book, *Hobson and imperialism*.

[100] 'Great Britain's foreign investments', *New Quarterly*, February 1910, as reprinted in JMK, XV, pp. 44–59.

Hobson added the rampant tendencies of British imperialism to his diagnosis of the British propensity to oversave. The export of capital noted by Mill as a counterbalance to Britain's capacity to accumulate capital rapidly, and celebrated by Bagehot as the archetypal manifestation of Britain's status as leader of the march towards mature forms of finance capitalism, was seen by Hobson as a symptom of a potential disorder that had remained concealed while Britain enjoyed unchallenged access to foreign and colonial markets for its exports of surplus goods and capital. With the encroachment of other capitalist nations on what had been a British preserve, the fallacy of unlimited saving became manifest and an unholy anti-democratic alliance between imperialism and the vested interests of a specific form of finance capitalism had been forged. By 1911, on the other hand, Hobson had reached an accommodation with cosmopolitan capitalism that enabled him to be almost as enthusiastic about its potentialities as Bagehot had been about the clever men in dark rooms who controlled Britain's destiny.[101] With a government that seemed to be committed to the redistributive programme he had always supported, Hobson could adopt an orthodox stance towards free trade. As the *Confessions* show, however, Hobson found it impossible to remain optimistic on this score during the inter-war period. When economic autarchy was a common feature of most developed nations' policies to deal with unemployment, he spoke of Britain's 'belated' recognition of the benefits of greater economic isolation and clearly felt that while Cobden's internationalist aims were still worth pursuing via the League of Nations, the cosmopolitan hopes that Cobden had entertained were no longer relevant to the modern world. Part of Britain's nineteenth-century inheritance was being overthrown by 'the two salient economic facts of our time, the unprecedented unemployment and the movement of every country towards economic isolation and protection of home markets'.[102]

* * *

Pursuit beyond 1914 of the last-mentioned thread would lead to an inter-war destination that Hobson came to share with Maynard Keynes – a 'New Liberal' of very different formation – and a new generation of economists confronting unprecedented levels of unemployment and world depression. As in the case of another common proleptic move, exploration of the influence of Hobson on Lenin's theory of imperialism,

---

[101] See p. 125 above.   [102] *Confessions*, pp. 34–5.

Hobson appears only in moonlight, in the light borrowed from a more powerful source. Admirers of Ruskin are apt to see him as the most important rival source of reflected sunlight in Hobson's universe, though one conclusion to be drawn from the above essay is that only a Ruskin thoroughly transformed by 'New Liberal' values could serve Hobson's purposes as spokesman for a humanistic version of economics. Not only did Hobson confront the authoritarian features of Ruskin's Xenophonic vision, he was also conscious of the potentially coercive implications of his own version of economic humanism – more so than Ruskin and more so, it could be argued, than Tawney, his friend and follower on these matters. He brought his *Confessions* to a close with some inconclusive musings on the issues at stake. Was it possible to substitute for what people actually want 'some higher estimate of what is "good" for them'? If there was danger in positing a social mind 'that is higher and better than the individual minds that seem to form this social mind', what scope was there for the exercise of 'expertism', allowing the future to be determined by 'disinterested experts'? While there might be increased opportunities for altruism in private dealings and for rational intervention in public affairs by humanitarian experts thinking organically, was there not a risk that well-meaning officials could obliterate human diversity?[103] The opposing elements are so evenly drawn that they leave scope for arguments about the liberal elements in Hobson's socialism and the authoritarian elements in his liberalism.

As we shall see in the concluding essay, Hobson's animus against the professional practitioners of economics in universities prevented him from entertaining the idea that economists might be capable of the same degree of disinterestedness that he posited in the organically minded social scientific experts on which his own vision of the future rested. The adversarial stance had become necessary to Hobson's self-definition.

---

[103] *Ibid.*, pp. 203–12.

Academic minds

I have sometimes felt regret that I was never able to pursue my economic studies in the quiet atmosphere of an academic life where I could have developed in a more orderly way my humanist theory, and tested it by lectures and discussions among serious-minded students.   John Atkinson Hobson, *Confessions*, p. 83

My fiftieth birthday! I find that now my whole nature is beginning to sway in the direction of leaving Cambridge. Two old impulses raise their heads and sing in tune with me: (1) the desire of travel, to know the world of West-European civilisation thoroughly and as a whole; and (2) the desire of literary independence, to be able to speak when I like as a man to men, and not three times a week as a salaried teacher to pupils.

Henry Sidgwick, journal entry, 31 May 1888, in *Memoir*, p. 489

I

Those who have spent their lives in academic employment are more likely to sympathise with Sidgwick's musings than Hobson's: they were based on experience of the everyday realities of university life rather than on imagination heightened by exclusion. And yet there is a clear sense in which both men were indulging in pipe-dreams. Sidgwick may have swayed in the direction of leaving Cambridge, but he was no more likely to obey the impulse during the dozen years that remained to him than he had during the preceding thirty-three. Indeed, after obtaining his fellowship at Trinity College at the age of twenty-one, the conscientiousness with which he performed his duties as teacher and administrator prevented him from spending more than one term away from Cambridge over the next forty years. A minor setback in 1872, failure to be elected to the Knightbridge Chair of Moral Philosophy, was righted in 1883. Unlike other academics who have appeared in these pages, then, Sidgwick did not have to move between universities to make his living or obtain his chair; he was a rare case of a prominent figure whose career was spent within the walls of one institution. And since he was never extra-mural he did not have to undergo a period of doubt as to whether he would succeed in completing the journey to an intra-mural post.

Hobson is a prominent case of someone who failed to complete that journey, but his exclusion and the way in which he publicised his outsider status make him a useful, if jaundiced witness to what was going on inside British academic circles for those who sought to be professional economists. There are more nuanced definitions, but 'professional' here means no more (nor less) than the privilege of being paid to engage in teaching and research on a full-time basis under conditions of reasonable security of tenure. The next two sections will concentrate on Hobson's reflections and experience before considering some institutional features of the professional existence of some of the academic insiders who have figured elsewhere in this book.

II

To the ambivalences noted in the preceding essay should be added another: Hobson was torn between wanting his own place in the academic world and arguing that the teaching of political economy in universities was marked by fatal types of deformation arising from sinister external pressures and what he diagnosed as the timid acquisitiveness of the academic mind. He was critical of 'the book-view of human nature', especially when it was associated with disciplines that had important normative implications for public life. In his opinion there was no longer a need to perpetuate the kind of artificial, protected, and specialised form of the life of the mind to be found in the seclusion and socially exclusive atmosphere of Oxbridge. Anticipating the views of generations of dedicated extra-mural teachers, he maintained that: 'The true ideal university shall make it possible for every man and woman . . . to be a student without ceasing to be a worker and a private citizen.'[1] Reflecting too on his own education in classics at Oxford, he maintained that a devitalised form of self-cultivation was being fostered at the expense of the kind of knowledge that could only come from engagement with people. This bred tentativeness and a fear of commitment that was really 'feebleness under the pretence of accuracy'. He added the following summary verdict on the

---

[1] 'The academic spirit in education', *Contemporary Review*, 63 (1893), 246.

effect of including economics within university curricula over the previous century:

The science is so modern, so unyielding to precise and priggish definitions, so amenable to practical applications; yet it cannot be wholly passed over. The academic mind sniffed at it for some time, as a dog might a hedgehog, touching it gingerly at this point and that, not daring to tackle it, yet unable to leave it alone. It has now reduced it to an academic study. For this purpose it must secure a rigid orthodox structure. This it has sought to secure by elevating Adam Smith, Ricardo, Mill, and one or two more recent writers to a position they neither claimed nor deserved as authoritative exponents of a cut-and-dried logical system. Here appears a paradox. The academic mind is prone to excess of caution. This very caution has bred rashness in economics. In the nature of things it is grossly improbable that a study involving so deep and delicate a knowledge of the changing social relations and desires of men could be raised into a sound scientific structure in a little more than a century after the publication of 'The Wealth of Nations'. Yet the academic mind is compelled to seem to have achieved this task. Although the very text-books which are taken as 'authorities' bristle with contradiction and antagonism upon the most essential points, yet by a judicious process of word-twisting, selection, and interpretation, a body of dogma has been improvised into a system presenting a specious show of consistency to the hasty observer, who is contented not to peer too curiously behind the scene.[2]

It is salutary to set this unflattering account beside the more dignified justifications for knowledge of economics provided by the insiders when seeking public support for their efforts – by Cairnes, by Sidgwick, and above all perhaps by Marshall when extolling the potential contribution of academic economists to public life.[3] Hobson struck another, more characteristically conspiratorial note when he announced that: 'No one who has faithfully followed the development of political economy can have failed to note how political or business interests, or else some academic bias, have warped and distorted the free natural growth of the study, making it subservient to the conveniences of some class or party cause.'[4] It has always been easier to assert than prove or disprove such all-purpose generalisations. By including 'some academic bias' alongside political and business interests as determining influences, Hobson made his charges unanswerable, though he denied that 'in dwelling upon bias of temperament or material interests as a ruling force in Political Economy' he was making accusations against or on behalf of any single class – a denial that allowed him to differentiate his position from that of Marx, who had

---

[2] *Ibid.*, 241–2.   [3] See pp. 213 and 270ff above.
[4] J. A. Hobson, *John Ruskin, social reformer* (London: J. Nisbet, 1898), p. 60.

spoken for an industrial proletariat.[5] Any science that purports to lay bare the material underpinnings of social life was itself likely to be subject to a materialistic analysis of its credentials. Such analyses were bound to deflate the pride of its professional guardians and – Hobson would have added reductively – material beneficiaries.

Hobson's heresies, coming on top of a lacklustre career as an under-graduate, ensured that his actual experience of academic life was confined to giving extra-mural courses and some invited lectures at the London School of Economics (LSE) based on what he was later to publish in the *Economics of distribution*. Looking back, he was inclined to count his blessings: the 'mixed life of lecturing, controversial politics, and jour-nalism' into which he had been driven had greater attractions. He had made contact with all walks of life and enjoyed a wider circle of political and intellectual acquaintances. He had avoided the fate of those who were committed by occupation to writing dull treatises and textbooks, not to mention the often mind-numbing routines of repetitive teaching and examining. He had been obliged to formulate opinions on public affairs in a manner that made them widely available to the general public. Most readers will confirm that Hobson's journalism, topical writing, and exer-cises in biography and autobiography are livelier than his efforts to master the more prosaic style required in works addressed to fellow economists. Some of his treatises aimed at this audience were dull without having the excuse of being par for the courses he was teaching.

Hobson's remarks about combining the role of student with that of worker and citizen were made with London in mind, and after 1895 the LSE, the institution founded by Sidney and Beatrice Webb, fitted his require-ments more closely than any other. If he had been appointed to the LSE he would have had two of his best friends as colleagues, Graham Wallas and L. T. Hobhouse, occupants of chairs in politics and sociology respectively. Instead, he was left to ponder ruefully on the irony that the founding bequest by the eccentric Fabian, Henry Hutchinson, a fellow native of Derby, was now being used to pay the salaries of Foxwell and W. M. Acworth to lecture, respectively, on the undesirability of socialising banking and nationalising the railways.[6] We do not know why Hobson was not offered more regular employment at LSE, but we do know that the first director, the historical economist William Hewins, who had co-operated

[5] See *The social problem: life and work* (London: J. Nisbet, 1900), p. 25.
[6] *Confessions of an econonomic heretic: the autobiography of John A. Hobson* (1938), ed. M. Freeden (Brighton: Harvester Press), p. 80.

with Hobson as a fellow lecturer on the Oxford extension circuit, was as unimpressed by the theory of underconsumption as Edgeworth and Foxwell were.[7] Though attracted to some aspects of this theory, the Fabians had been unwilling to 'venture on the mental revolution which its acceptance would require'.[8] There is also some evidence to suggest that Sidney Webb was not pleased to find that when Hobson expounded his other heresy on surplus income, he gave no credit to Webb for having anticipated the extension of the theory of rent to encompass capital and labour.[9]

The broad aim of the Webb partnership was to create an institution capable of providing the training in empirical research needed to enable experts to guide society towards its collectivist destiny, the one marked out for it by the forces of social evolution. Hobson could have no quarrel with this aim; his own programme became a highly interventionist one reliant on direction by social scientific experts like himself. But he did not share the confidence of the Webbs in factual or historical inquiries, and was to remain largely dependent on the empirical findings of others in his own writings. Sidney Webb, a civil servant turned politician, had a solid grounding in orthodox political economy, particularly that of Mill; and he admired much that Marshall accomplished in his *Principles*, including the consumers' surplus idea.[10] This meant that he was not as much of a sceptic on the virtues of economic theory as his wife; but Hobson may have seemed too much of a theorist for the Webb partnership's tastes, and a theorist whose credentials for accurate reasoning among other theorists were controversial at best. Edwin Cannan, the person responsible for teaching economic theory at the LSE, would not have disabused them on this matter. The new institution needed academic respectability of a kind that Hobson could not supply.

The Webbs also aimed to make the LSE an alternative to Marshall's Cambridge as a centre for economic research. As a by-product of this policy a number of economic dissidents were appointed, where one mark

---

[7] See his review of *Physiology of industry, Economic Review*, 1 (1891), 133–4.

[8] *Fabian News*, May 1895, as cited in A. M. MacBriar, *Fabian socialism and English politics, 1884–1918* (Cambridge: Cambridge University Press, 1962), p. 48.

[9] See S. Webb, 'The rate of interest and the laws of distribution', *Quarterly Journal of Economics*, 12 (1886–8), 188–208, and the response to Walker on pp. 469–72. Hobson's first articles on the same subject appeared later in the same journal: see 'The law of three rents' and 'The element of monopoly in prices' in 6 (1891), 1–24, 263–88. For Webb's possible annoyance, see A. M. MacBriar, *An Edwardian mixed doubles* (Oxford: Oxford University Press, 1987), p. 75n67.

[10] See Webb's remarks on the *Principles* in letters to Beatrice in *The Letters of Sidney and Beatrice Webb*, ed. Norman Mackenzie, 3 vols. (Cambridge: Cambridge University Press, 1978), I, pp. 163, 165–6, 171–2, 178.

of dissidence was rejection of Manchester school positions and support for tariff reform: Hobson fitted the former but not the latter condition. When Hewins resigned his post as the first director in order to act as economic adviser to Chamberlain as head of an unofficial tariff commission, Halford J. Mackinder, who was equally committed to tariff reform and imperial federation, took his place. With Foxwell and Cunningham providing some of the teaching in economics and economic history, the LSE was so well stocked with spokesmen on that side of the dispute that it became impossible to ask Ashley, another tariff-reforming historical economist, to follow Mackinder as director. Although Hobson was only one voice among many in opposing protectionism (arguably, Hobhouse took a more active position as secretary to the Free Trade Union), he became the principal spokesman for the anti-imperialist position during and after the Boer war. Imperial issues were divisive ones for the Fabians and others who were attached to the LSE. Appointing a spokesman for a pro-Boer position was a possibility (Hobhouse exemplifies this), but not perhaps someone who had conducted a noisy anti-jingoist crusade.[11] But there is little point in such speculations: there are too many reasons why Hobson was a dubious candidate for a regular appointment at the LSE – though it has to be emphasised that we do not know whether he ever applied or was considered for one. Hobson merely says that despite 'friendly contact' with the founders 'it was never suggested that I should go upon the staff'.[12]

III

The circumstances surrounding Hobson's exclusion from other aspects of British academic life are not accurately rendered in his *Confessions*, with the result that they convey a misleading impression of the general state of affairs. For example, he makes a point of saying that nothing of his appeared in the *Economic Journal* (*EJ*) despite his membership of the Royal Economic Society (RES), the implication being that membership should have been accompanied by an invitation to contribute. Before 1914 he did in fact write a couple of book reviews in the journal. This would have involved an editorial request, but it is unlikely that he would have been invited to contribute articles by the first editor, Edgeworth, or for

---

[11] The evidence on the complexities of LSE life in the early decades is judiciously surveyed in Ralf Dahrendorf, *A history of the London School of Economics and Political Science, 1895–1995* (Oxford: Oxford University Press, 1995). On Ashley and the tariff-reforming reputation of the School, see p. 109.
[12] *Confessions*, p. 83.

that matter by his successor, Maynard Keynes, who took over in 1911 and was not impressed by Hobson's excursions into his own special field of interest, monetary theory.[13] If Hobson submitted articles to the journal he might have encountered scepticism, but no outright barrier. As we shall see, it was the explicit policy of the RES to provide a forum for all schools of thought. In eschewing tests for orthodoxy among its 'fellows' the society followed a policy based on a mixture of tolerance and financial prudence: fellows could more accurately be described as subscribers, and the finances of the infant society needed these, sometimes badly, during its early decades. Two public figures, George Goschen and R. B. Haldane, occupied the presidency for the first thirty-eight years of the society's existence; and four of the first vice-presidents were politicians.[14] The academics on the council of the RES did not fill half the places until 1920; and it was not until 1929 that an academic – a retired one, Foxwell – was elected to the presidency. Any expectation that public figures would prove useful to the society had evaporated long before this: even the transition to a royal charter had mainly been the result of the efforts of Henry Higgs, a civil servant pupil of Foxwell with Downing Street connections. Indeed, most of the work that kept the RES going was done behind the scenes by two office-holders: the editor of the *EJ* and the secretary to the society. These consisted of the same three people exchanging the two hats for extended periods of office: Edgeworth, later assisted and succeeded by Higgs, who was in turn succeeded by Keynes as editor and then secretary.

For reasons considered later, eclecticism was the order of the day as far as articles were concerned, while the review pages of the *EJ* were, if anything, more miscellaneous than eclectic. It is in the review pages that we find Hobson appearing quite frequently as the subject of reviews that were invariably serious and in some cases sympathetic too.[15] This was

---

[13] See review of Hobson's *Gold, prices, and wages* (1913) in *EJ*, September 1913, as reprinted in JMK, XI, pp. 388–94. Keynes ruled himself out as the reader for Hobson's *Wealth and welfare* on the grounds that he took 'on the whole a very unfavourable view of his books'; see letter to Macmillan, 25 October 1913, Macmillan Archive, British Library.

[14] A. J. Balfour, H. C. E. Childers, Leonard H. Courtney, and John Morley.

[15] H. Llewellyn Smith welcomed the *Problem of poverty*, especially its 'expository and critical' parts, though he was mildly critical of the lack of evidence for some of the positions and the absence of specificity in the constructive proposals; *EJ*, 1 (1891), 583–6. L. L. Price praised the 'care with which [Hobson] had collected and examined his material, and the patience, independence, and subtlety with which he has formed his conclusions' in the *Evolution of modern capitalism*, while remaining mystified by the parts hinting at underconsumption in the treatment of the relation of machinery to depression; see *EJ*, 4 (1894), 673–6. C. F. Bastable, the author of the leading textbook on the subject, considered *International trade* to be a 'well-written and effective exposition of the principles of foreign trade', while questioning the validity of the law-like tendencies attributed

not the case with the first of them. *Physiology of industry* appeared before the *EJ* had begun publication in 1891, but Hobson's next statement of the underconsumptionist position in the *Problem of the unemployed* fell into the hands of Cannan, who treated its author as someone who was 'desirous of turning to account the unemployed agitation', the kind of charge that Hobson had been keen to deny when making his plea to Foxwell for the ban on his teaching extension courses in London to be lifted.[16] One of Marshall's prize pupils, Alfred Flux, delivered a critique of Hobson's theory at the meeting of Section F, the economics and statistics section of the British Association, in 1899; he said that he would have welcomed the chance to enter into direct discussion, 'had we been favoured with Mr Hobson's presence'. Presumably his presence had been expected. Instead, the controversy on 'saving and spending' appeared in the pages of a rival journal, proving, if nothing else, that the orthodox were prepared to argue for, rather than merely reiterate, the conclusions of their orthodoxy.[17]

With regard to his 'destructive' heresy, his theory of distribution, Hobson claimed he had not 'succeeded in gaining attention, even in the form of hostile criticism, from the orthodox economists'.[18] Some allowance must be made for memory lapse here. Flux, once more, took on the task of reviewing the *Economics of distribution* in the *EJ*, and Marshall and Edgeworth, as we have noted in passing, were sufficiently attentive for them to reprove Hobson's methods of interpreting their conclusions.[19] Hobson had chosen to work on a problem – of whether a unified theory of the prices of factors of production could be found – that was central to the work of an entire generation of Anglo-American and post-marginalist economists. It was a crowded field which he was not the first to enter and where what was most distinctive in his approach was the sweeping nature of the policy conclusions he drew concerning the suitability for taxation of the surpluses his theory had delineated.

Hobson attributed his failure to gain attention to the publication of his *Economics of distribution* in the United States. Though not exactly warring tribes at this time, Anglo-American relations between economists were often a matter of courtly diplomacy. Hobson undoubtedly received more active encouragement in academic circles across the Atlantic. Most of the

---

to empirical evidence on the declining significance of foreign trade; see *EJ*, 14 (1904), 609–11. E. J. Urwick's review of the *Industrial system* makes a conscientious effort to expound the peculiarities of Hobson's position; see *EJ*, 19 (1909), 441–4.

[16] For his plea to Foxwell, see p. 303 above; for Cannan's review see *EJ*, 7 (1897), 87–9.

[17] See the exchanges on 'Saving and spending' in *Economic Review*, 9 (1899), 174–85, 186–96, 342–50.

[18] *Confessions*, p. 168. [19] See p. 306 above and *EJ*, 10 (1900), 380–5.

articles Hobson wrote for professional audiences were published in American journals.[20] He made several visits with his American wife; he appropriated the opinions of Simon Patten in his early work and popularised the views of Thorstein Veblen in Britain; he was in harmony with 'progressives' and 'muckrakers' and became a close student of the American trust movement. If he had been prepared to move to the United States, he could have taken one of the posts he was offered in the larger and more pluralist university system that existed there.[21] For a time at least, Hobson established close relations with Richard T. Ely, president and founding figure in the American Economic Association, a body comparable to the Royal Economic Society in professional function, but unlike it in being modelled on the German Verein für Sozialpolitik. This was made clear in the first of its founding principles: 'We regard the state as an agency whose positive assistance is one of the indispensable conditions of human progress.'[22]

Ely sponsored Hobson's work in the United States by including the *Economics of distribution* in a series he edited; and he did so as a result of 'a feeling in this country that the English economists had not done justice to Hobson'. This was said in response to complaints from Marshall in 1901 that Hobson had misrepresented his views and failed to respond to the letters he had sent, accompanied by a copy of a later edition of his *Principles*. Marshall acknowledged that while there was 'an immense deal that is most fascinating about him', Hobson was a man in a hurry, 'and so he disappoints me whenever the only good work is slow work'. Ely confessed that his own experience in dealing with Hobson had led him to the same conclusion: 'There is enough in his "Economics of Distribution" for a very large volume, if the thought should be elaborated properly. I am disappointed, as you are, because he seems to lack continuity.'[23]

[20] Hobson's 'academic' articles appeared in the Harvard *Quarterly Journal of Economics*, the Chicago *Journal of Political Economy*, the *Annals of the American Academy of Political and Social Science*, and, in later years, the *Political Science Quarterly*. His sociological articles were published in the *American Journal of Sociology*. The only ones published in a British journal appeared in the *Economic Review*.

[21] See the essays by Malcolm Rutherford, Stephen Edgell and Rick Tilman, and Walter C. Neale and Anne Mayhew on the American dimension to Hobson's reputation, in J. Pheby (ed.), *J. A. Hobson after fifty years* (Basingstoke: Macmillan, 1994).

[22] For the opening statement of principles, see J. Dorfman, 'The Seligman Correspondence', *Political Science Quarterly*, 56 (1941), 110.

[23] The exchanges between Marshall and Ely in 1901 can be found in *Correspondence*, II, pp. 335–6. For an earlier complaint about Hobson's 'overwhelming haste', see Marshall's letter to Seligman, 13 May 1900, *ibid.*, p. 279. Marshall did not have a high opinion of Ely's own work; see letter to Phelps, 23 April 1891, opposing the award of an honorary degree to him at Oxford, *ibid.*, p. 34.

Hobson achieved security and the freedom to follow an independent (though not, as we have seen, a straight) line when he inherited a rentier income. He may have been right in thinking that freelance journalism conferred on him freedoms that many university teachers lacked, though editors could have more demanding expectations than senior colleagues and university trustees. It is hard not to believe that the content of Hobson's writings on foreign investment in 1911 was influenced by the nature of the journal in which it appeared.[24] Universities came under Hobson's critical gaze once more when he was assembling an account of the organised conspiracy of forces supporting imperialism, and when writing on 'millionaire endowments' in the *Crisis of liberalism* in 1909. Freed from the obligation to be subservient to Church and Crown, those employed by the ancient universities, especially in philosophy and economics, were now 'setting up new earthworks against the attack of the disinherited masses upon the vested interests of the plutocracy'.[25] Class interests were at work in 'the selection and rejection of ideas, hypotheses, and formulae'.[26] University endowments required the favours of the rich, and 'no bluff regarding academic dignity and intellectual honesty' could conceal the fact that only safe teachers using safe methods were employed.

That Hobson was still hankering after academic recognition can be gauged from his conclusion in *Imperialism* that it was hard now 'for a political economist with strong views on the necessity of controlling capital to be elected to a chair in economics'.[27] By the early 1900s, however, rejection combined with the inherent attractions of the more varied life of the political journalist had led to acceptance of the role of gadfly to the academic community. He had burned his boats and was, for the most part, not discontented with the outcome. During the inter-war period Hobson continued to write on sociology, psychology, and eugenics. But it may be more significant that in one of his later and most ambitious works, *Free thought in the social sciences* (1926), he devoted a third of the book to a restatement of his critique of orthodox political economy, marginalism, and neo-classical economics. As he recognised, he had entered the social sciences via economics and was justified in settling on *economic heretic* as the most descriptive label for his career.

---

[24] See pp. 328–9 above. [25] *Imperialism*, p. 218. [26] *Social problem*, pp. 218–19.
[27] *Imperialism*, p. 221; see also the *Crisis of liberalism: new issues of democracy* (1909) ed. by P. F. Clarke (Hassocks, Sussex: Harvester Press, 1974), ch. 4.

IV

Hobson's case was idiosyncratic, though parts of it reflect the mounting degree of academic professionalisation in economics he encountered at the turn of the century and during the next three decades. For an earlier generation, the experience of Jevons outlined in Essay 6 of this book gives a better idea of the opportunities available to someone who began as more of an outsider than Hobson. Jevons inherited family obligations rather than a private income: he had to find means of support for himself and his sisters after his father's bankruptcy and death. As a Unitarian, he could not be admitted to any Oxford or Cambridge college as an undergraduate. For the same reason he could not apply for the endowed chairs and fellowships at Oxford and Cambridge prior to 1871, when religious tests were removed. With no sense of taking second best, he went to University College London, sharing that experience with Bagehot and later with other economists from non-conformist backgrounds, Neville Keynes and Foxwell.[28]

But if repeal of the Test Acts came too late for Jevons (Keynes and Foxwell went on to take second degrees at Cambridge), one could still say that he benefited from an earlier piece of legislation: the acceptance of the meritocratic reforms arising from the Northcote–Trevelyan report commissioned by Gladstone in 1853, the report that recommended competitive examination as the chief means of entry into the civil service. The report was aimed at widening the field from which entrants into the civil service were recruited, improving their quality, and raising educational standards in the nation's schools and universities. As part of the attempt 'to quicken the progress of our Universities', the report had also recommended that in addition to 'the staple of classics and mathematics', proficiency in a range of other disciplines should be encouraged: 'history, jurisprudence, political economy, modern languages, political and physical geography, and other matters'.[29] Though he was not an applicant for civil service posts, Jevons's career is testimony to the prizes that could be gained via a system of competitive examinations. In common with other university teachers of 'modern' subjects his audiences and readership were swelled by those who needed to pass them. One of the reasons he felt aggrieved by his first exam result in political economy at UCL was because

---

[28] See Phyllis Deane, *The life and times of J. Neville Keynes: a beacon in the tempest* (London: Edward Elgar, 2001). Foxwell was educated at a Wesleyan college in Somerset before attending UCL.
[29] 'Report on the organization of the permanent civil service', *Parliamentary papers*, 27 (1854), 14.

he feared, wrongly as it turned out, that it would blight his chances of obtaining the scholarship that would help finance the next stage of his studies. It was with considerable later experience as an examiner, and some personal feeling as someone for whom success in examinations was his only means of gaining entry into the academic world, that he could defend what was often dismissed as mere 'cram':

any mode of education which enables a candidate to take a leading place in a severe and well-conducted open examination must be a good system of education. Name it what you like, but it is impossible to deny that it calls forth intellectual, moral, and even physical powers, which are proved by unquestionable experience to fit men for the business of life.[30]

Unfortunately, carrying off the top prizes at UCL in logic and the mental sciences did not, at first, earn Jevons much of a living. In the early years it was hard not to compare his situation with that of Fawcett, only two years his senior. Along with everybody else, Jevons could pay tribute to Fawcett's capacity for lucid exposition when dealing with a subject of common interest, the gold question. But in private he exulted in the fact that on this subject Fawcett had been converted by, and was heavily dependent on his own research.[31] Fawcett may have been present at the British Association conference in Cambridge in 1862 when Jevons gave the first public account of his new theory of value, where it was received 'without a word of interest or belief'.[32] At this time Fawcett was completing his *Manual of political economy*, a popularisation of Mill's *Principles* that was his only academic claim on the attention of the electors to the practically defunct (never properly activated) chair of political economy in Cambridge in the same year. Cambridge connections dating back to his undergraduate days and including a fellowship at Trinity Hall, plus Mill's testimonial, played a part in Fawcett's success, though in the end this was mainly due to the way in which his opponents bungled the election by splitting their vote.[33]

Fawcett was to occupy this post, chiefly addressing an undemanding, because mainly conscripted, audience composed of those sitting for pass degrees, until his death in 1884. As his friend and biographer, Leslie Stephen, pointed out when defending him from the charges of those in Cambridge who were interested in the newer ideas being propagated

---

[30] 'Cram', originally published in *Mind*, 1877, as reprinted in *Methods of social reform* (London: Macmillan, 1883), p. 97.
[31] PC, III, pp. 42–3.   [32] *Ibid.*, I, p. 188.
[33] See L. Stephen, *Life of Henry Fawcett*, 3rd edn (London: Smith Elder, 1886), pp. 116–22.

elsewhere: 'It is enough to say that . . . he discharged his duties vigorously and did his best to keep his hearers alive to the vast importance of the principles in which he believed by applying them to the great problems of the day.'[34] For these duties he earned £550 per annum (£300 from the chair plus £250 from his fellowship) for lecturing eighteen weeks of the year, and was not required to give up his career as an MP and later as a minister. It was an *ancien régime* appointment that did not conform to the Germanic idea of the research chair for which university reformers, like Mark Pattison in Oxford, were arguing during this period.[35] The Germanic idea was being pioneered at Manchester by Jevons's cousin, Henry Roscoe, professor of chemistry. Much as he would like to have followed this route, Jevons's initial appointment there departed from the German ideal in the opposite direction. In the early 1860s, and for some time after, his income was between £100 and £400 per annum (salary supplemented by student fees and dividends on railway shares). In return he had to give six lectures a week, together with evening classes on four nights, and had to cover logic and mental and moral philosophy as well as political economy. Even when he obtained his chair in 1866, the teaching hours, particularly in the evenings, proved onerous. For a conscience-driven man who found lecturing difficult, and who was engaged on original research across a broad front, the regime placed his health and equability under great strain.

Those like Jevons who were not subsidised by parental allowances or inherited wealth were obliged to supplement their incomes by private coaching or school teaching. Marshall did this for a time after he graduated to repay an uncle who had lent him the money he needed to finance his mathematical studies at St John's College, Cambridge. Would-be academics could write for the periodical press, a side-line that could be financially rewarding if they had the requisite talent and connections. Several of the economists who have been mentioned here read for the Bar, possibly as an insurance policy. This was true, for example, of Bagehot and Cliffe Leslie, though neither of them practised law. Alternatively, there was that other source of income which could be combined with teaching duties: examinerships in other institutions. When linked with writing the kinds of primers and textbooks that went with the new examination system

---

[34] *Ibid.*, p. 123. See also Phyllis Deane's defence of Fawcett's record in 'Henry Fawcett: the plain man's political economist', in L. Goldman (ed.), *Blind Victorian: Henry Fawcett and British liberalism* (Cambridge: Cambridge University Press, 1989), pp. 93–110.

[35] *Suggestions on academical organisation* (Edinburgh: Edmonston and Douglas, 1868).

in schools and universities, this could be lucrative. An examinership for entry into the Indian civil service, for example, could pay £150 per annum, making it a significant addition to an ordinary salary, such as Jevons eventually received in Manchester, of between £300 and £500, or even the £700 that came with Marshall's Cambridge chair. Jevons obtained such examinerships as his career advanced, but his most conspicuous successes came from writing elementary primers on logic, political economy, and money, which achieved sales of up to, and well over in some cases, the 100,000 mark – figures that can be compared with the less than 10,000 his best scientific works achieved over a longer period.[36] Given the amount of labour involved in this kind of work, however, Jevons always denied that there was much that could be described as profit in these earnings.

Fawcett had obviously capitalised on the commercial, pedagogic, and political possibilities presented by Mill's *Principles*. In a more indirect fashion, Jevons's success in writing books for use by students also owed something to Mill – an ardent supporter of the meritocratic reforms recommended in the Northcote–Trevelyan report – whose *Logic* and *Principles of political economy* became an essential part of the diet of those university liberals who came to maturity in the 1850s and 60s: the generation that spearheaded the movement for reform within Oxford and Cambridge, and collaborated in producing an agenda for a reformed parliament in 1867.[37] Fawcett's advice in his professorial inaugural in 1864, that his audience should make a diligent study of the *Principles* – 'the most complete and the most perfect treatise that has ever been written on the science' – was probably redundant as far as most of his serious auditors were concerned.[38] Pattison dated the beginnings of the decline in influence of the anti-science and High Church party at Oxford to the introduction of Mill's *Logic* as a textbook, a role for which it had not been written.[39]

Jevons's debt to Mill lay in the enhanced status now given to the fields of logic and political economy, of mental and moral philosophy, and in the place they had gained in the teaching and examinations for entry into the Indian civil service. There is no reason why Jevons should have felt or

---

[36] The figures are taken from Keynes's biographical memoir, JMK, X, p. 142.
[37] I am thinking here chiefly of the authors who produced *Essays on reform* and *Questions for a reformed parliament*. See C. Harvie, *Lights of liberalism* (London: Allen Lane, 1976) and C. Kent, *Brains and numbers* (Toronto: Toronto University Press, 1978), both of which stress Mill's influence.
[38] See 'Inaugural lecture on political economy, delivered at Cambridge, 1864', in *Fortnightly Review*, 9 (1863–4), 500.
[39] See his *Memoirs* (London: Macmillan, 1885), p. 166.

acknowledged such a general debt, though he gained access to Oxbridge circles through his role as examiner in precisely these fields. On one visit to Oxford in this capacity Jevons was pleased to see his *Principles of science* on display in the library at Balliol and copies of the second edition in the bookshops. Together with the news that it had been adopted as a textbook at Trinity College, Dublin, he could see that there was a chance of 'a steady sale for years to come'. It represented another step in his campaign to replace Mill. As Jevons wrote to his wife on this occasion: 'Mill's reputation is said to be rapidly declining in Oxford, in fact they say he is almost overlooked in the examinations.'[40]

V

In the essay on Jevons above (6), it was noted that one of his motives in moving to London was to enable him to attend meetings of the Political Economy Club.[41] At its foundation in 1821 the membership of this private dining club included most of the leading figures in the field. There were precious few academic posts devoted to the subject, none exclusively so, and only one of the original members, Robert Malthus, held such a post. By 1876, when the club acted as host during the celebrations of the centenary of the *Wealth of nations*, six honorary academic members were eligible to attend; the holders of the chairs at Cambridge, Edinburgh, King's College, London, Owens College, Manchester, Oxford, and Queen's College, Belfast. Looking through the minutes and attendance records of the club, it is clear that members drawn from politics, banking, and the civil service dominated the membership and probably, depending on the topic, much of the discussion as well. At one time a hope was expressed that the club would become a learned body, but as one member wisely noted in 1905: 'Had it been turned into an academy it would probably long ago have perished of excess of dignity and torpor.'[42] Overcoming torpor by bringing in younger members was still a problem. In 1901 the secretary of the club, Bernard Mallet, the civil servant son of Louis Mallet, approached Foxwell to see if he would support the suggestion of other members that Hobson should be elected to the club to enliven

---

[40] Letter to Harriet Jevons, 3 October 1878, PC, IV, p. 286.   [41] See pp. 158–9 above.
[42] Paper by Sir J. Macdonell in *Political Economy Club, minutes of proceedings, 1899–1920, roll of members and questions discussed, 1821–1920, with documents bearing on the history of the club,* (London: 1921), VI, pp. 342–3.

proceedings with a touch of heresy.[43] The nature of the response can be guessed but has not been found, and on this occasion Hobson's testimony is reliable: he allowed his name to go forward, but heard no more of the matter.[44]

Foxwell enjoyed his contacts with London bankers; it kept him in touch with a subject he taught at UCL and LSE. But some of these encounters must have reminded him of the clash between old and new generations dealt with in Essay 9, with the bankers taking a reactionary stance. The syllabus of the lecture that had obtained Marshall's approval on new responsibilities for the state received a very different response from a fellow member of the Political Economy Club, Henry Grenfell, Governor of the Bank of England. In sending it to Grenfell, Foxwell, with all the solemnity of a thirty-five-year-old, had said that 'what a great many of us younger men feel is that we cannot acquiesce in the actual condition of the great majority of the people, that that condition owes some of its worst features to the doctrinaire economists and their gospel of "laissez faire", and that judicious control and improved organisation may greatly ameliorate it'. The background to the exchange in 1884 was continued depression in manufacturing and trade, downward pressure on wages and prices, and signs of a revival of working-class interest in the ideas of Henry George and Hyndman's Social Democratic Federation. Grenfell's response, speaking as a sixty-year-old who had lived through the crisis of 1848, 'that year of dreams', was to emphasise the virtue of economists sticking to their last: 'Economical problems are as unalterable as a sum in common arithmetic. They are founded on the eternal necessity (if you want to live) to get your bread, and every one finding fault with competition must show a state of things somewhere where competition is not. I know of no such condition.' He could see little point in Foxwell's agenda for the state, and the idea that wages could be sheltered during depression showed that Foxwell lacked 'the faintest conception of the state of the manufacturing industry of England'. Lectures of this kind served only to 'stimulate mental dreams and hallucinations'. Indeed, Grenfell could not 'conceive anything more mischievous than giving lectures to the working classes on such subjects at all'. He clearly felt that academic chatterboxes should be discouraged; that economics was a practical business best appreciated by those who had experience of the world at large. Foxwell responded by claiming that he was not without

---

[43] Letter from Bernard Mallet to Foxwell, 11 January 1901, Freeman collection.
[44] *Confessions*, p. 84.

such experience, and that it was his academic duty to make the effort to explain economic problems to the working classes. He also managed to suggest that Grenfell might live to be grateful for such efforts: 'it is not impossible that a time may come . . . when the propertied classes will be glad to think that there are any reasonable persons, even unpropertied and unmarried lecturers [like himself at that time], who have any hold or control over the actions and affections of the masses of the people'.[45]

Marshall, as we have noted, wanted his works to be read by businessmen, and when founding the body that became the RES had said that while he did not want to recruit '"mere" business men', he was keen to include 'Bank Directors and others of the class who are for me at least the most interesting members of the Pol[itical]. Econ[omy] Club'.[46] He was less clubbable than Foxwell (who remained a bachelor until nearly fifty) and therefore not a regular participant in the club's affairs. Sidgwick, a shy man with a stutter who in clubbability was somewhere between the two, probably summed up the feelings of other academic members after enduring an evening in which the bankers took the lead: 'It is an exaggeration to say that they know *no* Political Economy; I think they read Mill some time ago, and look at him from time to time on Sundays.'[47]

Another club, a far less exclusive one, the Cobden Club, was dominated by civil servants of the calibre of Mallet, Farrer, and Robert Giffen. Some academics, notably Cliffe Leslie and Thorold Rogers, were also club stalwarts, but membership did not suit more fastidious tastes. We have noted Sidgwick's reservations about the work of Farrer, which probably helps to explain why he resigned from the club at an early stage in his career, in 1870. Marshall refused to join because the free trade message of the club was too crude.[48] The club's policy of buying large quantities of books and pamphlets for distribution, with or without its imprimatur, could give a healthy lift to the sales of some works.[49] And when the teaching of economics was gaining a foothold in a few universities, the

---

[45] See typescripts of speeches, correspondence etc. relating to club, 1883–97, *Political Economy Club files*, Box 4, LSE Archives, British Library of Political and Economic Science.

[46] Letter to Foxwell, March 1890, *Correspondence*, I, p. 314.

[47] *Memoir*, p. 408; see too his observation on p. 403 after another meeting: 'It is astonishing how little Political Economy these people know.'

[48] See p. 227 above.

[49] For example, 1,000 copies of Bastiat's essays were bought in 1874 and 11,000 copies of his *Sophismes économiques* were published as *Popular fallacies regarding trade* in 1882, a figure that puts in perspective the 500 copies of Fawcett's *Free trade and protection* bought in 1879 and the 5,000 copies of his *State socialism* pamphlet bought in 1884. Information derived from the minute books of the club held at the West Sussex Record Office.

award of a Cobden Club prize from 1875 onwards for a long essay on a suitable subject was a welcome addition to the established prizes in more traditional fields.[50] But like all forms of academic patronage exercised by external bodies it could give rise to friction over what constituted a suitable subject and whether the chosen one was compatible with the aims of the donor organisation. It took some time, however, for the ultimate question to be posed: was it possible for someone who was not a free trader to win the prize? Edwin Cannan, a free trader himself, threatened resignation as an examiner in 1912 when he learned that 'the essay chosen must not oppose the principles on which the Cobden Club is founded'. Somehow the issue was fudged because competition for the prize at the LSE continued to be held.[51]

VI

The need for larger annual gatherings of devotees, amateur and professional, had been met by Section F of the British Association, a body founded in 1831 and satirised in its early days by Dickens as the Mudfog Association for the Advancement of Everything. The section had been set up in 1856 and linked economic science with statistics. It was a marriage of convenience that, like many similar arrangements, proved inconvenient later. As Sidgwick said after presiding over the section's proceedings in 1885: 'The profound difficulty of making the talk of this section really scientific is that Statisticians and Economists are yoked together, and the Statisticians are weak or *arrière* in theory. It is worse than if the Physicists and Mechanicians were combined; but they have each a section.'[52] The annual conferences had a dual role as the venue where experts could speak to each other and as the forum where their knowledge could be displayed before a larger public as well. Here too there could be a clash of interests. The success of Section F in attracting large audiences was the source of a worrying episode in 1877, when Francis Galton, Darwin's cousin, the bio-statistician and originator of eugenics, proposed that the section should be closed on grounds of its lack of scientific credentials. An attempt was made in the following year by critics of political economy, led by Ingram and abetted by Cliffe Leslie, to exploit the episode as part of a campaign

---

[50] Information on the prize and its Oxbridge winners can be found in Alon Kadish, *Historians, economists, and economic history* (London: Routledge, 1989), pp. 79, 125, 129, 161, 170, 185, 187, 194.
[51] See exchange of letters with Lord Welby, 9 and 11 May 1912, Cannan Papers, 1022, fos. 46–9, 51–2, LSE Archives, British Library of Political and Economic Science.
[52] *Memoir*, p. 425.

against orthodox deductive methods, claiming that it represented 'an important crisis in the history of our Section'.[53] A closer look reveals something less dramatic: that the status of political economy was never in question, and that it was the popularity of the section that aroused concern.[54]

The nub of Galton's case lay in his belief that the theory of probabilities, the 'law of the frequency of error', had placed statistical science upon a new foundation capable of exercising 'the ingenuity of many generations of the ablest mathematicians'. None of the papers submitted to Section F in the period 1873–5 had dealt with the theory of statistics, and if one had been communicated, it would have been more appropriately discussed in Section A. Galton cited Jevons's paper on 'the influence of the sun-spot period upon the price of corn' as one that would have been more properly considered in this fashion. The mere fact that the papers were concerned with 'important matters of human knowledge' was no licence for existence: the same could be said of history, which all agreed was not a science. 'Usage has drawn a strong distinction between knowledge in its generality and science, confining the latter in its strictest sense to precise measurements and definite laws, which lead by such exact processes of reasoning to their results, that all minds are obliged to accept the latter as true.' There was some room for departure from these conditions, but they ought not to be 'too largely violated', as appeared to be the case with Section F. Not only was the section isolated within the Association, far more so than those devoted to anthropology and geography: it 'attracts much more than its share of persons of both sexes who have had no scientific training', running the risk that the reported discussions could bring discredit on the Association. A clinching argument turned on the existence of 'a more congenial and appropriate home', the Social Science Association, a body that had its origins in the London and provincial statistical societies formed in the 1830s and 40s, but which had organised annual conferences on the model of the British Association since 1857.

Galton elicited defences that conceded some of his facts while placing a different interpretation upon them. It had to be acknowledged that the

---

[53] See Ingram's presidential address to the section in 1878, 'The present position and prospects of political economy' in R. L. Smyth (ed.), *Essays in economic method: selected papers read to section F of the British Association for the Advancement of Science, 1860–1913* (London: McGraw-Hill, 1962), p. 41. Articles on the address appeared in *The Times* and the *Pall Mall Gazette*. Cliffe Leslie followed up with an article in *The Academy*, which went further in its criticisms of Section F than he intended; see his semi-apologetic letter to Jevons, 28 August 1878, PC, IV, pp. 272–3.

[54] See 'Considerations adverse to the maintenance of Section F' and the answers it provoked in *Journal of Statistical Society of London*, 40 (1877), 468–76.

section was attractive to large numbers of people, many of them women, who had no scientific qualifications; but it had been headed by a long list of distinguished figures.[55] Dr William Farr FRS, an epidemiologist and vital statistician, admitted that some papers of little interest or relevance had found their way into the proceedings, though the section was not unique in this. Speaking perhaps as someone who had collaborated in health matters with Florence Nightingale, Farr praised the enlightenment of the Association in welcoming women: 21 out of the 856 papers given since the section was founded had been given by those it was polite to describe as ladies, including papers by Nightingale and Mary Carpenter, the prison reformer and educationist. Farr estimated that the number of ladies who had attended recently was between 600 and 1,058, the precision of the latter figure suggesting that someone (appropriately for a section including statisticians) had taken the trouble to count.

The secretaries of the Statistical Society, Giffen and Hammond Chubb, also weighed in with a letter. It was essential to maintain a section that demonstrated the value of a scientific approach to 'other subjects of a far more complex and difficult character than those which are the subject matter of the physical sciences'. More stringent rules could be framed to discourage 'invasion' by those without scientific training; but they reminded their readers that the advancement of science included making its conclusions available to the 'unscientific multitude'. Edwin Chadwick, a past president of the section, rounded off the responses by looking forward to the day when a 'distinguished statist, sociologist, or professor of political economy' would occupy the presidency of the Association, mentioning the name of Mill as someone who could have filled that role. This risked being an own goal, for not only had Mill been dead for four years, he had preferred to support (though only rarely to attend) the Social Science Congress, chiefly because it had been sympathetic to women members from its inception.[56] Chadwick redeemed himself by making a suitably shrewd economic observation: there was a great deal to be said for a section in which more 'local and popular' subjects could be included 'in order to realise the required funds at the provincial meetings'. Section F brought in such funds and made few calls on the Association for its investigations. Its proceedings appealed to the working classes and they

[55] Among those mentioned were Charles Babbage, G. R. Porter, R. Whately, T. Tooke, Nassau Senior, W. Newmarch, E. Chadwick, J. E. T. Rogers, Stafford Northcote, W. S. Jevons, and H. Fawcett.
[56] For the most relevant letters of Mill on the subject, see CW, XV, pp. 553–4, 618, 626, 632–3, 683–4, 925; XVI, pp. 1021, 1030.

were widely thought to have helped put an end to a strike in Belfast when the Association held its meetings there in 1874. Finally, Chadwick (mischievously?) pointed out that the proceedings of Section F 'never in any way offend the religious prejudices of the nation', thereby providing 'a very striking set-off against the excitement produced by the bold utterances of the physical and biological sections' – a reference to some of the ructions associated with Darwin's discoveries.

Section F survived this minor crisis and after the demise of the Social Science Association in 1886 remained the only national body under whose auspices interested economists could meet at least once a year. The presidency of the section was one of those dutiful honorific parcels that could be passed around the leading figures, increasingly though still not exclusively those holding academic posts. Methodological pronouncements were a favourite, though somewhat divisive, topic for the presidential addresses, allowing the rival historical and theoretical camps to engage with one another almost up to the outbreak of the First World War. There was little scope for collaboration between meetings, though some *ad hoc* inquiries were started, one of which produced a report devoted to the state of 'economic training in this and other countries' in 1894. This brought the material underpinnings of the fledgling profession to the surface because it raised a bread-and-butter issue for academics looking for ways in which the demand for their teaching could be expanded and university posts created or confirmed. As one might expect, therefore, the report emphasised Britain's backwardness when compared with European countries as diverse as Austria, Belgium, France, Germany, Holland, Hungary, Italy, and Russia. In all these countries economics formed part of the state examinations for entry into the legal profession and/or the civil service.

Nothing similar existed in the United States. Even so, the report drew attention to the body of popular opinion there that viewed economics as a way in which the vital social and economic questions of American public life could be solved. The prejudices of the chairman of the committee, William Cunningham, fresh from his disputes with Marshall on the role of theory and history in economics, can be detected in the following comparison between Britain and America:

The American economists have not to shake off the half-uttered, half-silent opprobrium attached to their subject through the action of the more numerous though less conspicuous of their predecessors in their rigid adherence to incomplete or ill-founded theories. They are fortunate in entering upon their teaching at a time when the need of inductive inquiry and training is more fully recognised. This gives a more systematic aspect to the economic instruction demanded from them than was the case in England.[57]

There was no problem with the quality of instruction that *could* be made available in Britain: the problem was what a less decorous age would know as the lack-of-bums-on-seats problem. Finding employment for those who wanted academic jobs was becoming a relevant preoccupation.

VII

Marshall happened to be president of the section in 1890 when preparations (chiefly the work of others, especially Foxwell) for founding what became the RES and its journal were coming to a head. It enabled him to act as convenor for the final meeting to adopt proposals that embodied his views on the aims of the new body. More specifically, it allowed him to outmanoeuvre those who wanted the association to be a learned society with recognised qualifications for membership rather than simple payment of a subscription for the journal. Sidgwick, once more, found a middle position to occupy. At the inaugural meeting in 1890 he argued that while he hoped the new body would be 'as unexclusive as it could be consistently with its scientific aims', he still thought it desirable 'that a reserve power should be placed in the hands of the council to reject any obviously objectionable applicant'.[58] Marshall, on the other hand, wanted to avoid any suggestion of orthodoxy: 'an "orthodox science"', he maintained, 'was a contradiction in terms'. He hoped the association 'would start from an absolutely catholic basis, and include every school of economists which was doing genuine work'. The feeling seems to have been genuine: he invited his old enemy Cunningham and his wife to dinner during the launch period and was insistent on placing him on the council of the new body. For his part, the editor-designate, Edgeworth, announced that he would conduct the journal in a spirit that would be ' "British" in its love of fair play and free speech'. At the same time, however, Marshall reported the consensual view that the association should not, initially at least, commit itself to a policy of holding meetings. The reasoning behind

---

[57] 'Methods of economic training in this and other countries. Report of the committee, consisting of Professor W. Cunningham, Professor E. C. K. Gonner, Professor F. Y. Edgeworth, Professor H. S. Foxwell, Mr H. Higgs, Mr L. L. Price, and Professor J. Shield Nicholson', *Report on the proceedings of the British Association*, 1894, p. 381.

[58] *EJ*, 1 (1891), 10.

this may have been based on Section F experience and could hardly have
been put more tactfully: 'such discussions, unless conducted by a very
strong Association, might do harm: they might be attended chiefly by
people whose time was not very valuable'. A few meetings carrying the
impressive label of 'congresses' were later organised by the RES, but the
continued existence of Section F meant that one aspect of this role was
already being performed on a grander scale elsewhere.

It fell to the infant RES to continue making representations on the
issues connected with the professional status of economics. True to the
inner nature of the discipline, however, competition between rival suppliers rather than collaboration accounted for most of the early proselytising activity. The Webbs/Hewins alliance at LSE took an early lead
in 1895, followed by Ashley's commerce degree at Birmingham and
Marshall's Economics tripos at Cambridge in 1899 and 1903 respectively.
Hobson's 'millionaire endowments' and those prepared to serve 'the
vested interests of the plutocracy' were hard to find; there were not many
offers to buy or sell economists' souls. Ironically, two of the plutocrats
who made a bid to influence the shape of things in the 1880s and 90s –
Robert Miller, the Scottish engineer and philanthropist who funded the
Industrial Remuneration Conference and Hutchinson, whose bequest to
the Fabian Society helped Sidney Webb to finance the LSE's first steps –
were socialists. The bequest gave Webb some independent leeway when
negotiating with the London Chamber of Commerce and the Technical
Education Board set up by the London County Council to obtain their
support for vocational courses in commerce that would put the first bums
on seats. As in the case of the provincial civic universities, responding to
the needs of local commercial and manufacturing interests was the only
way forward for institutions that had no endowments or buildings and
limited access to local authority funds. Oxford and Cambridge had
endowments and buildings, but new subjects had to fight against established ones to obtain a share. Marshall had to use his professorial salary
to create prizes designed to lure promising students into apprenticeship
roles; he also paid for the post occupied by Pigou after 1900.[59] A City
livery company, the Girdlers', took over this commitment later, but when
Pigou succeeded to the chair he continued Marshall's financial commitment by spending nearly a third of his income paying for posts that
initially went to Maynard Keynes and Walter Layton.

---

[59] See letter to Roberts, 22 August 1910, *Correspondence*, III, p. 261.

Webb's initiative and political skills in using the Hutchinson money gave rise to protests from socialists, especially Bernard Shaw and Ramsay MacDonald, who accused Webb of malversation: funds that should have been used for socialist propaganda were being diverted into further and higher education. Another threat to Webb's ambitions came from Foxwell, supported by his former UCL students, Clara Collet and Higgs. In 1902 they mounted a campaign against Webb and the LSE within the newly federated University of London, partly on the ground that its endowment had been supplied by an organisation committed to socialism. Webb was able to deflect this by showing that other philanthropic sources were more significant, one of them being Lord Rothschild. Like most intra-university disputes, personal animosities lurked beneath the appeal to constitutional and even nobler-sounding principles. In this case there was an inter-collegiate battle between an older institution within which economics had had a long but rather exiguous existence and a young upstart, UCL versus LSE. The newer organisation had stolen a march on the older one and, under Webb's energetic leadership, looked like securing a monopoly of the externally-funded teaching. The objectors called for the senate of the University of London to investigate 'whether more than one School of Economics should be allowed to survive; and whether, if only one is desirable, it should be an isolated economic academy or a department of a university institution giving instruction in other Faculties'.[60]

It did not need much inside knowledge to identify which terms applied to LSE, which to UCL. A little more was needed to interpret the academic snobbery behind the concluding remark that these important issues should be determined by seeking 'the views of economists with university experience'. When this was written Foxwell still had a full set of Cambridge connections and the economics department he headed at UCL nestled among several other faculties. In private correspondence he described Webb, whose formal education had been via London extension classes, as 'a man whose conception of a University does not rise beyond that of a loosely federated aggregation of technical schools'.[61] He was able to thwart Webb's desire to incorporate the library of rare economics works Foxwell had collected into the British Library for Political and Economic Science at LSE by having it entrusted to the care of the University of

---

[60] See letter written by Clara Collet, December 1902, in Passfield Papers, 101212. For comment on the episode, see Janet Beveridge, *An epic of Clare Market* (London: G. Bell and Sons, 1960), pp. 48–52.
[61] Letter to Seligman, 6 January 1902, Seligman Papers, Columbia University Library.

London, where, as the Goldsmiths' Library, it became a long-standing source of friction between himself and the custodial body. In all other matters Webb saw off the Foxwell-inspired attack with as much success as he had seen off the attack from within the socialist camp. And as we have noted, Foxwell himself eventually appeared on the books of the LSE (doing so reluctantly, or so he reported to friends) after he had exiled himself from Cambridge economics and now needed whatever income he could get from his London teaching and examining.[62]

During the decade or more that preceded 1914 the student population of the colleges of the University of London (4,026) rose to just over half the total number of Oxbridge students (7,704), with the provincial civic universities taking a share that was quickly catching up on Oxbridge (6,498).[63] In other words, much of this non-Oxbridge expansion was taking place in new and newish universities and university colleges that owed their existence to local industrial and commercial support, notably so in the cases of Birmingham, Liverpool, Manchester, Nottingham, Reading, and Sheffield. In two of these cases, Birmingham and Manchester, faculties of commerce were created in which economics and economic history was taught alongside vocational subjects that included accountancy, foreign languages, and commercial law. Ashley's faculty at Birmingham had close connections with the Chamberlain family and local industry. At Owens College, Manchester, Sydney Chapman, one of Marshall's pupils, succeeded another former pupil, Flux, as Jevons Professor, a chair created in 1899, and built up a faculty with support from the cotton industry. While it might seem as though Marshall had successfully colonised Manchester, the same could not be said of either Birmingham or LSE; and in all three places the atmosphere was distinctly and in some respects defiantly antagonistic to those traditions of liberal education that had developed at Oxford and Cambridge.

One side of Hobson, the failed classicist, might have been heartened by the modernity and down-to-earth qualities of these developments, though there was probably equal scope for some Hobson-style muckraking if he

---

[62] As he wrote to Sir Walter Prideaux, 7 July 1902: 'As regards my own connecton with the School, it is no doubt subject to misunderstanding. It is the most humiliating passage in my life, due simply to pecuniary necessity, the School having appropriated the whole of the public money out of which I was led to believe my chair would be endowed.' University of London, Special Collections, MS 790/77.

[63] The figures are taken from M. Sanderson, 'The English civic universities and the "industrial spirit", 1870–1914', *Historical Research*, 61 (1988), 90–104. See too his much larger study, *The universities and British industry, 1870–1981* (Liverpool: Liverpool University Press, 1981).

had shown more interest in provincial universities.[64] The 'millionaire endowments' he seems to have known most about were in the United States. Apart from a footnote on the likely effect on the teaching of colonial history at Oxford of the donations made by the South African financier, Alfred Beit, most of his comments on the effect on intellectual freedom of plutocratic sponsorship were of an a priori nature. He can hardly be blamed for following a tradition of being fixated on what was increasingly becoming the minority experience of Oxbridge. To those who were part of the system, however, and most especially to Marshall as he was assembling his case for an Economics tripos at Cambridge, the situation was troubling for other reasons. In 1902 he saw himself at sixty as an old man with no time to waste. The science to which he had devoted himself was 'drifting under the control of people like Sidney Webb' in London and under the influence of the Chamberlain family in Birmingham. In the sixteen years of his tenure of the Cambridge chair – as a result, he thought, of the restraints of the curriculum – he had not been able to attract, Chapman apart, 'one single high class man devoting himself to economics'.[65]

Marshall had to do battle for his proposals within Cambridge and publicise the benefits of the new tripos in the market he thought could most easily be tapped. This consisted of those 'who are proposing to devote their lives to the professional study of Economics', and secondly those who are looking forward to a career in the 'higher and more responsible positions in industrial and commercial life'.[66] In the first category there might be a few more, like Chapman and Layton, to add to Pigou and Maynard Keynes, who could conquer new academic worlds for Cambridge economics, or, as happened in Layton's case before he left to begin a career in the civil service and industry, remain there to teach the teachers of the future. But it was clearly in the second category that numbers were to be expected, hoped for at least. Here the emphasis had to be on '*higher* branches of business', where this contrasted with the 'technical training suitable for the lower ranks'. The latter kind of training was best left to other institutions who could supply it 'more easily, and with less harm to themselves than Oxford and Cambridge can'. Since Marshall privately despaired of Oxford's capacity to respond to the new situation, it would have to be at Cambridge where the next generation

[64] There was at least one prominent academic freedom case; see A. W. Coats, 'John Elliotson Symes, Henry George, and academic freedom in Nottingham during the 1880s' in *The sociology and professionalization of economics* (London: Routledge, 1993), pp. 289–312.
[65] Letter to J. N. Keynes, 30 January 1902, *Correspondence*, II, p. 352.
[66] *The new Cambridge curriculum in economics* (London: Macmillan, 1903), p. 22.

of captains (as opposed to non-commissioned officers) of industry was educated. Here, in a 'residentiary' setting, in addition to what their courses taught them, they would develop 'strength and sincerity of character'. Potential employers and parents would see 'how, on the river, and in the football field, the student learns to bear and to forbear, to obey and to command'.[67]

Leaving aside the almost ritual opposition that came from Cunningham, Marshall's main task was to keep his own increasingly fractious team (Foxwell and Neville Keynes) onside while obtaining suitable endorsements from leading figures in business, banking, and public life, using letters to *The Times* for publicity purposes and for fending off those who rudely pointed out that his Economics tripos seemed to lack some essential ingredients for a training in business, such as courses on accounting.[68] Although he eventually achieved his ambition by establishing a set of courses that allowed for specialisation in economics, he put great strain on the patience of those with whom he had dealings. After hearing some of the objections of his colleagues on the senate of Cambridge University to having to read or listen to the views of the prominent businessmen he had collected as external supporters, he gave them the following reminder (a materialistic one at heart) of the new and more competitive twentieth-century world in which they were now living:

if this University should refuse to do what business men required: if in return they should, as it was said they were already doing, tend more and more to send their sons to new Universities (even though thereby the glorious training of Oxford or Cambridge corporate life were lost); and if, in consequence, the rising generation of wealthy business men became the loyal sons of the newer and not the older Universities, then he thought this University might regret too late that it had seemed somewhat indifferent to the opinion of business men.[69]

Hobson professed not to be enamoured of Oxbridge privileges or impressed by the dignified pretensions of the liberal educational ideal. With his propensity to accept conspiracy theories he might have had a field day if he had heard or read how far Marshall was prepared to go in qualifying that ideal in his quest for a larger place in the Cambridge sun for economics.

---

[67] *Ibid.*, p. 17.

[68] See letters to *The Times*, 20 November, 14 and 27 December 1905, *Correspondence*, III, pp. 118–21.

[69] Speech to Senate, 7 May 1903, in *Correspondence*, III, p. 402. Marshall had predicted that Cambridge would continue to be 'money-starved' if it failed to make room for what businessmen wanted when unveiling his plan for a separate tripos in 1901; see letter to Foxwell, 8 May 1901, *Correspondence*, II, p. 315.

VIII

As it grew in authority and its finances were put on a sounder footing, the RES took on a number of roles in serving its clientele. From the outset it was understood that the clientele was not confined to those holding academic posts. In this respect economics differed somewhat from other academic groupings that were professionalising their activities at this time. Unlike its two predecessors and closest comparators, the *English Historical Review* and *Mind: A Quarterly Review of Psychology and Philosophy*, the *Economic Journal* had to address the needs of a penumbra of interested parties in the non-academic world that made more specific demands than the 'general reader'. The penumbra included bankers, businessmen, civil servants, clergymen, journalists, politicians, and trade unionists, all of them having knowledge and responsibilities as actors in the economic world. It followed that the *EJ* could not be aimed exclusively at a specialist academic readership, and that many of its contributors would be drawn from those whom William Ashley spoke of in gratitude as being 'unhampered by the duties of the professional teacher of economics'.[70] Those who contributed articles to the first two issues of the *EJ* convey some idea of the mixture that obtained in the pre-1914 period before the academics became an international guild numerous enough to dominate, though never to the complete exclusion of others. The academics constitute a majority, but only by adding foreign contributors (Gibbs, Mayo Smith, Taussig, and Wieser) to the domestic ones (Bastable, Cunningham, Munro, Nicholson, and Price). Civil servants are the next largest group (Burnett, Farrer, Giffen, Higgs, and Schloss), followed by politicians and journalists (Webb, Courtney, and Rae), with a Quaker banker-barrister-historian (Seebohm) to bring up the tail. Theoretical articles were decidedly in the minority, less prominent than articles on economic history and the history of economics. Half of the theoretical articles during this period were the work of a single person, the editor. Much of the journal's space was devoted to applied economics and official reports, notably in the field of industrial relations.[71]

---

[70] In his presidential address to Section F in 1907 he listed Frederick Seebohm, Charles Booth, Seebohm Rowntree, R. H. Inglis Palgrave, Sidney Webb, J. A. Hobson, Chiozza Money, and [?] Welsford as examples; see his 'Survey of the past history and present position of political economy', in Smyth (ed.), *Essays in economic method*, p. 243.

[71] See the essays by Alon Kadish and R. D. Freeman, John Maloney, Ian Steedman, Peter Newman, and Donald Moggridge in John D. Hey and Donald Winch (eds.), *A century of economics: 100 years of the Royal Economic Society and the Economic Journal* (Oxford: Blackwell, 1990).

No. I   *MARCH* 1891   Vol. I

THE

ECONOMIC JOURNAL

THE JOURNAL OF

The British Economic Association

EDITED BY

F. Y. EDGEWORTH

CONTENTS

London
MACMILLAN AND CO.
AND NEW YORK
1891

Price Five Shillings

Fig. 12. Two covers of the *Economic Journal*, March 1891 and June 1891.

No. 2   *JUNE* 1891   VOL. I

THE

ECONOMIC JOURNAL

THE JOURNAL OF

𝕿𝖍𝖊 𝕭𝖗𝖎𝖙𝖎𝖘𝖍 𝕰𝖈𝖔𝖓𝖔𝖒𝖎𝖈 𝕬𝖘𝖘𝖔𝖈𝖎𝖆𝖙𝖎𝖔𝖓

EDITED BY

F. Y. EDGEWORTH

𝕷𝖔𝖓𝖉𝖔𝖓

MACMILLAN AND CO.
AND NEW YORK

Publication of the *EJ* was the most important continuous activity of
the RES. For all its necessary eclecticism the journal offered an oppor
tunity to read the latest communications of economists and economic
historians free from the distracting heterogeneity of the 'generalist'

periodicals.[72] The proposal to form the association sent out by Marshall in 1890 accurately depicted the publishing niche to be filled:

Every other country in which economic studies are pursued with great activity, offers facilities for the publication of thorough scientific work by persons who have not the time, or are unwilling, to write a formal treatise. Since isolated pamphlets, however able, seldom obtain any considerable circulation, Englishmen who have something to say that is too technical for the ordinary magazines, and too short for a book are sometimes compelled to give their views to the world in the columns of a foreign periodical, or as a publication of the American Economic Association.[73]

Marshall might want an outlet for the specialist, but he was also more than usually knowledgeable on the economics of publishing generally, as his correspondence with Macmillan and Company over pricing and the status of his *Principles* as the first book to be published under the net book agreement indicates. In writing to Macmillan about the journal, Marshall justified its length by saying that since it aimed to have 'a clientele among the general public', it was necessary 'to give a fairly good quantity of print for our price, whatever that might be'. To expand sales he thought the journal should be available at newspaper shops, bookstalls, and circulating libraries.[74] His advice to Edgeworth on the contents of the journal centred mostly on the notes and memoranda section aimed at improving the quality of information available to readers on current economic developments. After all, as he said on one occasion, short memoranda were written because the author had something to report, 'whereas "Articles" are often written because some one wants to write an article', an activity Marshall made to sound like self-indulgence.[75] He was also uneasy about the policy of paying contributors (10 shillings per page for articles, 5 shillings per page for reviews), and made it clear that he would use whatever he was paid to benefit a wider public.[76]

By making the journal the main activity of the RES and entrusting its management to a paid editor Marshall secured another victory: over those who wanted to assemble a 'guarantee fund' and issue the journal as a

---

[72] As an indication of this, here are the titles of the articles that appeared beside Sidgwick's two earliest contributions to the *Fortnightly Review* 31 (1879) on 'Economic method' and on 'Money': 'Shall we give up Greek?'; 'The Loyal League: a Japanese romance'; 'Agricultural depression'; 'Matthew Arnold's address to the Ipswich Working Men's College'; 'The plain story of the Zulu war'; and 'Conventions at whist'.
[73] Letter to potential members, 24 October 1890, *Correspondence*, I, p. 343.
[74] Letter to Macmillan, 23 January (?June) 1891, Macmillan Archive, British Library.
[75] See e.g. letters to Edgeworth, 26 March 1895, January 1896, and 10 June 1896, *Correspondence*, II, pp. 123–4, 145, 169.
[76] See letters to Higgs, 27 March 1893 and 1 April 1898, *Correspondence*, II, pp. 93, 228.

private concern. This idea had been floated some years earlier when it was learned that Miller was prepared to allow the balance of his donation to the Industrial Remuneration Conference to be used to create an economic journal. That did not please Marshall for reasons connected with Miller's land nationalisation and socialist sympathies; it led him 'to fear that [Miller] might want more room for people like Wallace – to say nothing of Hyndman – than either Keynes or I shd think right'.[77] This can be read in two ways, only one of which fits Hobson's reductive suspicions. Marshall was anxious about loss of academic independence and catholicity as a result of Miller's socialist bias. Secondly, however, since he hoped at that time that the editorship would be accepted by Neville Keynes, he wanted a controlling body over which he could exercise some influence when making the appointment.

Having been tardy by American, French, and German standards in founding a dedicated journal, the British economics community, broadly conceived, acquired two in the space of a few months. Another group, the Oxford branch of the Christian Union, launched its own journal, the *Economic Review* (*ER*), in January 1891, pipping the *EJ* to the post by a couple of months (and, incidentally, charging 10 shillings per annum rather than the 'professional' guinea required for the *EJ*). The clerics may have had more speed and flexibility because they began with a more unified conception of how their journal would advance their goals as a Christian organisation. The economists faced the problem of having to reconcile widely differing expectations and cover a broader spectrum of intellectual approaches. Marshall gave a formal welcome to the *ER*, a welcome that was in turn thanked by the editors in their first issue. There was 'ample room', they said, for both ventures; they represented 'complementary points of view, and lay stress on different aspects of social life'. Both groups put the best face on a coincidence that could have been embarrassing in showing a divided front. Only Cunningham took positive pleasure in the potential embarrassment to Marshall's plans, playing up the division as one involving a long-standing contrast between Oxford's interest in the study of man and Cambridge's concern with things, an updated version of Toynbee's dichotomy between human beings and economists.[78]

---

[77] Letter to Foxwell, 26 July 1886, *Correspondence*, I, p. 213. Marshall correctly diagnosed Miller's support for Wallace's scheme of land nationalisation, see letters sent by Miller to Foxwell, 9 and 16 November 1883, Freeman collection.

[78] Presidential address to Section F, British Association for the Advancement of Science, 1891, *Report of proceedings*, pp. 723–34.

Marshall would have preferred the Oxford group to have chosen some such title as the *Journal of Social Reform* to emphasise the absence of direct competition between the two journals.[79] But whatever was said on this subject, there was bound to be overlap, partly because the *EJ*'s inclusive approach to economics was matched by the *ER*'s unwillingness 'to draw a sharp line between the spheres of the Economic Moralist and of the scientific Economist'.[80] Since most of the potential audience was to be found in the middle, it is not surprising that both journals aimed for that position. A hot topic in applied economics, such as the eight-hour day, would have to be covered by both journals. Socialism and co-operative enterprises occupy more space in the *ER*, but not by a large margin. Ashley and Cunningham, both having church affiliations, appear in both journals with articles on the history of economic thought. Over the longer term, however, the *EJ* published more articles in this field, possibly because the reference in the editorial programme of the *ER* to 'those who believe in the possibility of a body of Economic teaching based in large part on the labours of bygone Economists' was not exactly welcoming. The two journals did eventually cultivate separate audiences and lists of contributors that matched their different origins and aims; they also developed different international affiliations.[81] Interpreted crudely as a Darwinian struggle for survival, victory eventually went to the *EJ* when the *ER* became a casualty of the outbreak of war in 1914. Under the editorship of Maynard Keynes the *EJ* enjoyed an increase in the number of its subscribers that continued throughout the war and into the inter-war period. When he took over in 1911 the membership stood at 563, lower than the peak year of 1893–4 when it was 750. It regained this level in 1915 and rose steadily to 4,502 by the beginning of the Second World War. Before his death in 1946 Keynes had overseen an era in which it would not be hard to show that economic problems shaped the entire agenda of domestic and international affairs – very much, it has to be said, as Marshall had predicted when making the case for his Economics tripos before the First World War.

---

[79] Letter to L. R. Phelps, 31 October 1890, *Correspondence*, I, pp. 345–6.

[80] See the editorial programme in *Economic Review*, 1 (1891), 2.

[81] For discussion of the content of the *EJ*, see Keith Tribe, 'The *Economic Journal* and British economics, 1891–1940', *History of the Human Sciences*, 5, 4 (1992), 33–58. Some early results of work on the *Economic Review* can be found in Julien Vincent, 'The commerce of ideas: protectionism versus free trade in the international circulation of economic ideas in Britain and France around 1900', in C. Charle, J. Vincent, and J. Winter (eds.), *Anglo-French attitudes: comparisons and transfers between English and French intellectuals since the eighteenth century* (Manchester: Manchester University Press, 2007).

In the years that separate Mill's first attempts to capture the high moral ground for political economy from Marshall's efforts in the same cause, the period covered by these essays, the shift towards academic definitions of the task, and academic deployment of the troops required to carry it out, was the single most important change in their respective circumstances. Mill's *Logic* and *Principles* appeared on many student reading-lists in the English-speaking world, but the only academic post he ever held was an honorific one as Rector of St Andrews. It is by no means an insignificant fact too that in his *Principles* Mill called for state funding of universities on the basis of their contribution to the nation's cultural and scientific life; and that he discharged the duties of his honorary post by delivering a three-hour locution justifying a more liberal or non-vocational conception of higher education than anything Marshall's generation of struggling academic entrepreneurs could afford – almost literally – to uphold. State funding was a long way away in 1848 and not much closer in 1867 when the rectorial address was given. Alexander Bain, an academic friend of Mill who heard the address, was particularly scathing about Mill's tendency to dogmatise about universities 'in total ignorance of their working'.[82] Mill was not as meddlesome as Jevons believed. Nor was he indifferent to what was happening to political economy in universities. But what mattered to him was the state of the *public* mind on political economy and related matters of social policy. The state of the *academic* mind was subservient to that. In this respect, at least, Mill had more in common with some of the non-academic critics who have featured here: Ruskin and Mallet, even Hobson.

This points to complexities in the larger story. Just as there was no simple division between issues that were the province of political economy and those raised by its opponents – as the essays in this book have shown, topics, preoccupations, and values cut across this artificial dichotomy in various ways – so there was no straightforward contrast to be made between academic and non-academic contributors to economic debate, even though by the end of this period institutional and professional pressures were making themselves felt more strongly than they had in the middle of the nineteenth century. These complexities were already evident in the careers of Mill's two most faithful followers, Fawcett and Cairnes: both held professorial chairs, though neither could be said to

[82] For Mill's case for public funding, see *Principles*, CW, III, pp. 969–70. The address can be found in CW, XXI, pp. 215–57. For Bain's comments on Mill's ignorance of the realities of university life, see his *John Stuart Mill, a criticism* (London: Longmans, 1882), p. 46.

have altogether abandoned the public and political concerns of their
master. That was most obviously the case with Fawcett, whose tenure of
his Cambridge chair was no impediment to his successful parliamentary
career and who was widely regarded, by Cairnes, as well as others, as a
mere populariser. Cairnes's career followed what was to become the more
orthodox route, gaining his first academic appointment as holder of the
Whately chair at Trinity College, Dublin by competitive examination,
and following this by moving to other posts on the basis of the reputation
of his published work. None of this signalled a retreat from the public
domain: his book on the question of slavery, for example, was addressed to
(and reached) a wide non-specialist public during the American civil war.

Something similar might be said of Jevons, simultaneously a professor
and a public controversialist, as it clearly could for the historical economists, Cliffe Leslie, Cunningham, Hewins, and Ashley, all of whom
exhibited a strong commitment to the public deployment of economic
argument in support of their conception of a flourishing national polity.
And Sidgwick and Marshall, for all their differences of intellectual style
and character, both displayed an ambivalent attitude towards participation in wider public debate – increasingly concerned to maintain the
dignity and disinterestedness of their academic calling, though selectively
willing to deploy that authority in the public realm. In these respects,
Hobson was right to point to an enduring tension in providing an academic home for economics. The issues were still seen as too important to
become a purely professional or technical preserve. Toynbee's epigram-
matic formulation of the opposition between economists and human
beings was to prove an influential way for later critics to summarise much
of the history covered here; but it was nonetheless fundamentally misleading. In the continuing debates over wealth and life no one group had
an exclusive monopoly over either category.

Mr Gradgrind and Jerusalem

I

No sympathetic reader of Dickens's *Hard times* is likely to credit Mr Gradgrind with the ability to build Jerusalem among the dark satanic mills of Coketown. Dickens did not, of course, share William Blake's visions: his own version of Jerusalem would probably have been a cheerier, less corrupt, and more efficient version of the society in which he lived and prospered. Nevertheless, he certainly hoped that the combination of utilitarianism and political economy embodied in the Gradgrind caricature would provide his readers with a thought-provoking statement of the problems of life in the Coketowns of his day.[1] Judging by the legacy of the image he created, Dickens succeeded beyond his own intentions and inclinations.

By inscribing *Hard times* to Carlyle – the leading abominator of the worship of Mammon, the scourge of the 'cash nexus' and of the 'dismal science' that appeared to reflect or celebrate these features of modern life – Dickens was aligning himself with a powerful anti-utilitarian current in the debate on the 'condition-of-England' question. He did so effectively enough for Ruskin, a fellow admirer of Carlyle, to commend the novel to his own readers when he decided to unmask the fallacies of the soi-disant science of political economy in *Unto this last* (1862).[2] All three authors were still sufficiently in tune with one another to collaborate

---

[1] '[*Hard times*] contains what I do devoutly hope will shake some people in a terrible mistake of these days, when so presented. I know it contains nothing in which you do not think with me, for no man knows your books better than I.' Letter to Carlyle, 13 July 1854, in *The letters of Charles Dickens*, 10 vols. (Oxford: Clarendon Press, 1965–98), VII, p. 367.

[2] '[Dickens] is entirely right in his main drift and purpose in every book he has written; and all of them, but especially *Hard times*, should be studied with close and earnest care by persons interested in social questions.' First published in *Cornhill Magazine*, 1860, and repeated in *Unto this last*, 1862; see JRW, XVII, p. 31n.

in opposing the campaign to prosecute Governor Eyre in 1865–6. The campaign was being mounted by Mill and his 'radical' associates, and it provided Carlyle and Ruskin with an opportunity to repeat their criticisms of the canting qualities of the science with which Mill's name was then so firmly linked.[3] Dickens could also describe himself as a 'radical', and yet, as Humphrey House argued many years ago, there must be some doubt as to how firmly Dickens can be recruited into any intellectual grouping.[4] Having encapsulated, for his own purposes, the contrast between a utilitarian and what has come to be thought of as a 'romantic' outlook on life, Dickens was later found by his co-adjutors to be unequal to the task of drawing the right conclusions. Hence Ruskin's mature judgement that Dickens was 'a pure modernist – a leader of the steam-whistle party *par excellence*'.[5]

This problem invites the attention of the intellectual historian as well as of the literary scholar. It concerns the power of symbolic representations to define allegiances and form part of a canon that remains, if only by tireless repetition, a significant part of Our Island Story. Instead of returning directly to the nineteenth-century schism between romantics and utilitarians, the main focus of this essay will be on the legacy of the Gradgrind caricature during the second half of the twentieth century. For it was via a number of interpreters of that legacy that the original schism was transmitted to us, acquiring additional features in the process. The central figures chosen here to illustrate a highly influential mode of transmission are F. R. Leavis, Raymond Williams, and E. P. Thompson. Jerusalem can be linked with Gradgrind in their cases because each of them entertained earthly visions that could only be articulated by returning to the scene of nineteenth-century crimes – crimes of sentiment as well as intellect of the kind that Dickens sketched, however inadequately, in *Hard times*.

Dickens's inadequacy as standard-bearer for the causes later associated with *Hard times* can be detected in his treatment of Gradgrind himself. Not only was Dickens prepared to acknowledge the kindly instincts that lay beneath this 'man of facts and calculation', but he allowed him to undergo a painful process of redemption. In one of his suspiciously frequent attempts to mollify those who might take the caricature amiss, Dickens wrote: 'I often say to Mr Gradgrind that there is reason and good

---

[3] 'Radical' was Ruskin's term. For his charges against political economy during the campaign, see JRW, XVIII, pp. 437–45, 550–4.
[4] See *The world of Dickens*, 2nd edn (Oxford: Oxford University Press, 1942; reprinted 1960).
[5] Letter of 19 June 1870 written after Dickens's death; see JRW, XXXVII, p.7.

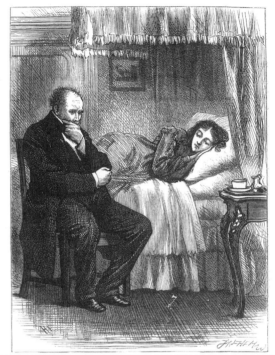

"I ONLY ENTREAT YOU TO BELIEVE, MY FAVOURITE CHILD, THAT I HAVE MEANT TO DO RIGHT."

Fig. 13. An illustration from Dickens's *Hard times* by Henry French.

intention in much that he does – in fact, in all that he does – but that he over-does it. Perhaps by dint of his going his way and my going mine, we shall meet at last at some half-way house.'[6] Far less forgiveness, far less willingness to believe that there were *any* halfway houses has been shown by twentieth-century readers who have accepted Gradgrind as the embodiment of a repellent mentality. With this came the catastrophic interpretation of Britain's experience of urban industrialisation, with political economy and utilitarianism being treated as complicit with the worst aspects of this experience. Gradgrind thus became a scapegoat for past errors and a persisting obstacle to any humane conception of a future social order, with the further implication that Jerusalem would be constructed on the high moral ground that stood above vulgar economic facts and calculations.

[6] Letter to Henry Cole, 17 June 1854, *Letters*, VII, p. 354.

As so often happens with caricatures, what Gradgrind has been taken to
symbolise has expanded to include dimensions Dickens could not have
envisaged and would probably have been alarmed to contemplate. The
commonest form of inflation has been the use of Coketown's MP, the
would-be social and educational reformer, as shorthand for any ruthless
Victorian employer, thereby confusing his role with that reserved for
Bounderby in the novel.[7] Retaining their separate identities enables two
other possibilities to be registered. First, by not preventing his daughter
Louisa from marrying the odious Bounderby, Gradgrind completes the
ruin of her life that began with her unimaginative education at his hands
at home. Secondly, the marriage can be taken as an emblem of union
between utilitarianism and industrial employers, thereby creating an alliance between an apologetic political economy and the interests of an
exploiting class. While the first of these possibilities belongs squarely
within the realm of Dickens's moral imagination, it is by no means clear
that the second does.

Mid twentieth-century interpreters, from F. R. Leavis onwards, have
been more confident in attributing broader ideological significance to the
marriage. Leavis regarded *Hard times* as 'the supreme document in cre-
ative literature, where Victorian utilitarianism and its part in Victorian
civilization are in question'.[8] As a consequence, perhaps, he judged the
Louisa–Bounderby marriage to be 'a just observation about the affinities
and practical tendency of utilitarianism'. The 'comprehensive vision' that
Dickens expressed for the first time in *Hard times* was 'one in which the
inhumanities of Victorian civilization are seen as fostered and sanctioned
by a hard philosophy, the aggressive formulation of an inhumane spirit'.[9]
Benthamism exemplified this 'indifference to essential human interests',
with 'disastrous consequences' for those interests.[10]

---

[7] For a surprising example, see Eric Hobsbawm's statement that: 'The indictment against early
nineteenth-century capitalism becomes no less black if we assume that every capitalist was like
Dickens' Brothers Cheeryble, and that there were no Gradgrinds at all.' 'History and the "dark
satanic mills"', as reprinted in his *Labouring men: studies in the history of labour* (London: Weidenfeld & Nicolson, 1964), p. 115.

[8] See his introduction to *Mill on Bentham and Coleridge* (London: Chatto & Windus, 1950), p. 34,
first published under the more informative title, 'Mill, Beatrice Webb and the "English School"',
Scrutiny, 15 (1949), 104–26.

[9] See *The great tradition* (London: Chatto & Windus, 1948), p. 228.

[10] *Mill on Bentham and Coleridge*, p. 31.

With the help of Elie Halévy's account of philosophic radicalism, Leavis identified the ancestry of utilitarianism as running from Newton to Adam Smith before being passed to Bentham. It constituted 'an important line of intellectual history' that achieved fruition in 'laissez-faire individualism'. Thus characterised, it could be connected, in quasi-Marxian fashion, with 'the classes associated with the expanding capitalist enterprise of eighteenth-century England' who regarded paternalistic forms of government as an obstruction to their interests. Having secured the Reform Act of 1832, the Benthamites and the middle classes they represented proceeded to oppose 'the sharing of its privileges and the reduction of its power'. Their most solid achievement was the new Poor Law of 1834, which became the

symbolic embodiment of all that was most rationally and righteously inhuman in orthodox utilitarianism, with its implacable Malthusian logic. Utilitarianism, in fact, provided the sanction for the complacent selfishness and comfortable obtuseness of the prosperous classes in the great age of Progress: they were protected by righteous rationality from the importunities of imaginative sympathy.[11]

Righteous rationality and imaginative sympathy provide the backdrop to Leavis's rehabilitation of *Hard times*, though in analysing the novel he concentrated more on the educational theme than the industrial ones. The Sleary circus embodies 'fancy' and 'wonder' in contrast to the sterile numeracy of the Gradgrind regime, providing a 'spectacle of triumphant activity that, seeming to contain its end within itself, is, in its easy mastery, joyously self-justified'.[12] A parallel insight by D. H. Lawrence is added immediately, and readers of Leavis would have recognised that what was being commended here was a version of George [Bourne] Sturt's *The wheelwright's shop* (1923), one of the classics chosen by Leavis and Denys Thompson for use in the teaching of English in schools in *Culture and environment: the training of critical awareness* (1933).

As a disillusioned Ruskinian socialist, reflecting on his experience in the 1880s, Sturt provided a direct link between nineteenth- and twentieth-century versions of the conflict between utilitarians and Romantics. Under the influence of Ruskin's *Fors clavigera*, Sturt had believed that 'man's only decent occupation was in handicraft'. Yet when he took charge of the wheelwright's shop, and attempted to run it along profit-sharing lines, without regard to cost estimates and what competitors could offer, neither his workmen nor his customers were willing to

[11] *Ibid.*, p. 34.   [12] *The great tradition*, p. 228.

collaborate with his 'Ruskinian absurdities'.[13] The book is, therefore, not merely an evocation of a world that was passing in the early years of the twentieth century, but a precise economic diagnosis of why the enterprise failed as a result of resistance to technological change and the encroachment of competitors on what had previously been a local monopoly. Unsurprisingly, this was not the side of Sturt's book that Leavis and Denys Thompson noticed; they saw it more as a 'memory of the old order' that could act as 'the chief incitement towards a new' – adding rather forlornly, 'if ever we are to have one'.[14] While recognising that there could be no return to a pre-machine age, Leavis consistently declined all challenges to delineate his own version of Jerusalem. Such a task was incompatible with the function of criticism. Yet by choosing to remain silent on the nature of the new order, Leavis's vision continued to be treated as nostalgic lament – much to its originator's annoyance.[15]

Some of the above is based on Leavis's introduction to Mill's essays on Bentham and Coleridge, a work intended as an extension of arguments mounted in *Education and the university: a sketch for an 'English school'* (1943). Mill's essays, plus the *Autobiography*, were commended as the kind of 'extra-literary' sources best calculated to broaden the study of nineteenth-century English literature at Cambridge. Indeed, Mill was favoured over the prose writings of Coleridge, Carlyle, and Ruskin, despite the 'enduring honour' attached to 'Ruskin's destructive analysis of orthodox political economy' – an analysis better read in Hobson's secondary account than in the original.[16] Notwithstanding 'the restrictive

---

[13] See *The wheelwright's shop* (Cambridge: Cambridge University Press, 1993), pp. 12, 53, 200.
[14] *Culture and environment* (London: Chatto & Windus, 1933), p. 97.
[15] Resistance to the demand to 'show our colours', whether coming from the left or right of the political spectrum, was defended in the 1930s; see for example 'Under which King, Bezonian?' in *Scrutiny*, 1 (1932), 205–14. Although Marxism was a prominent target for Leavis during this period, he did make one significant concession: 'Let me say, then, that I agree with the Marxist to the extent of believing some form of economic communism to be inevitable and desirable, in the sense that it is to this that a power-economy of its very nature points, and only by a deliberate and intelligent working towards it can civilisation be saved from disaster'; see *For continuity* (Cambridge: Minority Press, 1933), pp. 184–5. But the chief problem remained one of developing 'an autonomous culture, a culture independent of any economic, technical or social system as none has been before' (p. 168). What form 'economic communism' would take was never made clear, but the rejection of 'Morrisian archaizing' and 'garden-suburb handicraftiness' was sustained in *Nor shall my sword* (London: Chatto & Windus, 1972), pp. 81, 85; and the dislike of any nostalgic tag upheld in letters to the press; see *Letters in criticism by F. R. Leavis*, ed. J. Tasker (London: Chatto & Windus, 1974), pp. 100–1.
[16] *Mill on Bentham and Coleridge*, p. 36; see also J. A. Hobson, *John Ruskin, social reformer*, 3rd edn (London: J. Nisbet, 1904).

rigours of his father's educational experiment', Leavis judged Mill to be 'no unqualified Benthamite'. The encounter with Coleridge and Carlyle had made Mill a sensitive interpreter of the intellectual currents of his age. 'Technologico-Benthamite' became Leavis's compendium term for everything about the modern world that needed to be countered by the values embodied in his version of the 'English School'. More broadly, the campaign against technologico-Benthamism was Leavis's response to the cultural decline which had accompanied mass civilisation, a process that began with the industrial revolution and was continuing apace in the twentieth century. It is clear then that the niceties of Victorian intellectual history and of the benefits to be derived from extra-literary studies were merely part of that much larger battlefield on which, in 1962, Leavis was to confront C. P. Snow, the latest apologist for Gradgrind values. In dividing the world into two cultures, scientific and literary, Snow had characterised 'literary intellectuals' as Luddites in their attitude to the industrial revolution and the rising living standards associated with economic growth. *Nor shall my sword* (1972) brought Leavis's causes together by enlisting all his heroes, from Blake to Lawrence (while, incidentally, abandoning Carlyle, Ruskin, and Morris, those who *might* be guilty of Luddism), and by encompassing all those modernist enemies who were guilty of upholding 'statistico-egalitarian reductivism'.[17]

III

By then, however, Leavis's enhanced summation of the schism between Romantics and utilitarians had been taken up by others who can legitimately be described as his successors. Raymond Williams's *Culture and society* (1958) surveyed the 'traditional great debate' provoked by urban industrialisation from 1780 to 1950, taking in Leavis himself *en route*. *Hard times* was credited with an understanding of the 'dominant philosophy of industrialism', with some dubious real-life identifications of the objects of Dickens's satire being added. Whereas Leavis detected the grim presence of James Mill in the Gradgrind system of education inflicted on his son, Williams was 'certain that Dickens had the son's *Political economy*

---

[17] *Nor shall my sword*, pp. 107–8, 110, 119–20, 149, 151. On this phase of Leavis's career, see Stefan Collini, 'The critic as anti-journalist: Leavis after *Scrutiny*', in J. Treglown and B. Bennett (eds.), *Grub street and the ivory tower* (Oxford: Oxford University Press, 1998), pp. 151–76. On the Snow–Leavis debate, see Collini's introduction to the reprint of C. P. Snow, *The two cultures* (Cambridge: Cambridge University Press, 1993), pp. xxiii–xxv, xxix–xliii.

very much in mind in his general indictment of the ideas which built and maintained Coketown'.[18] Less enthusiastic than Leavis, however, Williams saw the novel merely as one of a number of its kind, 'more a symptom of the confusion of industrial society than an understanding of it', though he conceded that it was a significant symptom and, more vaguely, a 'continuing' one.

Culture and society owed much of its early success to its claim that recovery of a critical tradition could provide resources for a truly common culture that would incorporate working-class achievements based on the ideals of solidarity and community.[19] Williams rejected the 'Coleridgean' or minority view of culture, and with it those exclusively literary con- notations associated with Leavis's deployment of the great tradition. He also rejected the nostalgic and reactionary implications of the idea of a lost 'organic community' – a theme pursued in his other writings on the *Long revolution* (1961) and the *Country and the city* (1973). Jerusalem was still a vision to be actively pursued, or more accurately perhaps, to be pursued by political activists, provided they were unencumbered by the cultural pessimism and elitism associated with Leavis. After *Culture and society*, partly as a result of the resounding success of the book, Williams embarked upon a more overtly political career as leader of the left, mending his fences with the newer forms of Marxism that came into fashion in the late 1960s, though never with quite enough scientistic rigour to satisfy the zealots who entered New Left circles after 1968. The label accurately applied to Williams's early position was 'left Leavisism'.[20] Those who employed it on his Marxist left, however, were more dis- missive of Leavis, adding charges that Williams's modifications to the original continued to be tainted with a series of 'isms' that belonged to

---

[18] *Culture and society* (London: Penguin Books, 1961), p. 105. No evidence is cited in support of this certainty; the date given for publication of Mill's *Principles of political economy* is wrong; and the succeeding comment citing one of Mill's reactions to Dickens ('that creature') leaves the impression that this was Mill's response to *Hard times*, no evidence for which exists. The remark was in fact Mill's response to Dickens's ridicule of the 'rights of women' in an earlier novel, *Bleak house*; see letter to Harriet Taylor, 20 March 1854, CW, XVII, p. 190. He added that it was 'the only one of [Dickens's novels] I altogether dislike'; and his comment on the death of Dickens was that he regarded it as 'like a personal loss, even to those who only knew him by his novels'; see letter to Charles Eliot Norton, 26 June 1870, CW, XVII, p. 1740.

[19] For Williams's own retrospective view of *Culture and society*, see *Politics and letters: interviews with New Left Review* (London: Verso, 1979), pp. 97–132.

[20] Williams described the object of the journal he edited in 1947, also called *Politics and letters*, as being to 'unite radical Left politics with Leavisite literary criticism'; see *Politics and letters*, p. 65.

the polemics of new and old New Left politics at that time: romantic populism, moralism, subjectivism, culturalism, and literary idealism.[21]

E. P. Thompson, the figure who joined forces with Williams as the joint leader of the intellectual left in the early 1960s, was to be on the receiving end of similar criticisms, and his responses were much less conciliatory than those given by Williams.[22] In his own review of Williams's work Thompson regretted the absence of the element of 'struggle' in the idea of 'culture', speaking ironically of 'The Tradition' as 'a procession of disembodied voices' whose meanings had been 'wrested out of their whole social context'. This was a politer form of a more common Marxist charge, namely that Williams had paid insufficient attention to the class location and reactionary opinions of some of his bourgeois cast. What, for example, were such noted anti-progressives as Burke and Carlyle doing as part of The Tradition? Why had Williams evaded any encounter with Marx and Marxism, or indeed 'with an historian, an anthropologist, a sociologist of major stature'? Did that account for the impression that the forces at work behind the creation of the tradition were being treated impersonally? Thompson also asked why there were 'no good or bad men in Mr Williams' history, only dominant and subordinate "structures of feeling"'? No one could possibly charge Thompson with failing to make such moral discriminations in his own work. Nevertheless, these criticisms of Williams were 'comradely' in the best sense; they respected common aims and contained an insight into the differences between the trajectories of their respective autobiographies – Williams's journey from working class to middle class being, so to speak, reversed in Thompson's case.[23]

As a formative influence, they also had Leavis in common. Thompson drew attention to his own debt to Leavis in one of his last writings, an introduction to a reprint of Sturt's *The wheelwright's shop* published in 1993. Before he went up to Cambridge to read English he had been

[21] See, for example, T. Eagleton, 'Criticism and politics: the work of Raymond Williams', *New Left Review*, 95 (1976), 3–23.

[22] See especially the title essay and 'The peculiarities of the English', in *The poverty of theory, and other essays* (London: Merlin Press, 1978), written in 1978 and 1965 respectively. These essays can be compared with Williams's semi-apologetic answers to the questions posed by his New Left interviewers in *Politics and letters*.

[23] See Thompson's review of Williams's *Long revolution* in *New Left Review*, 9–10 (1961), 24–33, 34–9. Thompson later stated that the theoretical differences between his position and that of Williams at this time were so sharp that he wanted to be relieved of the reviewing task; see 'The politics of theory', in R. Samuel (ed.), *People's history and socialist theory* (London: Routledge & Kegan Paul, 1981), p. 398.

introduced to Sturt by a Leavisite school-teacher. Another of the bonds that linked Williams and Thompson was a shared interest in 'the Romantic critique of utilitarianism'.[24] This common preoccupation originated with Leavis and was nurtured by their apprenticeship as adult education teachers under WEA auspices. Unknown to each other, they both taught courses involving literature and history along Leavisian lines, with *Hard times* featuring among the romantic texts, and with *Culture and environment* providing a means of organising the teaching material.[25]

IV

Gradgrind certainly became early mental shorthand for Thompson. The opening chapter of his first book, *William Morris*, is entitled 'Sir Launcelot and Mr Gradgrind'. It was published in 1955, a year before Thompson left the Communist Party over the Soviet invasion of Hungary. Although there are interesting differences between the original and revised editions, the portrait of Gradgrind serves the same purpose: to introduce the enemy Morris found it necessary to combat. Thompson's praise for *Hard times* as a portrait of the enemy is a magnified version of Leavis, but with the same overtones of class conspiracy when speaking of political economy and the Victorian bourgeoisie:

Dickens's picture may be a caricature: but it is of the best order of caricature, which delineates the essential lines of truth. Mr Bounderby, the coarse and avaricious mill-owner of *Hard times*, was giving way to his more sophisticated cousin, Mr Gradgrind. Gradgrind not only has power and wealth: he also has a theory to justify and perpetuate exploitation. The Victorian bourgeoisie had constructed from bits of Adam Smith and Ricardo, Bentham and Malthus a cast-iron theoretical system, which they were now securing with the authority of the State and the Law, and sanctifying with the blessings of Religion. The laws of supply and demand were 'God's laws', and in all the major affairs of society all other values must bend before commodity values.[26]

---

[24] See Postscript to *William Morris: romantic to revolutionary* (London: Merlin Press, 1976), p. 769.
[25] For studies of what both Thompson and Williams taught during these years, see P. Searby and the editors on 'Edward Thompson as a teacher: Yorkshire and Warwick', in J. Rule and R. Malcolmson (eds.), *Protest and survival: the historical experience* (London: Merlin Press, 1993), pp. 1–23. On Williams, see R. Fieldhouse, 'Oxford and adult education', in W. J. Morgan and P. Preston (eds.), *Raymond Williams: politics, education, letters* (Basingstoke: Macmillan, 1993); and F. Inglis, *Raymond Williams* (London: Routledge, 1995), ch. 6. The contribution of Williams to adult education, and its contribution to his own work, is dealt with in L. Goldman, *Dons and workers: Oxford and adult education since 1850* (Oxford: Oxford University Press, 1995), pp. 286–98.
[26] *William Morris*, pp. 8–9.

Although Thompson's next book on *The making of the English working class* (1963) ends with the class having made itself by the early 1830s, twenty years before Dickens's delineation of the 'essential lines of truth', utilitarianism and political economy provide an antithesis to the main thrust of that story as well. It is not surprising then that the spontaneous pleasures of the working class, instanced by the 'circus folk' in *Hard times*, make a brief appearance, and that Gradgrind himself was judged to be 'most certainly out and about after 1815'.[27] As the insensitive spokesman 'for efficiency, cheap centralised government, laissez faire, and sound "political economy"', his entry on the scene predated the triumph of British capitalism after 1851. There was more than a hint, however, that Gradgrind might have been deprived of victory if things had turned out differently after the crucial period covered by Thompson's book. In its peroration he stressed the fact that the class whose fortunes he had traced 'suffered the experience of the Industrial Revolution as articulate, free-born Englishmen' whose consciousness had been forged, Burkean fashion, over several centuries. They had even achieved a temporary victory in the struggle 'between a capitalist and a socialist political economy' while 'Marx was still in his teens'. Here the native heroes were men such as Thomas Hodgskin and others who articulated a truly working-class version of the science. As a result of the 'collective self-consciousness' formed during the industrial revolution, where they 'met utilitarianism in their daily lives' – the ideology of their employers – they had 'fought, not the machine, but the exploitive and oppressive relationships intrinsic to industrial capitalism'. The characteristic independence of the artisan had gradually given way to a sense of 'community' and 'cooperation' adapted to the new conditions of production and capable of resisting the 'blind operation of the market-economy'.[28]

At the end of this tribute to the native working-class tradition, however, attention was drawn to that other theme in the book, 'the great Romantic criticism of utilitarianism' which was 'running its parallel but altogether separate course'. The finale is worth recalling because it contains much that signals Thompson's own interest in the Romantics and working-class consciousness – a theme that parallels Williams's *Culture and society*. Since nobody could doubt that Thompson was active in the continuing historical processes he was recounting, the importance of

---

[27] *The making of the English working class* [hereafter MEWC] (London: Penguin Books, 1968), pp. 64, 376.
[28] *Ibid.*, p. 913.

straddling these two worlds was as important to him as it was to his historical protagonists.

After Blake no mind was at home in both cultures, nor had the genius to interpret the two traditions to each other. It was a muddled Mr Owen who offered to disclose the 'new moral world', while Wordsworth and Coleridge had withdrawn behind their own ramparts of disenchantment. Hence these years appear at times to display, not a revolutionary challenge, but a resistance movement, in which both the Romantics and the Radical craftsmen opposed the annunciation of Acquisitive Man. In the failure of the two traditions to come to a point of junction, something was lost. How much we cannot be sure, for we are among the losers.[29]

The references to the self-taught 'culture of the craftsman' which precede this ending, and the emphasis on a lost sense of community before work and life were set asunder by 'violent technological differentiation', echo Leavisian (Sturtian) values, with Blake and D. H. Lawrence continuing to act, as they did for Leavis, as sources of inspiration. This could account too for the fact that, when faced with Williams's critique of Leavis's lament over urban industrialism (instead of the real enemy, capitalism) in *Country and the city*, Thompson felt that Williams 'could have looked more scrupulously than he does at the values at stake in that central Leavisite text, George Sturt's *The wheelwright's shop*'.[30] Moreover, Thompson's defence of these values, on this occasion and later, bears a distinct family resemblance to the one originally given by Leavis himself.[31] The 'disenchantment' of the Lake poets after the failures of the French revolution reminds the reader of Thompson's interest in Wordsworth and Coleridge, and of his frankness in hinting at the parallels with his own experience in breaking with the Communist Party.[32]

An interesting analysis of Thompson's narrative style by Renato Rosaldo has drawn attention to its Dickensian qualities, whereby the reader is moved 'more by the sentimental heroics of victimization than by the heroics of superhuman feats'. It is a form of melodrama that invites

---

[29] *Ibid.*, p. 915.

[30] 'A nice place to visit' (a review of Williams's *Country and the city*), *New York Review of Books*, 6 February 1975, reprinted in *Persons and polemics* (London: Merlin Press, 1994), pp. 244–55.

[31] *Ibid.* 'It may . . . be seen as a vast reserve of unrealized, or only partially achieved, possibilities – a past that gives us glimpses of other possibilities of human nature, other ways of behaving (even "organic" ones)'.

[32] See MEWC, especially pp. 103–4, 109, 172, 180–1, 192–3, 243, 378–9. The reference to those 'exposed to similar experiences of revolutionary disenchantment in the past twenty-five years' (p. 109) is echoed more movingly in the distinction Thompson made between disenchantment and apostasy in 'Disenchantment or default? A lay sermon', in C. C. O'Brien and W. D. Vanech (eds.), *Power and consciousness* (London: University of London Press, 1969), pp. 149–81.

the reader 'to take sides in Manichaean battles between virtue and vice', with the consequence that they 'enter a field of combat where the middle ground has been eroded'.[33] Methodism is the best-known casualty of this approach, but the same can be said for that other pair of enemies, utilitarianism and political economy. On occasions the two targets are combined, as when Dissenters are found to be addicted to 'the dogmas of free trade': hence the permeation of the movement 'by the values of enlightened self-interest which led on, in such a man as Francis Place, to the acceptance of a limited Utilitarian philosophy'.[34] As the organiser and annalist of the London Corresponding Society, Place has an important part in Thompson's story. His career becomes a moral tale about what happens when self-educated working men betray their class by allowing the 'self-respecting virtues' to lead them in a Malthusian and Benthamite direction, especially when compared with men of firmer resolve such as Thomas Hodgskin.[35] Having been given an early warning of the fatal defect in Place's character, the reader is prepared to be told that he was sitting for 'his own portrait as the White Man's Uncle Tom', with James Mill as his portraitist.[36] Although Place is credited with repeal of the Combination Acts, his motives are judged to be tainted by political economy.[37]

That there could be no middle ground on which any genuine leader of working-class opinion could stand in the struggle between capital and labour was an orthodox Marxian conclusion, though if Marx had been Thompson's actual source he might have had to consider why Ricardo was exempted from the 'vulgar' category of defenders of capital. Thompson did accept, however, that Place, Ricardo's pupil, represented a 'new phenomenon' by virtue of his vain attempt to make utilitarianism the 'ideology of the working class'. Why in vain? Because 'it is scarcely possible to think of middle-class utilitarianism without thinking also of Malthus and of orthodox political economy', with the result that: 'If utilitarianism was to enter working-class ideology it would make it captive to the employing class.'[38] Once more, then, we have returned to Leavis's Gradgrind with Marxian emphases.

---

[33] 'Celebrating Thompson's heroes: social analysis in history and anthropology', in H. J. Kaye and K. McClelland (eds.), *E. P. Thompson: critical perspectives* (Cambridge: Cambridge University Press, 1990), pp. 103–24.
[34] MEWC, p. 58.
[35] *Ibid.*, p. 63. For the contrast between Place and Hodgskin, see pp. 569, 818, 854–7.
[36] *Ibid.*, p. 170. Readers of the unrevised version, before 1968, would have had even less doubt: 'Trusty Nigger' appeared instead of 'Uncle Tom'.
[37] *Ibid.*, pp. 567–9.   [38] *Ibid.*, p. 850.

V

Another of the orthodoxies that Thompson sought to counteract was
Fabian versions of the history of the labour movement. Despite his
admiration for the work of J. L. and Barbara Hammond, he lumped them
together with Graham Wallas and Beatrice and Sidney Webb as 'men and
women of Fabian persuasion'.[39] As was the case with Wallas after 1904,
the Hammonds were, in fact, 'New Liberals' – another sign, perhaps, of
Thompson's indifference to distinctions between those occupying the
middle ground.[40] Nevertheless, he was generous in defending the Hammonds against common enemies, as can be seen in his spirited defence of
their catastrophist interpretation of the industrial revolution. Thompson
upheld their findings against the 'empiricist orthodoxy' of those twentieth-
century successors of Gradgrind's calculating mentality, the authors of
revisionist economic history based more on the statistics of living conditions
than on qualitative evidence.[41] A characterisation of the conflict between
some working-class perceptions and political economy in the late eighteenth and nineteenth centuries, therefore, exactly prefigures the ongoing
battle against their twentieth-century successors.

Although Thompson regarded the Hammonds' *Skilled labourer* (1919)
as a book of 'outstanding importance', he rejected their 'Fabian' tendencies
when dealing with Luddism. On matters of broad intellectual history,
however, when diagnosing the bourgeois mind during the nineteenth
century, he drew deeply on a chapter on 'The mind of the rich' in the
Hammonds' *Town labourer* (1914).[42] In the retelling, however, the story
acquired a different complexion. For the Hammonds, the chapter forms
an essential part of their story of 'resignation' by the 'governing classes' in
the face of catastrophe, a process aided by *selective* use and misunderstanding of the teachings of political economy by the property-owning
classes (landowners as well as capitalist employers), leaving aside those
parts that carried uncomfortable conclusions during a period when fears
of the contagion of the French revolution were at their height. They also
acknowledged that the policies recommended by political economists –
abolition of the Corn Laws, cheap and efficient government, and the
extension of the suffrage – were matters of concern for the poor. Thompson's

[39] *Ibid.*, p. 647.
[40] On the political affiliations and sympathies of Wallas and the Hammonds, see P. Clarke, *Liberals and social democrats* (Cambridge: Cambridge University Press, 1978).
[41] MEWC, pp. 213–15, 226–38, 366–7, 370–5, 916, 934.
[42] Chapter 10; for Thompson's use of this chapter, see MEWC, pp. 376ff.

account has no room for such qualifications, and his treatment of the 'conscience of the rich', the title of the next chapter in the Hammonds' book, concentrates less on evangelicalism and dissent as humanitarian sources (dissent had already suffered an 'appalling declension' in its social conscience) than on the 'cultural mutation' to be found in 'Tory paternalism' and the 'disappointed Romanticism' of Wordsworth and Southey. Hence it is between Jacobin and Tory that 'sparks of feeling and of argument are continually exchanged', and they do so across the bleak middle space occupied by all political economists (save Hodgskin and other 'Ricardian' socialists), reformers such as Brougham and Chadwick, the Methodists and the Mechanics' Institutes, Whigs like Macaulay, treacherous ex-radicals such as Place, Wade, and Edward Baines proved to be, and naïve apologists for technological progress, of which Andrew Ure was the best-known example.[43]

Thompson also made use of the work of a close friend of the Hammonds, Tawney's *Religion and the rise of capitalism* (1926), but did not tar him with the Fabian brush, despite his early connections with the Fabian Society. He endorsed the Weber–Tawney account of 'the interpenetration of the capitalist mode of production and the Puritan ethic'; and noted Tawney's linkage of puritan dogmas with arguments, especially on the subject of work discipline, bringing Methodism in as the prime manifestation of this alliance in the nineteenth century. But it may be more significant that Tawney's account of paternalist legislation in the period before the Church retreated in the face of the market and its secular apologists enabled Thompson to appreciate 'the shadowy image of a benevolent corporate state' that was being dismantled by the advocates of *laissez-faire* individualism in the nineteenth century.[44] Despite its restrictive and punitive features, this corporate state, with its 'legislative as well as moral sanctions against the unscrupulous manufacturer or the unjust employer', prefigures Thompson's work on food riots and the decline of a 'moral economy' in the face of Smith's political economy during the eighteenth century.[45] The handloom weavers and Luddites in *Making of the English working class*, like the organisers of food riots earlier, were performing a rearguard action against market imperatives and in favour of those paternal-deference relationships that had previously protected them.

[43] *Ibid.*, p. 379.   [44] *Ibid.*, p. 594.
[45] See 'The moral economy of the English crowd in the eighteenth century', originally published in *Past and Present* in 1967, later included in *Customs in common* (London: Merlin Press, 1991), pp. 185–258.

Thompson does not refer to Tawney's *Acquisitive society* (1921), the more overt political companion to his historical work on *Religion and the rise of capitalism*, but the reference to 'acquisitive man' noted earlier sounds very much like a nod in its direction. Tawney, no friend of the economics of his own day, also made no secret of his dislike for 'the melancholy mathematical creed of Bentham and Ricardo and James Mill'.[46] The clear moral echoes of Ruskin in Tawney's writings earned him a place between Lawrence and T. S. Eliot in Williams's account of the twentieth-century continuators of the great tradition. For his pioneering role in relation to the WEA alone, Tawney could have expected a sympathetic hearing from Thompson and Williams, but the fact that he provided a direct link in the chain connecting them with those who had taken a moral stand against the injustices of capitalist society during the nineteenth century sealed their allegiance.

Leavis was entitled to similar honours from both men. He had discerned the significance of the anti-utilitarian element in English literature from Blake to Lawrence, and had used similar sources – Ruskin, Hobson, and the Hammonds – when painting the historical background. Despite his own later rapprochement with Marxism, Williams was never as enthusiastic in his denunciation of Leavis as the newer literary-critical recruits to Marxism on his left became. It is a sign too of Thompson's generosity in recognising allies in a continuing struggle that he included a reference to the Snow–Leavis exchanges which occurred the year before *Making of the English working class* appeared.[47]

As Thompson later made clear, his book was engaged in two polemics. The first was against a tradition 'contaminated with capitalist ideology' that ran from Smith to modern economic history; and the second was 'against abbreviated economistic notions of Marxism', according to which the working class were 'processed into so many yards of class-conscious proletarians'.[48] While the former polemic occupies the surface, more inside knowledge was required to detect undercurrents of the latter – until, that is, Thompson took up cudgels against his 'structuralist' Marxist critics in defence of his version of socialism with a human face that was

---

[46] See *The acquisitive society* (London: Fontana, 1961), p. 21.

[47] 'When Sir Charles Snow tells us that "with singular unanimity . . . the poor have walked off the land into the factories as fast as the factories could take them", we must reply, with Dr Leavis, that the "actual history" of the "full human problem [was] incomparably and poignantly more complex than that".' MEWC, p. 486. Gareth Stedman Jones informed me that Thompson presented a copy of the book to Leavis, drawing attention to specific points of agreement. This copy was on sale in Cambridge in the early seventies.

[48] See *Visions of history*, ed. H. Abelove *et al.* (Manchester: Manchester University Press, 1983), pp. 6–7.

also peculiarly English. Although the real heroes and villains emerge clearly enough, the retrospective account of the targets does not prepare the reader for Thompson's reliance upon and generosity towards some of his 'Fabian' sources. In the end, of course, these have to be condemned for their middle-class assumptions and, more importantly, for their essential continuity with utilitarianism. Thompson here was able to call upon his work on Morris and the conflict between the Social Democratic Federation and the newly-formed Fabian Society in the 1880s. No-one who had read Thompson's account of this period, especially that given in the first edition of his book, would have any doubt that he too condemned the Fabian strategy for its rejection of revolutionary class struggle in favour of parliamentary gradualism and municipal socialism, and for its identification of socialism with state action.[49]

Williams and Thompson were not in contact with one another when writing their early books; there are no references to Thompson's work in Williams's *Culture and society*; and their assessments of Morris's contribution to the traditions that interested them varied. Nevertheless, though with less certainty than he was later to command, Williams cast some doubt on the Fabian position in the short section devoted to Bernard Shaw and the Fabians. He had wondered – without, one suspects, any genuine surprise at the likely answer – 'what a typical Fabian feels when he is invited to condemn Gradgrind, not as an individual but as a type'. Since Sidney Webb was 'the direct inheritor of the spirit of John Stuart Mill', the reader was being reminded that Mill had been shown to be capable only of an 'intellectualist' appreciation of culture, an inadequate form of 'humanized' utilitarianism. Shaw may have been capable of seeing something deeper at stake, but in becoming a Fabian he was 'telling Carlyle and Ruskin to go to school with Bentham'.[50] When Williams and Thompson combined forces, notably in producing the *May Day manifesto* (1966, revised in 1968), this earlier conviction that the labour movement had taken a wrong historical turning became the basis for what they condemned as 'Labourism', the flaw that had led successive post-war Labour governments to abandon real socialism.[51]

Here too there is a parallel with Leavis's long-standing opposition to the Bloomsbury and Fabian attitudes to literary culture which he

---

[49] See *William Morris*, pp. 499–506, 537–41, 577, 607–8, 682, 726. Starker judgements on Fabianism are passed in the 1955 edition, see pp. 586, 630–1, 667.

[50] *Culture and society*, pp. 79, 105, 183–4.

[51] For Williams's criticism of the Fabian influence on Labour, see *Resources of hope: culture, democracy, socialism*, ed. R. Gable (London: Verso, 1989), pp. 68–70, 74–5, 138.

associated with H. G. Wells: he had damned it by equating it with
'Babbitry' and the Americanisation of English life and popular culture.[52]
Similar anti-American sentiments were expressed by Thompson when he
was still a member of the Communist Party.[53] His enduring contempt for
the Fabian position can be detected in his dismissal of Richard
Wollheim's pamphlet on *Socialism and culture* (1961) for its 'sustained
mediocrity'; it reminded him that 'Fabians too could draw upon a long
heritage of literary criticism' instanced by Bentham's view of poetry as
prose that did not reach the edges of the page.[54]

There is also a link with Leavis's commentary on the ironies of Beatrice
Webb's career. Her autobiography was praised for its perceptive account
of her early life, and for its recognition that novels were a more satisfying
source of insight into her own society than she could derive from the
literature of social science.[55] As enemy of the technologico-Benthamite
tendencies of the modern world, however, Leavis pointed out that she had
ended her career by endorsing Soviet communism. In attempting to escape
from the 'unchastened individualism' of her Benthamite upbringing,
therefore, she had only succeeded in giving her blessing to 'that endless
growth in the range and complexity of state organization and bureaucratic control which makes the individual feel so helpless and so insignificant in the modern world'.[56]

For his own reasons, Thompson too had abandoned belief in Soviet
forms of communism, and had exposed the reductive tendencies of the
orthodox Marxist approach to literature in a manner that has a family
resemblance to Leavis's strictures in the 1930s and 40s. The experience of
'disenchantment' with Soviet-style communism underlines Thompson's

---

[52] See 'Babbit buys the world' and 'D. H. Lawrence and Professor Irving Babbit', in *For continuity*.
The first of these essays attacks H. G. Wells (and, incidentally, J. M. Keynes, for praising Wells's
William Clissold). Opposition to Americanisation continued in *English literature in our time and
the university* (London: Chatto & Windus, 1969), pp. 24, 33–5, 180–2; and in *Nor shall my sword*,
pp. 133, 149, 159, 184–5.

[53] Thus, having recounted a meeting with an American professor with crass materialist ambitions, he
wrote: 'The "American dream" really is as childish and as debased as this and its poison can be
found in every field of American life. Those who have never been to the United States and who
fool themselves . . . that Hollywood, the Hearst Press and the comics, represent only a lunatic
fringe of the American bourgeoisie, sometimes suggest that *Babbit* is an out-of-date joke on the
'twenties: unfortunately it only foreshadows the horror of today.' See 'William Morris and the
moral issues today', *Arena*, 2 (1951), June–July, 25.

[54] On Wollheim, see 'The long revolution', *New Left Review*, 9 (1961), 36.

[55] Though, as John Gross pointed out, the novels appreciated by Beatrice Webb were not ones that
figure in the Leavis canon; see *The rise and fall of the man of letters* (London: Penguin Books, 1973),
p. 301.

[56] *Mill on Bentham and Coleridge*, p. 27.

message to left activists on the subject of law – a message that informs his later work as historian. As a member of the Communist Party he had rejected talk about 'human rights' as the cover under which public opinion was turned against the Soviet Union, China, and the 'new democracies' being formed behind the Iron Curtain.[57] During the last two decades of his life, however, he advanced a highly sophisticated argument to show why the rule of law mattered to socialists, given 'the historical evidence of this century of the appalling powers a socialist state, or a so-called socialist state, can acquire'.[58]

Whigs and hunters (1975) became the place where Thompson worked out his position on this most effectively, concluding that law was 'a true and important cultural achievement of the agrarian and mercantile bourgeoisie, and of their supporting yeomen and artisans'.[59] It provided a language and other resources that could never be entirely subverted and converted to its own use by the rich and privileged. Together with *Customs in common*, Thompson's incursion into the Walpole decades of the eighteenth century in *Whigs and hunters* enabled him to locate the origins of Tory paternalism in the nineteenth century and to break through to the point where his earlier work on the English Jacobins in the 1790s had begun. It can also be seen as a search for other versions of the Sturtian community embodied in 'custom' and 'culture' before the industrial revolution produced a new set of antagonisms. Expressed in Marxist terms, it was still an inquiry into communities where 'use-values' rather than 'commodity-values' dominated.

But if one had to label the direction in which Thompson journeyed in the final part of his career, it would probably be as much towards anthropology as law. And here again there is a link with Leavis: their common concern with the world of 'custom', especially rural custom, the world destroyed by the industrial revolution, licensed a search for societies in which Sturtian values continued to prevail. Anthropology was one of the social sciences towards which Leavis was tolerant: it held a favoured place among the 'extra-literary' inquiries he encouraged, and those of his pupils who took up this discipline did so with his blessing – though it

---

[57] 'And (since the old lie that Socialism "can't work" was shattered for good when the Red Army routed the Nazis at Stalingrad) it is under cover of the same talk about "human rights" and so on that they try to turn the minds of the people of Britain and America against the Soviet Union, China and the new democracies'; see 'William Morris and the moral issues today' (p. 28).

[58] *Visions of history*, p. 9. See also his defence of the English jury system against the usual Marxist charge that it represented only 'bourgeois liberty' in *Writing by candlelight* (London: Merlin Press, 1980), pp. 165–71.

[59] *Whigs and hunters* (London: Penguin Books, 1990), p. 265.

came with a 'noble savage' notion of what could be learned from studying 'primitive' cultures.[60] Thompson's approach to anthropology was often critical, but it was based on a deeper understanding than Leavis's. His return to the eighteenth century involved rediscovery of the folklorist tradition and concentration on the symbolic interest attached to criminal punishment and such practices as 'rough music' and wife-sale.[61] Nevertheless, Thompson, while confessing to a weakness for the archival research which this entailed, never relinquished his claims to be addressing the pressing problems of his own day. In *Customs in common* these were identified as the North–South divide and the 'ecological catastrophe' being wrought by economic man. As in the case of Leavis's 'new order', he admitted that there could never be 'a return to a pre-capitalist human nature'. Historical-cum-anthropological studies such as his own could still serve, however, as 'a reminder of its alternative needs, expectations and codes'; they might therefore 'renew our sense of our nature's range of possibilities'.[62] Gradgrind's dominion, now extended to the globe, could still be resisted, if only by drawing attention to societies in which his economistic notions either did not prevail or could be counteracted.

VI

The above sketch of how a nineteenth-century schism was given renewed relevance by some leading mid twentieth-century partisans of the Romantics is no more than that. It certainly does not pretend to be an adequate account of the intellectual biographies of those mainly responsible. Nevertheless, a good case could be made for the significance of the episode to the cultural and political history of Britain. That my three authors generated large followings is reflected by the bio-bibliographical industries begun since their deaths (Leavis in 1978, Williams in 1988, and Thompson in 1993).[63] Singly and in combination, then, they provided a potent

---

[60] Former Leavis pupils who became anthropologists were: Paul Baxter, Godfrey Lienhardt, Malcolm Ruel, David Pocock, and R. O. C. Winkler. Leavis's lack of appreciation can be judged perhaps from a single question posed in *Nor shall my sword*, to which only one answer seems possible: 'Who will assert that the average member of a modern society is more fully human, or more alive, than a Bushman, an Indian peasant, or a member of one of those poignantly surviving primitive peoples, with their marvellous art and skills and vital intelligence?' (p. 60).

[61] See 'Anthropology and the discipline of historical context', *Midland History*, 1, 3 (1972), 41–55; and 'Folklore, anthropology, and social history', *Indian Historical Review*, 3 (1978), 247–66.

[62] *Customs in common*, p. 15.

[63] See, for example, C. Baldick, *The social mission of English criticism, 1848–1932* (Oxford: Oxford University Press, 1983) and *Criticism and literary theory, 1890 to the present* (London: Longmans, 1996); and Francis Mulhern, *The moment of 'Scrutiny'* (London, 1979). For broader appraisals, see

means by which an interpretation of the industrial revolution, with its inescapable mixture of myth and reality, has been appropriated and diffused.

The story clearly has special resonances for historians of the British left and those concerned with the cultural mission of English literature, but the significance extends beyond these communities. Complementary stories can and have been told about the industrial revolution as social catastrophe. But for those who are not primarily concerned with the fate of literary criticism or even with the social and economic history of Britain, other questions can be posed. Does the story support and is it supported by what we know about Victorian intellectual life? And how should we, as denizens of the early twenty-first century, come to grips with the original schism between romantics and utilitarians? There can be no easy routes through such treacherous, because well-trodden, territory. In what follows I will chiefly seek to raise some questions future travellers may need to bear in mind.

An obvious objection should be countered at the outset. None of the figures with whom I have been concerned would have claimed that intellectual history was their main interest; they wrote as cultural and literary critics, social historians, or political theorists and activists, or some combination of all these things. Nevertheless, each of them found it necessary to advance or borrow ambitious versions of nineteenth-century intellectual history to support their case. Of my three authors, Thompson was the one most acutely aware of, and frequently exasperated by, the criticisms of intellectual historians.[64] As Marilyn Butler has shrewdly observed, however, Thompson could be 'ultra-suspicious of tendencies which most tempt him'.[65] His criticisms of the 'disembodied' nature of

---

Rule and Malcolmson (eds.), *Protest and survival*; B. D. Palmer, *E. P. Thompson: objections and oppositions* (London: Verso, 1994); Harvey J. Kaye, *The British Marxist historians: an introductory analysis* (Cambridge: Cambridge University Press, 1984); and *The education of desire: Marxists and the writing of history* (London: Routledge, 1992). See also A. O'Connor, *Raymond Williams* (Oxford: Blackwell, 1989); G. McCann, *Theory and history: the political thought of E. P. Thompson* (Aldershot: Ashgate, 1997); and N. Stevenson, *Culture, ideology and socialism: Raymond Williams and E. P. Thompson* (Aldershot: Avebury, 1995). To this can be added J. McIlroy and S. Westwood (eds.), *Border country: Raymond Williams in adult education* (Leicester: National Institute of Adult Education, 1993).

[64] See especially the answers to A. W. Coats and Istvan Hont and Michael Ignatieff in 'Moral economy reviewed', in *Customs in common*, pp. 268–87. Williams's *Keywords* (London: Croom Helm, 1976) was subjected to close scrutiny by Quentin Skinner in 'The idea of a cultural lexicon', *Essays in criticism*, 29 (1979), 205–24, and his response was simply to make a number of unannounced changes to later editions; see Inglis, *Raymond Williams*, pp. 245–8.

[65] 'E. P. Thompson and the uses of history', *History Workshop Journal*, 39 (1995), 73.

the Williams version of The Tradition are essentially those of an intellectual historian, and he showed himself to be no mean exponent of stratospherically 'high' intellectual history when defending British empiricism later.[66] Thompson was also the one who most often found it necessary to engage with intellectual history for reasons partly connected with his interest in biography (Blake as well as Morris), but largely by virtue of the very nature of his enterprise, recapturing the consciousness of the past for the purposes of rescuing his chosen protagonists from 'the enormous condescension of posterity'.[67] The antagonists too were owed no less, though it was not Thompson's duty to undertake a task he believed had been only too well performed by others. By recognising the importance of 'struggle' and the dialectical qualities of consciousness, however, he was committed to understanding the cross-currents within which and against which the forms of consciousness that interested him defined themselves. Indeed, as his work moved increasingly in an anthropological direction this commitment grew.[68] He certainly claimed that listening to the disparate voices of historical actors was an essential part of his own practice in recapturing consciousness.[69]

   To describe the composite portrait of utilitarianism and political economy that emerges from the work of Leavis, Williams, and Thompson as tendentious is to overlook the warm-blooded normative intentions of their work. But an optic on the intellectual past that was serviceable for exercises in aerial bombing, 1940s style, would hardly commend itself to those wielding scalpels, and not just for purposes of performing cosmetic surgery. Those seeking a more nuanced picture of the lines of force at work in Victorian thinking need something more appropriate to the task, a better ear, more tolerance, and less overt partisanship. Regard for complexity does not have to be associated with personal sympathies, still less does it mean endorsing the 'apologetics of a ruling class'.[70]

---

[66] See, for example, 'The peculiarities of the English', especially pp. 266–74.
[67] MEWC, p. 13.
[68] Notably in *Whigs and hunters* and *Customs in common.*
[69] 'If he listens, then the material itself will begin to speak through him'; and 'The historian may tend to be a bit too generous because a historian has to learn to attend and listen to very disparate groups of people and try and understand their value system and their consciousness.' See *Visions of history*, pp. 14, 16.
[70] *Ibid.*, p. 8. Significantly, however, Thompson followed this crude charge with a warning against treating all history as ideology: it involved a 'precise discipline that entails distancing and objectifying – becoming aware of the questions one is asking', thereby preventing the intrusion of 'one's attitudes and values'.

VII

We no longer believe that Leslie Stephen, Elie Halévy, and A. V. Dicey were right, according to their different lights, in attributing to philosophic radicalism such exclusive and persistent influence over Victorian legislation and public administration. As William Thomas has shown, in the process of rescuing the philosophic radicals from the 'ism' attached to the collectivity later, even during the brief period when they were attempting to act as a political force, they were disunited and largely ineffectual.[71] Bourgeois most of them may have been, but their cause would have benefited from being *more* attuned to the interests and beliefs of the new electorate after 1832. A stronger sense of the emerging class basis of English politics, outside the landowning classes, against whom much of their fire was concentrated, would have improved their prospects – as it did those of Cobden and Bright in the 1840s and beyond. Instead, they spoke a doctrinaire *philosophe* language of public good, priding themselves on standing above the crudities of class interest – a stance that separated them as much from the middle classes as it did from the working classes. *Pace* Leavis, then, far from opposing the sharing of the privileges obtained in 1832, their continuing efforts to destroy such privileges conflicted with the hopes and anxieties of a new electorate made fearful by Chartism. Robert Lowe provides an extreme example of the kind of utilitarian who opposed the extension of the suffrage. Perhaps that is why he complained most bitterly about the ingratitude of the middle classes towards his efforts on their behalf.[72] But one Lowe does not make a winter.

Gradgrind was certainly busy during the early decades of the century, arguing the case for 'good government', but he was rarely running the show.[73] Similarly with the single-issue politics of the day, those centring on legal and penal reform, education, the Poor Law, public health, the Factory Acts, and the creation of a meritocratic civil service, where

[71] W. Thomas, *The philosophic radicals: nine studies in theory and practice, 1817–1841* (Oxford: Oxford University Press, 1979). For a more extended treatment of Halévy's misunderstandings of English politics, see Thomas's 'L'utilitarisme et le libéralisme anglais au début du XIXieme siècle' in M. Mulligan and R. Roth (eds.), *Regards sur Bentham et l'utilitarisme: recherches et rencontres* (Geneva: Droz, 1993), pp. 39–58.

[72] See A. P. Martin (ed.), *Life and letters of the Right Honourable Robert Lowe, Viscount Sherbrooke*, 2 vols. (London: Longmans, 1893), I, pp. 5–6.

[73] See P. Harling, *The waning of 'old corruption': the politics of economical reform in Britain, 1779–1846* (Oxford: Oxford University Press, 1996). See also P. Harling and P. Mandler, 'From "fiscal-military" state to laissez-faire state, 1760–1850', *Journal of British Studies*, 32 (1993), 44–70.

backroom tactics proved more influential, the philosophic radicals often played second fiddle to others – to Whigs (Scottish and English), to Tories, and especially to those with Evangelical and Dissenting affiliations that were distinctly at odds with the atheistic materialism of Bentham and his immediate disciples. Thompson's treatment of the religious dimension of nineteenth-century social thought concentrated more on its moral declension than its positive influence on public dispositions. Leavis and Williams paid it little attention, as the latter recognised when he confessed to 'tone-deafness' on the subject.[74]

Nor is it self-evident that Benthamism was indifferent to human interests. The efforts of Chadwick, Southwood Smith, and James Kay-Shuttleworth as Factory and Poor Law Commissioners were not entirely nugatory. It is also conceivable that they were fired by compassion and a genuine concern for injustice. It seems unreasonable to deny that imaginative sympathy *as well as* righteous rationality played a part in the public objects to which, after all, they (not us) devoted most of their lives.[75] This may be more difficult to credit in the case of Bentham, whose normal procedures were undoubtedly rationalist, and whose plans for paupers and prisoners provide opportunities to reveal our superior humanity. Nevertheless, precisely the same kind of rationalism resulted in highlighting forms of exclusion and oppression – for example, of women, homosexuals, and Jews – that often lay beyond the more conventional public sympathies of Victorians.[76] Dickens's private verdict on Gradgrind now seems nearer the truth than that passed by admirers of his novel.

The equation of Benthamism with *laissez-faire* individualism owes much to Dicey's *Law and public opinion in England during the nineteenth century* (1905), whose standards for admission to this club were notoriously lax, part of his own polemical attempt to stem the tide of late nineteenth-century collectivism.[77] During the period he assigned to Benthamite hegemony, 1825–70, everyone became a common-sense utilitarian without knowing it. The well-documented and influential example of Gladstone now provides the best test case here. Though clearly more inclined towards Coleridge than Bentham for confessional reasons, Gladstone's credentials as the spokesman for free trade, sound finance,

---

[74] *Politics and letters*, p. 130.
[75] On the 'conscience', see the contribution of D. Roberts to P. Marsh (ed.), *The conscience of the Victorian state* (Syracuse, NY: Syracuse University Press, 1979), pp. 39–72.
[76] See L. Campos-Boralevi, *Bentham and the oppressed* (Berlin: W. de Gruyter, 1984).
[77] On the background to Dicey's work, see S. Collini, *Liberalism and sociology* (Cambridge: Cambridge University Press, 1979), pp. 13–42.

and *laissez-faire* are impeccable. But Colin Matthew also taught us to appreciate that the Gladstonian idea of state, though minimal in its economic role, contained some powerful *étatist* features. It aimed to be strong and autonomous in relation to major interest groupings, where preservation of autonomy entailed reliance on municipal and voluntary agencies in a manner that was at least as 'corporatist' as the mercantile state Gladstone did so much to dismantle.[78]

Although Halévy's superior scholarship could be used to counter Dicey's emphasis on *laissez-faire* by showing the *dirigiste* aims of Benthamism, Halévy confirmed the prejudices of its opponents in another way. He absorbed political economy so thoroughly into utilitarianism, making Smith an honorary Benthamite *avant la lettre*, that Leavis can be forgiven for mistaking the ancestry. Halévy also succeeded in assimilating all political economists, radical, Whig, and Tory, into the Benthamite camp. He accepted Bentham's claim that he had indirectly sired Ricardo's economics, ignoring the fact that Ricardo and James Mill had severe doubts as to Bentham's orthodoxy as a political economist.[79] Moreover, as Boyd Hilton has shown, there was a large army of Christian or evangelical political economists whose thinking was more closely attuned to that of many Tory and some Whig politicians than the ungodly abstractions of Ricardo.[80]

By being treated as a composite set of doctrines, little scope existed for recognising any development in its separate elements, where development could entail decline as well as refinement. The versions of utilitarianism that emerged from the pens of Mill and Sidgwick belong to the latter category, but Mill's efforts to refine Ricardian theory came to an end when he acknowledged some fundamental defects in the logic of the wage-fund doctrine in the 1860s, leaving a ruin that required the attentions of a new generation of economists before it could become habitable once more. In the oft-quoted phrase of Bagehot, speaking in 1876, political economy lay 'dead in the public mind'.[81] During the next three decades, its orthodox supporters were engaged in furious methodological

---

[78] See H. C. G. Matthew, *Gladstone, 1809–74* (Oxford: Oxford University Press, 1986); and *Gladstone, 1875–98* (Oxford: Oxford University Press, 1995).

[79] See T. W. Hutchison, 'Bentham as an economist', *EJ*, 66 (1953), 288–306; D. Lieberman, 'Political economy and Jeremy Bentham', unpublished paper, 1982; R. D. C. Black, 'Bentham and the political economists of the nineteenth century', *Bentham Newsletter*, 12 (1988), 24–36.

[80] See *Corn, cash, commerce: the economic policies of the Tory governments, 1815–1830* (Oxford: Oxford University Press, 1977); and *The age of atonement: the influence of evangelicalism on social and economic thought, 1785–1865* (Oxford: Oxford University Press, 1988).

[81] *Economic studies*, in CWWB, XI, p. 224.

and political debate with their historicist critics. When political economy regained confidence under its new banner, Economics, in the early decades of the twentieth century, it had acquired a different agenda. Leavis's 'technologico-Benthamite' category was too all-encompassing to take account of such refinements, but as the residual category for all that was despised one might have expected Williams and Thompson, as overt political animals, to pay more attention to these shifts of focus, if only to show how devilishly cunning the enemy could be.

VIII

For the period during which the schism between utilitarians and romantics was a central issue, everyone agrees that Mill was still the crucial figure, whether or not they regard his bridge-building efforts as successful. Leavis was hardly being over-generous when he stated that Mill was no unqualified Benthamite. What Mill's mature version of utilitarianism lost in philistinism it may have gained in priggishness, but the result can hardly be described as 'complacent selfishness'. As Stefan Collini has shown, the moral requirements of duty and altruism could be strenuous in the extreme.[82]

Mill's reformulation of Ricardian political economy led to the espousal of many ideas that would have seemed distinctly peculiar to his mentors, not least in the explicit attention given to the claims and future of the labouring classes. Neither Leavis nor Williams seems to have made any effort to comprehend the *Principles of political economy*. For if Dickens really had this work in mind when indicting Coketown, he might have joined Williams in being disappointed to find how little Mill has to say on the subject of industrialisation and urbanisation. An underlying assumption in *Hard times* that relations between capital and labour ought to be regulated by benevolence and mutual understanding appears in popular versions of political economy, but not in Mill's examination of co-operative forms of socialism. These were commended precisely as a means of overcoming the *essentially* conflictual relations between capital and labour.[83] Speaking as someone capable of appreciating the technological wonders of his day, Dickens might have been dispirited also by Mill's statement that 'it is questionable if all the mechanical inventions

---

[82] See especially 'The culture of altruism', in his *Public moralists: political thought and intellectual life in Britain, 1850–1930* (Oxford: Oxford University Press, 1991), pp. 60–90.
[83] *Principles*, CW, II, Book IV, chapter 7.

yet made have lightened the day's toil of any human being'.[84] One wonders too how Dickens would have reacted to other well-known pronouncements in that book: against paternalistic attempts to guide the labouring classes, and in favour of measures that would 'pull down all large fortunes in two generations'.[85]

Many of Mill's contemporaries were bemused by his speculations about a world in which economic growth would no longer exhaust the energies of humankind for reasons connected with the quality of life and what was much later labelled as ecological catastrophe.[86] As public moralist, Mill regarded it as his duty to explore new potentialities for human nature that were beyond present horizons. His record as seer may have been no better than most practitioners of this trade, but he devoted more effort to diagnosing future possibilities than to golden pasts and cannot be accused of wearing rose-coloured spectacles when looking at Britain's industrial society in the late forties and beyond. In one of his rare references to Mill, Thompson spoke of him as being 'revolted in disgust against the ethic of capitalism', but betrayed his normal expectations by prefacing it with a fatal 'even'.[87]

While a history of Victorian political economy and utilitarianism without Mill resembles a princeless *Hamlet*, Rosencrantz and Guildenstern also played their parts. Just as there were some Gradgrind schools, so there were popular exponents of political economy such as Mrs Marcet and Mrs Martineau, and unregenerate dogmatists like Lowe.[88] Equally, there were some 'cast-iron theories' purporting to explain the unalterable character of the laws of supply and demand, the harsh realities of wage determination, the harmful effects of restricting adult hours of work, and the benefits of machinery. Such theories were frequently employed to silence socialistic and 'sentimental' voices during the period when novel urban forms of industrialisation were receiving most attention from a middle-class public. We may wince at W. R. Greg's review of *Mary Barton*, his patronising lecture to Mrs Gaskell on the social economics of the

---

[84] *Ibid.*, p. 756.
[85] Mill's description of the likely result of his proposals concerning taxation of rents and bequests, as reported to his friend Alexander Bain; see Bain's *John Stuart Mill* (London: Longmans, 1882), p. 89.
[86] *Principles*, Book V, chapter 6. It seems symptomatic that Williams's article on 'Socialism and ecology' mentions the romantic figures in the anti-capitalist tradition, but overlooks Mill entirely; see *Resources of hope*, pp. 210–26.
[87] *William Morris*, p. 243.
[88] On the schools, see R. Gilmour, 'The Gradgrind school: political economy in the classroom', *Victorian Studies*, 11 (1967), 207–24.

1842 depression. But what he has to say about the level of wages paid in Manchester, and the need and capacity for manufacturers with large fixed capitals to keep their businesses going longer during depression, still makes economic sense. What is less often noticed is Greg's related lecture to Mill on the non-viability of co-operative enterprises, where Sturt's later experience in finding that his workers rejected his 'Ruskinian absurdities' could be cited in Greg's support.[89]

It is hardly surprising that when employers defended laying off men during slack periods, or made attempts to cut wages or quicken the pace of work in response to competition, they appealed to the one science that purported to explain the need for so doing. Mill was sympathetic to trade union activities before and after his recantation of the wage-fund doctrine, which meant that trade unionists, like employers, were not averse to claiming that legitimacy had been conferred on their activities by the science of political economy.[90]

On one occasion at least, Thompson recognised that Tom Paine and Adam Smith provided a joint revelation to his artisans, but his understanding of and sympathy with later versions of political economy was severely limited.[91] More generally, his response to arguments advanced by historians of economic thought was to draw a distinction between their focus on 'intention' and his own concern with 'ideological interest' and 'historical consequences'.[92] This had the polemical advantage of requiring the critic to show that the industrial revolution and the new Poor Law did not have the material consequences attributed to them by Thompson and his chosen protagonists. Only the most dogged apologist for capitalism would deny that the industrial revolution had a disastrous effect on some groups of workers and possibly on a large section of the working classes at some time during their lives. But we are not obliged to reach a definitive conclusion on the 'standard-of-living' controversy before deciding whether the opinions of contemporary commentators have been registered without distortion. To expect this would be like making it a requirement of Thompson that he should give an economic analysis of the causes and remedies for a depression before registering the claims of the victims, and

---

[89] See Greg's review in the *Edinburgh Review*, 89 (1849), 402–35.
[90] See E. Biagini, 'British trade unions and popular political economy, 1860–1880, *Historical Journal*, 30 (1987), 811–40.
[91] MEWC, p. 105.
[92] *Customs in common*, pp. 202n, 270–1. In another formulation, he also spoke of being more interested in the 'sociology' of ideas than their 'identity'; see MEWC, p. 857n.

without recourse to the question-begging assumption that in Jerusalem such things would not happen.

Nor is it surprising that some leaders of the working classes were impressed by the self-respecting virtues. The native English forms of radicalism, socialism, and working-class political economy were as diverse as the versions associated with Owen, Chartism, Hodgskin, and Place suggest. When dealing with a phenomenon that had no precedent and might have a different future we should expect some versions of working-class political economy to appeal to well-established political diagnoses of corruption and injustice; and to recall acceptable precedents by looking backwards, with or without nostalgia, to an earlier memory of greater autonomy and stability in working conditions. By paying attention to the plurality of languages to be found among the Chartists, for example, Gareth Stedman Jones was able to make sense of the theory of unequal exchange that underpinned much of their thinking, while at the same time showing why the Charter looked to a political solution to the social and economic problems being diagnosed.[93] A muddled Owen and a treacherous Place have certainly obtained more sympathetic hearings from others than they received from Thompson.[94] It is also unfortunate for Thompson's contrast between Place and Hodgskin that the latter's career should have ended as a supporter of the anti-Corn Law League and as an assistant editor of *The Economist*. Hodgskin's theological commitments to a natural order made him a better member of Boyd Hilton's cast than Thompson's: he was a radical-Liberal rather than a socialist, Ricardian, Smithian, or Lockean.[95]

IX

Finally, there is my second question: how should we now regard the original schism between romantics and utilitarians? While it may have been crudely posed and artificially widened, nothing said so far supports the conclusion that it can be easily resolved. That a schism came into existence; that there was indeed a 'steam-whistle party', of which Dickens

---

[93] 'Rethinking Chartism', in his *Languages of class: studies in English working class history, 1832–1982* (Cambridge: Cambridge University Press, 1983), pp. 90–178.

[94] On Owen, see, for example, G. Claeys, *Machinery, money and the millennium: from moral economy to socialism* (Cambridge: Cambridge University Press, 1987); and on Place, see D. Miles, *Francis Place, 1771–1854: the life of a remarkable radical* (Brighton: Harvester Press, 1988).

[95] See D. Stack, *Nature and artifice: the life and thought of Thomas Hodgskin* (London: Woodbridge Boydell, 1998).

may or may not have been a fully paid-up member, cannot be denied. A portrait taken from the other side would contain some sharp character-isations of the romantic opposition, suggesting that an actual battle was taking place. Mill strove to achieve an open mind, but could not conceal his belief that on political economy Coleridge wrote like an 'arrant driveller'.[96] Macaulay, the scourge of utilitarian theories of government, ridiculed Southey's pessimism and ignorance of political economy. He also dismissed *Hard times* as 'sullen socialism', a remark that gains rather than loses point by noting that he had applied much the same description to Wordsworth's *Prelude* in 1850.[97] Ruskin's articles attacking political economy were discontinued after the public had registered dislike of their tone, and Bagehot's review of *Unto this last* carried a title that hardly suggests a desire to cultivate the middle ground: 'Aesthetic twaddle versus economic science'.[98]

There have, indeed, been those who have maintained that there can be no middle ground in any dispute between romantics and utilitarians. Resting, as they think it does, on a category mistake, they maintain that there can be no mediation between the two positions. It was on such grounds, for example, that De Quincey dismissed the criticisms of political economy made by the Lake poets.[99] Others have claimed that there could be no accommodation between a cultural stance that seeks an enduring holistic position on values and a social scientific perspective in which empiricism dictates that what may be true of some aspects of social life today may be false tomorrow.[100] Some aspects of the nineteenth-century dispute can be clarified by distinguishing between explanations for what existed and justifications for what might exist. Poetry and economic cal-culation may not belong on the same spectrum, but there has to be some means of mediating between what poets and economists said when they were talking about the same actual social conditions. However inad-equate we may find Mill's attempts to bridge the gap, the effort was worth

---

[96] 'Coleridge', in CW, X, p. 155.
[97] See *The life and letters of Lord Macaulay*, ed. George Otto Trevelyan (London: Longmans Green, 1901), p. 614. The remark about *The Prelude* was that it was 'to the last degree Jacobinical, indeed Socialist'; *ibid.*, p. 541.
[98] See CWWB, IX, pp. 315–29.
[99] Since political economy was self-consciously limited to questions involving the 'production and circulation of wealth', it had nothing to do with ethical questions concerning 'estimates of social grandeur'. See *Recollections of the Lake Poets* (London: Penguin Books, 1970), pp. 244–5.
[100] This was Noel Annan's reason for regarding as mistaken the attempts of Basil Willey, Leavis, Williams, and Dorothea Krook to treat Mill as someone who 'tried and failed to spiritualise utilitarianism'. See 'John Stuart Mill', in J. B. Schneewind (ed.), *Mill: a collection of critical essays* (London: Macmillan, 1968), pp. 22–45.

making. And if we are to confront the intellectual history we have, rather than the one we think we ought to have had, we cannot follow Williams in complaining about Mill's tendency to talk about 'civilisation' when what we think he ought to have been talking about was 'industrial society'.[101]

Much the same can be said of Thompson, whose attentiveness to the languages of his protagonists did not extend to all participants in the conversation. As Rosaldo has said of Thompson from an anthropologist's standpoint, 'the historian's notions have been conflated with those of his subjects'.[102] Thompson often wanted the novelist's freedom to achieve an ending that was incompatible with his professed aims as historian-anthropologist, where this entails recognition that there are no endings, merely persisting but not unalterable practices. Similarly with Dickens, with whom Thompson has been compared as narrator: as readers we can ask whether Dickens's sociological grasp exceeded his psychological reach, whether it is preferable to retain the holistic power of his darker social symbols by overlooking the bourgeois sentimentality of his happy endings.[103] Intellectual historians, however, in common with anthropologists, do not enjoy this freedom to ignore the teller of the tale.

Leavis was incensed by a response to his interpretation of *Hard times* that suggested it simply amounted to saying that 'all work and no play makes Jack a dull boy'.[104] It seems worth asking whether another reductive commonplace can be applied to the schism depicted by my trio: man does not live by bread alone. Expressed thus, it is hard to think of anyone on either side of the schism who thought differently, though their priorities as between bread and other sources of life might differ. Even those heartless men of 'facts and calculation', those statisticians Dickens caricatured, were aware that percentages told you nothing about the human tragedy that lay behind them. A cheap laugh at their expense could easily become a sign of seeking cheap grace. The high moral ground is appropriated by accusing your opponents of something they would not have denied.

Living in the kind of society we have enjoyed or suffered for at least the past two hundred years or so, there is a persistent need to be reminded that market values are not the sole arbiter. It is also possible to go one step

---

[101] See *Culture and society*, p. 67. Annan, writing from the opposite point of view, makes much the same criticism of Mill.

[102] In Kaye and McClelland (eds.), *E. P. Thompson*, p. 114.

[103] An argument employed, for example, by J. M. Brown in *Dickens: novelist in the market-place* (Totowa, NJ: Barnes & Noble, 1982), pp. 11–13, 26, 41–4, 74.

[104] John Holloway's comment in his essay on *Hard Times* in J. Gross and G. Pearson (eds.), *Dickens and the twentieth century* (London: Routledge, 1962), p. 166. For Leavis's response, see F. R. and Q. D. Leavis, *Dickens the novelist* (London: Chatto & Windus, 1970), pp. 208–12.

further by arguing that the market systematically perverted values for the kind of reasons suggested by Ruskin's contrast between 'wealth' and 'illth' – a contrast not unknown to Adam Smith that was given substance by Mill, and later by a generation or two of welfare economists writing in the 1880s and beyond. The great strength of the British romantic moralists, whether on the left or right of the political spectrum, has lain in such reminders, particularly when delivered at historic moments when the market was either failing or threatening to carry all before it. But it also seems to be another characteristic of the same moralists that they extend their protest to include all those who have studied how everyone's bread has been earned. If there is a moral to the story told here, it lies in the persistent unwillingness of the moral tradition to be defiled by the pitch associated with such vulgar consequentialist calculations, while suggesting that they know the answers anyway. Unwillingness to comprehend the workings of markets, it has been argued, has been a persistent weakness of the British socialist tradition.[105] Those on the left who assumed that Marx provided the correct analyses occupied a more defensible position. When Thompson criticised *Culture and society* for its failure to call upon the insights of a historian, anthropologist, or sociologist of note, it was inconceivable that he could have added an economist to this list – apart, that is, from Marx. He confessed to his own 'weakness in economic theory', but could rely on the understanding of his allies on the Marxist left.[106] Once this faith had weakened, however, not much was left apart from a conventional rejection of the coarse apologetics of the economics Gradgrind was taken to represent. Economic man now had to be exiled for the economism to be found in the versions of Marxism that had been rejected, as well as for his supposed capitalist ancestry. It would be an interesting exercise in virtual history to ask what would have happened if Thompson had been willing to extend to economics the kind of understanding he showed in his later work towards anthropology and the rule of law.[107] Moral protest may serve the purposes of allowing a Jerusalem to be conceived, but it does not enable the failures of existing societies to be analysed or the foundations for new ones to be constructed.

---

[105] See, for example, N. Thompson, *The market and its critics: socialist political economy in nineteenth-century Britain* (London: Routledge, 1988).

[106] 'The politics of theory', p. 404.

[107] That this need not be an entirely frivolous counterfactual can be seen in one of Thompson's answers to the Anderson–Nairn thesis, where he pointed out 'the distinctive contribution of English ideology in the late eighteenth century was neither traditionalism nor empiricism, but a naturalistic political economy most notably with Adam Smith'; see *Poverty of theory*, p. 254.

Bibliographic abbreviations and notes

The following abbreviations, followed by volume and page number, are used for each of the classic editions of the main figures in the essays.

CW: *The collected works of John Stuart Mill*, 33 vols. (Toronto: University of Toronto Press, 1965–91).

CWWB: *The collected works of Walter Bagehot*, edited by N. St John-Stevas, 15 vols. (London: The Economist, 1965–86).

Correspondence: *The correspondence of Alfred Marshall, economist*, ed. John K. Whitaker, 3 vols. (Cambridge: Cambridge University Press, 1996).

EEW: *The early economic writings of Alfred Marshall, 1867–1890*, ed. J. K. Whitaker, 2 vols. (London: Macmillan for the Royal Economic Society, 1975).

EJ: *Economic Journal*.

JMK: *The collected writings of John Maynard Keynes*, 30 vols. (Cambridge: Cambridge University Press for the Royal Economic Society, 1971–89).

JRW: *The complete works of John Ruskin*, ed. E. T. Cook and Alexander Wedderburn, 39 vols. (London: George Allen, 1903–12).

Memoir: *Henry Sidgwick: a memoir by A[rthur] Sidgwick and E[leanor] M[ildred] S[idgwick]* (London: Macmillan, 1906).

Memorials: *Memorials of Alfred Marshall*, ed. A. C. Pigou (London, Macmillan, 1925)

PC: *Papers and correspondence of William Stanley Jevons*, ed. R. D. Collison Black and Rosamond Könekamp, 7 vols. (London: Macmillan in association with the Royal Economic Society, 1972–81).

PE: Marshall's *Principles of Economics*, 9th variorum edition with annotations by C. W. Guillebaud, 2 vols. (London: Macmillan for the Royal Economic Society, 1961).

For each essay or pairing of essays the following notes record secondary sources that could be of interest to anyone wishing to do further work on a specific economist or public issue.

PROLOGUE

The term 'public moralist' was first used in 1984 by Stefan Collini in his introduction to Mill's *Essays on equality, law, and education* in CW, XXI.

He then employed it as the basis for a larger study; see *Public moralists: political thought and intellectual life in Britain, 1850–1930* (Oxford: Oxford University Press, 1991). For its further use in connection with Mill, see Bruce L. Kinzer, Ann P. Robson, and John M. Robson, *A moralist in and out of parliament: John Stuart Mill at Westminster, 1865–68* (Toronto: Toronto University Press, 1992). On the origin of 'industrial revolution', see the title essay in D. C. Coleman, *Myth, history and the industrial revolution* (London: Hambledon Press, 1992). Gareth Stedman Jones has provided a more thorough treatment of the Franco-German background to Engels's work in 'National bankruptcy and social revolution: European observers on Britain, 1813–1844', in Donald Winch and Patrick K. O'Brien (eds.), *The political economy of British historical experience, 1688–1914* (Oxford: Oxford University Press, 2002). On the late nine-teenth- and twentieth-century historiography of the industrial revolution, see, D. Cannadine, 'The present and the past in the English industrial revolution, 1880–1980', *Past and Present*, 103 (1984), 131–72; and D. C. Coleman, *History and the economic past: an account of the rise and decline of economic history in Britain* (Oxford: Oxford University Press, 1987). On the disparate elements that went into Toynbee's lectures, see Alon Kadish, *Apostle Arnold: The Life and Death of Arnold Toynbee, 1852–1883* (Durham, NC: Duke University Press, 1986). On the marginal revolution, see R. D. C. Black *et al.* (eds.), *The marginal revolution in economics* (Durham, NC: Duke University Press, 1973).

ESSAYS 2 AND 3

Mill's political economy has generated a vast literature. Two comprehen-sive overviews are Pedro Schwartz, *The new political economy of J. S. Mill* (London: Weidenfeld & Nicolson, 1968); and Samuel Hollander, *The economics of John Stuart Mill*, 2 vols. (Oxford: Blackwell, 1985). On col-onisation and the Wakefield connections, see Donald Winch, *Classical political economy and colonies* (London: G. Bell, 1965). For contemporary accounts of the Commons Preservation Society, see L. Stephen, *Life of Henry Fawcett* (London: Smith Elder, 1885), ch. 7; and G. J. Shaw Lefevre, *English commons and forests: the story of the battle during the last thirty years for public rights over the commons and forests of England and Wales* (London: Cassell, 1894). On the National Trust, see G. Murphy, *Founders of the National Trust* (London: Christopher Helm, 1987); and J. Gaze, *Figures in a landscape: a history of the National Trust* (London: Barrie and Jenkins, 1988). On the conservationist activities of Wordsworthians, see the final chapter in S. Gill, *Wordsworth and the Victorians* (Oxford: Oxford University Press, 1998). See too Jonathan Bate, *Romantic ecology. Wordsworth and the environmental tradition* (London: Routledge, 1991); and for a general study of Victorian environmentalism, see James Winter, *Secure from rash assault: sustaining the Victorian environment* (London: University of California Press, 1999). For a useful short compendium on land tenure reform, see David Martin, *John Stuart Mill on the land question* (University of Hull occasional papers, 1981). On Ireland the classic study remains R. D. C. Black, *Economic thought and the Irish question, 1817–1870* (Cambridge: Cambridge University Press, 1960). On Mill and Ireland the large literature can now be approached via an excellent overview in B. L. Kinzer, *England's disgrace: J. S. Mill and the Irish question* (Toronto: Toronto University Press, 2001). On India, see Martin I. Moir, Douglas M. Peers, and Lynn Zastoupil (eds.), *J. S. Mill's encounter with India* (Toronto: Toronto University Press, 1999). See also Zastoupil's *John Stuart Mill and India* (Palo Alto: Stanford University Press, 1994). For connections between thinking on Ireland and India, see R. D. C. Black, 'Economic policy in Ireland and India in the time of J. S. Mill', reprinted in *Economic theory and policy in context: the selected essays of R. D. Collison Black* (Aldershot: Edward Elgar, 1993). Two unpublished dissertations deal with the activities of the Wallace and George associations; see A. J. Peacock, 'Land reform 1880–1919: a study of the activities of the English Land Restoration League and the Land Nationalisation Society', MA thesis, University of Southampton, 1961; and S. B. Ward, 'Land reform in England, 1880–1914', PhD thesis, University of Reading, 1976. On Mill and Fabianism, see A. M. Macbriar, *Fabian socialism and English politics, 1884–1918* (Cambridge: Cambridge University Press, 1966) and W. Wolfe, *From radicalism to socialism: men and ideas in the formation of Fabian socialist doctrines, 1881–1889* (New Haven: Yale University Press, 1975).

ESSAY 4

The best short treatment of the main theme of this essay is still that of John Tyree Fain, *Ruskin and the economists* (Nashville: Vanderbilt Press, 1956). See too J. C. Sherburne, *John Ruskin or the ambiguities of abundance: a study in social and economic criticism* (Cambridge, MA: Harvard University Press, 1972); and Willie Henderson, *John Ruskin's political economy* (London: Routledge, 2000). Ruskin is well served by his biographers, the latest being Tim Hilton; see his two volumes, *John Ruskin: the early years, 1819–1859* and *John Ruskin: the later years* (New Haven: Yale University

Press, 1985 and 2000). For studies of the practical influence of Ruskin's ideas, see the essays by Jose Harris and Lawrence Goldman in D. Birch (ed.), *Ruskin and the dawn of the modern* (Oxford: Oxford University Press, 1999).

ESSAY 5

On *The Economist*, see Ruth Dudley Edwards, *The pursuit of reason: The Economist 1843–1993* (London: Hamish Hamilton, 1993); and Scott Gordon, 'The London *Economist* and the high tide of laissez-faire', *Journal of Political Economy* 63 (1955), 461–88. On Maine, see a useful collection of essays by A. Diamond (ed.), *The Victorian achievement of Sir Henry Maine* (Cambridge: Cambridge University Press, 1991). On Lowe, see John Maloney, *Political economy of Robert Lowe* (Basingstoke: Palgrave Macmillan, 2005). On the Anglo-Irish *Methodenstreit*, see S. Collini, 'Particular polities: political economy and the historical method', in S. Collini, D. Winch, and J. Burrow, *That noble science of politics* (Cambridge: Cambridge University Press, 1983); and G. Koot, *English historical economics, 1870–1926* (Cambridge: Cambridge University Press, 1987). On Cliffe Leslie, see R. D. C. Black, 'The political economy of Thomas Edward Cliffe Leslie (1826–82): a reassessment', *European Journal of the History of Economic Thought*, 9 (2002), 17–41.

ESSAY 6

R. D. C. Black, the editor of Jevons's papers and correspondence, has also written authoritative accounts of his economic writings, several of which are now included in his *Economic theory and policy in context* (Aldershot: Edward Elgar, 1995), part III; see also 'Jevons, marginalism and Manchester', *Manchester School*, 40 (1972), 1–8; 'Jevons, Bentham and De Morgan', *Economica*, 39 (1972), 119–34; and his chapter on Jevons in D. P. O'Brien and J. R. Presley (eds.), *Pioneers of Modern Economics in Britain* (London: Macmillan, 1981), pp. 1–35. There have been several major general studies of Jevons published in recent years, chiefly from a history-of-science standpoint; see Margaret Schabas, *A world ruled by number: William Stanley Jevons and the rise of mathematical economics* (Princeton: Princeton University Press, 1990); Sandra Peart, *The economics of W. S. Jevons* (London: Routledge, 1996); Harro Maas, *William Stanley Jevons and the making of modern economics* (Cambridge: Cambridge University Press, 2005); Bert Mosselmans, *William Stanley Jevons and the cutting edge of economics* (London: Routledge, 2007).

ESSAY 7

On Cobdenism and the Cobden Club, the best source is Anthony Howe, *Free trade and liberal England, 1846–1946* (Oxford: Oxford University Press, 1997). Howe is also editing *The letters of Richard Cobden*, the first volume of which, 1815–1847, was published by Oxford University Press, 2007. For a modern biography of Cobden, see Nicholas C. Edsall, *Richard Cobden: independent radical* (Cambridge, MA: Harvard University Press, 1986). For a recent collection of essays, see Anthony Howe and Simon Morgan (eds.), *Rethinking nineteenth-century liberalism: Richard Cobden bicentenary essays* (Aldershot: Ashgate, 2006). For a comprehensive study of the part played by free trade in British civic and political culture, see Frank Trentmann, *Free trade nation: commerce, consumption, and civil society in modern Britain* (Oxford: Oxford University Press, 2008). On trade treaties, see P. T. Marsh, *Bargaining on Europe: Britain and the first common market, 1860–92* (New Haven: Yale University Press, 1999). On the Liberty and Property Defence Leagues, see N. Soldon, '*Laissez-faire* as dogma', in K. D. Brown (ed.), *Essays in anti-labour history* (London: Macmillan, 1974); E. Bristow, 'The Liberty and Property Defence League and individualism, 1882–1914, *Historical Journal*, 18 (1975), 761–89; and M. W. Taylor, *Man versus the state: Herbert Spencer and late-Victorian individualism* (Oxford: Oxford University Press, 1992).

ESSAY 8

Bart Schultz, *Henry Sidgwick: eye of the universe. An intellectual biography* (Cambridge: Cambridge University Press, 2004); Stefan Collini, 'My roles and their duties: Sidgwick as philosopher, professor, and public moralist', in Ross Harrison (ed.), *Henry Sidgwick*, Proceedings of the British Academy, 109 (Oxford: Oxford University Press, 2001); and Stefan Collini, 'The ordinary experience of civilised life; Sidgwick and the method of reflective analysis', in Collini, Winch, and Burrow, *That noble science of politics*. Cairnes is now well served by Tom Boylan and Tadhg Foley (eds.), *John Elliot Cairnes: collected works*, 6 vols. (London: Routledge, 2003). See too the editors' article on 'John Elliot Cairnes, John Stuart Mill and Ireland', *Hermathena*, 135 (1983), 96–118.

ESSAYS 9 AND 10

Keynes wrote biographical essays on Foxwell as well as Marshall; see *Essays in biography*, JMK, X. For a full-scale modern biography of

Marshall, see Peter Groenewegen, *A soaring eagle: Alfred Marshall, 1842–1924* (Aldershot: Edward Elgar, 1995). On Foxwell, see Audrey G. D. Foxwell, *Herbert Somerton Foxwell: a portrait*, Kress Library of Business and Economics, publication no. 1 (Boston, 1939); and Richard Freeman's entry in the *Oxford Dictionary of National Biography*. D. P. O'Brien, 'Marshall's work in relation to classical economics', in J. K. Whitaker (ed.), *Centenary essays on Alfred Marshall* (Cambridge: Cambridge University Press for the Royal Economic Society, 1990) is the most thorough of the treatments of its theme. Another collection of essays edited by Rita McWilliams Tullberg, *Alfred Marshall in retrospect* (Aldershot: Elgar, 1990) contains useful articles, especially those by P. D. Groenewegen on taxation and Phyllis Deane on free trade. *The Elgar companion to Alfred Marshall*, ed. Tiziano Raffaelli, Giacomo Becattini, and Marco Dardi (Aldershot: Elgar, 2006) is a compendium based on the most recent research by economists and historians of economics. I have also benefited from reading unpublished work by Simon Cook; see 'Poetry, faith, and chivalry: Alfred Marshall's response to modern socialism', to appear in *History of Economics Review;* and his forthcoming book, *'A rounded globe of knowledge': the intellectual foundations of Alfred Marshall's economic science.* The pioneering study of the tariff reform controversy is that of A. W. (Bob) Coats, 'Political economy and the tariff reform campaign of 1903', originally published in 1968, now included in his collected essays *On the history of economic thought: British and American essays* (London: Routledge, 1992). The best recent account of the background to Marshall's memorandum on fiscal policy can be found in Peter Groenewegen (ed.), *Official papers of Marshall: a supplement* (Cambridge: Cambridge University Press, 1996). On 'The appointment of Pigou as Marshall's successor', see the articles by R. H. Coase and A. W. Coats in *Journal of Law and Economics*, 15 (1972) 473–95. On Cambridge welfare economics, see Roger Backhouse, 'Sidgwick, Marshall and the Cambridge school of economics', *History of Political Economy*, 38 (2006), 15–44; and Steven Medema, 'The hesitant hand: Mill, Sidgwick and the evolution of the theory of market failure', *History of Political Economy*, 39 (2007), 331–58.

ESSAY 11

For Hobson's bibliography and other assessments, see J. Pheby (ed.), *J. A. Hobson after fifty years* (London: Macmillan, 1994). Another useful collection is M. Freeden (ed.), *Reappraising J. A. Hobson: humanism and welfare* (London: Unwin Hyman, 1990). For studies of Hobson's contribution to

'New Liberalism', see M. Freeden, *The new liberalism* (Oxford: Oxford University Press, 1978); and Peter Clarke, *Liberals and social democrats* (Cambridge: Cambridge University Press, 1978). See too J. Allett, *New liberalism: the political economy of J. A. Hobson* (Toronto: Toronto University Press, 1981). The most recent full-scale study is that by Peter Cain, *Hobson and imperialism: radicalism, new liberalism, and finance, 1887–1938* (Oxford: Oxford University Press, 2002). On eugenics, see M. Freeden, 'Eugenics and progressive thought: a study in ideological affinity', *Historical Journal*, 22 (1979), 645–71. For the interest in eugenics shown by Marshall, see Groenewegen, *A soaring eagle*, pp. 479–86, 510–12. Hobson's welfare economics is covered in J. Maloney, *Marshall, orthodoxy and the professionalisaton of economics*, ch. 7, and is the subject of Roger Backhouse and Steven Medema, *The hesitant hand* (Princeton: Princeton University Press, 2008).

ESSAY 12

The pioneer student of the professionalisation of economics in Britain and the USA was A. W. (Bob) Coats, whose various studies are now reprinted in *The sociology and professionalisation of economics: British and American economic essays* (London: Routledge, 1993). See too Alon Kadish, *The Oxford economists in the late nineteenth century* (Oxford: Oxford University Press, 1982); Alon Kadish, *Historians, economists, and economic history* (London: Routledge, 1989); John Maloney, *Marshall, orthodoxy and the professionalisation of economics*; John D. Hey and Donald Winch (eds.), *A century of economics: one hundred years of the Royal Economic Society and the Economic Journal* (Oxford: Blackwell, 1990); Keith Tribe and Alon Kadish (eds.), *The market for political economy: the advent of economics in British university culture, 1850–1905* (London: Routledge, 1993). On the science associations, see J. Morrell and A. Thackray, *Gentlemen of science: early years of the British Association for the Advancement of Science* (Oxford: Oxford University Press, 1981); Roy MacLeod and Peter Collins (eds.), *The parliament of science: the British Association for the Advancement of Science, 1831–1981* (Northwood, Middlesex: Science Reviews, 1981); and Lawrence Goldman, *Science, reform, and politics in Victorian Britain: the Social Science Association 1857–1886* (Cambridge: Cambridge University Press, 2002).

Acknowledgements

This book has been written since I retired from the University of Sussex. That was in 2000, and since then I have been grateful for research grants from two funding bodies that do not regard age as a disqualification. I was given an emeritus award by the Leverhulme Foundation that covered travel costs and other incidentals for three years; and the British Academy awarded me a small grant for the same purposes in 2004. I was thankful for this award because a sizeable portion of the Leverhulme grant had gone towards the editing costs of a collective enterprise that was part of the centenary celebrations of the British Academy and involved collaboration between economic historians and intellectual historians. My co-editor, Patrick O'Brien, and the contributors to *The political economy of British historical experience, 1688–1914*, greatly improved my knowledge of the subjects covered there, though at the expense of time that I might have spent on this book.

A few of the essays here have been published elsewhere in different form. Parts of Essay 5 appeared as 'A very amusing book about old times' in Antoin Murphy and Renee Prendergast (eds.), *Contributions to the history of economic thought: essays in honour of R. D. C. Black* (London: Routledge, 2000). Some of the material in Essays 3 and 4 appeared in 'Thinking green, nineteenth-century style: John Ruskin and John Stuart Mill' in Mark Bevir and Frank Trentmann (eds.), *Markets in historical contexts: ideas and politics in the modern world* (Cambridge: Cambridge University Press, 2004). A version of Essay 7 appeared as '"Between feudalists and communists": Louis Mallet and the Cobden creed' in Anthony Howe and Simon Morgan (eds.), *Rethinking nineteenth-century liberalism: Richard Cobden bicentenary essays* (Aldershot: Ashgate, 2006). A slightly shorter version of the essay in the Appendix appeared in Stefan Collini, Richard Whatmore, and Brian Young (eds.), *Economy, polity, and society: essays in British intellectual history, 1750–1950* (Cambridge: Cambridge University Press, 2000). With the exception of the last-mentioned, all these essays were written with an eye to inclusion alongside others as part of this book.

I would like to record my thanks to various libraries for permission to cite manuscript materials: the British Library; the London School of Economics archive centre; the Wren Library, Trinity College, the King's College archive centre, the Marshall Library, and the University Library in Cambridge; the Bodleian Library, Oxford; the Balliol College Library and the Mallet family for the Mallet papers; the John Rylands Library in Manchester; the West Sussex and Surrey Record Offices for the Cobden and Farrer papers; the special collections section of the library of the University of Sheffield for the Hewins papers; the library of Columbia University for the Seligman papers; the Baker Library at Harvard for the Foxwell papers; and Richard Freeman for his hospitality and access to material in his private collection of Foxwell letters. I would also like to think that those who write on these subjects in future will benefit from another project that has delayed appearance of this book: the creation of a website (www.economistspapers.org.uk) devoted to a guide to archive sources.

The photograph of John Ruskin appears by permission of the National Portrait Gallery. Bagehot's portrait is taken from the Warren J. Samuels Portrait Collection at Duke University. The photograph of Jevons holding the tools of the assaying trade he practised in Australia during the gold rush of the 1850s appears by permission of the John Rylands University Library, Manchester. The photograph of a drawing of Sir Louis Mallet by Philip Homan Miller appears by permission of the British Library. The photograph of Sidgwick appears by permission of the Master and Fellows of Trinity College, Cambridge. The photographs of Marshall in 1865 and of Foxwell in 1936 appear by permission of the Master and Fellows of St John's College, Cambridge. The photograph of Foxwell as a young man was lent to me by Richard Freeman. The photograph of Marshall in his eighties and the hand-drawn diagram of consumers' surplus by Marshall, a copy of which was lent to me by John K. Whitaker, appear by permission of the University of Cambridge, Faculty of Economics. The photograph of Toynbee appears by permission of the Master and Fellows of Balliol College, Oxford. The photograph of Hobson appears by permission of the London School of Economics archives.

I have enjoyed the support and advice of old friends and some new acquaintances. Roger Backhouse read the book for Cambridge University Press and waived his right to anonymity, which meant I could inflict unfinished essays on him. Jeff Lipkes and Simon Cook commented helpfully on earlier versions of two of them. The essay in the Appendix was the subject of supportive conversations with two of my oldest Sussex colleagues and friends, Laurence Lerner and the late David Pocock. As in the case of *Riches and poverty*, however, my greatest debt is to another friend and ex-Sussex colleague, Stefan Collini. Frequent references to his work will show that he has preceded me with exemplary studies of some of the figures who feature here. More to the point, when spirits have flagged he has invariably responded with support and valuable suggestions for surmounting problems. Åsa Söderman was generous with her time and expertise when it came to putting the book into electronic shape. The dedication acknowledges another kind of debt that cannot be discharged by words alone.

Index

IDEAS IN CONTEXT

Edited by QUENTIN SKINNER AND JAMES TULLY